The

FINANCE
CURSE

Nicholas Shaxson

The
FINANCE
CURSE

How Global Finance Is Making Us All Poorer

Grove Press
New York

Originally published in Great Britain by The Bodley Head in 2018, this edition has been revised for American publication.

Published simultaneously in Canada
Printed in Canada

First Grove Atlantic hardcover edition: November 2019

This book was set in 11-pt Janson Text by Alpha Design & Composition of Pittsfield, NH

Library of Congress Cataloging-in-Publication data is available for this title.

ISBN 978-0-8021-2847-8
eISBN 978-0-8021-4638-0

Grove Press
an imprint of Grove Atlantic
154 West 14th Street
New York, NY 10011

Distributed by Publishers Group West

groveatlantic.com

19 20 21 22   10 9 8 7 6 5 4 3 2 1

For Emma, Oscar, and George

Contents

Introduction

In the early 1990s I was the correspondent for Reuters and the *Financial Times* in mineral-rich Angola in west Africa, which was then supplying more than 5 percent of all US oil imports and which the United Nations reckoned was suffering the world's worst civil war. Angola was, on paper, one of Africa's wealthiest countries, but on standard measures of human development it was almost the poorest. As UNITA rebels rampaged across the countryside, digging up diamonds to pay for their war machine, I flew into besieged cities in the interior in corkscrew dives to avoid antiaircraft fire, to try to make sense of what was going on. In the government-held capital of Luanda I remember the sight of upside-down legs kicking and wriggling from the tops of stinking hot garbage Dumpsters, as scab-encrusted war orphans in diesel-soaked clothes dived for food and other treasures discarded by the beneficiaries of the oil wealth. These kids, some of whom slept at night in sewers to hide from robbers and the police, would surround me on street corners, tickling my elbows, wheedling for cash, crooning *"Amigo! Amigo!"* to try to establish a friendship with the white man. Often, though, they used two different words: *"Chefe!"* or *"Patrão!"* the Portuguese words for "boss" or "patron." This would, they reasoned, oblige me to fulfill my assigned role and look after them as my loyal underlings. Most days, I'd donate something to Kwanza and the boys, six or seven cheerful rascals who lived on my hotel's street corner, and they defended me fiercely against all comers. Sometimes, I felt as if they would have fought to the death to protect me.

These kinds of relationships were woven into the country's economic and political tapestry, especially in the hierarchy of political power, where the rich and influential handed out goodies to their underlings in exchange for their support. At the time, oil and diamonds made up more than 99 percent of Angola's exports, and it was quickly obvious to me that economic theories about supply and demand and interest rates that were being taught in Western schools made no sense here. To begin to understand an economy so extremely dependent on minerals, it helps to picture it as a swollen river, which fans out into a widening delta system of ever more numerous rivulets. Flotillas of boats loaded with treasure—meaning the oil wealth, in Angola's case—glide downstream, and gatekeepers extract tolls from the passing boats. The big diversions occur far upstream, and as the river flows onward and splits and branches, there is steadily less to go around. These street children lived out at the furthest end of the river delta, where all that was left for them lay at the bottom of a bug-infested dumpster.

Every Western visitor to Angola had a version of the same question: How could the people of a country with such vast mineral wealth be so shockingly destitute? War and corruption were part of the answer, of course. A venal leadership in Luanda was stealing the oil money, eating lobster and drinking champagne on Luanda's beaches, while its ragged and malnourished compatriots slaughtered each other out in the dusty provinces. But something else was going on too. I didn't know it then, but I was getting a frontline view of a grand new thesis that academics were just starting to put together, now known as the "resource curse."

Many countries dependent on income from natural resources tend to grow more slowly and suffer more corruption, greater conflict, more authoritarian politics, steeper inequality, and greater poverty than their resource-poor peers. It's not just that powerful crooks steal the nations' mineral bounty and stash it offshore, though that is also true. The big point is that all this money flowing from natural resources such as oil can make their populations *even worse off* than if those riches had never been discovered. In short, more money can make a country poorer. That's why the resource curse is also sometimes known as the "paradox of poverty from plenty." The curse affects different countries in different ways; some countries, like Norway, have apparently benefited from their minerals, but few in war-ravaged Angola back in the early 1990s doubted that the minerals were a curse.

As I was writing about the destitution and the bloody carnage in Angola, John Christensen, the official economic adviser to the British tax haven of Jersey, was reading my articles and noticing some weird parallels with what was happening at home. "I was fascinated by this counterintuitive concept that too much oil and gas wealth could make you poorer," he recalled. Jersey, which was dominated not by oil but by a swollen offshore financial industry based on secrecy and low- or zero-tax facilities, was suffering some of the same symptoms. "The more I read about it, the more I thought, 'But this is Jersey!'" he said. And he understood a bigger point: it wasn't just finance-dependent Jersey that was suffering something akin to Angola's resource curse. Other countries whose financial sector had grown too dominant—such as Britain and the United States—were exhibiting some of these same symptoms. Christensen had by then left Jersey, horrified by the venality and corruption he had witnessed in this little British tax haven, and set up the Tax Justice Network, an organization dedicated to understanding and fighting against offshore finance.

We met in 2006 and began to discuss the similarities between oil-rich countries and finance-dominated ones. We resolved to work together to create a new analysis, which we began to call the "finance curse."

The nations of Africa's oil-soaked western coastline provide a good starting point for understanding the finance curse. Traveling extensively in those regions between 1993 and 2007, I watched the oil sector pump up some parts of their economies and drain life out of others. For one thing, high-salaried oil jobs were sucking the best-educated and most talented people out of industry, agriculture, government, civil society, and the media, damaging them all. Something similar has happened in the United States. Back in the 1960s and early 1970s, bankers didn't earn that much more than teachers or doctors. Then, around the 1970s, this ratio began to rise. By 1990, the average financial sector worker earned three times as much as the average American, a ratio that hasn't fallen despite the global financial crisis.[1] And that's just the *average* worker in finance; the top players earn hundreds of times more.

Now "finance literally bids rocket scientists away from the satellite industry," wrote the authors of a study by the Bank for International Settlements on the impact that the rise of finance has had on economic growth. "The result is that people who might have become scientists, who in another age dreamt of curing cancer or flying people to Mars, today dream of becoming hedge fund managers."[2] As we'll soon see, America contains many experts in corporate strategy, whose talents lie in reengineering and fixing up failing firms and making them sing again. Yet many if not most of these experts have been sucked into the private equity sector, where they are incentivized to engage not in productive corporate reengineering but in damaging financial engineering that sucks out maximum profits from these firms at the cost of long-term viability. The financial brain drain out of politics and into highly paid finance is also a big reason we have so many mediocre politicians: many excellent candidates have been diverted into banks and hedge funds, their talents washed away by a deluge of money.

In Angola, those clever people who did stay in government soon lost interest in the difficult challenges of national development, and politics became a corrupting, conflict-ridden game of jostling to get access to the flow of oil money. Wall Street has achieved something similar in the United States. Whole swathes of the political classes have turned their attention away from the tough slog of fostering a stronger manufacturing sector or creating a level playing field to allow local media to flourish and prevent its wholesale capture by the billionaire class. Now our politicians are enraptured by the power and wealth and business models of the likes of Citigroup, Goldman Sachs, private equity firms, and hedge funds, which have very different agendas. Big money has captured policy making, and finance has played a central role. With this great shift of political focus, balanced national development has taken a second hit.

The cascading inflows of oil wealth in Angola also raised the local price of goods and services, from housing to ham sandwiches to haircuts, in a "Dutch Disease," a phenomenon named after the economic dislocation that hit the Netherlands after it made large gas discoveries in the 1960s. This high-price environment caused a third wave of destruction to local industry and agriculture, which found it ever harder to compete with cheaper imported goods. Likewise, large inflows of money into Wall Street and into real estate markets from overseas can raise local price levels, making it harder for many local businesses to compete with foreign firms.[3]

As if all this were not enough, these curses of resources or finance produce a more destabilizing problem. I remember watching cranes festoon the Luanda skyline at times of high oil prices, then, when prices crashed, I saw weeds grow in the lobbies of half-finished concrete hulks whose owners had gone bankrupt. Massive borrowing in the good times and a buildup of debt arrears in the bad times magnified the problem. The equivalent in the United States was the euphoria of the 1990s that culminated in the global financial crisis. This boom-bust was differently timed and mostly caused by different things, but as with oil booms, it had a ratchet effect. In good times, the dominant sector can curse alternative economic sectors for reasons I've already given, and when the bust comes the chaos magnifies the damage. And those lost sectors, once destroyed, aren't easily rebuilt. Meanwhile, bankers—who famously will lend you an umbrella when it's dry but want it back once it starts raining—reinforce this instability by turning on the credit taps during booms, creating endless new financial vehicles to help households and businesses take on more debt, amplifying the exhilaration, then whipping away credit when things go bad, deepening the slump.

Alongside all this, there's another whole array of damage to consider.

In our traditional view of the US economy, wealth is created throughout the economic system by many people and businesses working in diverse fields: in manufacturing, construction, banking, fishing, tourism, or catering, trading with each other in competitive markets. Finance, creating helpful linkages between these players, supports workers, consumers, and businesses alike. Meanwhile, the government supplies the police, roads, schools, sewers, and so on and upholds the rule of law to support all this activity. To pay for these services, governments need to bargain with voting citizens and with businesses to raise the taxes, and this bargaining has, since the days of the Boston Tea Party, fostered healthy lines of political accountability. This is a story of healthy *horizontal* relationships between the many different actors in an economy. With a mineral-dependent economy, though, it's different. Return to that image of the river delta: when oil money sluices downward from the top of the political system, rulers don't need to bargain with their citizens anymore. These are *vertical*, hierarchical relationships. As it flows downward, the oil money washes away checks and balances, institutions, and accountability, replacing them with a crude political and economic formula: rulers allocate wealth, or permissions to access wealth, downward in exchange for loyalty. And if your citizens complain, the oil money pays for paramilitary police to keep them in their place. This is why oil economies like Russia's, Venezuela's, or Angola's are often rather authoritarian.

Finance, it turns out, is starting to have similar effects in the United States. While America has a vastly more diversified economy than Angola's, its economy is seeing an ever-larger share of wealth spout out at the apex of the system—not from oil pipes inserted into the ground as in Angola, but from pipes jammed into the lifeblood of the real economy—and into your pocket. Back in the 1950s and 1960s, assets held by the financial sector in the United States were worth around one year's GDP, and financial corporations earned little more than a tenth of all corporate profits. Now the financial sector's assets are worth more like five years' GDP, and around a third of all corporate profits flow to finance—a proportion that is rising. As all this has happened, bankers and other financial players, cheered on by the Clinton, Bush, Obama, and now Trump administrations, have hoovered up companies across the economy and assembled the pieces together in anticompetitive mergers or cartel-like arrangements, or run their financial affairs more aggressively through tax havens to sidestep tax bills or irritating regulations. Each move flushes more wealth out at the top, while the other parts of the economy that are being extracted from grow weaker and find it ever harder to compete with the giants. All this increases the top-down flows of money and power, generating the core fact of economic discrimination that underpins all those better-understood forms: racial, gender, sexual, and geographical discrimination. Our financial sector should serve our economy, but it's increasingly the other way around.[4]

The costs of the finance curse are staggering. Since around 2010 a diverse range of academics at the International Monetary Fund (IMF) and elsewhere have begun putting together a new strand of research now known as "Too Much Finance," which shows a remarkably consistent pattern across the world over time. As a country's financial sector develops, it tends to contribute to the development of the economy—but only up to a point, after which it starts to reduce economic growth and inflict all sorts of other damage. The graph of the relationship between the size of a financial sector and economic growth is an inverted U shape, with a "sweet spot" of maximum, ideal size in the middle. It turns out that the United States, Britain, and many other Western economies passed this optimal point long ago. According to a 2016 estimate by Professor Gerald Epstein and Juan Antonio Montecino of the University of Massachusetts at Amherst, the excess bloat in the United States' financial sector will have cost the US economy a cumulative $12.9 to $22.7 *trillion* between 1990 and 2023. That calculation, a first approximation of the costs of the finance curse, is equivalent to a net $105,000 to $184,000 loss for the average American family. Had the financial sector been at its optimal size and performing its traditional useful roles, and had this lost wealth been spread equitably among the people, the typical US household would have doubled its wealth at retirement.[5] The US economy would be stronger today if the US government had paid its highest-paying financiers their full salaries, then sent them off to live in luxurious gated communities to play golf all day.

The great financial crisis that first erupted in 2007 was a part of this damage. But the finance curse has multiple layers. Once you know what to look for, you'll find its distortions, schemes, and abuses all over the place. For instance, the five largest US technology behemoths spent around $150 billion in 2018 just on *buying their own stock*, instead of investing in improving their businesses. Since 1995 IBM has spent well over $160 billion buying back its own stock—yet at the time of this writing, the company was worth little more than $100 billion. IBM stockholders got rich, while company investment stagnated. More broadly, the S&P 500 firms spent $720 billion on share buybacks just in the twelve months before September 2018, a gigantic "anti-stimulus," sucking money out of the productive economy, that is comparable in size to Obama's economic stimulus package approved in 2009 to respond to the financial crisis. If you add dividends to these buybacks, the total rises to $1.2 trillion, which is 1.3 times the size of the US defense budget in 2018. When oil companies spend their money on financial games like buybacks instead of investing in oil rigs, it's called "drilling on Wall Street." Across the Atlantic, a study of 298 companies in the S&P Europe 350 share index found something similar: they spent €350 billion—equivalent to 110 percent of their net income—on shareholder dividends and stock buybacks in 2015. The comparable figure for the UK was 150 percent. This is what Bank of England economist Andrew Haldane meant when he said firms were "eating themselves."[6]

What on earth is going on? A simple, crude answer is that when a company buys its own shares or pays bumper dividends it boosts its share price and, with it, corporate executives' short-term stock options and bonuses. With over a third of all stocks and other financial assets owned by the richest 1 percent of Americans (and around 80 percent held by the top 10 percent), share buybacks and bloated dividends are syringes jammed into the veins of the real economy, sending torrents of wealth skyward.[7] But a more interesting answer lies in a word that finance academics now use: "financialization." This is a process that first properly emerged in the 1970s and has slowly, silently, crept up on us all. Financialization involves two main trends: first, a massive growth in the size and power of the financial, insurance, and real estate (FIRE) sectors; and second, the penetration of financial techniques, markets, motives, and ways of thinking into the economy, society, and even culture. In this era the bosses of companies that create real wealth in the economy—making widgets and sprockets, finding cures for cancer, or selling mass-market holidays—have been turning their attention away from the hard slog of trying to boost entrepreneurship, productivity, and genuine efficiency toward the more profitable sugar rush of financial engineering, monopolization, and unproductive "tax efficiency" to tease out more profits for the companies' owners, always at somebody else's expense. As this has happened, the rate at which new job-creating businesses are formed has halved since 2006, just before the global financial crisis.[8] Private equity titans buy up healthy companies, load them up with debt, and drive them into the corporate graveyard—yet get ridiculously rich in the process. Airlines often make more money speculating on fuel derivatives than on selling you tickets to Atlanta. Banks buy and sell trillions of dollars' worth of derivatives and other exotic financial instruments to each other—and they, too, mysteriously get richer. Are they creating wealth inside this closed circle? Or are they extracting it from others elsewhere?

Half a century ago it was widely accepted that the job of a corporate CEO was to generate wealth to serve several goals: to produce profits, to create and maintain good jobs, to contribute taxes to support roads and schools, and so on. All these things enriched healthy communities and made a stronger nation—and this formula ultimately made for stronger corporations too. Back then, CEOs at big firms earned twenty to thirty times what the average worker did. But financialization has whittled down the purpose of business to little more than a single-minded focus on maximizing the wealth of shareholders, the owners of those companies, often at the expense of employees, suppliers, or the wider community. This shift has unleashed gushers of profits for owners—and for CEOs, who now earn two to three hundred times the average worker's paycheck. And as the bosses' rewards have soared, the underlying economy—the place where most of us live and work—has stagnated. When adjusted for inflation, Americans' real hourly earnings have barely budged since the 1970s. The profits and the stagnation are two sides of the same coin: wealth extraction by those at the top from the rest. "It is not short term versus long term; that is not the distinction," says William Lazonick of the University of Massachusetts at Lowell, one of America's best-known experts on corporate strategy. "It is value creation versus value extraction." Financialization is a central part of the finance curse. Its consequences include lower economic growth, steeper inequality, less efficient and more distorted markets, eroded public services, greater corruption, the hollowing out of small towns and small businesses, and widespread damage to democracy and society.

To compensate for this economic sluggishness, and to escape from politically difficult choices, successive governments have filled the holes with policies of financial loosening, which have unleashed oceans of credit into the economy in the past forty years, puffing up finance. You'd expect a larger financial sector to be a fountain of investment capital for other sectors in our economy, but in fact the opposite has happened. As recently as 1995 over half of bank lending went to small businesses, which are the economy's lifeblood, creating two out of three jobs. Now the share is less than a quarter. Most of the credit now unleashed on the economy has been circulating inside the financial sector, unmoored, disconnected from the real economy and from the people it is supposed to serve. This book will show how these self-serving parts of finance have increasingly overshadowed and even preyed on other parts of the economy, which must struggle to survive, like seedlings starved of light and water under the canopy of a giant, deep-rooted, and invasive tree.

And there's another whole dimension to this, which the academics have hardly measured in any useful way: the rise in global organized crime and abusive quasi-legal activities that spew out of modern finance. It's impossible to convey the scale of this, but one approach can be found in a list entitled "Robert Jenkins' partial list of bank misdeeds," a kind of running score regularly updated by a former Bank of England official.[9] Each element on his list is a shocker. There are many elements that are widely known: "mis-selling interest rate swaps" and "mis-selling of mortgage-backed securities" ("mis-selling" is a euphemism for "fraud"). Coming in at number 11, there's "abusive small business lending practices," a hallmark of modern finance. At number 16, there is the humble "aiding and abetting tax evasion"—a sport that has cost treasuries around the world hundreds of billions. Next comes "aiding and abetting money laundering for violent drugs cartels," a reference to, among other things, the role played by HSBC in washing hundreds of millions of dollars for Russian gangsters and Mexico's Sinaloa cartel. Number 19 is "manipulation of Libor," referring to the numbers used to calculate payments in the $800 trillion derivatives market and a lot more besides. Number 61 is the less weighty "offers to procure prostitutes to curry favor with SWF [sovereign wealth fund] clients." Tucked away at number 114, there's "facilitating African money laundering on a grand scale." At the time of this writing, the list contained 144 items; each represents a large can of villainous worms. And this is only a *partial* list of the misdeeds—and even then, this refers only to *banks*. There's a whole zoo of "shadow" financial players outside the regulated banking system whose members enjoy less oversight, so often behave even worse (we'll meet some of them soon). And the list hardly touches on the national security aspects of oversized finance, as shadowy foreign players use secretive Delaware shell companies to insert silent crowbars into America's economy and political system. Trying to get your arms around the scale of all this damage feels a bit like trying to convey to a child the distances between galaxies in the known universe.

The transformation that has happened in the era of financialization has had little to do with the needs of ordinary business and ordinary people. Financial cheerleaders would like us to believe that Wall Street is the wealthy goose that lays America's golden eggs. The finance curse shows it to be a different bird: a cuckoo in the nest that is crowding out other parts of the economy.

We all need finance. We need it to pay our bills, to help us save for retirement, to redirect our savings to businesses so they can invest, to insure us against unforeseen calamities, and also sometimes for speculators to sniff out new investment opportunities in our economy. We need finance, but the measure of its contribution to our economy isn't whether it creates billionaires and big profits, but whether it provides useful services to us at a reasonable cost. Imagine if telephone companies suddenly became insanely profitable and began churning out lots of billionaires, and telephony grew to dwarf every other economic sector—yet our phone calls were still crackly and expensive and the service unreliable. We'd soon smell a rat. All this wealth is a sign of sickness, not health.

To unpack the idea of the finance curse, we'll go on a century-long journey that spans the globe, from the era of robber barons in the early twentieth century, to the City of London as it rediscovered a role for itself after the fall of the British Empire as a crime-infested, deregulated offshore playground for Wall Street in the 1950s, to the birth of modern tax havens in the Caribbean in the 1960s, to the myth of Ireland's Celtic Tiger economy (contrary to received wisdom, it wasn't based on low corporate taxes), to the shocking truths about London's role in generating the global financial crisis—something that parochial Americans have spent too long ignoring. After the crisis we travel to South Dakota and the peculiar world of wealth managers, then follow twisting corporate trails leading from a shattered local newspaper in New Jersey up to the glittering offices of secretive private equity titans and hedge fund moguls in Manhattan, and from there to Iowa's bitter, financialized, hog farming communities. And we will see how, all along the way, evidence has been beaten, twisted, and abused to perpetrate a great hoax upon the public, persuading us that all this activity is normal, necessary, and even a good thing. It is anything but.

CHAPTER ONE

Sabotage

Some economists behave like aliens who sit in spaceships high above Earth, watching us through powerful telescopes. They record all the scurrying back and forth, then build theories and mathematical models about what we're up to, without properly accounting for folly, cruelty, sex, friendship, patriotism, credulity, and the general rough-and-tumble of our crazy, emotional lives.

One economist who perceived both the economic behavior and the emotional complexity, and can consequently help us understand the finance curse, was an early-twentieth-century Norwegian American called Thorstein Veblen, an extraterrestrial of a different kind. An unlikely figure, he perched himself outside the normal range of human experience, and this enabled him to sit far enough back from humanity to observe our foibles clearly, so he could use them as a starting point for properly understanding the world of money and business. Veblen rebelled against the conventional wisdom. He has been called an American Karl Marx and the Charles Darwin of economics, but in truth his varied output is too diverse and weird to categorize. Yet his nuanced understanding of messy human behavior is exactly what makes his ideas so remarkable—and useful. By linking economics with uglier truths about how we as humans really behave and think, he discerned many of the deepest principles that underpin the finance curse.

Veblen was an economist, sociologist, womanizer, and misfit. He made his own furniture but didn't make his bed in the morning, and he would let his dishes pile up in tottering heaps before washing them all in a barrel with a hose. It is said he once borrowed a sack from a neighbor just so that he could return it with a hornet's nest inside. In his florid, peculiar writing style he described religion as "the fabrication of vendible imponderables in the nth dimension," the main religious denominations as "chain stores," and their individual churches as "retail outlets." At the fiercely religious Carleton College in Minnesota he poked fun at mathematical economics by asking a student to calculate the value of her church to her in kegs of beer, and he provoked uproar with a speech entitled "A Plea for Cannibalism." A lank-haired weirdo genius, he observed society unencumbered by strictures of religion, economic conventions, or the petty airs and graces of the early twentieth century that kept the grubby workers down and the landed gentry in their rightful place. His apartness let him see things others couldn't and helped him say the unsayable.

Born to Norwegian immigrant parents in rural Wisconsin in 1857, Veblen was the sixth and the smartest of twelve children. The farmstead where he grew up was so isolated that when he left he was, as one historian put it, "emigrating to America." His brilliance took him from these humble beginnings to Yale, where he got a PhD in 1884, before going to ground and mooching around listlessly for several years. "He read and loafed," his brother remembered, "and the next day he loafed and read." Some said he was unemployable because he hated Christianity or because he had a prejudice against Norwegians. His oddball, sardonic wit surely didn't help, nor did his open contempt for economists and other academics. He clashed repeatedly with university authorities but also relished scholarly cut and thrust, calling himself "a disturber of the intellectual peace" and "a wanderer in the intellectual no-man's land."[1]

It wasn't all solitude, though. He was later ejected from the University of Chicago for marital infidelities with colleagues and students.

As one story goes, the dean summoned Veblen into his office in 1905 for a chat.

DEAN: We have a problem with the faculty wives.
VEBLEN: Oh yes, I know. They're terrible. I've had them all.[2]

Veblen's womanizing prowess wasn't due to his looks. Longish hair was plastered down on either side of a center part; bushy eyebrows and a roughly cut mustache and beard suggested he hadn't tried very hard to discard his Norwegian peasant-farmer upbringing. One lover apparently described him as a chimpanzee. Others remembered a weird domestic charisma. "Lounging about in his loose dressing gown and looking not nearly as anemic and fragile as in his street clothes, he reminded one, with his drooping moustaches and Nordic features, of nothing so much as a hospitable Viking taking his ease at his own fireside," a visitor recalled. "At such times, he was at his best, doling out curious information, throwing off a little malicious gossip which, in view of his seclusiveness, he must have picked miraculously out of the air, mixing picturesque slang with brilliant phrases of his own coinage, solicitously watching out for his guests' comfort."[3]

This charisma extended to the realm of ideas and gained him a following that has endured more than a century after his death. He vivisected capitalism, impaling Victorian and neoclassical economists, who regarded humanity as a set of identical, perfectly informed, "utility-maximizing" individuals and firms pursuing their own self-interest, to be treated as data inputs for their mathematical sausage-making machines. In these economists' hands, he acidly observed, a human became "a lightning calculator of pleasures and pains, who oscillates like a homogenous globule of desire of happiness under the impulse of stimuli." Such economists, he jeered, would take "a gang of Aleutian Islanders, slashing about in the wrack and surf with rakes and magical incantations for the capture of shellfish," and shovel them all into equations about rent, wages, and interest. Bring back history, he lamented. Bring back politics. Bring back real life. He had a point then, and he would still have a point today.[4]

Veblen's best-known book, *The Theory of the Leisure Class*, published in 1899, is a vicious exposé of a world where productive workers toiled long hours and parasitic elites fed off the fruits of their labors. The wealthy also engaged in "conspicuous consumption" and "conspicuous leisure"—wasteful activities to show others they were so rich they didn't need to work. Plutocrats always wanted more wealth and power, he noted, and, worse, their petulance and excesses generally provoked not anger but reverence! The oppressed masses didn't try to overthrow their social betters; they wanted to copy them. (The popularity of shows like *Keeping Up with the Kardashians* might be the modern equivalent.) Twentieth-century man, he concluded, wasn't that far removed from his barbarian ancestors.

Veblen's next big book, *The Theory of Business Enterprise*, published in 1904, got less attention but was more radical and more important.[5] In it, he contrasted industry and the "machine process"—the productive engineers and entrepreneurs who rolled their sleeves up and made useful stuff—with what he called the "business" of making profits. Above the foundation of production rose a financial superstructure of credit, loans, ownership, bets, and markets to be controlled and milked. While Marx had focused on tensions between workers and factory owners, Veblen concentrated on a different but related struggle: between wealth *creators* and wealth *extractors*. Makers versus takers; producers versus predators. If it helps, picture a group of old men in top hats, manipulating a Rube Goldberg–like contraption of spindly pipework perched on top of the economy, hoovering up coins and notes and IOUs from the pockets of the workers and consumers toiling away underneath.[6]

Generations of economic thinkers had known about this distinction at least as far back as the publication of Adam Smith's *The Wealth of Nations* in 1776.[7] The main problem, though, was that people disagreed about who the wealth creators were. A conservative tradition holds that they are the rich, the owners of money and capital, who build the factories, then get taxed by government, which redistributes their wealth to the poor and to the recipients of handouts. It's a view that had long been promoted by the likes of John C. Calhoun, a former US vice president and secretary of war who had been a leading defender of slavers and plantation owners. Calhoun, the "Marx of the Master Class," did everything he could to try to safeguard "the rights of the radical rich," as the historian Nancy MacLean puts it: the rights of wealthy elites against "oppression" by democracy and by the "tyranny" of majority voting.[8] Calhoun's modern equivalent would be today's billionaire classes, who lobby, finance think tanks and political candidates, and even create media empires so as to skew and rig the laws of the land in their favor. In their view of history, it's the poor and disadvantaged who are the leeches, preying on the capitalists.

But Veblen was having none of it. He compared the rich wealth extractor to a self-satisfied toad who "has found his appointed place along some frequented run where many flies and spiders pass and repass," and he then went a whole step further, into more controversial terrain. Many businessmen get rich, Veblen went on, not just through extraction, like the lazy toad catching passing flies, but through active sabotage—or, as he put it in his spiky language, "the conscientious withdrawing of efficiency." These players, he said, interrupt the regular flow of outputs, shaking the tree so they can more easily make off with the fruit.[9]

Nonsense, the critics sneered. Who'd do such a rotten, foolish thing?

Lots of people, it turns out. Veblen had brutally exposed one of capitalism's great open secrets. Here it is: big capitalists don't like efficient competition, and they don't like free markets. They *say* they do, but genuine competition drives down prices and drives up wages—and so reduces profits. What they really like are markets rigged in their favor and against workers, consumers, and taxpayers. That's where the big money is. Instead of competing against each other they conspire against consumers: "It became a competition not within the business but between the business as a whole and the rest of the community." This conflict is at the heart of the finance curse.

The Theory of Business Enterprise came out in the wake of what was then, and may still be, the most impressive feat of investigative journalism in world history. This was an exposé of John D. Rockefeller's Standard Oil monopoly by the journalist Ida Tarbell, who uncovered a conspiracy and cartel the likes of which the world had never seen. Rockefeller, she revealed, was a master of Veblenite sabotage, rigging markets in the production and distribution of oil and its refined products, buying or elbowing out rivals in a ruthless and sometimes violent quest to build an America-wide monopoly. Her articles, serialized in *McClure's* magazine from 1902 to 1904, opened with a picture of rugged young men carving out new frontier towns in the Pennsylvania oil fields.

> Life ran swift and ruddy and joyous in these men. They were still young, most of them under forty, and they looked forward with all the eagerness of the young who have just learned their powers, to years of struggle and development. They would make their towns the most beautiful in the world. But suddenly, at the very heyday of this confidence, a big hand reached out from nobody knew where, to steal their conquest and throttle their future. The suddenness and the blackness of the assault on their business stirred to the bottom their manhood and their sense of fair play.[10]

In one Rockefeller operation a hundred ruffians descended on Hancock, a town in Delaware County, New York, in 1892 to prevent a competing pipe from being laid. As another account put it,

> Dynamite was part of their armament, and they were equipped with grappling irons, cant-hooks, and other tools to pull the pipe up if laid. Cannon . . . are used to perforate tanks in which the oil takes fire. To let the "independents" know what they were to expect the cannon was fired at ten o'clock at night with a report that shook the people and the windows for miles about.[11]

The independents abandoned Hancock. A more overt act of business sabotage is hard to imagine.

Tarbell's explosive articles were an obsessive labor of love and loathing. She had watched her own father, a small-time oilman named Franklin Tarbell, transmogrified by Rockefeller's ruthless tactics from genial, loving father into a grim-faced, humorless shell. "Take Standard Oil stock, and your family will never know want," Rockefeller crooned to the victims of his semilegal practices. He would offer to swap their degraded business interests for Standard Oil stock, offering the equivalent of pennies on the dollar, while assuring them that they would be much better off with him because, he admitted, "I have ways of making money you know nothing of." Franklin Tarbell held out and paid a heavy price, so much so that his business partner killed himself. Ida's father "no longer told of the funny things he had seen and heard during the day," she remembered. "He no longer played his Jew's harp, nor sang to my little sister on the arm of his chair."

Rockefeller paid bribes and kickbacks. He eliminated rivals through spying, smear tactics, thuggery, and buyouts with menaces. He sabotaged producers of oil barrels, hoarded oil, and squashed middlemen. He secretly financed politicians and haughtily dismissed requests to appear at official inquiries. He covered his tracks, delegating questionable tasks to juniors and avoiding compromising language on internal documents. He expanded overseas, dodging regulations and gaming gaps in the global tax system to become, as one biographer put it, "a sovereign power, endowed with resources rivaling those of governments."

It takes time, Tarbell noted, to crush men who are pursuing legitimate trade:

> But one of Mr. Rockefeller's most impressive characteristics is patience. He was like a general who, besieging a city surrounded by fortified hills, views from a balloon the whole great field, and sees how, this point taken, that must fall; this hill reached, that fort is commanded. And nothing was too small: the corner

grocery in Browntown, the humble refining still on Oil Creek,
the shortest private pipe line. Nothing, for little things grow.[12]

In the early days of Rockefeller's business operations, corporations
weren't allowed to do business across state lines, but he had found a
loophole. He brought all his different state corporations together under
the ownership of a trust, a flexible and powerful mechanism of central
control that could operate at a national level and in great secrecy. (This
is why anti-monopoly laws and actions have been known as "antitrust"
measures ever since.) Through his trust mechanism, Rockefeller soon
controlled over 90 percent of the oil refined in the United States, extracting vast wealth from consumers and generating fountains of profit, which
were funneled beyond the core business into railroads, banking, steel,
copper, and more.[13] If this reminds you of today's Amazon, you're on the
right track. It is no coincidence that Rockefeller was America's biggest
monopolist and also its first billionaire—and that Amazon's boss, Jeff
Bezos, is the richest person in world history. Monopoly was, and still
is, where the big money is.

Rockefeller was in fact just one of several robber barons dominating
the American economic landscape in Veblen's day. There were monopolies in beef, sugar, whiskey, shipping, railroads, steel, cotton, textiles, and
furs, and the rulers of these fiefdoms amassed fortunes so great that their
names (Rockefeller, Carnegie, Vanderbilt) still resonate today.

But one force eclipsed them all, a financial monopoly. In 1913,
nearly a decade after Veblen published *The Theory of Business Enterprise*, a US congressional committee produced its now famous *Money
Trust Investigation*, a report exposing a grand conspiracy of American
business leaders to rig half the national economy. Rockefeller was
implicated, but it was bigger than him or Standard Oil. The *Money
Trust* documented a monstrous interlocking lattice of at least eighteen
major financial corporations and more than three hundred crosscutting
directorships and secret lines of control that governed much of industrial America and manipulated the financial clearinghouses and the

New York Stock Exchange.[14] It was based on a rogues' charter known insidiously as "banking ethics," by which the conspirators agreed not to compete with one another. Atop it all sat a banker, John Pierpont Morgan.

The report warned chillingly that there were forces more dangerous than monopoly in industry: the greater danger was monopoly in finance, control of the means by which credit was allocated to industry and across the economy. If you controlled credit, it warned, you controlled it all. "The acts of this inner group [have] been more destructive of competition than anything accomplished by the trusts, for they strike at the very vitals of potential competition in every industry that is under their protection," it said, adding, "The arteries of credit [are] now clogged well-nigh to choking by the obstructions created through the control of these groups." Finance doesn't have quite the same brutal style or degree of control today, but as this book will show, it has gone a long way in this direction.

When the *Money Trust* report went public, national fury ensued. Political cartoonists drew octopuses with their tentacles wrapped around buildings, men in top hats grasping the globe, bankers sitting on sacks of money while the poor queued up to hand them their savings. Devils with pitchforks pranced with bags of cash. A scowling eight-armed J. P. Morgan cranked eight handles turning machinery inside eight banks; or he was a giant Pied Piper, leading great crowds in a merry dance into the wilderness. Louis Brandeis, the best-known lawyer of Veblen's era, summarized the report's findings with a perfectly aimed metaphor for the wealth extraction:

> The goose that lays the golden eggs has been considered a most valuable possession. But even more profitable is the privilege of taking the golden eggs laid by someone else's goose. The investment bankers now enjoy that privilege. The dominant element in our financial oligarchy is the investment banker. . . . We must break the Money Trust or the Money Trust will break us.[15]

Brandeis pointed to something else too: a lesson that recurs again and again in the story of the finance curse. At the heart of all the extraction and predation there usually lies a genuinely useful function. The central problem isn't finance but *too much* finance, the *wrong kind* of finance, and finance that is *too powerful*, unchecked by democracy.

Beyond monopolies, there were many other varieties of sabotage around in Veblen's time, many of which were international in scope. One of the biggest, which the *Money Trust Investigation* didn't even mention, also involved Morgan's bank. This saga began in 1899, when William Cromwell, Morgan's legal counsel, incorporated a new company, the Panama Canal Company of America. At the time, Panama was a province of Colombia and had a profitable railroad running across the narrow isthmus connecting North and South America. Cargo ships could unload on the Atlantic side, have their goods shipped by rail to the Pacific coast, and avoid sailing around the entire South American continent. President Theodore Roosevelt, in league with Morgan, armed and supported separatists who wanted to wrest Panama away from Colombia and get their hands on those lucrative rail transit fees. And if they could build a canal to replace the railroad, why, the profits would multiply. To cut a long conspiracy short, Panama won independence from Colombia, but only under effective US control. The Panama Canal opened in 1914, and the new country's first official fiscal agent was J. P. Morgan. "Wall Street planned, financed and executed the entire independence of Panama," summarized Ovidio Diaz Espino, a former Morgan lawyer who wrote a book about the affair entitled *How Wall Street Created a Nation*. This episode "brought down [the] Colombian government, created a new republic, shook the political foundations in Washington with corruption and gave birth to American imperialism in Latin America."[16]

Essentially, Wall Street interests had harnessed their government's military resources to build and operate a mighty tollbooth at the biggest choke point in one of the world's great trade arteries. Communities of

American financial toads soon became happily ensconced there, with the flies and spiders of Veblen's imagination replaced by giant ships. In 1919, as Panama was taking the first steps in setting up its deregulated, ask-no-questions shipping registry, Veblen summarized the game, where the wealth extractors got their government to support them as if it were its patriotic duty:

> In this international competition the machinery and policy of the state are in a peculiar degree drawn into the service of the larger business interests; so that, both in commerce and industrial enterprise, the business men of one nation are pitted against those of another and swing the forces of the state, legislative, diplomatic, and military, against one another in the strategic game of pecuniary advantage.[17]

This was sabotage, he said, appealingly wrapped in the flag. To help the national champions "compete" on a global stage, the common man must shoulder the burden and, in doing so, should be made to swell with patriotic pride.

Veblen wasn't talking about Panama, but he might as well have been. And he identified what was then and remains today one of the most important and misunderstood themes of international finance: the "competitiveness" of nations. This term could mean many things, but Veblen understood that big banks and businesses loved to promote a particular meaning of the term, which I call the "competitiveness agenda." Under this view, America is in some sort of giant global economic race, in which our biggest international firms must constantly be given subsidies—corporate tax cuts, deregulation, a free pass to let them build monopolies or abuse their American suppliers or employees, or whatever—in order that they can better compete in this race. If we don't give them these handouts, these interests warn, they'll run away to more "competitive" places like London, Hong Kong, or Geneva. I will show how this competitiveness agenda goes a long way toward explaining why some modern banks are too big to fail, why big bankers are too important to jail, why our schools aren't getting funded, why your favorite local bookshop closed down, and why tax havens seem so hard to tackle. I'll expose the fallacies, misunderstandings, and hypocrisies that underpin the competitiveness agenda and reveal it to be one of the most confused and dangerous economic myths of all time.

Veblen understood these fallacies clearly, even if he couldn't anticipate all the various schemes that financialized capitalism would create. One of these was the world of offshore tax havens, a tool of sabotage that was in its infancy in Veblen's day. There's no general agreement as to what a tax haven is, though the concept can usefully be boiled down to "escape" and "elsewhere." You take your money or your business elsewhere—offshore—to escape the rules and laws at home that you don't like. These laws may involve taxes, disclosure, financial or labor regulations, shipping requirements, or whatever, so "tax haven" is a misnomer; these places are about so much more than tax.

Let's take tax and a classic tax haven trick that had already begun to emerge in Veblen's day called "transfer pricing." Imagine it costs a Spanish multinational $1,000 to produce a container of bananas in Ecuador, and a supermarket in Santa Barbara, California, will buy that container for $3,000. Somewhere in this system lies $2,000 in profit. Now who gets to tax that profit? Well, the multinational sets up three subsidiaries: EcuadorCo in Ecuador, which produces the bananas; USACo in the United States, which sells the bananas to the supermarket; and PanamaCo, a shell company with no employees and based in a tax haven. These companies inside the same multinational sell the container to each other: first, EcuadorCo sells it to PanamaCo for $1,000, then PanamaCo sells it to USACo for $3,000. Where does the $2,000 profit end up? Well, it cost EcuadorCo $1,000 to produce the container, but it sold the container for $1,000 to PanamaCo, so there's zero profit—hence no tax—in Ecuador. Similarly, USACo bought the bananas from PanamaCo for $3,000 but sold them to the supermarket for $3,000, so there's no profit or tax in the United States either. PanamaCo is where the action is. It bought the container for $1,000 and sold it for $3,000, making $2,000 profit. But because it's in a tax haven, the tax is zero. Presto! No tax anywhere!

In the real world it's obviously much more complicated than this, but this is the basic concept, and indeed Panama was one of the pioneers in this game in Veblen's lifetime. It's clear that nobody anywhere in this financial game has produced a better, more efficient way to grow, transport, or sell bananas. This is simply wealth extraction: a shift of wealth away from taxpayers in both rich and poor countries toward the businesses and some lawyers' and accountants' fees. But it's also sabotage, because it rigs markets in favor of the large multinationals who can afford to set up these expensive international schemes, at the expense of their smaller domestic competitors who can't.

Two brothers who became pioneers of this kind of multinational tax strategy were Edmund and William Vestey, who founded the Union Cold Storage Company in Liverpool, England, in 1897. Meat monopolists extraordinaire, the Vesteys ran cattle operations in South America at one end, where they crushed the unions on their extensive holdings. At the other end, in Britain, they crushed rival meat traders—including one of my great-great-uncles[18]—and monopolized the retail trade. In between, they dominated certain shipping lines, not least through their Panama Shipping Company Inc., and rigged the international tax system in their favor. "If I kill a beast in the Argentine and sell the product of that beast in Spain," William Vestey taunted a British royal commission in 1920, "this country can get no tax on that business. You may do what you like, but you cannot have it."[19]

From those early beginnings in the 1920s, tax havens would grow to offer a wider ecosystem of market-cornering possibilities. And with the growth of mobile global finance, particularly after the 1970s, the possibilities for sabotage would multiply, in the United States and around the globe.

As the twentieth century progressed, Veblen's views that sabotage and wealth extraction were central organizing principles of capitalism would be vindicated again and again. Take, for instance, the great American streetcar scandal, when a consortium of oil, bus, car, and tire companies came together in a loose arrangement to buy up streetcars and electric mass-transit rail systems in forty-five major US cities, then kill them off. (The scandal inspired the Hollywood film *Who Framed Roger Rabbit*.) Antitrust lawyers argued that the ensuing destruction of rail-based urban transport was part of a "deliberate concerted action" to push America into dependency on cars, buses, tires, and oil. To the extent that they were right, this helped pave the way for, among other things, massive climate change.

Financial players also sabotage markets where we buy and sell stuff *all the time*. The less regulated these markets are, and the less attention regulators pay, the more rigging. That helps explain why, when regulators' attention was elsewhere engaged during the financial crisis, crude oil prices rose from $65 a barrel in June 2007 to nearly $150 in July 2008. Yet this happened amid falling demand and a world oil glut, exactly the opposite of what the textbooks tell us ought to happen. On September 22 alone, the price rose over $18 a barrel, then dropped nearly $15 the next day. By December, it was down to $30, then back up over $70 by the following June. An internal Goldman Sachs memo in 2011 suggested that speculation accounted for about a third of the price of oil—equivalent to $10 extra on every American driver's fill-up. The speculators weren't buying up actual barrels of oil to sell them later at a profit, not least because there are physical limits on just how much oil there is available to buy. Instead they were employing financial instruments, which can be used to bet without limit: one bet piled upon another, upon another. Each bet tends to push the oil price either up or down. This created unreasonably large price swings, which were then worsened by herd behavior: if Goldman Sachs was buying, people reasoned, then they ought to as well. As hedge fund officials and other market watchers noted, the mayhem—which ricocheted to oil consumers around the world—greatly benefited large financial players, who had the best information to buy and sell ahead of everyone else: they made out like bank robbers.

Meanwhile, in the aluminum market, Goldman Sachs indulged in some bizarre market sabotage when in 2010 it bought up Metro, a metals storage company regulated by the London Metal Exchange, the standard-setter for the aluminum industry. Before the purchase, customers who bought aluminum from Metro had to wait some forty days for it to be delivered from the warehouse, but within a couple of years they were having to wait ten to fifteen times as long—674 days at one point, according to investigations by the US Senate and the *New York Times*. Metro's customers would also have to pay to store the aluminum for two years before they could get their hands on it. What is more, prices went haywire. MillerCoors, a big user of aluminum for drinks cans, reckoned the dysfunctional market had imposed an extra $3 billion cost on users; some industry experts estimated American shoppers had paid $5 billion extra from 2010 to 2013 through a thousand tiny price hikes in the cans, automobiles, and other aluminum products. Over this time, Goldman was ramping up its trading of financial products linked to aluminum, and other players—notably Germany's Deutsche Bank, JP Morgan, a British hedge fund called Red Kite, and the Swiss-based commodity trader Glencore—inserted themselves into and milked this strange market. All of this was overseen and approved from London, a den of rogue regulators that we'll meet properly in chapter seven and that hosts the London Metal Exchange.[20]

Britain also provides an even more blatant, brazen example of sabotage. There, a unit of Britain's giant Royal Bank of Scotland used the crisis to hit thousands of fragile small businesses with crippling, unexpected fees, fines, and interest-rate hikes. It became known as the bank's "Vampire Unit": under its Project Dash for Cash, financial terms were engineered to make more struggling businesses fail, so it could get hold of their assets cheaply. "Rope: sometimes you need to let customers hang themselves," one internal bank memo said. An independent report said the bank wasn't alone either: it found "profiteering and abhorrent behavior" all across retail banking. "Some of the banks," it said, "are harming their customers through their decisions and causing their financial downfall." This sabotage led to family breakdowns, heart attacks, and suicides.[21]

Veblen made an observation about such behavior that remains relevant today. The fountains of profit that can ensue from this kind of rapacity and market rigging underpin what he sneeringly called "business sagacity." We hear "business sagacity" every day from the leaders of politics, industry, and finance. We hear it when CNN or Fox brings out know-nothing bankers or financial pundits to applaud the latest merger-driven rise in the stock market, the latest deregulatory or tax-cutting gift to Wall Street, or a surge in banker bonuses or private equity activity, as if these things benefit the country.[22] To the extent that these soaring profits are extracted from the veins of our economy, they are signs of rigged markets and economic atrophy, not health. As Veblen famously put it, "business sagacity reduces itself in the last analysis to the judicious use of sabotage."

Veblen and Tarbell were often pilloried by their contemporaries, yet they were both proved correct again and again, throughout the twentieth century and beyond. After her exposé of Standard Oil, Tarbell was vilified by sections of the media. "The dear girl's efforts . . . are pathetic," wrote one academic. She and her followers were "sentimental sob sisters," wrote another. Rockefeller called her "Miss Tar Barrel," a socialist, and "that misguided woman." She pretended to be fair, he said, but "like some women, she distorts facts . . . and utterly disregards reason." The vilification made her long to "escape into the safe retreat of a library" and be liberated from "harrowing human beings confronting me, tearing me."[23] But in 1911 her investigations bore fruit. Standard Oil was broken up into thirty-four different companies, to become the forerunners of today's oil giants ExxonMobil and Chevron, and even a part of British Petroleum. The breakup didn't last, though: at a meeting in 1928 at Achnacarry Castle in Scotland, the heads of some of the biggest fragments of Standard Oil got together with some foreign rivals and hammered out a secret criminal deal to carve up the world's oil industry into profitably collaborating fiefdoms.

Veblen died in 1929, a few weeks before the great financial crash vindicated his big ideas. The crash, and the ensuing turmoil, fed dark forces that eventually plunged the world into bloody global warfare, still in the lifetime of Tarbell, who died in 1944. The work of Tarbell and Veblen, and history, contain warnings: these great financialized malignancies of capitalism must be tackled.

CHAPTER TWO

Neoliberalism without Borders

Sometime in the mid-1950s a disagreement took place in the cafeteria of Northwestern University, in Chicago's northern suburbs, between Meyer Burstein, a conservative economist, and his colleague Charles Tiebout, a high-spirited left-winger who was teaching microeconomics on the faculty there. The argument, when it started, was simply about high rents, but by the end it had developed into something bigger: a grand and influential new theory about how states and nations "compete" with each other. The two colleagues got on well enough as friends, but Tiebout was irritated that Burstein had become one of the fast-growing band of what he called Friedmaniacs, a group that blindly followed Milton Friedman, the Chicago School economist who was then on his way to becoming America's financial godfather of the Right.

Tiebout was "one of the funniest guys I have ever known," said Lee Hansen, one of his only surviving close friends. Tiebout would imitate academic bigwigs in his classes, give them silly nicknames, and turn up to meetings in dungarees despite the university's traditional suit-and-tie uniform. When a student's father complained about a "socialist" book Tiebout had assigned as part of his course, Tiebout impishly got the dean to send a letter back stating, "This is to inform you that Professor Tiebout is not a socialist; he is a communist."[1]

Tiebout was not in fact a communist; he was just a mischief-maker. Back then, though, communism was a risky thing to even joke about: Senator Joseph McCarthy had been conducting anticommunist witch hunts in Hollywood, government, academia, and other parts of American society. He had even accused George Marshall—originator of the Marshall Plan to block global communist expansion by providing aid to Europe after World War II—of having communist leanings.[2]

Behind the fun, though, Tiebout did believe that government could do good. And at that lunch in the Northwestern cafeteria he felt the need to defend this belief when Burstein started griping about the high rents in the part of Chicago where he lived, which reflected high property taxes that paid for public services he didn't use.

"Why should I pay for good schools when I have no children?" Burstein asked.

"But Meyer," Tiebout said, "you don't have to pay those high rents! Why don't you just move to Rogers Park?"[3]

Later that day Tiebout was chatting with an undergraduate student, Charles Leven. "You know, Chas," Tiebout said, "I was absolutely right. People do have a choice over their local public goods and a way of showing it through their revealed preference simply by moving. In fact, that's a damn good idea. I should stick to my guns and write it up!" In less than a week he had written a first draft, and he submitted it to the conservative *Journal of Political Economy*, which published it in October 1956 under the dull title "A Pure Theory of Local Expenditures." Tiebout could not know it then, but his hastily drafted article would become, a few decades later, one of the most widely cited articles in economics.[4]

A phrase in that conversation with Leven—"revealed preference"—ought to twitch the antennae of any mainstream economist. Tiebout was referring to Revealed Preference Theory, a concept the US economist Paul Samuelson had put forward in 1938. The basic idea was that while you can't insert psychological probes directly into people's minds to figure out their consumer preferences, you can do the next best thing: if you study their buying habits you can reveal their preferences and plug this data into the Chicago School's elegant mathematical models and graphs. This data will allow you to study the effects of government policies and subject them all to the penetrating analyses of market economics.

By the 1950s Revealed Preference Theory was already quite widely used for understanding consumer behavior. But when you switched away from consumers and markets and tried to apply the model to public services like schools, roads, or hospitals, there was a problem, which Samuelson himself had laid out in a paper in 1954. And it was a big one: the so-called free-rider problem. People will happily consume public services, Samuelson explained, but they like to dodge the taxes that pay for these things. The free-rider problem means that you can't get people to reveal their preferences regarding taxes and public services, so you can't shoehorn this stuff into the Chicago School's elegant mathematical models to determine optimal levels of taxes and public spending. Government and democratic politics had to step in and deal with this one, and the economists wouldn't get a shot at it. Ouch.

Tiebout's 1956 paper claimed to have found the riposte. There *was* a way to envisage a market for public services and taxes after all, he explained. Samuelson might be right that you couldn't apply market analysis to the US *federal* government, Tiebout reasoned, but you could do so with *local* governments. After all, each state or local government zone offers a different package combining a particular bundle of taxes with a particular bundle of public services, and people can move among these jurisdictions according to which mix of taxes and public goods works best for them. (Burstein, as it happens, did move to Rogers Park. He paid less rent and "was happy as a clam and stayed there.") Shopping for better public services like this was, Tiebout wrote, like shopping in a mall: public services are analogous to consumer goods, while taxes are akin to the prices of those consumer goods. Communities will "compete" to provide the best mixes of tax and public services, just as in a private market.[5]

If people can vote with their feet, he went on, then not only could economists reveal Americans' preferences for the right mix of public goods and taxes and fit this data into their mathematical models, but you'd also get a "competitive sorting" of people into optimal communities, thus bringing the efficiency of private markets into the government sphere. With a little mathematics, governments could discover the ideal equilibrium, balancing taxes against public services. Countering the rising tide of antigovernment Friedmaniacs, Tiebout felt he had shown how government could be efficient after all. Tax cuts weren't the magic elixir to entice productive companies and people to move across borders; those firms and people needed good tax-financed public services too. It was a trade-off, and when people moved across borders to make this trade-off work best for them, this improved overall welfare. All this amounted to a rather progressive agenda—or so he thought.[6]

Tiebout himself never really pursued his idea; for him it was "just another paper," technically elegant but hardly rooted in the real world.[7] And for a long time it didn't take off. Political centralization was in vogue, so nobody cared much for theories about local politics, and the media usually brought up local government only in the context of desegregation, incompetence, or corruption. The story might well have ended there—and for Tiebout it did: he died of a heart attack in January 1968, aged forty-three.

When the world finally started to wake up to Tiebout's paper, the year after his death, it would kick off a debate about one of the most important questions in the modern global economy: What happens when rich people, banks, multinational firms, or profits shift across borders in response to different incentives like corporate tax cuts, financial deregulation, and so on? When states "compete" by offering incentives like corporate tax cuts, is this a good thing, or the recipe for an unhealthy race to the bottom, as states scramble to offer ever-bigger incentives? In this debate, Tiebout's ideas would be magnified and distorted, then wielded to support arguments that this kind of "competition" is a good thing. And these arguments, in turn, would serve as the ideological underpinning for a wide range of harmful policies that generate the finance curse. Which is not what the leftist Charles Tiebout would have wanted at all.

History shows that inequality usually gets properly upended only after large, violent shocks.[8] For Tiebout's generation, it was World War II that provided the shock. The financial crisis and Great Depression of the 1930s had discredited the old certainties of free trade, financial deregulation, and laissez-faire economics that had given the market saboteurs like Rockefeller and the Vesteys such freedom to operate. Workers who had spilled their blood on the battlefields of France were in no mood to pander to moneyed elites anymore; they wanted their countries to give something back to them. The end of the war in 1945 provided a unique political opening to put into practice the progressive, revolutionary ideas of the British economist and polymath John Maynard Keynes.

Keynes knew that finance had its uses, but he knew that it could also be dangerous, especially when it was allowed to slosh around the world at will, unchecked by democratic controls. If your economy is open to tides of global hot money—rootless money not tied to any particular real project or nation, that is—then it is harder to pursue desirable policies like full employment. This is because if you try, for instance, to boost industry by lowering interest rates in a country that is open to flows of financial capital, then money will simply sluice out, looking for better returns elsewhere. Capital will become scarcer; the value of the currency will tend to fall; and interest rates will be forced up again. If governments wanted to act in the interests of their citizens, Keynes knew, there was no alternative but to curb those wild, speculative flows. "Let goods be homespun whenever it is reasonably and conveniently possible," he famously said. "Above all, let finance be primarily national." Keynes carefully distinguished between cross-border *trade*, which was often beneficial, and speculative cross-border *finance*, which he knew was far more dangerous. It wasn't just governments at risk; the great crash of 1929 had exposed how cross-border speculative flows could wreak havoc with the private sector too. "Experience is accumulating," he added, "that remoteness between ownership and operation is an evil in the relations among men, likely or certain in the long run to set up strains and enmities which will bring to nought the financial calculation." If distant foreign financiers control your business, he was saying, the damage is likely to outweigh whatever profits might emerge.

Keynes's ideas about the dangers of cross-border finance carried such intellectual force that by the time World War II got under way they had become mainstream wisdom. Governments and general public opinion accepted that if countries were to avoid a repeat of the economic and military horrors that had occurred in recent years, they were going to have to transform the global financial system. So in 1944, under the intellectual guidance of Keynes and in the dominating presence of his US counterpart Harry Dexter White, the world's most advanced countries got together at Bretton Woods in New Hampshire and hammered out an agreement to set up a global system of negotiated cooperation, to curb flows of financial capital across borders and to protect countries from these destabilizing tides of hot money. The system had a shaky start: from 1945 to 1947 Wall Street interests forced through a brief financial liberalization, which caused huge waves of capital flight from war-shattered Europe, as rich Europeans sent their wealth overseas to escape having to pay for reconstruction. But fears of a communist takeover in Europe soon focused policy makers' minds, and the system was at last given teeth.

Bretton Woods was a remarkable arrangement and almost unimaginable today. Cross-border finance was heavily constrained, while trade remained fairly free. So cross-border financial flows were permitted if they were to finance trade, real investment, or other accepted priorities, but cross-border speculation was discouraged. A vast administrative cooperative machinery was set up to make the system work, to prevent destabilizing flows of hot money, and to open space for war-shattered democratic societies to put in place progressive policies. In his book *Moneyland*, the British writer Oliver Bullough uses the image of an oil tanker as a metaphor for the system. If it has just one huge tank, the oil may sluice back and forth in ever-greater waves until it knocks the vessel over. But if divided into many smaller, separate compartments—each compartment being analogous to a country in the Bretton Woods system—the oil could shift about a bit inside each compartment "but would not be able to achieve enough momentum to damage the integrity of the entire vessel."[9]

One of the overall aims of this giant global safety mechanism was, as US Treasury secretary Henry Morgenthau famously declared, to "drive the usurious moneylenders from the temple of international finance." Another related goal was to keep Europe growing and keep communist influences out. Curbing finance was then—and should be today—treated as a matter of national security.

The Bretton Woods system was leaky and troublesome, but it held together for roughly a quarter century after World War II. With finance bottled up in its national compartments, governments felt free to act in their countries' best interests, without fear that all the money would flee overseas. Taxes for the wealthy were high, sometimes very high: average top income tax rates fluctuated around 70–80 percent in the United States between the 1950s and 1970s (and in Britain, having reached 99.25 percent during the war, stood at 97.5 percent for most of the 1950s, falling to 80 percent only in 1959). Domestic financial regulations were amazingly robust too: the New Deal in the United States, combined with vibrant anti-monopoly laws, split up mega-banks and hedged bankers with all kinds of restrictions. Massive government-led technological developments during the war were also unleashing waves of industrialization, and governments continued to invest aggressively in research considered too risky for the private sector.[10] Health services and government-funded welfare provision blossomed across the Western world; labor unions were mighty; and developing countries successfully nurtured infant industries behind trade barriers. It is hard to imagine now, but investment bankers weren't paid outrageously more than teachers.[11]

Amid all this massive, coordinated government intervention and in some cases astonishingly high tax rates, economic growth in both rich and poor countries was collectively higher—much higher—during this period than in any other age of human history, before or since. Western economies grew at an average 5.5 percent a year during 1950–73: astonishing by modern standards. Trade flourished, even as speculative capital flows were repressed. The era is now often known as the Golden Age of Capitalism.[12] As growth powered ahead, economic inequalities fell, inflation was tamed, debts shrank, and financial crises were small and infrequent. The history books are full of references to France's *trente glorieuses* (glorious thirty), Italy's *miracolo economico* (economic miracle), Germany's and Austria's *Wirtschaftswunder* (economic wonder), and plenty of others. "Most of our people have never had it so good," purred British prime minister Harold Macmillan in 1957. "Go round the country, go to the industrial towns, go to the farms and you will see a state of prosperity such as we have never had in my lifetime—nor indeed in the history of this country."[13] Growth in developing countries picked up too. This was the American dream on a global scale. Rebuilding after the destruction of war was a part of the story, to be sure, as was a large shift of women out of unpaid work at home into the paid workforce, but controlling global financial flows was an essential ingredient, preventing crises and speculative attacks on countries that tried to put in place progressive economic policies. The Bretton Woods system was a vast, explicit, brassy administrative and political antidote to the curse of overweening finance and to the freewheeling policies of the earlier robber-baron age. Finance would be society's servant, not its master. Keynes never got to see his ideas so thoroughly vindicated—he died in 1946. But Keynes's ideas would not go uncontested for long. A counterrevolution determined to shackle governments and unleash the full power of money and finance again was already well under way.

This pushback from the banks was organized around a simple idea that had come in a "sudden illumination" in 1936 to an Austrian economist called Friedrich Hayek. Within a couple of years this idea had a name: neoliberalism. For many people, "neoliberalism" isn't a serious term but a political swear word brandished by people on the Left against anyone to their right whom they don't like. (It's also not to be confused with the term "liberal," which some in the United States seem to wield as a term of abuse against anyone to their left whom they don't like.) The word "neoliberalism" has a particular history and meaning, which in terms of its practical effects has meant financial deregulation, privatization, and globalization actively promoted and protected by governments that have fallen under the sway of these ideas.

Neoliberalism is an outgrowth of classical liberalism, which dates back a couple of centuries. There's political liberalism, which is all about citizens having equal democratic rights in a system of sovereign law, and there's economic liberalism, which starts from Adam Smith's "invisible hand," by which free exchanges or trade in properly functioning—that is, unsabotaged—markets are supposed to make society better off overall. The more liberal (or free) the exchange, in this view, the better for society as a whole; government's role is to provide basic functions like defense, to enforce property rights, and to keep a watchful eye out for monopolies, but otherwise to get out of the way. Political and economic liberalism are fairly separate realms, but in each case freedom is foremost.

Neoliberalism put these ideas on steroids and gave them a rather large twist. Its starting point was the theory that government inevitably amasses ever more power and heads toward tyranny. At the time Hayek had his sudden illumination, this fear was understandable. The Nazis loomed over Europe, and Soviet totalitarianism was just over the hill. The Thought Police from George Orwell's hit novel *Nineteen Eighty-Four*, published in 1949, also hung like a leering specter over Western culture. Hayek began with the idea that competition in markets delivered efficiency and collective benefits for all. Then he took a giant leap of faith and argued that this conclusion could be, and even should be, true not just of markets and commercial exchange but of other aspects of life. What if you could reengineer society and laws into a giant market or set of markets, he wondered, using government scissors to cut the social fabric into separate fragments, then pitching these fragments into competition with one another? The simplest example of this is privatization, where governments sell off state assets to the private sector in the hope that they will compete and become more efficient. If you can achieve this, Hayek argued, then the market can become a tool for finally taming government, the handmaiden of tyranny.

Hayek's most famous book, *The Road to Serfdom*, laid this all out. Competition and the price system were the *only* legitimate arbiters of what was good and true, he said. And this soon became a neoliberal mantra. Cut taxes, deregulate, privatize, and launch all these pieces into competition with one another, then let it all rip. Not just banks or companies, but also health services, universities, school playing fields, environmental protection bodies, prisons, military capabilities, regulators, lawyers, shell companies, and the kitchen sink—all of it could be, should be, *must be*, shoehorned into the same competitive framework, to be sorted and judged by the only true test of virtue: the test of the market. In this framework, explained the writer Stephen Metcalf, humans are transformed from being "bearers of grace, or of inalienable rights and duties," into ruthless profit-and-loss calculators, sorted into winners and losers. Society is no longer a space for political debate or collective action but a universal market that harnesses the benefits of competition to work as a giant, all-knowing mind, a sort of organically emerging intelligence in which the market constantly figures out the best way to distribute scarce resources among competing priorities to deliver the greatest good for all. Government is, in this view, not necessarily weakened but instead reengineered as an agent for making markets penetrate as deeply into society as possible. Things like citizenship and traditional notions of justice and even the rule of law are swept aside and replaced with technocratic measures like productivity, risk, and returns on capital. Neoliberalism is "the disenchantment of politics by economics," as the British political thinker Will Davies put it: "an attempt to replace political judgement with economic evaluation. . . . [T]hrough processes of competition it becomes possible to discern who and what is valuable." By doing so, he concludes, "competition, competitiveness and, ultimately, inequality, are rendered justifiable and acceptable."[14] This was a wholly new notion of justice. A more revolutionary idea is hard to imagine.

The neoliberal revolution was born in earnest at a historic meeting of American and European intellectuals at Mont Pèlerin near Geneva in 1947, just a few years after the Bretton Woods summit. The meeting was attended by Hayek and many other famous economists and thinkers, including Milton Friedman, Ludwig von Mises, George Stigler, Frank Knight, Karl Popper, and Lionel Robbins. The meeting was financed by Switzerland's three largest banks, its two largest insurance companies, the Swiss central bank, the Bank of England, and City of London interests.[15] Hayek himself, after leaving the London School of Economics in 1950, "never held a permanent appointment that was not paid for by corporate sponsors."

The ambition of the Mont Pelerin Society (MPS), born at that meeting, was utopian, even messianic, envisaging private-sector heroes overturning the dark forces of authoritarian state control. "We must raise and train an army of fighters for freedom," declared Hayek, "to work out, in continuous effort, a philosophy of freedom." Economic freedom would deliver political freedom. A tide of corporate money began to flow into a new network of radical think tanks, which pushed these ideas. This began as a trickle with the MPS in Switzerland but soon spread to London, with the launch of the Institute for Economic Affairs, which became immensely influential there, and then shifted rapidly further afield and offshore, buoyed by financial and corporate donations in each place. The MPS's intellectual momentum morphed and branched into an international chain of think tanks and supporters, which in the United States would be guided by the ideas of extreme anti-government thinkers like James McGill Buchanan and heavily funded by billionaire members of the family that founded the commodity trading firm Koch Industries. Globally, they would become the backbone of the Atlas Network, a syndicate of nearly five hundred think tanks and institutions promoting libertarian, anti-state ideas, also funded by myriad billionaires, millionaires, and financial and large corporate institutions. This loosely connected coalition would form the engine of neoliberalism and the pushback against the Keynesian consensus.[16]

In terms of raw power, neoliberalism takes authority away from politicians and hands it to economists and to moneyed interests. At the apex of this new form of authority sit the financial players who buy and sell global companies, exerting a kind of veto power over governments that have drunk the neoliberal elixir. Perhaps the most pervasive and insidious outcome of this ideology is the broad-based phenomenon I mentioned in the introduction, financialization, a central element of the finance curse, which involves not just the growth in size of the financial sector but also the injection of financial techniques and competition into pretty much anything that can't be nailed down—and a lot that can be.

These ideas enraptured growing numbers of people, including a British woman called Margaret Roberts, the president of the Oxford University Conservative Association. Half a century later, long after she had married, taken the surname Thatcher, and become Britain's first female prime minister, she would call Hayek's *Road to Serfdom* the book "to which I have returned so often." The ideas would also percolate through to Ronald Reagan, who famously declared that "government is not the solution to our problem; government *is* the problem." As the historian Nancy MacLean and the journalist Jane Mayer have documented, these ideas were carefully networked, targeted, and funded in the United States and beyond, to help produce the money-tainted political systems we have today.[17]

But the ideas' influence went far beyond money. Many politicians love neoliberalism because the "verdict of the market" absolves them of responsibility for making hard choices, helping them sidestep troublesome notions like fairness or justice. Having dislodged all those prisons, crime laboratories, or fragments of the education system from the grasping arms of government and into competition with one another, the politicians can lean back with their feet on their desks and eat popcorn, while they watch the laissez-faire machinery of "the market" sort out all that noisy, sweaty, difficult kerfuffle. And this hasn't been so hard to sell to the public either; after all, who doesn't like competition? To borrow a few words from Keynes, "nothing except copulation is so enthralling." When television presenters on CNBC or Fox take the government policies of the day and say, "Let's see if Wall Street thinks this is a good idea," they aren't just promoting what Veblen sneeringly called business sagacity. They're embracing neoliberalism and its *political* judgments about what is good.

Yet the ambition of neoliberals did not stop at shoehorning people, companies, and parts of our societies into the great sausage machine of the price system; they wanted to shovel in whole countries. And Tiebout opened up this wonderland for them. Like two powerful magnets brought into close proximity, the two bodies of thought—the neoliberals arguing that parts of society *should* be made to compete (efficiently) with one another, and Tiebout arguing that states and jurisdictions *could* compete efficiently with one another—were inevitably going to come together.

The full merger happened when a Princeton economist called Wallace Oates wrote a paper in 1969 with some measurements that seemed to confirm Tiebout's thesis.[18] Oates looked at fifty-three communities in New Jersey and studied their property taxes, along with local authority spending on schools. Then he looked at how this related to local house prices. And his results were just as Tiebout had predicted: higher local property taxes seemed to mean lower house prices, while more school spending meant higher house prices. People did "vote with their feet" after all, moving in and out of communities in response to taxation and spending packages. Tiebout, it seemed, was right!

Oates's results may not seem so surprising today, but this idea was radically new then. As the scholar William Fischel put it, "everyone knew that Americans were mobile, but no economist had previously connected mobility with demand for the services of local government." The model grew and grew in stature and has now become, according to Fischel, "pretty much the touchstone for local public economics in the United States . . . its influence has expanded beyond economics and beyond the public sector."[19] Those arguing for greater tax and spending powers for local governments around the world draw support from this model born out of Tiebout's and Oates's work. Behind the scenes, Tiebout's big idea is everywhere.

For the neoliberals, the idea of states "efficiently sorting" was thrilling: a mechanism for shoveling districts, states, and even whole countries into their competitive models at last, enabling them to declare the whole process a good thing. Even better, it could justify the view that public services and tax systems and even laws were just another commodity to be bought and sold in the marketplace. "Law became one of many 'assets' through which a nation can compete," wrote Will Davies; tax "becomes nothing but a 'cost' for the [company-nation] to minimize."[20]

It's not hard to see how subversive all this was. The rule of law has a monetary price, and so does your corporate tax rate and regulatory environment. Once this awesome intellectual land grab by corporate and financial interests began to enter mainstream politics in the late 1970s, it would lead inevitably to corruption, oligarchy, bank bailouts, and the growth of international organized crime.

As these changes unfolded, a series of events was starting to play out on the ground in the United States that would expose Tiebout's ideas in ways he would never have intended. Rather than local governments competing with one another and thus increasing efficiency, as he had once thought, the emerging "competition" among the states was revealing itself to be a powerful tool for big financial and corporate interests to get what they wanted from states by playing them against one another in a vicious race to the bottom. (For the rest of this book, I will call this latter form "competition"—with scare quotes—as opposed to competition between private actors in markets.)

In 1973, just four years after Oates published his paper, Idaho's Democratic governor Cecil Andrus had a meeting with David Packard, the boss of the fast-growing computer company Hewlett-Packard. The company was looking to build a major new computer plant and had narrowed its options down to Idaho or Oregon. Andrus described in his autobiography how he pitched his state's attractions in the face of an attractive counteroffer from Oregon. "Packard listened politely," Andrus remembered, "then asked in a level voice, 'What type of tax concessions is the state willing to give?'" Andrus's answer would seem quaint today.

> I took a deep breath and set out to sell him on a difficult argument. "We don't believe in existing businesses subsidizing new businesses," I told him. "When you come to Idaho you become a citizen, and we all play by the same rules. A few years down the line and you'll be an old-timer. Do you want to subsidize the next guy who comes along?" It was a nervous moment. After a brief pause, Packard grunted: "Makes sense. That's the way to go." He moved on to other questions. We captured the computer plant and gained a top-notch corporate citizen.

At that time the old consensus was still alive, which held that corporations were not just machines for creating profit but had a wider purpose: they were stable social institutions that created useful goods and services, well-paying jobs, tax revenue, and, ultimately, thriving communities.

That consensus was about to come under threat and eventually change beyond all recognition. One of the least well-known instruments of change was a new industry that was already stirring in America by the time Andrus spoke. This industry had first emerged in 1934 when a businessman called Leonard Yaseen created the Fantus Factory Locating Service in New York. The company set out to provide expert local guidance for companies that wanted to relocate or expand into unfamiliar parts of the country. This was in itself a perfectly reasonable idea. The problems soon began, however, when companies went beyond looking for the good stuff that benefits everyone in a locality, such as strong infrastructure or a healthy and educated workforce, and into searching for wealth-extracting free rides such as special tax treatment, exemptions from pro-union laws, lax environmental standards, or outright financial inducements from politicians at the expense of local taxpayers.

By the time Oates popularized Tiebout's paper in the late 1960s, the relocation industry was already maturing, with secretive consultants playing local areas off against one another and constantly pushing states to get the "business climate" right—which meant extracting maximum subsidies from local taxpayers. In the words of Greg LeRoy of the US nonprofit group Good Jobs First, a veteran observer of these changes, these consultants are now "the rock stars in expensive suits at economic development conferences," or "the speaker-bait that brings in hundreds of public officials who hang on their every word"; they are the "shock troops of the corporate-orchestrated 'economic war among the states' that is slashing corporate tax rates and manipulating state and local governments everywhere." While "cities and states are 'whipsawed' against each other to maximize subsidies," they "have played our state-eat-state system like a fiddle."[21]

LeRoy outlines fourteen free-riding scams the site consultants deploy, including job blackmail, creating a "bogus competitor," receiving "payoffs for layoffs" in the form of subsidies while firing workers, and paying poverty wages while sticking taxpayers with hidden costs. A presentation by Ernst & Young, one of the players in this game, was entitled "Turning Your State Government Relations Department from a Money Pit into a Cash Cow." Since the 1970s this race among US states has been getting faster and faster, and today the system has run amok.

One of the best petri dishes for studying this at close quarters is Kansas City, where the state border between Kansas and Missouri runs through the middle of town. Companies here can relocate across the state line simply by crossing the street, and this has sparked especially fierce local border wars on incentives, even calls for "cease-fires." On a visit to the Kansas City area one icy December morning in late 2016, I met Blake Schreck, president of the Chamber of Commerce in Lenexa, a prosperous municipality in Johnson County on the Kansas side of the border. Soft-spoken and genial, Schreck reminded me of Apple's founder, Steve Jobs: tall and silver-haired, wearing a turtleneck and wire-framed glasses. He operates out of an office in a beautiful white-painted former farmhouse with Harrods-green shutters and set among lush clipped lawns, and his job is to persuade businesses to move to the area: first Lenexa, then Johnson County, then Kansas State. He seems to have been effective. Lenexa is a haven of high-end business parks, sprawling low-rise office buildings, and industrial centers, nestled among pretty suburban developments chock-full of architects, engineers, and bioscientists living comfortably behind white picket fences. Employment in Johnson County has been growing by over 4,000 jobs on average a year, and its median income is 40 percent above the national average.[22]

When I met him Schreck outlined a number of traditional reasons so many businesses come to the area. "We have had good elected officials who are not afraid to get infrastructure out ahead of growth: streets and roads and sewers and all these kinds of non-sexy things. Over the years it has paid off," he told me. But the excellent local public school system is key, he said. "The hard Right come here and say all that matters is the lowest possible taxes. But here in Johnson County we are the antithesis of that. It is about total community development. Here they are paying for excellence in a safe neighborhood. We have proven that that is the model that works. Honestly and truly," he continued, "in thirty years of doing this I have never had anyone telling me the taxes in Kansas are too high. It has never been an issue. When I started here, we looked down our noses at anyone who even dared ask for an abatement or incentive: we thought, 'If you want to be in our community you pay your way and join the community.'" Idaho's governor Cecil Andrus would have approved.

But the conversation then turned darker. Certainly by the 1990s, Schreck said, he had noticed direct contact with potential businesses being replaced by a more aggressive brand of consultant, who rudely and ruthlessly changed the calculations. "Instead of 'Hey, come on in and have a beer and a steak, and let's get to know each other and see if you like our community,' the whole process is more cold and clinical now. You're put in a matrix on some consultant's spreadsheet, and you want to get into their top ten. You have to be ready to respond to these data-heavy requests: they want information overnight on a five- and ten-mile demographic slice and study. Everything is now driven by the consultants. That is the big change in the industry. Incentives coalesced around and became part of this whole culture when the consultants started driving the relocation train."

A culture of secrecy has crept in along with the consultants, and in their hands it is a deadly weapon for jimmying more corporate subsidies from the public purse. Secrecy helps the consultants exaggerate and lie about what rival places are offering while preventing you from checking, so they can squeeze the last drops out of your desperate state or city. Schreck pulled out some files and riffled through them, reading out project names like Bigfoot, Redwood, and Maple, each with ironclad confidentiality clauses attached. "We've had big deals here where six to ten people come in from a company, and we're not even allowed to know their *first* names," he said. Schreck and his colleagues gave them names from the Quentin Tarantino movie *Reservoir Dogs*: Mr. Pink, Mr. Orange, and so on. "These are the extremes we've been driven to."

In LeRoy's long experience, companies nearly always decide where they want to relocate to before they start playing the states against one another, but with consultants earning up to 30 percent of the value of the subsidy package, they have every incentive to deceive and exert undue pressure, and around 90 percent of the value of incentives gets gobbled up by big businesses; small businesses hardly get such opportunities.[23] Not only that, but the tax incentive game is notorious for corruption, with public officials being paid off or receiving campaign "donations" for rubber-stamping juicy deals. There are many revolving doors.[24] The Missouri-controlled part of Kansas City, for instance, has set up an arm's-length economic development corporation (EDC) whose avowed goal is "a competitive, vibrant and self-sustaining economy," but its staff members rotate in and out of the big law firms negotiating the handouts. The EDC also gets a cut of each deal, while tax abatements come out of someone else's budget: the classic free-rider problem.

Johnson County, Schreck said, now typically gives a 50–55 percent property tax abatement for incoming businesses, but aggressive companies have squeezed out more: the restaurant chain Applebee's got 90 percent for ten years by playing the we'll-move-to-Missouri card. The Missouri Port Authority gives up to 100 percent. Even more remarkably, the Promoting Employment Across Kansas (PEAK) program peels off—get this—as much as 95 percent of the withholding taxes levied on employees' payrolls and, instead of handing those taxes over to the hard-pressed state, funnels these sums back to the companies employing them for up to ten years. Other deals allow companies to get their sales taxes paid in their projects. Such deals are becoming increasingly common across the United States, and they've got a nickname: "paying taxes to the boss." There are other goodies, such as zero-interest loans or outright grants from states. "We are now at a point where there is an expectation pretty much from every company that comes along that there is going to be some financing," Schreck said. "There are other states that blatantly pay you—we aren't close to that point." Yet the race seems to be speeding up, and different tax jurisdictions are increasingly at each other's throats. "We've traditionally been great partners, but it's put us at odds with each other. Put a bunch of rats in a box and if there's plenty of cheese, no problem. But take away the cheese, and they start biting each other."

Just a few miles east of Schreck's offices, immediately across the state line, is Jackson County, Missouri, where I met Bruce Eddy, executive director of the Community Mental Health Fund. This is a public sub-fund that channels a little over $10 million per year into charities serving some fifteen thousand victims of domestic and sexual violence and people with mental health needs.[25] Most of its revenues come from a single stream, local property taxes. This is different from most tax systems around the world, where various taxes flow into the maw of a general public budget, then get mixed up and spat out in different spending allocations, so you can't see the direct effects of any given tax cut. But here property taxes railroad straight through to particular spending lines, such as this fund. So competitive tax abatements have direct victims.

Eddy's work is intensely political, and he reports to elected officials, so he was guarded talking to me, but it was soon clear how badly the property tax abatements slice into his budget. "It's like a hydra," he said. "There are many tax abatements, and I have to fight for revenue to serve mentally ill people. This is not a sport." "Competitive" tax cutting has become like a mania. "There's a circular discussion going on here. Cutting taxes is good. Why? Because it's 'competitive.' Why is 'competitive' good? Because it means lower taxes! That plays into the neoliberal agenda that doesn't like the common good. The notion of being a human that merits some reasonable standard has been totally dismantled. And it's getting worse."

This game has spread across the United States and the world. One of the bleakest recent tales concerns Amazon, which in 2017 announced plans to build a second headquarters, dubbed HQ2, and asked cities to submit secret bids stuffed with incentive packages. Amazon knew where it wanted to set up all along—somewhere that offered deep pools of educated workers and executive expertise and maximum access to political power.

Yet it deliberately kicked off a ferocious beehive of bidding, as 238 cities scrambled to offer ever-bigger packages. Much of the bidding was shrouded in secrecy to maximize the anxiety, but of the details that emerged we know that Newark, New Jersey, offered a $7 billion package, and Chicago offered to let Amazon receive up to 100 percent of all income taxes paid by its employees. St. Louis, Missouri, offered $7.3 billion, and Montgomery County, Maryland, offered $8.5 billion for the $5 billion project. (Jamie Dimon, the CEO of JPMorgan Chase, said he would watch to see who won the bidding, then call up their lawmakers and demand the same.) In the end, though, Amazon didn't go with any of the high-bidding places. In November 2018 it announced that it had split the bid between Long Island City in Queens, New York, and Crystal City in Arlington, Virginia, just seven minutes' drive from the Pentagon, probably its most profitable client, and fifteen minutes from the White House. The combined bid came to a measurable $4.6 billion in subsidies to Amazon, plus a range of unmeasurable or hidden costs, including a potentially very large tax break for high net worth individuals with long-term investments in Amazon stock—people like Amazon's CEO, Jeff Bezos. (Amazon's three headquarters will also be an average of just 6.4 miles from Bezos's three main residences.) "Just as Amazon has crawlers and algorithms to find the lowest price on any brand, they have created an offline algorithm pitting cities against each other," said Amazon expert Professor Scott Galloway of the NYU Stern School of Business, ahead of the awards. "Amazon already knows where they want to be, and they are creating this kind of Hunger Games environment to mature the best term sheet possible—then give it to the city's mayor where they want to be."[26]

The Amazon example highlights two more crucial points about the race to the bottom that happens when states "compete" by offering tax cuts, deregulation, and subsidies to mobile businesses. First, *the race does not stop at zero*. Once corporate tax payments are down to nothing, it keeps going: you start getting into grants, peeled-off sales and payroll taxes, and other financial chicanery—an ever-growing pile of wealth extracted from taxpayers and handed to ever-larger corporations. There is literally no limit to the extent to which corporate players and the wealthy wish to free-ride off the taxes paid by the rest of us. Cut their taxes, give them subsidies, appease them, and they will demand more, like the playground bully. Why wouldn't they?

A second point is the winner's curse, an idea well understood by economists. This is a common phenomenon in auctions, where the winning bidder is often the one who overpays substantially, because he doesn't understand the value of what he is bidding for or what he is giving away; because he's cajoled, bullied, or bribed into overpaying; or because he wants to be seen as catching the big fish—and he doesn't care about the cost because he's using other people's money. A detailed 2016 study found that the pursuit of corporate megadeals (such as Amazon's HQ2)—known as "buffalo hunting" in economic development circles— was costing US states an average of $658,000 per job directly created: a massive overall loss for these states. For technology data centers, the average cost was $2 million per job. When President Trump in July 2018 broke ground on a new manufacturing plant for Foxconn, the company claimed it would create between 3,000 and 13,000 jobs, which generated a range of positive headlines in Wisconsin. Yet the subsidy package was worth an estimated $4.8 billion—up to $1.6 million per job. And Foxconn has a long history of backing out of promised investments like this and of replacing workers with robots—what the company itself calls "Foxbots." The cost per job could be higher still. By contrast, US states spent less than $600 per worker on training schemes, which are known to be vastly more effective than tax incentives in creating jobs.[27]

This chapter poses three big questions for policy makers. The first is: Will tax cuts and other goodies attract out-of-town business investment to *my* area? The answer is pretty clear and obvious: yes, sometimes.

Since Oates's 1969 paper came out, this question has been measured and confirmed over and again.[28] It doesn't just happen with US states; it happens with whole countries too.

The second question is: When states or countries "compete" to attract businesses or citizens, is this efficiency good for the world at large, or is it a harmful race to the bottom among the participating states?[29] As I've explained, the neoliberals used Tiebout's big idea combined with ivory-tower Chicago School mathematics to argue that such "competition" is healthy and efficient. And if you're a nerd like me who looks for this argument, you'll find it all over. For example, in 2013 Switzerland's president, Ueli Maurer, told the World Economic Forum at Davos, "Locational competition exists within our own borders. Diversity stimulates competition: that is not only the case in business, but also in politics. This leads to good infrastructure, to restraint in creating red tape and to low taxes." This idea can be boiled down to an appealing sound bite: competition is good; if it works for companies, then it works for countries. Tiebout, Oates, and the Chicago School lent academic credibility to the idea that states and countries can compete as if they were businesses, generating prosperity. This idea has been massively, world-changingly influential.

But there is one small snag with Tiebout's argument: it's hogwash. Utter nonsense. Even Tiebout said his model was unrealistic. Indeed, people who were at the seminar where Tiebout first presented his theory to the academic community said he offered it as an inside joke on the conservative economics establishment. He certainly found it delicious to have his paper accepted by the right-wing *Journal of Political Economy*. Tiebout reportedly said, "I don't think those fuckers know I'm a liberal and they'll feel compelled to publish it!"[30]

And the paper itself is clear about its limits. "Those who are tempted to compare this model with the competitive private model," wrote Tiebout "may be disappointed."[31] It turns out that each of the major flaws in the model is fatal; collectively they are a catastrophe. For starters, a moment's thought reveals that "competition" between countries or tax systems bears no resemblance *whatsoever* to competition between companies in a market. To get a taste of this, ponder the difference between a failed company like Toys 'R' Us (which filed for bankruptcy in 2017, partly due to competition from the market-hogging Amazon) and a failed state like, say, war-shattered Syria. When a company fails it is sad, but hopefully its employees will get new jobs, and the "creative destruction" involved when companies compete in markets can be a source of dynamism for capitalism. But a failed state, a place of warlords and murder and nuclear trafficking, is an utterly different and more dangerous beast, which never disappears, only festers. The only thing the two kinds of competitive failure really have in common is a shared word in the English language. Even if you believe, as I do, that competition between private actors in unsabotaged markets can be a great thing, this says nothing *at all* about the state-versus-state kind.

Not only that, but the Tiebout model requires eye-watering assumptions to make its "efficient sorting" work. In fact, Tiebout himself laid most of these out in black and white. For one thing, it assumes that hordes of citizen-consumers will flit back and forth from state to state or country to country at the drop of a tax inspector's hat, selling and buying their homes costlessly and tearing their kids into and out of local schools at the latest tweak to tax rates. Second, it assumes that tax havens don't exist, that corporations don't use them to shift profits around the world or even threaten to shift them in order to terrify politicians into giving them unwarranted tax cuts and other goodies. In Tiebout's model rich people don't dodge tax or free-ride off public services. Crime, pollution, and other bad things don't spill across borders. There is only one kind of tax—property taxes—and everyone lives off dividend income alone, while infinitely wise community leaders, in harmony with all other political forces, guide infinitely wise citizens. Company executives pondering where to relocate are never swayed in their decisions by free hookers sent up to their hotel rooms or cash-filled brown envelopes stuffed under doors on their location scouting trips, and corruption is absent from local politics.

To avoid the free-rider problem, everyone must go to school and college or university in one place, then work, live, pay taxes, and grow old in the same locality, exclusively, for their whole life; otherwise jurisdictions will free-ride off each other's education or pensions systems—and people can't vote with their feet after all. So there's no room in this model for people like the technology billionaire Peter Thiel, who has railed against high taxes and encouraged the United States to "compete" aggressively on its tax rates for big businesses and rich people like him—then in 2011 went and became a citizen of New Zealand, likely as a backup plan if politics ends up making life at home unbearable.[32]

Tiebout's assumptions, in turn, rest on a whole archaeology of other rickety assumptions required to make the general "efficient markets" theories work. In a nutshell, humans must be rational, wise, and self-interested, and markets are infallible.

None of this makes any sense, outside of a professor's blackboard. In a world of rising inequality this kind of "competition" is *always* generically harmful, for it rewards the big multinationals, global banks, wealthy individuals, and owners of flighty capital, who can easily shift profits or themselves across borders, shopping for the best deal, the lowest taxes, the weakest worker protections, the greatest secrecy for their financial affairs, or the most lax financial regulations, and then threaten to go elsewhere if they don't get state handouts. Your local car wash, your barber, your last surviving mom-and-pop fruit and vegetables merchant, or your average worker can't jump (or credibly threaten to jump) to London or Hong Kong if they don't like their tax rates or their hygiene regulations. So the big players get the handouts, and the small fry are forced to pay the full price of civilization—plus a surcharge to cover the costs of catering to the roaming members of the billionaire classes who are too important to contribute. This "competition" systematically shifts wealth upward from poor to rich, distorting our economies and undermining our communities and democracies. The free-rider problem is "one of those things you hear about in your first term of economics, then never hear about it again," says John Christensen, who cocreated the finance curse concept with me. "It is one of the biggest dark continents in economics."

The answer to the second of my three questions for policy makers then is clear: "competition" among states on corporate taxes is indeed a race to the bottom that increases inequality and harms the world at large. It is not efficient, and it benefits a few rich folk at the expense of much larger, poorer communities.

The third question is bigger and thornier. In fact, it is one of the thorniest economic questions of all time. It is this: Whether or not "competition" is a harmful race to the bottom that hurts the world at large, does it make sense for *my* country or state to "compete," from the perspective of local self-interest?

Schreck used to think not, at least for his area, but now he seems less certain. "In Lenexa we used to just say no," he said. "But you have to get in the game, and once you're in the game, it's hard to get back out, the argument being that half of something is better than all of nothing. There are states, especially in the Deep South, which are much more aggressive, with amazing incentive packages. It's a little whirlpool sucking on all of us. If you tried to swim out of it, you know, could you make it?"

There is a deep and pervasive belief that holds firm to the idea that yes, the giveaways are sadly necessary from a local perspective and we should play beggar-my-neighbor. The notion that countries have no choice but to be "competitive" in areas such as corporate tax or financial regulation has been the basis of some of the main national economic strategies of Britain and the United States for the past few decades. As Bill Clinton once put it, each nation is "like a big corporation competing in the global marketplace." Donald Trump has repeatedly touted plans to "make America more competitive, to reduce taxes, to roll back regulations." David Cameron, a former British prime minister, put it in even starker terms: "We are in a global race today. And that means an hour of reckoning for countries like ours. Sink or swim. Do or decline."[33]

This belief system is, however, flatly wrong. Like Tiebout's theory, it is underpinned by elementary economic fallacies. In general terms countries can opt out of this race unilaterally, with no economic penalty—in fact with a net national benefit. Beggar-my-neighbor is in reality beggar-myself. The only good move is not to play.

To see why this is so, it is necessary to leave the relatively calm waters of individual US states and venture into rougher, wilder, more perilous global seas. Here we will find that of the two major players in the global economy, Britain and the United States, Britain decided to play this game harder, faster, and more ruthlessly. In the process it has caused devastating damage to the international economy, and it has also beggared itself.

CHAPTER THREE

Britain's Second Empire

For centuries the City of London, the cash-pumping financial center at the heart of the British Empire, ran the greatest system of wealth extraction ever devised. Royal Navy gunships supported the predations of City-based groups like the East India Company, a trading organization that evolved into a bloodthirsty and unregulated operation with a private army, which in the eighteenth century looted the Indian subcontinent. At the Battle of Plassey, in 1757, the company defeated the nawab of Bengal; it then loaded the Bengal treasury's gold and silver into a fleet of over a hundred boats and sailed off with it down the Hooghly River. British imperial rule in India was founded on this gigantic international monopoly, and its control over India's industry, trade, and money would enable one of the greatest systems of wealth extraction ever devised. (That's the very same East India Company that provoked the Boston Tea Party in 1773 and helped pave the way to the American Declaration of Independence.)

The City's core principle underpinning these imperial adventures was freedom—specifically, freedom for finance and trade to flow unmolested across borders. "It is the business of government," one British prime minister declared in 1841, "to open and secure the roads for the merchant." The City's devotion to this principle was so extreme,

in fact, that it became the unofficial religion of empire. "Free trade is
Jesus Christ, and Jesus Christ is free trade," declared Sir John Bowring,
a former City trader who became governor of the British territory of
Hong Kong, as Britain sought to bludgeon open the mouthwateringly
large Chinese market for its goods and services. Britain fought and
won the two Opium Wars, in 1839–42 and 1856–60, enabling it (and
other European powers) to impose on China its drug-dealing system
of free trade.[1]

As with everything in finance, the City's imperial role was not a
simple tale of good and evil. Alongside all the militarized predation, the
City financed railways, roads, and many other beneficial projects in the
empire and far beyond, lending to France, Russia, Prussia, Greece, and
the new South American republics. London was, as the financier Nathan
Rothschild put it, "the bank for the whole world." Its relentlessly international outlook was also the bedrock of Britain's relatively tolerant multi-
culturalism, which has for centuries made London one of the most diverse
and exciting cities on the planet and contributed to Britain's decision to
send out its warships in support of policies to end the international slave
trade. "[In London] the Jew, the Mahometan, and the Christian transact
together," the French writer Voltaire declared in 1733, "as though they
all professed the same religion, and give the name of infidel to none but
bankrupts." The American Revolution, which ended in 1783, drastically
curbed the City of London's presence in the United States, which rapidly
developed its own financial system interests, so much so that by the mid-
nineteenth century the North American colonies held their reserves not
in London but in New York City. Yet the London banks continued to
lend and trade heavily with the countries around the United States. "In
a very real sense," explains one classic historical account, "the colonies
became part of the invisible financial and commercial empire which had
its centre in the City of London."[2]

Yet all these riches flowing into the City of London didn't necessarily benefit Britain as a whole; they benefited certain interest groups
in Britain, often at the expense of others. Clashes and tensions between

finance and the other parts of the economy happened again and again over the centuries. For instance, free trade benefits financial interests that profit from servicing both imports and exports, but it potentially harms local manufacturers, who benefit from protective barriers against cheaper foreign imports. For all the free-trade rhetoric, protectionism was central to the successful industrializing strategies of the United States, Britain, Japan, South Korea, and many others. The outward focus also meant that while the City was great at serving colonies, it often severely neglected British domestic industrialists outside London, something that continues today.[3]

The sinews of empire—British cunning, diplomacy, money, and violence—were finally broken by World War II, as Britain spent its national strength and treasure defending itself against Nazi Germany. So when the world's leading nations put together the Bretton Woods architecture at the end of the war, curbing speculative flows of capital across borders to give governments the space to put in place policies their war-weary populations demanded, power had shifted decisively across the Atlantic to Washington, DC, and Keynes and the British establishment failed in their attempts to fashion the new system in a way that would restore Britain to its self-appointed place at the center of world economic affairs. The empire staggered on for a few years, but by then it was an empty shell, ready to crack.

It may seem counterintuitive, but Britain and the United States entered their greatest period of broad-based prosperity and economic growth at precisely the moment the City of London and Wall Street were at their lowest, most heavily regulated ebb. This was no coincidence, for it was a reflection of the age-old clash between finance and other parts of the economy. The Bretton Woods restrictions on speculative financial flows across borders and the remarkable set of New Deal regulations inherited from the 1930s brought this clash into sharp relief.

An old and profitable set of relationships between Wall Street and London had been decisively interrupted. The City, looking with envy at the giant, fragmented, yet fast-growing global marketplace that the

Bretton Woods controls had now mostly placed out of its reach, was bottled up inside Britain's war-shattered domestic economy, plus a few remaining British territories and outposts that still used the pound sterling. Heavily constrained and highly taxed, the City was suffused with lethargy. Oliver Franks, the chairman of Lloyds Bank, lamented that his daily job was "like dragging a sleeping elephant to its feet with your own two hands." For the next couple of decades Britain and the countries participating in the Bretton Woods system would collectively enjoy the strongest, most broad-based, and most crisis-free economic expansion in history, with growth running at nearly 4 percent in the advanced economies and 3 percent in developing nations, more than twice the rate that had been attained in a thousand years of history.[4]

British elites, still basking in old imperial and financial glories, dreamed of remaking their system with the City of London at its heart. As Britain's future prime minister Harold Macmillan put it in 1952, "This is the choice—the slide into a shoddy and slushy Socialism . . . or the march to the third British Empire."[5]

Yet these elites were due for another set of shocks. The British Empire was crumbling. India became independent in 1947. Then, in 1956, everything changed. Egypt's feisty president, Gamal Abdel Nasser, took over the Suez Canal. Britain and France joined Israel in an invasion of the canal zone, but the United States, which had lost patience with European imperialism and fretted that the escapade would inflame pro-Soviet passions in the Arab world, forced the invaders to withdraw. The colonies realized how weak Britain now was and that it was possible at last to break free. Ghana gained its independence in 1957, followed by Nigeria in 1960, then Uganda, Kenya, Northern and Southern Rhodesia, Bechuanaland (now Botswana), Nyasaland (now Malawi, where I was born), Basutoland (now Lesotho), and a host of others.[6] Those last streams of easy profit from the colonies, backed by British gunboats, were now permanently out of reach—or so the newly independent countries thought.

*   *   *

Nobody could guess it then, but in 1956, the year of Britain's greatest imperial humiliation, a new financial market was born in London that would nurture itself on the City's old religion of freedom, and also reinvent the City as a global financial center. This market would grow so spectacularly that it would come to replace and even surpass the empire as a source of wealth and prestige for the City establishment. And this market in London would also create a new offshore playground that would in the decades to come play a central role in Wall Street's quest to reassert its own dominance over the US government and establishment and the rise of an all-American finance curse.

A few months before the Suez Crisis, some officials at the Bank of England noticed that the Midland Bank (now part of HSBC) was taking US dollar deposits unrelated to any commercial or trade deals. Under Bretton Woods this was classified as speculative cross-border activity, breaches between the separate national safety compartments of the global oil tanker, and this wasn't allowed. The City of London in those days was an old boys' network of elaborate rituals and agreement by gentleman's handshake. Financial regulation was achieved, often quite effectively, by the Bank of England governor inviting people in for tea and using raised eyebrows and other discreetly English signals to let them know if they were out of line. Midland's chief foreign manager was called in, and whether throats were politely cleared in his direction, a subsequent Bank of England memo noted that Midland "appreciates that a warning light has been shown." Yet Midland's new cross-border business was unusually profitable, so it pressed quietly on.[7]

Any central bank trying to implement the Bretton Woods system needed enough foreign exchange or gold reserves on hand to defend its currency at the fixed level against the US dollar. The Bank of England was constantly anxious about those reserves running out and making it hard for Britain to source essential foreign goods if things came to a crunch. Midland's dodgy activities were generating healthy dollar fees, bolstering Britain's dollar reserves, so the Bank of England decided to look the other way. Slowly, as more dollar profits tumbled in, this temporary indulgence solidified into a permanent tolerance. In effect, Britain had decided to host, but not regulate, a new market for dollars in London. Yet this new business wasn't regulated or taxed by the United States either. So who *was* regulating it? The answer was: nobody.

Ironically, some of the first users of this über-capitalist market were Soviet and Communist Chinese banks, delighted that their transactions weren't being regulated or overseen by Western governments during the Cold War. But soon their funds were swamped by far bigger tides, as American banks realized they could come to London and do things they weren't allowed to do at home, bypassing tight New Deal financial regulations in the States.[8] In short, these bankers could take their business elsewhere to escape the rules they didn't like at home. Amid high anxiety about the loss of empire, the City establishment had quietly turned Britain into an offshore tax and financial haven.

As word got out, more and more banks, especially American ones, got in on the action. The Americans gave this business an appropriate name, the Eurodollar markets, or the Euromarkets. This didn't have anything to do with today's euro currency; a Eurodollar was simply a dollar that had escaped Bretton Woods controls and was being traded in these new libertarian markets, mostly located in Europe. Eurodollars were a new form of stateless money and, as a London banker put it, "completely isolated from the monetary mass" of the rest of the UK. Bankers in London would simply keep two sets of books: one for offshore Eurodollar deals in foreign currencies, where (mostly) dollars got borrowed and re-lent around the world, and a second book for deals in sterling hooked into the British economy.

So Eurodollars were in one sense dollars like any other, but in another sense they were different because they had escaped into a market outside government control, where they could behave freely. It's a bit like helping someone escape from their conservative family home environment in the suburbs and taking them to Las Vegas, then offering them whiskey and cocaine. They are the same person but also different—more fun but also more irresponsible. This is a good way to understand not only Eurodollars but also offshore tax havens.

As London created this profitable offshore market, other pre-existing tax havens in the neighborhood—notably Switzerland and Luxembourg—also joined the Eurodollar party.

Switzerland was the granddaddy of the world's tax havens, having harbored the wealth of European elites in secret for centuries. This dark history is directly connected to the country's famous political neutrality and also to its snow-capped Alpine geography. After becoming a unified country in 1848, Switzerland was always riven by internal divisions, as hardy and self-reliant Alpine valley communities, often speaking different languages and practicing different religions, were separated from one another by forbidding snow-covered mountain ranges. A German-speaking part around Zurich in the north, center, and east, bordering Germany and Austria, sits next to a very different French-speaking zone in the west, dominated by Geneva and up against the French border, and an Italian-speaking area in the smaller southern segment, above Italy. So if a European war were to break out between France and Germany, for instance, this could pitch Switzerland's French- and German-speaking zones into conflict with each other. To counter this threat, the Swiss had to adopt political neutrality in all foreign wars. But they also created a remarkable constitutional machinery to minimize internal conflicts, including a major decentralization of power to the cantons and regions, plus a system of government based on rule by consensus between the main parties, called Concordance. These two mechanisms—neutrality and this unique political machinery to curb latent internal linguistic, religious, and cultural antagonisms—have been so successful that they have made Switzerland into one of Europe's most stable countries. And on this bedrock, a great tax haven has been built.

When Catholic French kings took large loans from heretical Protestants, it was Swiss bankers who acted as the intermediaries, helping them hide the money trails. When European wars broke out, elites in opposing countries looked to discreet Switzerland, not just as a place to stash their gold in the event of banking catastrophes at home but also as a place to continue to do profitable business with the enemy. Even more important, European governments at war needed to raise taxes to pay for their armies, and the elites looked to Swiss bankers to hide their wealth and shelter it from those war taxes: let the lesser classes send their sons to die and pay for the costs of fighting and subsequent reconstruction. The first real flows of offshore wealth came during the Thirty Years' War of 1618–48, and this was followed by larger rivers of money during the Franco-Prussian War of 1870–71. Then World War I came and brought a flood. World War II brought great dirty tides of it, helped by the fact that in 1934 Switzerland had codified its long traditions of banking secrecy into an ironclad law, with dire penalties for transgression.

Swiss bankers love to tell a story that their banking secrecy law was put in place to protect Jewish money from the Nazis. In fact, pretty much the opposite was true. During the war the Swiss banking establishment protected Nazi loot, and when Jewish survivors tried to reclaim their money after Germany surrendered, the Swiss stonewalled them for decades. It was only in the 1990s that the US government finally started putting pressure on them, and they began to disgorge at least some of that stolen money. The story about Swiss banking secrecy being put in place to protect Jewish money was first created by a bulletin of the Schweizerisches Kreditanstalt (now Credit Suisse) in 1966, and it was eagerly embraced and trumpeted by Swiss officials and bankers as a convenient myth to wrap around themselves to justify helping the world's dictators, cronies, and crooks pursue their dark sports with impunity.[9]

In early 1945, as the war wound down, the Swiss signed a new agreement with the Nazis to accept three more tons of looted gold, some from melted-down dental fillings and wedding rings from Jews and other victims of Nazi concentration camps. The US government heaped pressure on Switzerland to open up the books, and the Swiss promised to cough up information on Nazi gold, but it was a ruse. Allied lawyers soon spotted loopholes and evasions, but Swiss officials knew they had a powerful friend among the Allied forces: the British banking establishment. So Swiss officials began musing publicly that amending Swiss banking secrecy laws would reveal British secrets too. British officials began backpedaling. A crackdown, the Brits reckoned, might risk disclosure of certain numbered Swiss accounts that they didn't want opened up. Furious correspondence went back and forth between the British treasury, the prime minister's office, and diplomatic offices. "We need to go slow on this," one official said. "We don't want to be forced to reveal Swiss banking secrets." An urgent telegram came flying back: "You are not (repeat not) doing anything that would lead to requests for disclosure of information from British banks." American diplomats, many fresh from the horrors of confronting the Nazi war machine, were flabbergasted.[10]

Swiss banking laws were not only about secrecy of bank deposits and other assets, but also about a deliberate lack of official oversight and regulation of all kinds. So when the Euromarkets first appeared in London, it is hardly surprising that the Swiss were among the most enthusiastic followers. A Bank of England memo in those early days explained the Euromarkets' attractions: freedom from local supervisory controls such as banking regulations to restrain risk-taking; freedom from foreign exchange controls; low taxes for the players and for their customers; deep secrecy; and "very liberal company legislation" to let company directors get away with operating outside standard democratic rules. While the Euromarkets were mostly disconnected from mainstream economies, the unrestricted interconnections among the emerging centers were intense, effectively creating a single rootless nowhere zone of finance. (Think of it as being a bit like cloud banking.) It was an unaccountable, profitable, seamless global financial adventure playground, overseen by nobody—and growing like a virus on speed.[11]

This rules-free paradise was ideal for tax cheats, scammers, and criminals. But there was another big attraction. The banking system in any country constantly creates new money when banks make new loans to customers. As the economist J. K. Galbraith put it, "The process by which money is created is so simple that the mind is repelled." To stop banks running amok, governments put brakes on money creation by enforcing reserve requirements, which restrict how much they can lend out in relation to their deposits. The Euromarkets had none of these brakes. Eurodollar lending, a Bank of England memo noted, "is not controlled, as regard amount, nature or tenor: reliance is placed on the commercial prudence of the lenders." Prudent bankers won't indulge in an orgy of reckless lending, whatever the official constraints are, but the British were assuming that everyone operating in the Euromarkets was prudent.

US authorities soon began to notice these new Atlantic ripples, and in 1961, two years after US banks joined the party in London, US officials warned the Bank of England that the market posed a "danger to stability." Benjamin J. Cohen, then at the Federal Reserve Bank of New York, remembers being asked to look into Eurodollars in 1962. "It was in the manner of 'There's this development over in London we want to understand better,'" Cohen recalled. "'Go over there and find out about it.'" It was quickly obvious that this interconnected system of financial centers was already amplifying and propagating financial shocks, sluicing rising tides of financial capital back and forth across the world. Worried US officials began calling the markets "disruptive forces" and a dangerous "transnational reservoir" of rootless money. By 1963 messages were flying between Washington and New York as higher interest rates in the Euromarkets drew dollars out of the United States to London and beyond. A memo from the time lamented "the undercutting of New York as a financial center" and slammed the Euromarkets for generating the same kinds of risks that caused the crash of 1929. The Federal Reserve Bank of New York and the US Treasury complained that the markets were making "the pursuit of an independent monetary policy in any one country far more difficult" and aggravating a "world payments disequilibrium." Robert Roosa, a top US Treasury official, told US bankers using the markets that they should "ask themselves whether they are serving the national interest." But others in the US administration, more in favour of Wall Street interests, were gung ho for the new market. Hendrik Houthakker, a junior staff member of the Council of Economic Advisers who wanted to alert President Kennedy to the market, was told "no, we don't want to draw attention to it." As one analysis of the markets put it, it was "almost as if [US authorities] wanted to create a financial centre outside their own shore."[12]

At the start of the 1960s, Euromarket deposits already amounted to $1 billion, the equivalent of perhaps $50 billion in today's money. Between 1960 and 1970 the dollar sums circulating in these markets multiplied tenfold.[13] A top Bank of England official captured the spirit of the City in a comment to a financier setting up an Italian bank in London in that decade: the banker could do whatever he wanted, as long as he didn't "do it in the streets and frighten the horses." In the late 1970s Roosa warned of speculative global capital flows moving around the globe "in magnitudes much larger than anything experienced in the past, massive movements." Then, from 1970 to 1980, volumes expanded tenfold *again*.[14]

The Vietnam War, which heated up in the early 1970s, added to the flames, as the United States was sending more dollars overseas for military spending than it was receiving back in foreign earnings. The result was a growing overhang of dollars in the global system, feeding the Euromarkets further. The twin oil price shocks of the 1970s accelerated the flows, generating giant new surges of petrodollars—more accurately, petro-Eurodollars—which the large banks recycled out of the oil-producing countries via the giant turntable in the City of London back into disastrous, crime-soaked cycles of Third World lending. Those loans would often be looted by national elites through bogus development schemes or outright theft and sent back for safekeeping into the Euromarkets, where nobody would ask questions about the money's origins, and then re-lent *again* back into those looted countries. With each turn of this whirligig, the bankers took a profitable cut.

When Mexico's Harvard-educated president Miguel de la Madrid took power in 1982, he lectured his fellow citizens about "belt-tightening" while starting to accumulate tens of millions in his own foreign bank accounts—$162 million in 1983 alone, according to US intelligence reports. Most of this was first obtained by squirrelling away the proceeds from official Mexican loans via the Euromarkets, and pretty much all of it was then stashed offshore via the Euromarkets in Geneva, London, and elsewhere. "You have many friends here, not least in the City of London," gushed British prime minister Margaret Thatcher at a luncheon for him in London in 1985. "We shall continue to offer the widest possible trade opportunities to you."[15]

As the murderous Jean-Claude "Baby Doc" Duvalier of Haiti and the grasping Ferdinand Marcos of the Philippines looted their treasuries, American and British bankers in London and Zurich got rich. By some estimates, over half the money borrowed by Mexico, Venezuela, and Argentina in the late 1970s and early 1980s "effectively flowed right back out the door, often the same year or even month it flowed in." In Venezuela it was nearly dollar for dollar. The ordinary citizens of these countries had to shoulder the burden of crushing debt repayments. In the unpoliced Euromarkets, there was nobody to stop it.[16] The American financial system was increasingly intertwined in complex webs with those of other countries, "no more reducible to Wall Street than the manufacture of iPhones can be reduced to Silicon Valley," as one account put it.[17] Tax evasion, crime, bad accounting, bank scams, gray-zone semilegal rip-offs, pump and dump schemes, and especially lax financial regulation: it all came together in one unholy, messy, fast-growing festival of finance centered in London.

Long after the formal trappings of the British Empire had crumbled, here was another giant looting machine run out of the City of London. It needed no British soldiers and was predicated on tight secrecy. It was all but invisible.

The Euromarkets grew some more and just kept growing. The Bank of England routinely rebuffed American requests for ideas on how to tackle the growing problems and tensions. "However much we dislike hot money we cannot be international bankers and refuse to accept money," a Bank of England memo said. "We shall do lasting damage." The Americans pressed further, and the British screw-you became more explicit. "It doesn't matter to me whether Citibank is evading American regulations in London," said James Keogh, a top Bank official. "I wouldn't particularly want to know."[18]

Like a slow-motion explosion, the Euromarkets rapidly accelerated financial globalization. They metastasized beyond Britain, beyond dollars, and beyond anyone's control, morphing into a frenzied financial battering ram, which would combine with Hayek's and Friedman's ideological pushback against government intervention to smash holes in exchange controls and the cooperative international infrastructure. More and more cracks were appearing in the walls of the dam, and the massive oil price surges of the 1970s threw everything into further confusion. The Bretton Woods system was rubble. And so began a new era of free finance, engendering massive profits for the financial sector— and in turn much slower global growth, rising inequality, global crime, and more frequent financial crises across the Western world.[19] It was precisely what Keynes had warned about.

As this chaos had been unfurling, another set of darker developments, umbilically linked to the Euromarkets, was gathering pace. This particular variety of mayhem goes back as far as you like, but a good place to start is with the Wall Street financier Wallace Groves, an associate of the Meyer Lansky crime syndicate that was operating casinos out of Miami in the 1950s. The US Mob ran offshore gambling and crime operations in nearby Cuba and had thoroughly corrupted the government there, ultimately triggering a populist revolt that began in 1953 and eventually brought the Communists to power under Fidel Castro.

Groves had settled in the nearby Bahamas, an old offshore pirates' den that had once hosted the notorious Blackbeard and the bloodthirsty

Henry Morgan (who was so successful as a pirate that the Queen knighted him and appointed him lieutenant governor of Jamaica). Groves set up casinos and other profitable businesses in the British-ruled Bahamas, catering heavily to American clients outside the reach of US law enforcement, and he deployed his profits to subvert the thuggish Bahamian elite, known as the Bay Street Boys. As the Communist threat to the Mob's Cuban operations grew, the Mafia turned its attentions to the Bahamas as an alternative. In 1955 the Bay Street Boys gave Groves a two-hundred-square-mile concession to develop a port and free-trade zone, exempt from taxes until 1980 (subsequently extended to 2054) and largely free of the rule of law too. This anything-goes, libertarian free-for-all tax haven prospered greatly, though it contributed relatively little to the rest of the Bahamas, apart from corruption and some jobs, which mostly went to shady expatriates. A British official in 1968 worried that it had become "a separate city state." As the empire crumbled, British officials were reluctant to alienate the elites in another potentially restive colony by outlawing this lucrative and fast-growing offshore activity.

All this would have been troubling enough for the US and British governments. But other British territories in the region had noticed the money pouring into the Bahamas tax haven and wanted to copy it. A race to the bottom got under way, led by an unholy triumvirate of money-scenting local colonial elites, a few (mostly American) promoters of tax haven schemes, and a coterie of (mostly British) accountants and offshore lawyers to help set it all up.

The British National Archives for this period tell a remarkable story, with officials from government departments becoming aware of tax haven activity popping up like Caribbean mushrooms on island after island, then engaging in a whirlwind of official correspondence, chasing after it all. Different departments pushed and pulled in different directions. The treasury, for its part, fretted about losing tax revenue to these tax havens, while seeming quite unconcerned that tax and crime-fighting authorities in the United States and elsewhere were being undermined and cheated. The Bank of England seemed most worried about shoring up exchange controls and the Bretton Woods architecture—these places were obvious points of leakage. But again, it showed little or no concern for North or South American governments and citizens, whose countries' tax and crime-fighting systems were being undermined by these British havens, mostly known as British overseas territories. The Foreign Office seemed delighted with the dirty-money game, since it would help these tiny territories become self-sustaining, so they weren't a drain on British foreign aid budgets.

Aside from the Bahamas, the main territories in question were (and still are) the last fragments of the British Empire: fourteen semi-independent nations including seven global tax havens—Anguilla, Bermuda, the British Virgin Islands, the Cayman Islands, Gibraltar, Montserrat, and the Turks and Caicos Islands. Alongside the tax havens of Jersey, Guernsey, and the Isle of Man around the British mainland, known as the Crown dependencies, these colonies did not cut all their ties with Britain when the empire collapsed.[20]

In many of these places banking was conducted in both pounds sterling and US dollars, which were supposed to be kept separate under the safety hedge of the Bretton Woods system. Banks were supposed to keep two sets of books for the different currencies and implement exchange controls carefully between them. But arbitrage between currencies was highly profitable, and these libertarian paradises didn't want to play by the rules, especially if there was big money to be made. By the 1960s all sorts of curious creatures were scurrying through the holes in the Bretton Woods boundary hedge that ran right through the middle of all these tax havens. Among the best known and the earliest of these creatures were the Beatles, whose film *Help!* was shot in 1965 in the Bahamas because the band had to live there for a while in order to make it work as a tax shelter. There's a memo in the archives from a Bank of England official in 1969 that quivers with alarm:

> Events, however, seem to be moving rather faster. The potential
> gaps in the Exchange Control hedge can no longer be contained

by occasional visits. The smaller, less sophisticated and remote Islands are receiving almost constant attention and blandishments from expatriate operators who aspire to turn them into their own private empires. The administrations in these places find it difficult to understand what is involved and to resist tempting offers. . . . Tax haven proposals by a US resident are leading them to have second thoughts about the need for Exchange Control at all. We might need to station a man somewhere in the area.[21]

Fabulous and enticing promises began to mount. The memos going back and forth are ferocious by crusty British civil service standards, describing a game of whack-a-mole in these outgrowths of the Euromarkets, an offshore whirligig running faster and faster, driven by foreign criminals, shady characters, and anti-regulation bankers. Someone from the Overseas Development Ministry was gung ho for secret banking and seedy shell-company business because it "attracts entrepreneurs and financiers," he said, arguing that this was a fine way for these Caribbean microstates to develop their economies—without apparently sparing a thought for the hundreds of millions of North Americans, Latin Americans, Africans, and many others paying a murderous price for Britain helping their elites, drug gangs, and kleptocrats to ransack their national coffers. These activities, he said, were "mainly aimed at North American companies" and "may have little adverse effect on the UK." Screw you, America.

The Bank of England quietly welcomed foreigners stashing money in the territories, generating foreign currency fees just as the Euromarkets were doing in London. The same Bank memo urged the authorities "to be quite sure that the possible proliferation of trust companies, banks, etc. which in most cases would be no more than brass plates manipulating assets outside the Islands, does not get out of hand." But as long as exchange controls were not breached, "there is of course no objection to their providing bolt holes for non-residents." That last sentence is, of course, code language for welcoming shady money. Especially North and South American shady money.[22]

The correspondence shows a mounting range of scams and schemes building up in Britain's havens. One memo described a "financial pirates' nest" being set up in the British Virgin Islands, used for drugs and gunrunning, while another opposed a plan by an American consortium of "investors," with the innocuous name of Global Risk Underwriters Inc., to take over Antigua's satellite island of Barbuda, to set up a free port and an investment bank with numbered accounts and exemption from any investigation, along with unregulated gold refining, gambling, and, officials suspected, drug smuggling.[23] Officials in London discovered that an American financier called Clovis McAlpin was proposing a scheme in the Turks and Caicos Islands that would amount to "exclusive rights which would virtually turn him into the uncrowned king of the islands." (The scheme came to nothing.) They fretted that the Caymans had been "literally raided by an expatriate tax council, who overnight persuaded them to enact trust legislation which goes beyond anything yet attempted elsewhere." (This council has evolved and still exists today, and it largely writes the Caymans' tax haven laws.) One memo slammed Cayman's Trust Law of 1967 as "quite uncivilised," while another lamented the role of the accounting firm Price Waterhouse, which had been urging nearby Montserrat to set up an "objectionable" brass-plate business, again catering mostly to Americans. There were new laws on shell companies in the British Virgin Islands, whose users would be "immune for at least twenty years from all enquiries from any source," and this risked infuriating the US government.[24]

As one scheme followed another, the wrangling continued in London. The archives show how those supporting the offshore tax haven model slowly began to gain the upper hand. The merry-go-round continued, getting ever faster and more interconnected with the Euromarkets. More and more private operators flocked to the territories, urging each to compete fiercely with its rivals by putting in place ever more devious and criminal-friendly secrecy facilities, trust laws, and financial regulatory loopholes.

This era, from the mid-1950s to the early 1980s, was the great watershed between the two ages of the global system of tax havens, as the slow, discreet system of secret offshore banking dominated by the Swiss ceded ground to a more hyperactive, aggressive Anglo-Saxon strain, operating first out of the London-centered Euromarkets, then rippling out into the unpoliced and heavily criminalized British offshore network that still exists today. If you consider Britain and its tax haven satellites together as a network, it would soon constitute the world's biggest offshore tax haven. This network is like a spider's web, linking the City of London at the center to satellites like the Caymans or Gibraltar.[25] Fees or assets captured in the web, typically from jurisdictions near the haven in question, get fed upward to the City of London. So, for example, a Colombian criminal or American mobster might set up a shell company or bank in the Cayman Islands; or a French bank or energy company will establish a special purpose vehicle (SPV) in Jersey to hide assets from shareholders or from government regulators; or a Russian oligarch might set up a dodgy bank in Gibraltar. Sometimes illegal activity is involved, sometimes not. Each step needs lawyers, accountants, and banking services, which the British network happily provides. The most profitable heavy lifting happens in London, but it is often the haven that snared the business in the first place. A spider's web is a sinister analogy, but it is apt.[26]

In 1976 Anthony Field, the managing director of Castle Bank & Trust in the Caymans and the Bahamas, was arrested at a Miami airport, after a private eye hired by the IRS discovered that the bank had been helping two hundred rich Americans dodge taxes: Americans who included *Playboy*'s Hugh Hefner, the rock band Creedence Clearwater Revival, Chicago's Pritzker family, and members of the Cleveland Mafia. The Castle banker was told he faced jail if he didn't provide details about his American tax-evading clients. He refused, saying he'd be prosecuted in the Caymans if he did. To bolster Field's case, the Cayman government drafted a ferocious new secrecy law that could land you in jail not only for leaking confidential information to outsiders but for merely *asking* for it (a version of the law is still in place today). This Cayman law was an astonishingly brazen, London-approved, fist-pumping fuck-you to the United States. (In the end President Richard Nixon stepped in and appointed a new IRS commissioner from Cleveland, who squashed the whole case.)[27]

The close legal links these British havens have with London is crucial, providing the reassuring legal bedrock, political support, and familiarity that other fly-speck havens can't match. If there's a dispute over a Cayman-incorporated structure, for instance, British courts and British judges will rule on the case and have the final say. Why would you deposit your money in a banana republic bank when you can go to the Cayman Islands and have your stash protected by the British legal system? The importance of the British link was illustrated clearly when the Bahamas became fully independent from Britain in 1973 under a black nationalist premier, Lynden Pindling (who was also, as it happens, on Meyer Lansky's payroll). The money fled the Bahamas in droves, and most of it alighted in the nearby Caymans, which was still British. A London-based lawyer called Milton Grundy, who helped write laws of "labyrinth complexity" for tax havens like the Caymans, explained why the money left the Bahamas so fast: "It wasn't that Pindling did anything to damage the banks," he said. "It was just that he was black."[28]

The need for this British bedrock highlights how tax havens turn two faces to the world. On the one hand, they need to appear clean, trustworthy, and efficient, to reassure flighty clients that they're in safe hands. On the other hand, they want to get hold of as much dirty money as they can. They square this apparent contradiction with a simple offering to the world's stateless hot money, which goes roughly like this: "You can trust us not to steal your money, but if you want to steal

someone else's money, then you can also trust us to turn a blind eye."
This helps explain why Swiss people are famed around the world for
their punctuality, personal honesty, and efficiency—and yet Switzerland
is historically one of the world's greatest money-laundering sinks of
dirty money. And it's a similar story in Britain. British people are still
admired the world over for fair play, and British judges for their incor-
ruptibility, yet at the same time we find Roberto Saviano, Italy's most
celebrated anti-Mafia journalist, calling Britain "the most corrupt place
on Earth" because of all the City's dirty money. This contrast between
apparently clean officials and dirty money is no coincidence; it is the
heart of the offshore model.

With these financial arrangements in place, Britain was able to
make up for the loss of its ability to use its soldiers and gunboats to
extract riches from foreign countries. Professor Ronen Palan of City
University in the UK describes this spider's web as "a second British
empire which is at the very core of global financial markets today."[29]
This second financial empire has characteristics in common with Britain's lost territorial empire. First, the libertarian character of its escape
routes strongly echoes the old empire's evangelical devotion to freedom.
Criminals inevitably flock to libertarian, unpoliced free spaces to deal
in money, just as wasps will mysteriously turn up when you open a pot
of strawberry jelly at a summer picnic. Laws were carefully drafted to
achieve maximum secrecy, and when packing crates full of drug money
arrived in the Caymans or Panama, the police would be on hand to escort
them safely from the airport to the local banks. And as we will see, this
laissez-faire approach to money in the British tax havens would extend
far beyond handling the proceeds of drug deals and organized crime
and into high finance. The veteran US crime-fighting lawyer Jack Blum
remembers first understanding the links between crime and financial
deregulation on a trip to the Caymans in the 1980s: "I began to see that
drugs were only a fraction of the thing," he told me. "Then there was
the [other] criminal money. Then the tax evasion money. And then I
realized, 'Oh my God, it's all about off the books—off balance sheet.'"

By 1989 the Cayman Islands, with just twenty-five thousand inhabitants, would be on paper the world's fifth-biggest banking center, a position it more or less holds today.

The spider's web has enabled people connected to the City of London to make immense profits from illegal or immoral activities, typically involving American citizens and taxpayers, while using the overseas territories like barge poles—to hold the stink at arm's length. And whenever a bad smell has emerged, British officials have told their irate detractors, "Look, chaps, these places are largely independent from us; there's really not much we can do." Yet this claim of powerlessness is false. Her Majesty the Queen appoints the governors of these British overseas territories; all their laws were and still are sent to London for approval; and Britain has always had complete power to revoke these laws. Yet it almost never does.[30]

We should be outraged at this long-running British government strategy in support of the City of London. But not *too* outraged, because there's another large player in the tax haven game that may be just as bad, in its own way. The United States itself.

In 1967 Michael Hudson, then a balance-of-payments economist at Chase Manhattan Bank, was in a company elevator when someone handed him a State Department memo asking Chase to take the lead in helping turn the United States into a giant tax haven. "Like Switzerland, flight money probably flows to the US from every country," the memo began. The United States at that time was suffering outflows of dollars as US forces conducted bloody and expensive ground offensives in Vietnam, and it was looking to attract some money back. The memo listed its complaints: the US Treasury and FBI were too enthusiastic in their use of subpoenas and other tools to crack down on crime; taxes and regulations on foreign money were too high. Hudson was asked if he could estimate how much foreign illicit money the United States might be able to get its hands on. "The hot money wouldn't come directly into Chase, because that wouldn't be nice and very legal," remembers Hudson, now a finance professor at the University of Missouri at Kansas City. "What happened was that the Latin American criminals, other criminals, drug dealers, all sorts of organized crime would put their money in the offshore Caribbean banks, and these offshore banks would then deposit the inflow in the head office."

According to Hudson, "they were saying, 'We want to replace Switzerland. All this money will come here if we make this the criminal center of the world. This is how we fund Vietnam. We wanted the foreign criminal money, which is patriotic, but not the American criminal money.'"[31]

In fact, the United States already had some discreet laws to attract foreign money and had, since 1921, exempted from tax the interest income on bank deposits owned by foreigners. After World War II, there were widespread fears that if European economies collapsed again they might fall into communism and the Soviet orbit and also fears that enormous quantities of US aid to address this, under the Marshall Plan, might be undermined by wealthy Europeans seeking to escape paying their share. US policy makers in Congress deplored the "small, bloated, selfish class of [Europeans] whose assets have been spread all over the place" and asked "whether or not [the United States] should become a sanctuary for refugee money." Indeed, early drafts of the IMF's Articles of Association said countries should be "required" to help each other address capital flight, especially with transparency: telling European governments about their wealthy citizens' stashes of offshore wealth. Yet an alliance of US bankers, with some help from Treasury officials, fought back hard against such transparency, fulminating that these and other controls would do "maximum violence to our position as a world financial center";[32] in the end the IMF would no longer *require* countries to help each other track down offshore stashes, merely *permit* them to do so. Through this tiny loophole whooshed huge volumes of European treasure, much of it the proceeds of US Marshall Plan aid that had been sequestered by that small, bloated, selfish class of Europeans almost as soon as it landed, and sent back offshore to the United States: a total of at least $4–$5 billion in 1947, which in those days was a vast sum of capital lost to a Europe desperate for capital for reconstruction. Only a major new economic crisis in Europe in 1947, caused largely by these outflows, forced US policy makers to tighten up again.[33]

Over the ensuing decades, foreign capital continued to wash into the United States, much of it from Europe and much of it smuggled undetected alongside bona fide trade flows. Once the money was there, the US banking community was able to hold on to it by cloaking it in deep secrecy, for the United States didn't have any meaningful arrangements in place to tell foreign governments about their wealthy citizens' holdings. And it steadily put in place new federal-level regulations to bolster the attractions: by 1976, when a new US Tax Reform Act reaffirmed America's commitment to use tax haven secrecy facilities to attract capital to the United States, it was estimated that a third of all bank deposits were from Latin Americans evading taxes and controls at home.

And while this shift was happening at a federal level, mostly with respect to banking deposits, another whole set of games was going on at the state level, as places like Delaware and Nevada started passing laws to allow the creation of shell companies and other mechanisms that would be all but impenetrable to outsiders—including the IRS. In 1984 *Time* magazine summarized the changes: "America has become the largest and possibly the most alluring tax haven in the world." At any rate, it was giving the British postimperial spiderweb a run for its money.[34]

The Janus-faced offshore business model of trying to appear clean and well regulated while attracting as much criminal and dirty money as possible poses many problems for any country, like the United States or Britain, that hosts and encourages this kind of activity.

For one thing, it assumes you can sequester the dirt and the criminality safely away from the rest of the economy, from democracy, and from society. This, however, is impossible, for the two most dangerous parts of a political system are most likely to meet and become intertwined: the richest and most powerful members of society, who are of course the biggest users of tax havens, and criminals. Fish, as the saying goes, rot from the head. Crafting a national economic strategy that relies on offshore finance creates inevitable blowback, which has criminalized American and British elites in four main ways: it brings the wealthiest and most powerful into close proximity with criminals; it offers the elites permanent temptations to criminality; it makes criminals rich, enabling them to join the ranks of the elites; and, by making it easy to escape rules and laws, it creates a culture of impunity and a real sense of being above the law. Modern US politics, with sleazy revelation after sleazy revelation, exposes how dangerous this strategy has been.

All this history helps us answer a question that bothers many people about tax havens: Why don't governments just close these financial brothels down? Lee Sheppard, a leading US tax expert, summarizes the answer to this question as well as anyone: "We fuss about them, we howl that the activity is illegal, but we don't shut them down because the town fathers are in there, with their pants around their ankles."[35]

And this, in turn, brings us to a further major characteristic of these offshore territories: they are all, especially the smaller island tax havens, "legislatures for hire," as the British tax haven expert Prem Sikka puts it. Like the old colonies, their political and economic development is mainly dictated not by local democracy but by foreign interests, and in the case of tax havens this means rootless foreign offshore money. A memo in Britain's national archives from 1969 illustrates this problem, fretting about

> a flow of propositions involving Crown lands put daily and end-lessly to the government by private developers. These proposi-tions are inevitably propounded in an atmosphere of geniality, lavish hospitality, implied generosity and overwhelming urgency. They are usually backed by glossy lay-outs, and declaimed by a team of businessmen supported by consultants of all sorts. They are invariably staged against an impossibly tight deadline, with an implicit threat of jam today or none tomorrow. On the other

side of the table—the Administrator and his civil servants. No business expertise, no consultants, no economists, no statisticians, no specialists in any of the vital fields. Gentlemen vs Players—with the Gentlemen unskilled in the game and unversed in its rules. It is hardly surprising that the professionals are winning, hands-down.[36]

In small island tax havens, administrations staffed by former fisherfolk or owners or employees of bed-and-breakfast hotels are asked to scrutinize complex laws on special purpose vehicles or offshore trusts. Even in those rare cases where administrators do possess the technical knowledge to understand such laws, there is a wall of money pressuring them not to oppose any proposal. With Cayman-registered banks now holding $1 trillion in assets, equivalent to 100,000 percent of that microstate's gross national product, it is clear where the power lies. As a result, local administrators can usually do little more than rubber-stamp laws devised for the owners of the world's hot money. The Panama Papers leaks in 2015 revealed how Mossack Fonseca, the Panamanian firm at the center of the scandal, effectively wrote the tax haven laws of Niue, a tiny Pacific island of 1,500 people. Mossack Fonseca got an exclusive agreement to register offshore companies there, and this operation was soon generating 80 percent of that territory's government revenue. The logic, as described by the firm's cofounder Ramón Fonseca, was that "if we had a jurisdiction that was small, and we had it from the beginning, we could offer people a stable environment, a stable price." They certainly had Niue.[37]

It is also essential to understand how the business model of these places is *purposely* antidemocratic. A tax haven's deliberately constructed loopholes are not designed to help locals escape laws and rules but to help others, elsewhere, do so. Officials carefully write their laws to ensure that any resulting damage in unpaid taxes or evaded financial regulations is inflicted elsewhere, protecting the tax haven against self-harm. This "offshore" element means that the people who make the tax haven laws are always separated from those who are affected by those laws. So there is *never* democratic consultation between lawmakers in tax havens and the people elsewhere affected by their laws. That is the whole point of offshore. And it means that offshore is, almost by definition, the equivalent of the smoke-filled room, where business gets done by cigar-chomping gentlemen outside of, and indeed in opposition to, the democratic process. And they operate according to the golden rule: whoever has the gold makes the rules.

Rudolf Elmer, a Swiss bank whistleblower who was accused of passing information to WikiLeaks about shady arms brokers, Mexican officials linked to drug dealers, Saudi companies linked to the bin Laden family, and around forty American and other politicians accused of corruption, found out the cost of offshore dissent. Two men followed him to work, began watching his wife at home, and hung around his young daughter's day care and offered her chocolates in the street. The Swiss police declined to help; instead, they searched his house, and he ended up in prison. "I was an outlaw," he said. "I was godfather to a child whose father is in finance. He said I had to stop—'you are a threat to the family.'" After Elmer's release, the courts kept pursuing him, and in June 2015 he sent me a trove of documents that showed how Switzerland, under instructions from its banking establishment, had corrupted its judicial system to nail Elmer, despite the case having no legal merit because he had been working in the Caymans when he blew the whistle. The court declined to allow him to call witnesses, refused to accept documents to support his case, and used false evidence. A former Swiss judge told Elmer that his treatment reminded him of the Mafia. "Swiss bankers . . . simply do not go to court for their crimes," Elmer wearily told me. "They are a protected species."[38]

In tax havens like Switzerland, deference to offshore financial interests becomes reinforced by a ferocious social consensus to make sure everyone does the right thing, which is to keep bringing in the money. The wealthy high-society folk who run these places rarely do anything as crude as to throw opponents of offshore finance in jail. The threat usually lies in more discreet mechanisms, such as the knowledge that if you rock the boat, your employment opportunities will dry up or you will be ostracized. In the goldfish bowl of small-island life, where opportunities are often scant, that is usually enough to silence even the reddest of radicals. John Christensen remembers this pressure from his days as official economic adviser to the tax haven of Jersey. He recalls choking with anger during meetings, yet feeling immense pressure to conform to what offshore finance wanted from the island. "It took real strength to stand up and say, 'I'm sorry, I don't agree with this.' I felt like the little boy farting in church." Many years after leaving Jersey and setting up the Tax Justice Network to combat tax havens, he says he is still a hated figure in Jersey financial circles, pilloried as a traitor. In such places the capture of the tax haven by offshore financial interests —or financial capture—often extends into family life itself. A few years ago in the Alpine tax haven of Liechtenstein I spoke to a woman who had once spoken out publicly against her country's financial laws. After that, she said, her own sister crossed to the other side of the street to avoid meeting her.

These cultural changes have been a direct consequence of the race-to-the-bottom contagion, as countries like Britain and the United States have operated under the assumption that they need to "compete" to attract the world's hot money and have cleared away the political and cultural obstacles to make this happen. There has been no larger arena for this game than the Euromarkets, which, as one analysis put it, created a giant "transatlantic regulatory feedback loop that stimulated deregulation on both sides of the Atlantic . . . eroding the regulatory architecture of the postwar Keynesian state in Britain and destabilizing American New Deal regulations." This feedback loop helped generate a rising global wall of money and debt, which has steadily burrowed into the nooks and crannies of our economies and our political systems, driving a gravitational shift inside the United States toward the needs of finance and delivering a payload of financial techniques and methods that have transformed the way we think about businesses, our homes, our public services, and even the people we love.[39]

The hot capital flowing into the countries that played this game the hardest made some local bankers, lawyers, and accountants wealthy. But this hot money inflicted a wave of more invisible damage on the wider US economy and society, through all the different mechanisms of the finance curse: greater financialization and wealth extraction, the brain drain out of productive sectors and into banks and shadow banks in Miami, Chicago, or New York, and greater deregulation and risk-taking at taxpayers' expense, as American banks flocked to the London playground, then returned home with threats to move out wholesale if they didn't get what they wanted.

Worse was to come. As the tax havens and the Euromarkets began to flourish, another set of changes got under way in the United States that would turn out to be just as powerful a crowbar to undo the progressive reforms that had generated such widespread prosperity during the Golden Age of Capitalism. These would deliver a knockout blow not so much to the Bretton Woods system as to an older, yet no less powerful, democratic tradition: antitrust. These changes would help create the wealthiest robber barons in world history.

CHAPTER FOUR

The Invisible Fist

In April 2018 Mark Zuckerberg, of Facebook, facing a grilling from a Senate panel, took about as much care with his own information as Facebook does with your data: he allowed a photographer from the Associated Press to snap a photo of his crib notes. One of his arguments was aimed against anyone suggesting that Facebook should be broken up: "US tech companies key asset for America; break up strengthens Chinese companies."

There were other fascinating things in Zuckerberg's notes, and few people probed this particular tidbit very far. But his argument was odd, if you think about. He was calling for Congress to accept his monopoly, which profitably harvests and sells valuable and sensitive data about American users, in the interest of American competitiveness (and national security). Or, to put it more simply, to improve American competitiveness by restricting competition in America.

Lawmakers and commentators mostly fell over themselves to flatter Zuckerberg, and with a couple of honorable exceptions, they avoided the elephant in the room: Facebook's gargantuan monopoly, trapping us in a devil's bargain where we have no choice but to accept being subjected to secret surveillance if we want to connect with friends and neighbors this way online.[1] And that is because, until very recently, few were paying much attention to the awesome monopolistic powers of big firms like Facebook, Google, Amazon, and Netflix. The Obama administration was so cozy with Google that it may as well have given it the keys to the White House. The Trump administration is even worse.[2]

Most people still aren't paying attention. How did these remarkable blind spots come to exist? The perils of monopoly power have been clearly understood since long before Rockefeller built Standard Oil. "If we will not endure a king as a political power," said Senator John Sherman, who sponsored America's first proper antitrust law in 1890, "we should not endure a king over the production, transportation and sale of any of the necessaries of life." The New Deal program that followed the crash of 1929 had strong antitrust measures—a large and varied body of anti-monopoly laws to tackle big banks and great concentrations of economic power—at its heart. Yet in the modern era this has all been swept away. Who killed anti-monopoly?

There is, in fact, a clear answer to this question. We can trace the shift back to an ideological insurgency in the 1960s and 1970s, led by a group of Chicago School economists who would, as with a magician's trick of misdirection, shift attention away from the all-important question of whether corporations have too much economic and political power and toward a far narrower issue: whether the price is right. If the merger of two large companies doesn't lead to higher prices, the argument now goes, what's the problem? The services of Facebook and Google are free, apparently, so move along, folks, there's nothing to see here. This narrowing of focus has blinded us to many deeper issues, which are among the biggest drivers of financialization and the finance curse.

This revolution was sparked at a dinner party in 1960 at the Chicago home of Aaron Director, an American economist with a small mustache, horn-rimmed glasses, and a lightweight boxer's wiry frame. Director was a contrarian, pugnacious antigovernment fanatic, a former radical leftist union organizer who had crossed over and now seemed hell-bent on smashing the consensus that once fed his idealism. His politics were completely, purely free-market and even to the right of Milton Friedman, the godfather of libertarian free-market economics, who was married to Director's sister, Rose. "Family dinners at the Friedmans' house must have been a bundle of laughs," said Matthew Watson, professor of political economy at Warwick University in England. "There can't have been many house guests where Milton would have been accused of being too pro-government and too left wing." That particular night Director hosted twenty dinner guests, conservative thinkers including not just Friedman but George Stigler (who would go on to make a name for himself attacking government regulation), the British economist Ronald Coase, and a fire-breathing lawyer called Robert Bork.[3]

The University of Chicago was a bear pit, an arena of intense macho intellectual combat where academics were constantly struggling to outdo each other with clever theories about efficient markets—theories that often perched on toe-curling assumptions—to defend unconventional, even antisocial positions usually supporting big business and attacking government. Mathematical and logical elegance trumped the messy reality of life and the world. Director himself was one of the truest of true believers who thought pretty much anything worthwhile could and should be shoehorned into the price mechanism in the interest of "efficiency." His messianic zeal mesmerized many of his students. "I regarded my role as that of Saint Paul to Aaron Director's Christ," Coase said. "He got the doctrine going, and what I had to do was to bring it to the Gentiles." Bork, another disciple, said Director "gradually destroyed my dreams of socialism with price theory," adding that many of his colleagues "underwent what can only be called a religious conversion."

The guests that evening came to listen to Coase present a draft paper, "The Problem of Social Cost." Stigler remembered wondering "how so fine an economist could make such an obvious mistake." At the start of the evening Coase summarized his idea and a vote was taken. All twenty guests opposed him.[4]

Coase deployed a novel argument. Corporations in those days were supposed to be subject to the law—or at least the law came first. If a corporation was pumping illegal pollutants into a river, you went out and found the pipe or some incriminating documents, then wielded the law to stop it. Pollution is an externality, a consequence that affects other parties who aren't associated with the transactions or businesses involved. Markets can't generally solve externalities; it had long been accepted that governments and laws needed to step in to stop such failures in the market. Coase wasn't having this.

Imagine, he said, that a farmer's cattle ravaged his neighbor's wheat crop. If the law held the cattle farmer liable, he'd have to pay for a fence or negotiate compensation with his neighbor. If the law didn't hold him liable, the wheat farmer would pay for the fence. But from an overall efficiency perspective it didn't matter which farmer paid for the fence, since the cost of the fence was the same. So the law itself didn't really matter, he went on: laws should be subject to a sort of cost-benefit analysis where harm caused by the polluter or the careless farmer or the tax cheat should be weighed against the benefits derived by those actors who gained. It was enough to show that overall "welfare" was maximized to let this happen.

You could extend this logic. If there was a large banking monopoly, for instance, any losses to consumers or workers could be balanced out by gains to the bank and its shareholders, and there might be no net loss overall. Bring in gains such as economies of scale reaped by larger corporations, and monopolies might turn out to be a good thing! Monopolies were the natural way markets wanted to go, and it wasn't the job of judges to interfere. Once you took into account the apparent costs of regulation to the monopolizers, he said, it became hard to justify doing anything about them.

The guests were stunned. Until then antitrust—the large body of established law and theory that said monopolies were harmful and that governments should regulate them—was supported both on the Left of the political spectrum, where people fretted about giant banks and industrialists oppressing workers and customers, and on the Right too, where people were keen to protect and promote competition and the integrity of markets. Coase had just lobbed a bomb into this whole edifice—and into a few other edifices too.

The dinner progressed. The arguments mounted. "As usual, Milton [Friedman] did most of the talking," Stigler remembered. "My recollection is that Ronald didn't persuade us. But he refused to yield to all our erroneous arguments. Milton would hit him from one side, then from another, then from another." But then, as in the plot of *Twelve Angry Men*, the mood began to change. "To our horror," Stigler said, "Milton missed him and hit us." By the end of the evening they took another vote: all were for Coase. "I have never really forgiven Aaron for not having brought a tape recorder," Stigler said. "It was one of the most exciting intellectual events of my life."[5]

This violent attack on the foundations of legal authority—that laws should be subjected to economic cost-benefit calculations and rejected if they fail to pass muster—was a classic example of the Chicago School's "economics imperialism"—a power grab by economics professors with ambitions to colonize and dominate as many areas of social and political life as they could lay their hands on. It was at the same time an example of red-blooded neoliberalism, which argued that lawyers and laws should bow down to economists and economics and that everything had a price. The scale and success of this insurrection was made clear later on, in 1983, when a group of Chicago School economists was reminiscing about—one might say gloating over—this power grab. This short exchange between Bork, influential jurist and economist Richard Posner, and Henry Manne, another influential economist, gives a flavor.

> BORK: As far as I know, the economists have not yet done any damage to constitutional law.
> POSNER: We are working on that.
> MANNE: We'll chase you out of that too. [*laughter*][6]

It doesn't take a genius to see how elevating easy-to-massage numbers above the rule of law was likely to boost lawbreaking everywhere, not least in the financial sector.

These revolutionary ideas percolated slowly at first, but cheerleaders and corporate funders weren't hard to find. One early enthusiast was a partner at a Wall Street consulting firm who was already a fanatical devotee of the antigovernment novelist and libertarian guru Ayn Rand. "The entire structure of antitrust statutes in this country is a jumble of economic irrationality and ignorance, . . . confusion, contradictions and legalistic hairsplitting," he thundered in 1961. "The world of antitrust is reminiscent of *Alice in Wonderland.*" The problem wasn't big business, he said; it was big antitrust and big government. This irate Wall Street partner, whose name was Alan Greenspan, would later become chairman of the US Federal Reserve.[7]

The United States is the historical home of anti-monopoly, and trends around the world have been led by what happens there. Anti-monopoly has been hard-wired into the American psyche since the country's founding. America's rugged individualism emerged as a bulwark not only against oversized government but against overwhelming business and financial power too. The Boston Tea Party of 1773, which helped trigger the War of Independence from Britain, was in large part a protest against the monopolizing East India Company, "which, besides the trains of evil that attend them in the commercial view, are forever dangerous to public liberty," wrote Samuel Adams and John Hancock.[8] And this was always understood: monopoly wasn't just an economic problem but a fundamental threat to liberty and democracy.

Anti-monopoly zeal and monopoly power ebbed and flowed for centuries alongside shifting political tides. President Andrew Jackson launched a titanic struggle in the 1830s against what he called a "hydra of corruption"—a net of interlinked monopolies centered on the Second Bank of the United States—and his victory preceded a period of strong defenses against business predation and of tremendous economic dynamism. "The stranger is constantly amazed by the immense public works executed by a nation which contains, so to speak, no rich men," wrote the French political scientist Alexis de Tocqueville in 1840. "What astonishes me is not so much the marvelous grandeur of some undertakings, as the innumerable multitude of small ones."[9]

The Civil War in the 1860s was a fight against slavery and monopoly: the abolitionist senator Thomas Morris of Ohio called "slave power" the "goliath of all monopolies," and his fellow abolitionist Wendell Phillips railed against the "aristocracy of the skin" in the slave economies of the South. When the war ended, however, America drifted fitfully toward the "age of Caesarism," the era of the Rockefellers, Carnegies, and J. P. Morgan, who justified their power as necessary to "rationalize" their industries in more "efficient" ways.[10]

Democratic pushback emerged to confront these concentrations of economic and political power, often with geographical roots that are eerily similar to what we see today. Communities across rural and poor America saw large conglomerates sucking wealth and control away from their regions to benefit elites in mostly coastal cities like New York. The Sherman Antitrust Act of 1890, which empowered the government to finally break up Standard Oil in 1911, was partly inspired by these geographical iniquities. "If we would not submit to an emperor," declared Senator John Sherman, after whom the act was named, "we should not submit to an autocrat of trade."[11] The act was fairly broad and blunt, but its teeth were sharpened with new laws added over the coming decades.

The biggest wave of antitrust actions to date happened in the 1930s with Franklin D. Roosevelt's New Deal, a sweeping package of progressive political reforms in response to World War I and the great crash of 1929, which helped shift economic and political power away from finance and large corporations toward ordinary folk. The New Dealers created a carefully calibrated system of government checks and balances to mediate between competing social priorities, regionally and nationally, breaking up concentrations of power in different parts of the economy. Their flagship legislation was probably the Glass-Steagall Act of 1933, which forced banks to separate their commercial banking activities from the more speculative investment banking, breaking up the banking behemoths.

At every stage it was understood that this was not so much about economics as political power and protecting democracy. Economic efficiency was exactly the wrong goal; the point of antitrust laws, as the antitrust lawyer Louis Brandeis explained, "was not to avoid friction, but by means of the inevitable friction incident to the distribution of the government powers among three departments, to save the people from autocracy."

While Hayek and the neoliberals saw government as the agent of tyranny, with the post–World War II Soviet Union as the prime bogeyman, the anti-monopoly crusaders argued that large concentrations of private power bred tyrannical government, especially fascism. For them, Nazi Germany was the prime exhibit. "The liberty of a democracy is not safe if the people tolerate the growth of private power to a point where it becomes stronger than their democratic state itself," Roosevelt said in a landmark address to Congress in 1938, as war loomed in Europe. "That, in its essence, is Fascism—ownership of Government by an individual, by a group, or by any other controlling private power." The Nazi state, the corporatist Fascist Italian state, and the imperial Japanese economic system were all heavily cartelized; in fact the Nazis in 1933 had actively encouraged the formation of big industrial cartels as a way of enforcing top-down control, eliminating foreign competitors and juicing up profits for big firms backing the war effort. As trust-busting US congressman Emanuel Celler put it, "The monopolies soon got control of Germany, brought Hitler to power and forced virtually the whole world into war."[12]

When the war ended, a victorious America began to spread its doctrine of benevolent antitrust around the globe like a democratizing shock wave. The United States inserted anti-monopoly principles into the constitutions of the defeated aggressor countries as one of its "four Ds" for postwar governance: denazification, deconcentration, democratization, and decartelization. European countries adapted in their own ways. Britain took all this rather seriously too, though in its own way.

For Britain's financial sector, run by an old boys' network that had grown fat off the profits of empire and had been protected from international competition, the problem was less about monopolizing giants and more about gentleman's agreements to carve up turf, restrict competition, and pocket the resulting profits.[13] After the war, Britain's bloodied workers were in no mood for compromise, and the new economic regime that began to emerge wasn't so much about breaking up giant corporations as about full-scale nationalization, bringing the energy industries, the railways, the coal mines, and iron and steel under government control. And on the European Continent the 1957 Treaty of Rome, which laid the foundations for the European Economic Community, contained strong antitrust provisions modeled on the Sherman Act.[14]

But with the growth of the offshore Euromarkets in London, the steady resurgence of finance, and the rise of neoliberalism, the pendulum began to swing back again. US regulators began to notice British intransigence. "There was always a lot of trouble across borders," said the antitrust lawyer Jack Blum. US laws in this area were supposed to apply internationally, but "the British fought us tooth and nail on that proposition," he said. "That was with regularity. The UK passed laws to prevent the US investigating."[15] Yet these were minor difficulties when compared to the devastating blows that were to come, especially at the hands of Director's dinner guests, most obviously Robert Bork.

Bork was a cranky lawyer who had been growing steadily more agitated about impending moral collapse. He blamed America's ills on feminists, multiculturalists, gays, pornographers, fearmongering "race hustlers," and most especially leftist professors. He once asserted that "homosexuals, American Indians, blacks, Hispanics, women, and so on" had only "allegedly" been subjected to oppression, and that the list of victim groups "is virtually endless, including at one time everybody but ordinary white males."[16] The answer to modern moral turpitude, he said, was censorship.

With eyes alternately hooded and bulging, and sometimes both at the same time, if you can picture that, Bork was beefy, physically imposing, and, to many people, terrifying. One television critic said he "looked and talked like a man who would throw the book at you—and maybe the whole country." As US solicitor general, Bork fired the courageous special prosecutor in the Watergate scandal that would eventually bring down President Nixon in 1974, a dismissal that was later ruled illegal. Years later Senator Edward Kennedy would denounce him in these terms:

> Robert Bork's America is a land in which women would be forced into back-alley abortions, blacks would sit at segregated lunch counters, rogue police could break down citizens' doors in midnight raids, schoolchildren could not be taught about evolution, writers and artists would be censored at the whim of government, and the doors of the federal courts would be shut on the fingers of millions of citizens for whom the judiciary is often the only protector of the individual rights that are the heart of our democracy.[17]

Bork denied these charges and his record was a bit more nuanced than Kennedy's picture suggests but there is no doubting it: he was a piece of work.

His colossal contribution to the game at hand was a little firecracker of a book published in 1978 called *The Antitrust Paradox*. This built on work by Richard Posner and Ronald Coase, shifting the focus of antitrust law even beyond Coase's emphasis on "efficiency" to something simpler and narrower: prices for consumers. "The only legitimate goal of American antitrust law," he said, "is the maximization of consumer welfare." Channeling his guru, Aaron Director, he made some astonishing arguments based on the assumption that markets behave efficiently. Predatory pricing—in which players in a market collude to extract profits by restricting competition—was "a phenomenon that probably does not exist," he said, because monopolists making large profits would be instantly undercut by "entrants who would arrive in sky-darkening swarms for the profitable alternatives." It was "all but impossible" for actors to corner markets by buying up competitors, he asserted. (Try telling that to anyone who has tried going head-to-head with Amazon or Google.) If monopolies did persist, Bork said, it was only because they were more efficient, and if monopolists did raise prices, this was just fine because monopolists were consumers too! Traditional anti-trust concerns, he argued, were "nonsense ... mechanisms the law has imagined." The book was, as the US antitrust expert Gerald Berk put it, "vehemently anti-constitutional democracy." What is perhaps oddest about this episode is what Bork eventually became most famous for: arguing that the US Constitution should not be interpreted according to prevailing democratic spirits but instead should be taken literally, just as the founding fathers had originally intended, however much the country had moved on. Yet his arguments on consumer prices as the sole lodestar for antitrust were exactly contrary to what the framers of the constitution had intended. Indeed, the words 'consumer prices' don't appear anywhere in any of America's antitrust laws.[18]

What mattered to Bork was not reality but elegant models of reality. Boil everything down to price, ignore all this leftist claptrap about laws and rights and power, and efficiency would follow. Instead of regulating preemptively by focusing on the structure of markets and whether any players have too much power in those markets, regulation should happen only after the event, once an alleged monopoly had been established and you could measure its effects. Monopolies staring people in the face could be assumed out of existence because they just couldn't exist, and if they did, well, they might just be brilliant. Bork's book was so influential, says the Open Markets Institute, America's leading independent anti-monopoly group, that it became "the main guide to more than a generation of policymakers and enforcers."[19]

These ideas gained heavy tailwinds. The high inflation of the 1970s and early 1980s encouraged a worldview focused on lowering consumer prices. And big business and big banks loved Bork too, of course. A "Law and Economics" school set up in 1974, first in Miami and now at

George Mason University, also began to spread the ideas of applying cost-benefit analysis to laws, while its founder, Henry Manne, worked to raise corporate donations and, with Bork's help, spread the word. At George Mason, Manne joined forces with the conservative thinker James McGill Buchanan, another godfather of the libertarian Right who would join with Charles Koch and other antigovernment billionaires and corporations to fund and spread these ideas. (By 1990, according to the historian Nancy MacLean, Manne could boast that 40 percent of the U.S. federal judiciary had been treated to a Koch-backed curriculum.)[20] One Chicago consulting firm, Manne frankly admitted, "more than once expressed their appreciation to me for substantially boosting their business." These anti-antitrust attitudes spread and spread, not so much by transforming the laws themselves, which remained on the books, but by getting judges to interpret them in new, narrower ways.

When Republican Ronald Reagan became president in 1980, another old argument came to the fore—just like the one Mark Zuckerberg would later use to try to bamboozle the US Senate—that American national economic champions and "America's international competitiveness" weren't compatible with strong antitrust laws.[21] Let American giants exploit American consumers, workers, and suppliers more effectively, it argued, to boost their profits so they can better compete on the world stage.

Some US firms were then large vertically integrated companies guided by Fordism—a one-stop-shop production model named after the Ford Motor Company, which brought coal, iron ore, and other raw materials into one side of its vast River Rouge Complex and produced finished cars out the other. US antitrust authorities had until then recognized that in industries such as vehicle manufacture it was necessary to operate on a large scale, so they tolerated these behemoths but tried to ensure there were several competing against one another in any market. Europe, for its part, wanted its own champions to take on the Americans and the Japanese and set up projects like Airbus and the Ariane rocket program. European financial and market integration, it was calculated, would provide the expanded base for launching these cross-border Eurochampions into the world economy, going head-to-head with the Americans and Japanese. With these changes, anti-monopoly took another hit.

As the 1970s became the 1980s, American antitrust law shifted its focus away from worrying about the structure of markets, and the immense wealth and power that can be milked from rigged markets, to a narrower focus on simple metrics based on price. The authorities stopped writing detailed analyses of the industries and markets they regulated and came to understand less and less about how they worked or what made economies tick. A growing band of anti-antitrust academics also realized there was money to be made by selling consultancy services to big corporations and increasingly "seemed like paid apologists for wealthy corporate interests," says Kenneth Davidson, a veteran US anti-trust expert and former regulator. Many academics got rich in the Wall Street–led feeding frenzy of monopolizing mergers and acquisitions in the 1980s that would have been forbidden a few years earlier (and they continue to do so: economics professors today can earn over $1,000 per hour defending megamergers[22]). From 1981 to 1997 there were more than seven thousand bank mergers in the United States alone, almost unopposed. To understand how badly things went from there and why this matters so much to us now, it is necessary to delve further into the madness of the real world and look at how monopolies work.

Walk into a shopping mall today and you'll see Bork's progeny all around you. That brightly colored cornucopia of goods on your supermarket shelves, packaged under myriad different brands—most are made by a few goliaths like Unilever or Kraft Heinz. (Note the double-barreled name of that last behemoth, the product of a gigantic merger. Kraft Heinz even tried to take over Unilever, though in 2017 it became one of the few megamergers that failed, after Unilever officials put up a ferocious defense.)[23] Via the chocolates we buy, the phones we chatter into, the sunglasses or shoes we wear, the water we drink, the airlines we fly with, the railways we suffer on, or the social media platforms we're addicted to, we pay hidden "monopoly taxes" almost any time we open our wallets. Bork said predatory pricing wouldn't—couldn't—happen, but we are drowning in it, as businesses leverage their market power to screw us over in endless hard-to-see ways.

Countless situations and strategies exist. There's monopoly (a single seller), oligopoly (a few sellers), monopsony (a single buyer), oligopsony (a few buyers), predatory pricing and wage setting, patents, loose cartel arrangements, and more. These structures operate across all sorts of markets, market niches, and market micro-niches, locally, nationally, and across borders. To avoid needless complication, going forward I'll often lump these all together, inaccurately, as monopolies, their defining characteristic being that someone is exerting power and restricting competition in markets, usually to extract supersized profits.

The simplest and best-known version is the horizontal monopoly, in which companies buy out rivals making or doing similar stuff, or use superior financial reserves to sell below cost, undercutting their competitors and driving them off the cliff (the death of many Main Street family businesses at the hands of the large supermarkets and, more recently, Amazon is one example).

Slightly more complex are vertical monopolies. In these a big manufacturer, say, buys up the distributors and retailers of its products, then refuses to sell rival manufacturers' products. Take, for instance, the Italian eyewear giant Luxottica, which has integrated the optical business with the fashion industry to generate enormous wealth for its owners. Luxottica controls large parts of the spectacles industry, from design and product development to manufacturing, logistics, distribution, and retail. It owns the iconic Ray-Ban, Oakley, Vogue Eyewear, Persol, and Arnette brands and has exclusive agreements with Giorgio Armani, Emporio Armani, Bulgari, Chanel, Dolce & Gabbana, Prada Eyewear, Paul Smith, Polo Ralph Lauren, Valentino, Versace, and several others. That's horizontal monopoly. Now imagine you're at LensCrafters, which sells these brands and is owned by Luxottica. But you don't like the service—or the offerings, for that matter. So you go around the corner, to Pearle Vision. That's owned by Luxottica too. You don't like it either, so you go to Sunglass Hut or Sears Optical. They're owned by Luxottica too. It's not just the brands of sunglasses that are being monopolized here; it's the stores that sell them. That's vertical monopoly. And it goes deeper: as Luxottica itself admits, its grip extends from manufacturing, to distribution, to wholesale, to retail, to e-commerce, to lens processing.

And that gives this giant great power. In the early 2000s Luxottica stopped selling Oakley products in its stores, crashing Oakley's stock price and then buying the company cheaply. The comedian John Oliver in 2017 aired a clip of Luxottica's former CEO Andrea Guerra purring silkily, in response to a reporter's challenge that the Oakley episode represented a monopolistic shakedown: "I understand your theory, but they understood that life was better together." His comment reminded me of Rockefeller's offers to buy up the ownership shares of weakened rivals with Standard Oil stock, saying, "I have ways of making money you know nothing of." Oliver put it more plainly, stroking an imaginary white cat while repeating Guerra's words, adding at the end, ". . . Mr. Bond." Luxottica made nearly $6.4 billion in gross profits on $9.9 billion in sales in 2017, mostly from the United States: that's a whopping 65 percent profit rate as a share of sales. Even the monopolizing Walmart can manage only 25 percent. Competition in these markets has broken down. And public records show that plenty of Luxottica's profits come from financial trading activities, through snaking chains of corporate entities, far out of view—entities in Ireland and other tax havens, which essentially charge other parts of the Luxottica empire in the United States and elsewhere large royalties for the rights to use brands and trademarks, then allow those large payments to be deducted from the US affiliates' taxable profits while at the same time being received profitably in the tax haven, where little or no tax is paid. (This is a version of the same "transfer pricing" game I described earlier, with the banana company shifting profits into a tax haven.) The whole Luxottica shebang is ultimately controlled by a firm called Delfin SARL in Luxembourg, a secretive European tax haven.

So Luxottica squeezes customers through horizontal and vertical monopoly power, and it squeezes taxpayers through tax haven games. And this now goes deeper. Luxottica specializes in frames, while the French multinational Essilor controls nearly half the world's prescription lens business and says it supplies three to four hundred thousand retail stores around the world. In 2017 US and European regulators approved a merger to create EssilorLuxottica. "Forgive me," a long-time entrepreneur in the optical sector said. "But it is nothing short of control of the industry." The deal was completed in October 2018, so I should expect my next pair of glasses to be more expensive—and businesses supplying this behemoth should also expect to be rewarded less for their hard work.[24]

Another version is the home-base monopoly. Walmart, for instance, grew by focusing on towns too small to support two supermarkets, extracting supersized profits from customers and suppliers in those towns, then using those profits to expand. The game of regional or local monopoly has also been popular with banks, and arch-monopolizer Warren Buffett has also used it with local media organizations. "If you have a monopoly newspaper or if you have a network television station," said Buffett, "your idiot nephew could run it."

Different, but also familiar, are too-big-to-fail monopolies. Large institutions, usually banks, become so systemically important that a collapse would trigger mayhem, which is what happened in the global financial crisis of 2007–8. They milk markets by making profits from risky business, then get taxpayers to bail them out when the risks crystallize in a crisis. There is actually an official list of these monsters published by the Financial Stability Board, a global body based in Switzerland. There were twenty-nine too-big-to-fail banks at the last count in 2018, plus nine too-big-to-fail insurers, including JPMorgan Chase, Bank of America, Citigroup, HSBC, Deutsche Bank, UBS, Bank of China, Goldman Sachs, Wells Fargo, and Bank of New York Mellon. This is not just a matter for financial regulators: it is an antitrust issue. But in Europe and the United States the regulators are asleep, letting these goliaths stay intact. And here's a scary trend: while the top five US banks held 10 percent of all US banking assets in 1990, this share had risen to nearly half by 2016.[25]

There are many other varieties of financial monopoly, run by banks, hedge funds, or private equity firms. Today just three financial firms— BlackRock, State Street, and Capital Group—own 10–20 percent of most major American companies, including many that compete with each other. But Wall Street firms aren't just assembling market power by owning strategic stakes in markets; they are also the financializing machines that assemble mergers and build monopolies, earning huge fees.[26] Pick up any copy of the *Wall Street Journal* or *Financial Times* these days, and there's a good chance the top headline involves a megamerger.

The giant tech monopolies like Facebook, Google, and Amazon also resemble—indeed are—financial players in several important ways. As the *Financial Times* journalist Rana Foroohar explains, "They each sit in the center of an hourglass of information and commerce, taking a cut of whatever passes through." Amazon, like a big investment bank, can both make a market and participate in it. Both the big banks and big tech firms also have vastly more market data than the customers they deal with, and they trade on these "information asymmetries" ruthlessly—and the victims all share this subservient relationship, whether they are ordinary folk taking out variable rate subprime mortgage loans, cities like Detroit buying complex mortgage-backed securities, or booksellers trying to use Amazon's platform. "Like the house in a Las Vegas casino," wrote Foroohar, "they always win." Silicon Valley and Wall Street firms have been the biggest and most influential campaign finance donors in recent history, and both sides are suffused with an intense libertarian, anti-tax, anti-regulation worldview. (Facebook's unofficial motto, "move fast and break things," could hang happily above any testosterone-fueled Wall Street trader's desk.) Peter Thiel, arguably Silicon Valley's most influential investor, shares Buffett's contempt for competition; he even wrote a book praising monopolization, in which he declared competition "a relic of history." Silicon Valley and Wall Street also seem to enjoy and pursue the same above-the-law treatment: the Obama administration let bankers off the hook for the global financial crisis (the Trump administration has arguably been worse), and likewise the tech monopolies have had a free pass on antitrust with successive administrations, and now the main targets of antitrust law are such villains as music teachers, church organists, ice-skating instructors, home health aides, and truck and Uber drivers who try to organize to protect their livelihoods.[27]

Then there is the pincer monopoly, where you capture a closely related activity in the supply chain, then use that power to squeeze or kill a competitor in your first market. Or the leapfrog monopoly, where you innovate so fast or repackage an old business in new technology so well that flat-footed antitrust regulators can't keep up. Many technology firms, and some private equity firms, specialize in this.

Monopolies are contagious too. This is the case with defensive monopolies, where the only response to bigger players squeezing you out of your markets is to merge with others, to acquire the clout to be able to push back. One expected supermarket merger in May 2018, for instance, was billed by analysts as a strategy to create an "Amazon crusher" (as if that would stop that online steamroller).

There are natural monopolies, where so-called network effects permanently prevent competitors from breaking in. Facebook is one: you want to be on the platform where your friends are, not searching for them on five different platforms. Then there is the hydra monopoly, where if you control one part of a supply chain, you can hold the whole industry hostage. When a minor earthquake off Niigata in Japan crippled a monopolizing car parts producer making piston rings, it all but shut down Japan's automobile industry; Toyota alone produced 120,000 fewer cars in the following weeks. These monopolies can generate instability, with a limited failure at one monopolized node rippling out.[28]

Or try the offshore secrets monopoly. In this arrangement, commonly owned or closely collaborating financial interests pretend to compete by hiding their ownership of companies behind secretive shell companies in tax havens, while really controlling them all. The beauty of this strategy is that you can give government regulators secret personal stakes in its success. Who knows who might be using this mechanism to amass financial power over our economies? Monopolies are about power. Allowing opaque foreign interests to obtain monopolizing locks over parts of an economy can threaten national security, and such interests even venture out into the open. In Europe, Russia's Gazprom and Chinese state enterprises are acutely aware of the advantages of controlling bottlenecks in energy and technology markets; the European Commission is currently grappling with Gazprom over gas supplies in a case that has been called "the antitrust clash of the decade."[29]

There are also what might be called corrupt monopolies. A trader/manager at a major US bank in London told me how the bank would bribe clients in the tax haven of Singapore, where oil traders would buy "masses of hookers" for their clients. "We'd go to the Orchard Shopping Centre—they called it the Four Floors of Whores—where $200 gets you Russians, Chinese—whatever you want." Collaboration in markets depends on trust, he said, but of the honor-among-thieves variety. "If you want someone to trust you, you'd better be sleeping with a hooker at least—to get in as deep as they are." Money is made from sharing advance information among buddies, helping the banks to trade ahead of clients' moves; for example, getting your bank to buy jet fuel just before the airlines come shambling into the market, pushing prices up for them. "You talk to everyone, you know all that information, so you can move first. It's easy money if you have the size."[30] Who pays the price? You, when you buy an airline ticket whose price has been bumped up by this cozy and corrupt financial collusion. Then you'll get hit again, because the airlines are skimming off large monopoly profits after a series of megamergers left the four largest US airlines—American, Delta,

United, and Southwest—in control of four-fifths of domestic passenger traffic: Delta, for instance, has a more than 75 percent market share in Atlanta, Philadelphia, and Dallas–Fort Worth. (In smaller towns or cities, the routes are often dominated by a single carrier, and prices are especially high.) In Europe, where regulation is stronger, airfares are far cheaper. Or take health insurance, where in many states one or two firms have a combined 80–90 percent market share, and where a proper dose of competition, by one startling estimate, could save the average American family $9,000 a year. There's a similar problem with high-speed internet, and also with internet search, where Google has a 90 percent market share.[31]

A much bigger example of corrupt monopoly comes from finance, via the famous London Inter-Bank Offered Rate (LIBOR) scandal. LIBOR is a benchmark interest rate whose value, before the scandal erupted in 2012, was set by global banks under the aegis of the British Bankers' Association. A group calling themselves "the cartel" manipulated the rate to influence the prices of trillions of dollars' worth of securities pegged to that rate. (They say the problem is fixed, but it probably isn't.)[32] Who paid the cost of *these* supersized profits? You, ultimately, when the financial crisis hit.

Another massive source of market power comes through the ownership of patents, trademarks, and copyrights. The original intent of these was to carve out limited exceptions to antitrust laws so as to encourage firms to innovate, guaranteeing that for a fixed period of time only they could profit from something they had invested in. But such "intellectual property" has become a blanket license to profiteer and now often stifles innovation. The song "Happy Birthday," originally created by a Kentucky kindergarten teacher in 1893, was under copyright until a judge overturned it in 2016 after a long legal battle. Until then you were supposed to pay the copyright holders, a succession of companies including Warner/Chappell Music, royalties every time you sang it in public.[33]

Patents can be a matter of life and death. The American biopharmaceutical company Gilead's hepatitis C drug Sovaldi, for instance—priced at $84,000 in the United States for a twelve-week treatment (versus a manufacturing cost as low as $68)—has been parked in the corporate tax haven of Ireland. Despite sales of Sovaldi and a related drug, Harvoni, booming in 2015, the company's tax bill plummeted as it "engaged in a massive shift of American profits offshore," according to research by the nonprofit group Americans for Tax Fairness. By the end of 2015 Gilead was sitting on $28.5 billion in accumulated offshore profits, helped by huge royalty payments from Gilead's US affiliates to its Irish companies, sucking the profits offshore. Breaking such monopolies can have dramatic results. When South Africa broke a patent stranglehold and managed to cut the cost of antiretroviral drugs for AIDS sufferers from $15,000 per patient per year down to less than a hundredth of that figure, the country's average life expectancy surged from 53.4 years in 2004 to 62.5 in 2015. South Africa's statistician general at the time, Pali Lehohla, believes the change was largely owed to increased access to these drugs. With a $1,000 patent-protected pill, explains Matt Stoller, a US monopolies expert, "you aren't paying for health care. You are paying for yachts."[34]

Those are killer yachts.

In light of all this complexity, it is clear that the popular view—that tackling monopolies is just about breaking up cartels or big firms—is wrongheaded. Monopolies need to be understood and dismantled using a whole range of economy-wide strategies: empowering labor unions, reforming banking rules, addressing billionaire and financial control over the media, focusing on conflicts of interest among large audit firms, cracking down on tax havens that prioritize banks and large multinationals over small businesses, and plenty more. Breakup is important, but it's just one tool in the kit.

One of the first people to understand properly the potential of the relaxation of antitrust rules after Bork's vandalism—to have the vision to approach this through a financialized frame—was Jack Welch, the CEO of the American conglomerate General Electric. In the early 1980s it was common for large corporations like GE to be involved in many different and often unrelated activities, each contributing to overall profits. GE, for example, produced televisions, electric trains, lights, motors, X-ray machines, washing machines, hospital equipment, aircraft, and plenty more. The clue was in its name. But in 1981, three years after Bork's book came out, Welch inaugurated a new company strategy: GE would aim to be the number one or number two in every business line it was involved in.

He set about reshaping GE and, in the process, boosting its market power where possible. The company bought out competitors in related market sectors, created economies of scale to make it harder for competitors to break in, and sold off or closed business units that did not pass muster. In the pre-Bork era, antitrust laws would have stopped much of this, but no longer. Welch's strategy caught on, helping fuel the great Wall Street merger boom of the 1980s. Spurred by Bork's beefy message, the Reagan administration took the brakes off. "The general modus operandi was to break apart the old conglomerates that had been assembled in the 1950s and 1960s," says Barry Lynn, a US antitrust expert, "and then reassemble the parts in ways that better linked like to like. . . . [The] goal was to reduce competition as much as possible."[35]

This was profitable enough, but the transformation had a second stage. That was outsourcing, particularly the outsourcing of labor-intensive production facilities to cheap-labor countries like China and Bangladesh. This was driven especially hard by financial players and activist shareholders. And at the same time, bigger firms were aggressively expanding their use of tax havens to cut tax bills—also driven by financial players. These two related forms of offshoring—each involving taking money or operations elsewhere to escape paying out at home—gave large firms a killer cost advantage over their smaller, more domestically focused rivals, boosting their market power further. Old nurseries of jobs, skills, and technologies were being smashed open in cash raids, and big firms often began to look less like industrial manufacturers rooted in

communities and more like trading companies: loosely connected con-
glomerations of monopolies and near-monopolies focused on financial
returns rather than building up in-house strength and expertise. You
might call these firms middleman monopolies, inserting themselves at
the choke points linking many different actors in a market, just as the
giant supermarket chains position themselves between producers and
consumers, then try to use this position, if they can, to extract more
profit from both sides.

This can be especially scary for the small producers who supply
these giants and who sometimes have nowhere else to turn. For example,
Alicia Harvie of Farm Aid, a group that represents US family farmers,
said in 2017, "We can't overstate the level of fear and intimidation felt
by poultry growers that contact us or our partner organizations. If they
choose to speak up, they risk everything—their contract, their land,
their homes."[36]

These changes in the landscape of economic power have most
often been driven by investment funds, activist shareholders, and other
financial interests, which have forced firms to channel their growing
profits less into research and development and more into paying bumper
dividends. "The pressure from financiers to increase profits has resulted
in an ever swifter monopolization of the industrial systems upon which
we depend," wrote Lynn, and the new model of antitrust "builds vandalism right into the system." This process has been a central part of the
financialization of large corporations in country after country.

But this isn't just about industrial processes—far from it. At every
turn it has been about corporate power and its relationship with democracy and society. The monopolization of news has been especially dangerous because it eliminates ideological competition, leading to "a mushy
liberal sameness in every market," as the US economic historian Bruce
Bartlett once put it.[37] Haughty and distant from large parts of the population, large news organizations based in London or New York peddle
what often feels, to rural communities and the poor, like fake news.
As Facebook, Google, and other monopolizing internet behemoths

slaughter newspapers' advertising revenues, only the strongest news giants prosper, reinforcing these dangerous trends and fueling the furious new politics now convulsing large parts of the world.

In 2017 and 2018 the Trump administration rolled back protections against monopolies in local broadcast news, allowing a slew of stations to come under the control of the archconservative and pro-Trump Sinclair Broadcast Group. These stations quickly began parroting the centrally dictated line, so much so that a video overlaying the voices of a multitude of different local news anchors all saying precisely the same thing—attacking the mainstream media and Trump's critics—went viral.[38]

The power now being amassed is staggering. Amazon, the "Everything Store," thrills consumers with its convenience and low prices. It owns and sells books, toys, patents, cloud computing space, and endless other stuff, but it also owns much of the infrastructure for selling these things: "The thousands of retailers and independent businesses that must ride Amazon's rails to reach market," explains Lina Khan of the Open Markets Institute, "are increasingly dependent on their biggest competitor." Imagine if a giant trucking company owned most of America's roads and was allowed to charge drivers to use them. This is a vertical, horizontal, everything monopoly. Amazon once had a Gazelle Project to approach and buy competitors "the way a cheetah would a sickly gazelle," as Amazon's boss, Jeff Bezos, described it. Amazon's policy isn't so much buying its competitors as eating them and their markets, with little more than a burp. It is massacring competing stores: Toys 'R' Us is just one of many well-known businesses that Amazon helped put out of business, and in the process millions of good jobs are being replaced with smaller numbers of poorer, more menial, windowless, shelf-stacking, robotized ones, as it spreads relentlessly into new areas. Amazon's prices seem low, but it has such power that it can also manipulate its competitors' prices, thus weakening them and making it easier to pick them off.[39]

The behemoths often eke out "efficiencies" from economies of scale. But do these gains get passed on to consumers, employees, or taxpayers? In a competitive market, they should. But that's the whole point here: these aren't competitive markets. The more power these monopolies have, the more they can take these "efficiencies" for themselves. And this has powerful geographical effects: much, often most, of the wealth that the monopolizers generate is shipped out of local communities to mostly wealthy shareholders in places like London, New York, or Geneva, while local employees, suppliers, and distributors get crushed. We'll meet some of the victims a little later.

Monopolizing trends have hit workers hard in countries around the world. It used to be thought that this was largely caused by globalization, which pitted US workers against Chinese ones, driving down US wages. But there are now lots of more recent studies that point the finger at monopoly. Mostly, these studies look at how much of US national income goes to workers and how much goes to the owners of capital (very crudely speaking, the billionaire class). And here's the result of one of these studies: Eric Posner, Glen Weyl, and Suresh Naidu found that workers' wages have risen only 3 percent in real terms since the 1970s, while corporate profits have soared, and that the impact of monopolists exerting power in the labor markets is "huge." If labor markets were working properly, they reckoned, about three-quarters of national income should go to workers. Instead, only 50–60 percent does. To put this in more concrete terms, they said, the median annual wage for a US nurse is about $68,000—but if these markets worked properly, nurses ought to be earning between $90,000 and $200,000 a year. And if you are earning the average worker's wage of $30,500, you would instead be earning between $41,000 and $92,000 if market power were eliminated and proper competition reintroduced. The big corporate cause of inequality these days, it seems, isn't so much soaring CEO pay and bonuses as the rise of super-wealthy monopolizing firms that have left their competitors choking in their dust.[40]

And something telling and unexpected has been happening in poorer countries too. Trade theorists used to think that as companies in rich countries outsourced lower-skilled jobs to poorer countries, workers' share of income in those poorer countries would rise. But this hasn't happened either. This puzzle can be explained in large part by the growth of monopolizing international "lead companies" sitting (usually offshore) at choke points on long international supply chains for goods and services, trying to use their global market power at every niche to extract profits, replacing workers with robots where possible, keeping workers' wages low in all countries, rich and poor, and often escaping tax in the bargain. This game isn't just about big players taking a bigger share of the pie; the pie has actually shrunk as workers have lost purchasing power and thus found themselves less able to buy goods, sapping demand for corporate output. This in turn has refocused the attention of corporate managers away from investment and toward more financial engineering (and even more monopolization) to keep the profits flowing. Almost all industries are now becoming more concentrated, and since 1997 the number of listed companies in the United States has roughly halved, even as corporate profits have grown like gangbusters. "On this trend, by 2070 we will only have one company per industry," explained the authors Jonathan Tepper and Denise Hearn in their anti-monopoly book *The Myth of Capitalism.* "Or we may get social revolution."[41] Not only are big companies gobbling up smaller competitors; they are creating a rigged playing field that makes it exceptionally hard for start-ups to get past the first hurdles. Those that do end up like those freshly hatched baby turtles struggling down African beaches toward the sea, eaten by predators.

Under Bork's and the Chicago School's influence we have traded balanced economies, with plentiful, stable, well-paying jobs and thriving communities, for unbalanced economies, with zero-hour contracts, atomized communities, and cheap televisions—and they probably aren't much cheaper either. We've exchanged Adam Smith's invisible hand of the well-functioning market for the invisible fist of monopoly power. We have traded variety, balance, and resilience in our economy for a world of ever-narrower market sectors, where a dwindling number of ever-growing giants appropriate most of the proceeds, as investment bankers, private equity firms, and others hunt the market landscape for niches that haven't been sufficiently monopolized in order to bring them together and reap the dividends. Through this great finance-cursed, monopolizing package, we've made the rich richer and more powerful, and the poor and middle classes poorer and less powerful. We've reduced overall economic growth, undermined democracy, and damaged our national security.[42]

These changes joined with financial deregulation and the rise of the Euromarkets to create the typhoon-force winds filling the sails of large banks and multinationals. The tools that had underpinned the prosperity of the postwar Golden Age of Capitalism were being blunted, which created unprecedented challenges for the political parties of the Left. Infected by these new ideas, and dazzled by the oceans of credit now sluicing around the world, they began to look for new paths less hostile to financial capital and big business. "We have moved past the sterile debate between those who say government is the enemy and those who say government is the answer," said President Bill Clinton, who, along with his wife, Hillary, had studied under Bork at Yale Law School in the 1970s. "My fellow Americans, we have found a third way."

CHAPTER FIVE

The Third Way

In 1972, as the Golden Age of Capitalism was coming to an end, a fashionably dressed Pakistani banker called Agha Hasan Abedi confessed to a couple of colleagues a dream to set up "a world bank: a global bank for the Third World." Within ten years, he grandly promised, "you'll see: we will all be millionaires." That year he got start-up funding from the president of the United Arab Emirates, incorporated a new banking institution in the tiny European tax haven of Luxembourg, formed an international alliance with Bank of America, and began opening up branches and hoovering up deposits from around the globe. Within five years the Bank of Credit and Commerce International (BCCI) had 146 branches in thirty-two countries and a shiny new headquarters just a few minutes' walk from the Bank of England in the City of London.[1]

BCCI would do anything, for anyone, anywhere, using any methods. It trafficked in nuclear materials and secrets and in Chinese Silkworm anti-ship missiles. Alongside normal deposit-taking services for expatriates, it worked with Saddam Hussein, Manuel Noriega, Colombia's Medellín and Calí drug cartels, Hezbollah, heroin-trafficking Asian warlords, the Afghan mujahideen, and the North Koreans. And BCCI wasn't just a global octopus of murder and organized crime; it was also a giant Ponzi scheme, ripping off its depositors and investors in what turned out to be the biggest banking fraud of the twentieth century.[2] It bamboozled everyone by splitting its main operations three ways: between two separate holding companies in Luxembourg and the Caymans and its headquarters in London. It was the quintessential tax haven bank, and by this stage of the book it should be obvious why Abedi chose the Caymans and London.

Jack Blum, whose dogged investigations helped finally bring the bank down, remembers discussing it with officials from Pittsburgh-based Mellon Bank. "The entire senior international staff at Mellon just about threw up on the table" when he brought up BCCI, Blum remembered. Yet this radioactive bank seemed to be protected at the highest levels of the US political establishment. Blum came up against the CIA and "an army of people working in Washington on all sides."[3]

And not just in Washington. BCCI procured hookers, mercenaries, and assassins for clients, and bribes flowed like champagne wherever in the world it did business—including in its main global base of operations in London. "I would go to 101 Leadenhall Street [in the City of London] and see a man called ——," recalled a former employee who delivered bribes and payments. "He would smile at me and say, 'Sign this piece of paper.' I would write 'Mickey Mouse' on a piece of tissue paper, which was then thrown away. He handed me a bag of money, which I would then take back and distribute."[4] To whom the payments were distributed, he did not say, but a number of politicians from Britain's Conservative Party took BCCI's money. Robert Morgenthau, the Manhattan district attorney who led the attempts to close BCCI down, remembers the Cayman attorney general, "a crotchety British guy," refusing to help. The Americans turned to London, hoping to find a different attitude. "We had no cooperation from the Bank of England," Morgenthau remembers. "We tried to get financial records out of London; they didn't provide us with anything."[5] In fact, in April 1990, as Morgenthau's investigation into the rogue bank gathered pace, the Bank of England hatched a plot to help BCCI shift its headquarters, officers, and records away from Britain to secretive Abu Dhabi and rebuffed a formal request from the US Senate Committee on Foreign Relations for a full copy of the British government's internal report into the scandal, "on the ostensible ground that to do so would violate British secrecy and confidentiality laws." After the Bank of England was presented with evidence of BCCI's role in financing terrorism and laundering drug money, its response, according to a US Senate report, "was not to close BCCI down, but to find ways to prop up BCCI and prevent its collapse. This meant, among other things, keeping secret the very serious nature of BCCI's problems from its creditors and one million depositors." Robin Leigh-Pemberton, the Bank of England governor, revealed the British see-no-evil attitude: "If we closed down a bank every time we found an instance of fraud, we would have rather fewer banks."[6]

Remarkably, in 1990, the advisers to Britain's then prime minister Margaret Thatcher hatched up a plan to take over BCCI and even make her its president after leaving office. And she seems to have approved of the plan. In early 1991 Thatcher's son, Mark, and her closest advisers went to the Inn on the Park hotel in exclusive Mayfair in central London, where they met Ali Shorafa, a nominee of BCCI, and presented their plan for the Thatchers to take over. According to Mark Hollingsworth, the author of *Thatcher's Fortunes*, a book about her family's tax haven–diving financial affairs, Shorafa was keen on the plan to marry Thatcher with BCCI, but the scale of the scandal that erupted scotched the idea soon afterward. Yet according to Hollingsworth, who was briefed by someone present at the meeting, "she must have known in 1991 when she was considering this offer that BCCI was bent." Indeed she must have. This was "international global crime, of a level that boggles the mind," said Senator John Kerry, unveiling an astonishing US Senate report into the bank and into the UK authorities' attempts to protect it from the forces of law and order. "I'm saying very directly that the Bank of England had sufficient information to close BCCI 15 months earlier than it did [in July 1991]." By the time the Thatchers plotted their takeover, everyone in high circles knew how bad things were. And even *after* the bank exploded, in 1991, Margaret Thatcher went on to

meet the UAE president Sheikh Zayed, BCCI's cofounder, and told him
he had been "badly mistreated."

Thatcher's own personal finances, it turns out, were deeply
embedded in the crooked offshore world: her top personal financial
adviser was Hugh Thurston, based in the British island tax haven of
Jersey—"a remarkable guy who knew everything about Jersey and the
offshore world," Hollingsworth said—and "their accounts and offshore
companies were registered in Jersey, and in turn owned by offshore
companies." There remain deep mysteries about Thatcher's personal
financial affairs. For instance, records show that the house where she
lived on Chester Square in posh Belgravia in central London was
owned by a company called Bakeland, which in turn had Thurston
and Leonard Day, another Jersey-based financial adviser, as its main
registered shareholders. According to an investigation by the *Guardian*, Day and Thurston were holding it "as nominees for a trust with
concealed beneficiaries." When Day was asked why Thatcher owned
her home through such an arrangement, he said, "No one's going to
tell you about that."[7]

It isn't uncommon to find a politician, even one of Thatcher's global
stature, behaving in corrupt or shady ways. But there was something
else happening too. An ethos of "competitive" globalized finance was
starting to creep into political parties around the globe, first on the
Right, then increasingly on the Left.

It turns out that small tax havens are an excellent prism for understanding this phenomenon: in these places, the checks and balances
and messy political kerfuffle you find in large democracies get swept
aside, crystallizing some of the processes at play into clearer, more dis-
tilled forms. One of those small tax havens was the European mini-
state of Luxembourg, nestled between France, Germany, and Belgium.
Luxemburg is the fourth pillar of the BCCI edifice alongside London,
the Caymans, and the United Arab Emirates. But BCCI was just one
among many global scandals implicating Luxembourg. It was here that
the bearded American hustler and fraudster Bernie Cornfeld chose to

build up his now notorious Investors Overseas Services (IOS) in the 1960s. Operating out of a castle in Geneva built by Napoléon, Cornfeld surrounded himself with purring cheetahs and beautiful women, including leather-clad female chauffeurs, the actress Victoria Principal, and the famed Hollywood madam Heidi Fleiss. Like BCCI, IOS—before it collapsed in accounting scandals and fell into the hands of violent gangsters in 1971—hoovered up shady money from rich and poor countries and fed it into US securities via the Eurodollar market. Luxembourg was also home to the thoroughly rotten Banco Ambrosiano Holdings SA, the subsidiary at the center of the giant Banco Ambrosiano bank scandal, which involved the Italian Mafia, the Vatican, Masonic lodges, and, famously, the hanging of "God's Banker" Roberto Calvi under Blackfriars Bridge in London. The tiny country was key to the Elf affair, Europe's biggest corruption scandal since World War II, which involved the French state oil company Elf Aquitaine serving as a giant offshore slush fund, pumping secret finance to all the main French political parties and to the intelligence services and supplying bribes on behalf of French businesses all around the world, from Venezuela to Germany to Taiwan. The global fraudster Bernie Madoff ran some of his largest scams out of Luxembourg. In fact, most large-scale cross-border financial and political scandals since the 1960s have had a colorful Luxembourg chapter. And things haven't changed that much: as a *Financial Times* analysis put it in 2017, "Luxembourg sometimes resembles a criminal enterprise with a country attached."[8]

If anyone can be called the architect of the modern tax haven of Luxembourg, it's the man who served as finance minister from 1989 to 2009, as well as prime minister from 1995 to 2013, and is now president of the European Commission and in charge of Europe's Brexit negotiations, Jean-Claude Juncker. The son of a steelworker and trade unionist, Juncker is an ebullient, charismatic, chain-smoking, larger-than-life master manipulator. A short video from a summit of European leaders in Latvia in May 2015 points to his man-of-the-people appeal; Juncker stands, swaying and tittering, as a succession of heads of state and government walk past. As they greet him he slaps their cheeks roughly, grabs their ties, manhandles them, and lovingly kisses their bald patches. At the approach of Viktor Orbán, Hungary's hardline right-wing prime minister, Juncker offers a half-raised hand salute and follows up with a gangster handshake and the greeting "Dictator!" Then, beaming broadly, he slaps the stony-faced Orbán on the cheek. Juncker has denied rumors that he is an alcoholic, telling a French newspaper in 2016 that his occasional lurches and staggers are due to a leg injury he got in a car crash in 1989. (He chugged four glasses of champagne during that interview.) His outbreaks of irrational honesty are legendary. "When it becomes serious, you have to lie," he once said with a shrug in 2011, on live television. Juncker reached astonishing heights of popularity, with approval ratings sometimes over 80 percent.[9]

Juncker doubled down on Luxembourg's tax haven offerings, loosening nearly all controls on finance, offering ironclad secrecy to match Switzerland's to hoover up the world's dirty money, and also turning the country into a giant global tax-cheat factory for multinationals, which endures today. This exploded in the LuxLeaks scandal of 2014, where PricewaterhouseCoopers (PwC) in Luxembourg was revealed as having cooked up a feast of complex financial schemes to help the world's biggest multinationals cut their tax bills: Walt Disney, Koch Industries, Pepsi, Ikea, FedEx, Deutsche Bank, Blackstone, JPMorgan Chase, and more than three hundred others. Marius Kohl, head of one Luxembourg tax agency, would receive applications for tax rulings every Wednesday in batches of thirty or forty on a USB memory stick (when he started losing them and forgetting passwords, PwC gave him direct access to its system). When a journalist asked Kohl how he judged a complex scheme's legality, he simply licked his thumb and held it in the air. Juncker denied all knowledge of these games, yet he knew—*everyone* knew—and leaked diplomatic cables show that he fought tenaciously and successfully in Brussels to derail any crackdowns.[10]

And all this shadiness, in turn, was protected by standard tax haven systems of social control, underpinned by an attitude that characterizes every tax haven I've ever known: don't rock the boat, don't ask questions, and don't do anything to threaten offshore finance. Above all, the financial center must remain globally "competitive," and dissidents against this view face subtle but potent threats: an invisible melting away of job chances, a bias in the courts, family disapproval, social scorn. Some have been called *Nestbeschmutzer*—nest polluters, the dirtiest kind of traitor. Ahead of a trip to Luxembourg City in October 2011, I got an email from a local businessman who was in conflict with a Luxembourg bank. He told me of "the absolutely scandalous discrepancy" between Luxembourg's laws and how its judges applied them:

> The people involved fear retaliation from Luxembourg authorities when going public. I know by personal experience how bad this may turn out. You just don't make it in this country unless you've proven your absolute loyalty to the system in place, including being OK if not more with all of its malpractices. I also know by personal experience how difficult it is for foreigners to get a firm grasp of the Mafia-like functioning of Luxembourg. No foreigner can imagine how bad it really is.[11]

Luxembourg has the world's second-largest mutual funds sector after the United States, but a court system the size of a small provincial town's. It can't possibly police the financial oceans that roil through here—and it doesn't want to; "competitive" policing of finance is, after all, a big part of the offering.[12] Many of the international funds that channeled investors' savings into Madoff's giant Ponzi scheme were run out of Luxembourg. "The whole setup violated European law," said Erik Bomans, a partner in Deminor, a financial recovery firm representing some three thousand defrauded Madoff investors. "There were no control mechanisms, no yearly due diligence, nothing, nothing, nothing." When victims tried to get their money back, Luxembourg took the banks' side every time. "It is unbelievable, we have no access to justice," Bomans continued, "thanks to the Luxembourg judicial system."[13]

In Luxembourg, all this was immensely popular and the secret of Juncker's success. With one hand he nurtured a huge expansion in this Euro-beacon of offshore finance, neoliberal deregulation, laxity in policing financial crime, and national "competitiveness." With the other he used the wealth thus acquired to shower Luxembourgers with progressive spending and social policies. This seemingly contradictory behavior should be familiar to many of us, for it has formed the economic heart of an agenda that has enraptured a generation of Western politicians and underpinned the main economic strategies of many countries for more than a quarter of a century. This deregulate-and-redistribute model brought Bill Clinton's New Democrats to power in 1993, Tony Blair's New Labour to power in Britain in 1997, and a host of other leaders too, including in Australia, France, Germany, Italy, the Netherlands, Portugal, and Sweden. Those who adopted the formula often found themselves winning elections with large majorities. And it made tremendous fortunes on Wall Street and in the City of London. This was the Third Way.

The Third Way was a pretty simple idea: it was an attempt by the parties of the Left to stake out a new middle ground in politics. Globalization was inevitable, they argued, so countries should embrace it and adapt to it, hitching a ride on the growth of global financial markets, then shaving off the raw edges with progressive social policies and good old-fashioned redistribution, leavened with a personal-responsibility agenda. It was, Clinton's adviser Al From gushed, "the worldwide brand name for progressive politics for the Information Age."

But the Third Way was also an offshore model, driven by the competitiveness agenda, the idea, or ideology, that countries must constantly dangle enticements to large multinationals and banks and to rootless global money—tax cuts, financial deregulation, turning a blind eye to crime—for fear that they will disappear to more hospitable or "competitive" places like London, Dubai, Hong Kong, or Geneva.

There's no single genius or jarring event that brought about the Third Way. It was probably going to happen anyway. As financial globalization slowly caught fire from the 1970s, left-leaning politicians found themselves, like passengers on a sinking ship, looking for a way out. And they were delighted to see a retinue of white-gloved stewards beckoning them toward a glamorous exit route and life rafts. Luxembourg and London were already happily afloat and had grabbed themselves bottles of champagne. By the mid-1970s a new breed of liberal northern Democrat was emerging in the Democratic Party, vowing to clean up Washington after Watergate. Anti-banker sentiment had faded along with memories of the Great Depression; crusaders against big banks and monopolies—crusaders like Wright Patman, a tough, bespectacled old Texas Democratic populist who had been known as the Bane of the Banks before World War II—fell out of favor.

In with the new blood came Tony Coelho, a Portuguese American with a gift for fund-raising and a related fondness for large firms. Coelho became a leading defender of large agribusiness interests against small farmers and got elected to Congress in 1978, the same year that Bork wrote his bestselling book, *The Antitrust Paradox*. At the Democrats' annual party dinner Coelho raised fifty times the normal amount and, as a result, was soon appointed chair of the Democratic Congressional Campaign Committee. "Money is part of politics, and always will be," he declared as he cranked up a new Democratic corporate fund-raising machine. His key insight was that big business and rich folks weren't interested in supporting only Republicans, with their low-tax, free-market ideology; what the moneybags really wanted was special favors, tax breaks and loopholes, nods and winks to mergers, and juicy government contracts. And the Democrats were just as able to offer these as the Republicans were.[14]

Coelho opened the gates to a flood of new money into the Democratic Party. Some came from Don Dixon, a dealmaker who later went to prison for fraud after a lurid six-week trial with testimony describing call girls, hot tubs, yachts, and the gift of a $40,000 painting to the Vatican, which got him an audience with the pope. After the Democrats' devastating loss to Reagan in 1980, Coelho became even more single-minded about corrupting the party.[15] Back in the 1960s, less than 5 percent of members of Congress went on to become lobbyists. Today, it's closer to 50 percent.[16] At the same time the New Democrats shifted their attention away from working-class whites and labor issues toward civil rights and social tolerance. In 1982 the Democratic National Committee officially recognized seven new caucuses: women, blacks, Hispanics, Asians, gays, liberals, and business professionals. Behind this welcoming move lay a less salubrious calculation: if they could get enough of these cultural groups on board, they might be able to dispense with their traditional role as the guardians of the citizenry against big banks and monopolies and do what many influential and ambitious people in the party *really* wanted to do: cozy up to big business. The overall result of this sea change from progressive economics toward identity politics has been an enduring one, and it was crystallized by Hillary Clinton in an election rally speech in 2016.

"If we broke up the big banks tomorrow," she shouted, "would that end racism?"

"No!" her audience replied.

"Would that end sexism?"

"No!"

Although she did say she would tackle the banks if they misbehaved, hers was a pro–big bank message, couched as something progressive.[17]

Through these decades, a number of new academics emerged to support the changes on the Left. The best known was perhaps the Harvard Business School guru Michael Porter, author of several influential books and articles about corporate strategy, including a piece in the *Harvard Business Review* in 1979 arguing that the best business strategy is to avoid competition by finding monopolizing niches where others can't go.[18] Porter scaled up his insights about corporations to the level of the nation-state in an 850-page doorstop called *The Competitive Advantage of Nations* (1990), which was a bestseller. The book wasn't straightforwardly neoliberal. Countries should play to their strengths, they should create clusters of knowledge and innovation, they should avoid short-termism, Porter said, among many other mostly unobjectionable things. But the book also rested solidly on the idea that "competitive" countries and cities must look after business, and especially big business, to prosper. The emphasis, for instance, was not so much on education—the stuff that creates rounded, knowledgeable, social, politically engaged, and honest human beings—but skills, the part of education that business needs.[19] And by framing public policy strategies in corporate terms, Porter helped political leaders of the Left develop a common language and empathy with big banks and multinationals, while at the same time making the parties of the Left seem less scary to big business.

Less well known than Porter was a man called Antony Fisher, a wealthy former businessman whom Milton Friedman called "the single most important person in the development of Thatcherism"—and ultimately, his influence in the United States has been almost as great. Fisher was born into wealth, and his moment of great revelation came in 1945 when he read the *Reader's Digest* version of Friedrich Hayek's book *The Road to Serfdom*, the new bible for the fledgling neoliberal movement. For decades afterward he would be heard repeating a favorite phrase: "Communism is the poison offered to the people; socialism is the cup in which it is given; and the welfare state is the tempting label on the bottle." Well connected in financial and political circles in the City of London, Fisher easily secured a meeting with Hayek, who urged him to put his money toward financing intellectuals, or, as he put it, "second-hand dealers in ideas," to push the counterrevolution against big government and the Bretton Woods system. Fisher didn't do so straightaway: in 1950 he introduced factory-farming for chickens to Britain, after studying the nascent industry in the United States and illegally smuggling twenty-four fertilized White Rock eggs into the UK. This magnified his wealth and enabled him in 1955 to found and finance the

Institute of Economic Affairs (IEA) in London, which has been widely credited with shaping Thatcher's worldview about the importance of cutting taxes and deregulating finance. Fisher and his cofounders agreed to be "cagey" about the IEA's true aims, not least because being seen as partisan might put at risk their charitable status: "it is imperative that we should give no indication . . . of political bias," one wrote: it should all be couched as simply explaining the economics of the free market. A few days after she was elected in 1979, Thatcher sent the IEA a note, saying, "It was primarily your foundation work, which enabled us to rebuild the philosophy upon which our Party succeeded." After a brief foray into turtle farming in the Cayman Islands, which lost him a lot of money, Fisher met and married a rich widow, Dorian Crocker, helping him keep the dream of funding an intellectual counterrevolution alive. Fisher set up the Fraser Institute in Canada, which began pumping out Hayek's ideas to great effect there too. He was hell-bent on influencing "liberal" New York as well and set up the free-market Manhattan Institute in 1977 with Bill Casey, who would go on to become Reagan's campaign manager and director of the CIA.

But Fisher was only just getting started. In 1981 he set up what may be the world's most influential ideological organization that almost nobody has heard of, the Atlas Economic Research Foundation, which was to be an international network that would, as Fisher put it, "litter the world with free-market think tanks." Atlas, named after Ayn Rand's wildly popular libertarian novel *Atlas Shrugged*, had simple goals: to provide seed funding for think tanks in different countries, to teach them to grow organically and seek the most powerful avenues for influence, and to raise money from local banks and businesses. At the same time, Atlas would serve as a kind of "meta" think tank, keeping them all on the true path. It merged with Hayek's Mont Pelerin Society and, over time, began to intermingle with other, better-known sources of funding for libertarian think tanks in the United States: the Wall Street–funded Templeton Foundation, the networks of the hedge fund tycoon Robert Mercer (a supporter of Steve Bannon and *Breitbart News*), and what some call the "Kochtopus"—the tentacular nexus of political and financial links funded by the billionaire brothers Charles and David Koch. Atlas's membership includes the American Enterprise Institute, the similarly influential American Legislative Exchange Council (ALEC), the Cato Institute, the Freedom Foundation, the Heritage Foundation, and, at the time of this writing, over 180 more. And those are just the funding networks in the United States: Atlas has littered the world with 475 partner institutions—and rising.[20]

Meanwhile, world leaders had a new global forum at the exclusive Swiss ski resort of Davos—what *Time* magazine in 1981 described as their "magic meeting place," where politicians would discuss the state of the world with financial and business bosses, think-tank glitterati, and prominent journalists—incidentally providing Swiss bankers with fabulous opportunities to market their anti-tax, criminalized wealth-management services and offshore attitudes to the assembled global elites. The World Economic Forum (WEF), with Porter's help, began to issue annual competitiveness rankings and scores for countries, generating anxiety among policy makers about whether their country was keeping up in the global race. The answer was always no, even for top-ranked countries, because the pack was always there, snapping at their heels.[21]

By the end of the 1980s the Democratic Party was still split between a leftist old guard and a new centrist wing, but it was obvious which way things were going. At a meeting of the Democratic Leadership Council in 1990, Jesse Jackson tried to rally supporters with promises of higher taxes and spending, but he was savaged by the Democratic strategist Al From, who responded by saying, "We trust that a few people in the press have a brain in their heads." The fast-rising governor of Arkansas, Bill Clinton, intoned that "we don't think the Democratic Party should lead with class warfare."[22] In short order, the globalizing, liberalizing Clintonites decisively won this internal battle. And this reflected tectonic shifts in the intellectual zeitgeist. The political philosopher Francis Fukuyama famously summed up the changes in 1989, as the movement was gathering steam, with the declaration that the victory of market capitalism was "the end of history as such: the end point of mankind's ideological evolution and the universalization of Western liberal democracy as the final form of human government." For the mainstream Left, the Third Way was the only way.

Adding fuel to the globalist fires, the left-leaning US public intellectual Lester Thurow in 1992 weighed in with *Head to Head: The Coming Economic Battle among Japan, Europe, and America*, a book setting out an "American Game Plan" in a grand "win-lose" contest of nation against nation. Clinton chimed in with a declaration that each nation was "like a big corporation competing in the marketplace," shortly before he became president in 1993. A global economic race was on, and by now everyone knew it. "The fate of nations became entangled with the fate of enterprises, and vice versa," wrote the British political economist Will Davies of the new Davos era. "A new vision of political authority was invented, in which the nation or city or region was comparable to a corporation, of which the political leader was the CEO and the citizens were employees."[23]

As the 1990s progressed, world leaders steadily tuned in to the competitiveness agenda and to Third Way–ish ideas: embrace big banks, big business, and globalization; "compete" as a nation; and redistribute what you can. There was Australia's fratty prime minister Bob Hawke, who could have given Juncker a run for his money: Hawke once held the world speed record for drinking a yard of ale. There was Italy's Romano Prodi, Sweden's Göran Persson, the Netherlands' Wim Kok, and Germany's Gerhard Schröder with his project for *Die Neue Mitte*—the New Middle. Tony Blair, Britain's rock-star prime minister, elected in 1997, copied Clinton's model, promising reform, renewal, modernization, enterprise, and innovation—with a generous dose of redistribution and a new social agenda. Clinton had campaigned on a platform of investing in people: job training, health, and infrastructure. Robert Reich, one of his advisers, remembers how soon that changed. "Nobody [but me] could fit into the jump seat opposite Bill Clinton in his presidential limousine because I'm so short," he said. "[O]ther advisers would be quite annoyed with me for having that face time. I spent huge hours lobbying. That's what it really came down to—trying to make the strongest case I could for the principles that I thought Bill Clinton was elected on, but the response I got back from Bill Clinton and from others who didn't agree with me was number one, we have got to get the bond traders on our side."[24] Even former leftist firebrands like Jesse Jackson were giving way to the steamroller of modern finance. "Why are African Americans continuing to 'invest' in the bear lotto when they need to be included as participants in the bull market?" Jackson asked. "Why are our youths buying hundred-dollar Nike shoes instead of Nike stock?"[25]

Back in the UK, Blair wielded the C-word of "competitiveness" to devastating effect. "With foreign businesspeople and foreign journalists, he'd talk about all the opportunities of globalization: to attract overseas businesses to act as role models, to lift the competitiveness levels of the economy. He managed their expectations upwards: 'invest in Britain, come to Britain,'" explains Warwick University's Matthew Watson. But with domestic audiences it was a different message. It wasn't about opportunities but about imperatives and restraints on policy: how limited the opportunities would be to redistribute, tax and spend, and do the things that Labour was traditionally associated with. For the home audience "it was all about managing expectations downwards. There was a functional necessity for business interests to win out. It was an opportunity—or a threat. A chance for national renewal—or an imperative to follow blindly."[26]

One of Blair's most uncompromising statements on this subject came in a signature speech in 2005. The changing world, he said, was "indifferent to tradition. Unforgiving of frailty . . . replete with opportunities, but they only go to those swift to adapt, slow to complain. I hear people say we have to stop and debate globalization. You might as well debate whether autumn should follow summer." It didn't take a genius to see that this ethos, at the heart of the Third Way's economic approach, was a kind of surrender. Bow down to foreign hot money was the message: degrade the taxes and the laws and the oversight, and the money will come. Blair's government sold more than six hundred government tax office buildings to a company based in the tax haven of Bermuda, in the name of "efficiency." Blair even attacked Britain's financial regulator, the Financial Services Authority, which he said was "seen as hugely inhibiting of efficient business by perfectly respectable companies that have never defrauded anyone." He chided regulators' tendency "to restrict rather than enable. We pay a price if we react like this. We lose out in business to India and China, who are prepared to accept the risks." This was the leader of the *Labour* Party, officially representing the working classes, effectively urging Britain to degrade its laws and even its labor force to the level of developing-country sweatshops.[27]

All this, in country after country, was a replica of the Jean-Claude Juncker tax haven model: a selfish doctrine of dog-eat-dog national self-interest, a well-padded boxing glove of social solidarity covering a neoliberal fist, a technique for papering over the ugly truths of the finance curse.

As these ideas gathered pace, the US Treasury, USAID, and Western governments were exporting them not just to Western economies but to anyone who would listen. One of those countries was Russia, which was undergoing massive political convulsions after the official end of communism and the dissolution of the Soviet Union in 1991. At the tail end of the Republican administration, and especially after Bill Clinton's election in 1992, Western advisers urged a sweeping program of privatization there and in other former Soviet states, allowing a tiny elite, hooked into a fast-growing organized criminal underworld, to use the new chaos and a worldwide deregulatory ideology to engineer the largest and quickest transfer of wealth into billionaire hands in world history. The main beneficiaries of this privatization—which was, in effect, a cartelization by around twenty-five major kleptocratic oligarchs in banking, energy, ports, iron and steel, diamonds, and so on—included numerous Russian officials and also "leading gringo investors/advisers, Harvard professors,

USAID advisers, and bankers at Credit Suisse First Boston and other Wall Street investment banks," according to James Henry, a former chief economist for McKinsey & Co. and an expert in capital flight.[28] And so began a massive drain of wealth out of Russia, hundreds of billions of dollars bleeding from the open arteries of the Russian economy and pouring into banks, shares, and real estate in London and Miami, often via Jersey, Cyprus, Dubai, and the British Virgin Islands. And at the receiving end of this bargain: "shock therapy" for ordinary Russians.

These vast flows of capital flight, much of it looted from the former Soviet Union, were a godsend for one particular American businessman, who had just suffered a string of major business bankruptcies, including the $1 billion Trump Taj Mahal Casino in Atlantic City in 1991, then the Trump Castle, the Trump Plaza and Casino, and the Plaza Hotel in 1992. That businessman, Donald Trump, blamed his business failures not just on a widespread real estate crash but ultimately on his success:

> I began to socialize more, probably too much. Frankly, I was bored. I really felt I could do no wrong. Sort of like a baseball player who keeps hitting home runs or a golfer who keeps winning tournaments—you just get a feeling of invincibility. Ultimately, this invincible feeling, while positive at times, can be destructive. You let down your guard. You don't work as hard. Then things start to go in the wrong direction. And that's what happened to me.

The official story is that the businessman then resurrected his empire through fabulous dealmaking, raw energy and animal spirits, and some clever tax accounting. By 1993, he said, "Piece by piece, deal by deal, a beautiful picture was beginning to emerge." And this story is partly true. But what were those deals? It was, very often, taking advantage of those rivers of ill-gotten capital flight now pouring out of the former Soviet Union. As Trump's son, Donald Trump Jr., later explained: "In terms of high-end product influx into the United States, Russians make up a pretty disproportionate cross-section of a lot of our assets; say in Dubai, and certainly with our project in SoHo and anywhere in New York. We see a lot of money pouring in from Russia."

Yet neither Clinton nor Blair seemed especially concerned about these flows, even though anyone with any sense would know that actively assisting a bunch of crooks to plunder a giant nuclear-armed and oil-rich state with a long history of trying to destabilize Western democracies wasn't a great idea. The finance-cursed political implications of these inflows into our banks would become apparent only many years later. "The long-run consequence of careless interventions in other countries is that they often come back to haunt us," explains Henry. "In Russia's case, it just has."[29]

Blair and Clinton were ignoring, or perhaps even relishing, these inflows, for they had hitched their political wagons to the shiny modernity of new derivatives and securitization vehicles, private equity titans, and profit-gushing global banks—many of which were happily guzzling on the former-Soviet money drain too. Opening our economies to these flows was all part of a mission to become more "competitive" against this unstoppable, implacable wall of global money. And nobody was pointing out the obvious follies that were stacking up.

Well, almost nobody. In 1994, the year after Clinton took power, the economist Paul Krugman wrote an essay entitled "Competitiveness: A Dangerous Obsession." In it he declared, "The growing obsession in most advanced nations with national competitiveness should be seen, not as a well-founded concern, but as a view held in the face of overwhelming contrary evidence. And yet it is clearly a view that people very much want to hold." Krugman raked through various things "national competitiveness" might possibly mean: trade surplus, terms of trade, labor costs, David Ricardo's (very different) concept of comparative advantage, or simply the question of national power and global economic heft. Being as charitable as possible, he concluded that the concept boiled down to "a funny way of talking about productivity." Not relative to other countries, mind, just plain old productivity. "If we can teach undergraduates to wince when they hear someone talk about 'competitiveness,' we will have done our nation a great service," he continued. "A government wedded to the ideology of competitiveness is as unlikely to make good economic policy as a government committed to creationism is to make good science policy."[30]

The confusions at the heart of the competitiveness agenda stack up, one after another. Economies or tax systems or cities are nothing like companies and don't "compete" in any meaningful way. The only possible coherent meaning of the term is a military one, when one country "outcompetes" another by becoming strong enough to conquer it. But this isn't how economics works. Companies pursue profits, which then get taxed. What is the equivalent of profits for a nation? A budget surplus? A trade surplus? These can be signs of diseased economic policies such as unnecessary austerity or underconsumption. (And how would you tax a budget surplus?) The simplest way for a country to make cheaper exports is to devalue its currency. But companies don't have their own currencies to devalue. If a company shapes up and produces better, slicker products, it can put its rivals out of business, but if America improves its technology or education, that won't put Germany out of business. It could well make Germans richer. You improve education to make American people more productive, more equal, wealthier, and other good things, but not because you're in a race with Germany.

Now this is, admittedly, a tricky area. You can take any term in the English language, in this case "national competitiveness," and make it mean whatever you want it to mean. You can argue, for instance, the best way to support something you call "national competitiveness" is to upgrade education, build strong social protections, or control dangerous capital flows across borders. You could argue that a nation could become more "competitive" by adopting protectionism combined with carefully targeted industrial policies of nurturing productive domestic economic ecosystems—that is, after all, how the United States and many other countries industrialized in the first place. You could insist that "national competitiveness" must meet the test of productivity, good jobs, and a broad-based rise in living standards. There are strong, respectable arguments along all these lines.[31] But Clinton and especially Blair weren't making these arguments: they were pushing the competitiveness agenda, which was all about pursuing rootless capital in a globalized world. Give big banks and multinationals what they ask for, look the other way when they behave badly, then watch the wealth spring up and trickle down.

Another core confusion underlying the agenda is the idea that globalization is unstoppable and implacable, like the weather, and the best you can do is adapt your societies to the needs and whims of big banks and corporations and mobile rich people, then compensate the losers as best you can. This self-abasing belief, that we must bow down to global markets and run as fast as we can in some sort of a race to the bottom, is widely held, both on the Right—whose members see beneficent global markets reining in and disciplining grasping, incompetent governments—and also on the Left, which fears that governments are powerless to shield their people from nasty global forces. "Both agree that impotent politicians must now bow before omnipotent markets," explained Martin Wolf, chief economic commentator for the *Financial Times*. "This has become one of the clichés of the age. But it is (almost) total nonsense."[32]

People believe this nonsense because of other confusions. One is that they fail to see how the pro-finance changes that have happened with globalization have generally required active intervention, or deliberate nonintervention, by governments. Central banks have been actively freed from direct democratic controls, and their objectives have been deliberately changed from goals such as promoting full employment to targeting inflation. Financial deregulation has involved deliberately defanging laws that protect societies. Trade and investment treaties, deliberately negotiated and signed, tie the hands of governments and prevent them from intervening to shelter domestic industries. Governments have deliberately chosen to privatize huge swathes of public assets and to feed them into competitive, financialized frameworks. They have chosen to cut taxes on capital and to reduce workers' rights. Financial globalization isn't just about mobile capital inevitably flowing effortlessly through and around the restraining bonds of the state; it requires intergovernmental deals to guarantee that creditors will be paid back and endless decisions to remove impediments to these flows. All these are solid policy choices, made deliberately by states—and all are reversible.[33]

Yet there's a deeper confusion in the competitiveness agenda. This one hinges on a concept called the "fallacy of composition," which is where you think that the fortunes of your big businesses and big banks are identical to the fortunes of the economy as a whole. If government policy can make Goldman Sachs more globally competitive, the argument goes, this makes America as a whole more "competitive." Few people get beyond this simple, beguiling formula. Yet improving the fortunes of Goldman Sachs won't necessarily improve the fortunes of America, and this is especially true if a big chunk of Goldman's profits are extracted from other parts of the economy. Large banks, multinationals, and hedge funds, the biggest beneficiaries of this agenda, are not just competing in global markets; they are also competing against and killing their smaller domestic rivals, not just in markets where they sell stuff, but also in terms of the people they can hire. High wages on Wall Street suck talented, educated people out of often more genuinely productive areas of the economy. Instead of finding a cure for malaria, our best and brightest are getting rich as high-frequency traders. This is where the finance curse concept comes back into play: if *too much* finance reduces economic growth and causes other damage to your country, then the pursuit of *more* finance through policies that follow that agenda will most likely make things worse.

Language has proved a fabulous tool for bamboozlement here. One example is the standard confusion that conflates the market competitiveness of firms and the "competitiveness" of nations: two very different things. Some observers think that "national competitiveness" has something to do with the nineteenth-century economist David Ricardo's similar-sounding, but very different, concept of "comparative advantage"—a concept that points countries toward focusing on nurturing their most productive strengths, then trading with other nations to import the goods and services in sectors where they are relatively weaker.

Third Way politicians seem to love this false idea of a whole economy as a business or corporation facing merciless global competition, because it helps persuade people that there is an urgent "need" to make "tough choices" and cut back on health, education, or law enforcement in order to free up the resources to help "our friends" in big business or on Wall Street compete on a world stage. Yet we feel no corresponding need to lend such support to our local handyman or print shop, which isn't competing globally. In 2017 Trump wielded this fear-mongering tactic to great effect, praising China and "highly competitive" countries with "unbelievably low tax rates," who are "taking us, frankly, to the cleaners, so we must—we have no choice—we must lower our taxes." His administration went on to give US multinationals and billionaires the biggest collective tax cut in world history—taking the majority of the United States' taxpaying population to the cleaners instead. And there are voices out there who want to abolish corporate taxes completely.

Yet "competitive" corporate tax cuts have been a disaster, undermining markets and tax systems in endless ways.

You might also think that cutting corporate tax rates ought to curb corporations' appetite for diving into tax havens and cooking up schemes to escape tax, but if anything, the opposite has happened. A long-term set of cuts in corporation tax rates worldwide since the 1980s has been accompanied by a vast surge in tax-related profit shifting into tax havens—now costing governments $300–$650 billion per year, with poorer countries particularly hard-hit. The latest research shows that cutting corporate tax rates from, say, 25 to 20 percent doesn't make a damn bit of difference. Why would that tax cut stop businesses from lobbying for a further cut to 15 percent? And why would a corporation accept 20 when it can get zero in a tax haven?[34]

So corporate tax cuts don't curb tax avoidance. But they do inflict a range of harms. For one thing, the more you cut corporate tax rates, the more wealthy people will convert their ordinary personal income (like their salary) into corporate forms, so as to pay the lower corporate tax rate instead of the higher income tax rate. So corporate tax cuts can cannibalize the income tax. (In fact, in many countries this was the main reason for setting up a corporate income tax in the first place: for protection from the personal income tax.)[35]

Another malign effect of corporate tax cuts is that they favor large, wealth-extracting, profit-gushing corporations over small, struggling businesses, reinforcing monopoly. To illustrate this, let's make a quick detour to Marquette, a fading agricultural hamlet of six hundred souls deep in the flat Kansas countryside. In 2014, Marquette's last school closed as a direct result of the tax-cut policies of Governor Sam Brownback, who promised that extreme corporate and income tax cuts would be a "shot of adrenaline" in the heart of the Kansas economy. In the final school meeting, terrified parents held up pieces of paper with numbers on them to indicate how many children in their home were losing their school. Local businesspeople weren't cheering either. "For a business owner, you're better off having those teachers in those jobs here in Marquette, they shop in town and help you out that way," said Steve Piper, who owned the grocery store. "If your sales are down, if you are not making any money to start with, taxes mean nothing. It's a percentage of a smaller amount of money. When I sell my stores, is anyone going to want to buy a store in Marquette without a school in town?"[36] Piper had put his finger on a crucial and often ignored point about tax cuts. Taxes on businesses are levied on profits, which are essentially the difference between two large numbers: revenues minus costs. Even relatively small changes to one or the other side of that balance can have massive effects on your profits. Let's say, for example, your costs are 95 units and your revenues are 100, for a pre-tax profit of 5. If the profit is taxed at 30 percent, that leaves 3.5 units. A tiny 3 percent fall in revenues down to 97 units slashes the gross profit from 5 to 2: a full 60 percent. A 6 percent fall, down to 94 units, below costs, could bankrupt your business. By contrast, a huge corporate income tax rate cut from 30 to 20 percent will hardly move the needle: your after-tax profit goes up from 3.5 to 4, a gain of 0.5 units. (In fact, the IRS has estimated that all state and local taxes make up, on average, just 1.2 percent of the typical company's cost of doing business.)[37] Meanwhile, a nearby wealth-extracting monopoly or share-flipping high-frequency trader with few employees but huge profit margins—let's say revenues of 100 and costs of 50, for after-tax profits of 50—will gain a full 5 units from the same tax cut to 20 percent—ten times as much as the small business gets. The historical record of big business shows that much, if not most, of that boost flows into share buybacks, rather than investment. So tax cuts that lead to fewer public services can be especially damaging to small businesses and communities: they can mess heavily with revenues and the ingredients of success, while hardly reducing total costs. Not only that, but lower-margin businesses with big cost components, which tend to be hit hardest by tax cuts, are often the best kinds of business to have in your state, because large costs will tend to reflect a large and well-paid labor force or perhaps deep local supply chains—the stuff with which thriving local communities are built. In an exhaustive review of the evidence, the Center on Budget and Policy Priorities concluded, "Numerous academic studies find *no* correlation between state tax levels and various measures of state economic performance. . . . Other studies find that higher taxes are actually associated with *better* economic performance. . . ."[38]

In Europe, the obsession with "national competitiveness" may run even deeper. The EU's documents are full of declared intentions to make Europe "the most dynamic and competitive knowledge-based economy in the world by 2010" and "the easiest and cheapest place to do business." Whatever could this mean? Well, this vision is riddled with Euro-confusions. In 2007, for instance, Neelie Kroes, then Europe's top official for competition, gave a speech welcoming a recent "merger tsunami"—mergers, she said, that "must be allowed to run their course without undue political interference." Her job was to rein in and regulate monopolies, and yet she was welcoming a "merger tsunami" and declaring openly for the price-obsessed Chicago School approach. (The *Wall Street Journal* reported EU officials saying they had "never dealt with a commission candidate with such extensive business ties—and potential conflicts"—as Kroes.)[39] She wasn't exaggerating about the tsunami; by the turn of the millennium, by one measure, over 80 percent of all measured global flows of foreign direct investment involved mergers as opposed to productive new "greenfield" investment, as the former Soviet Union spewed forth a treasure train of fresh assets ready for weaving into monopolizing, labor-crushing, tax-escaping giants and investment funds. For rich countries, almost *100 percent* of investment flows happened through mergers.[40] Her second statement was shorter, but odder still. "Competition is the main driver for competitiveness." What does this mean? Well, it goes something like this. If you free up Europe's internal single market for multinationals, then finance, trade, and investment will flow more freely across seamless European borders, forcing European firms to compete more intensely with one another, creating efficiencies that would then help these firms compete more effectively on a global stage. This, in a nutshell, is Europe's rickety bridge between greater market competition and "global competitiveness."

But this argument raises new questions. How do firms create these "efficiencies"? Well, one way is to strip out costs. But what are those costs? Why, corporate taxes, workers' wages, pensions, financial regulations, social and environmental protections—the lifeblood of European democracy and society. Another way is to encourage monopolizing mergers, so companies can gouge workers and consumers even more comprehensively—and help these champions go head-to-head with the Americans and the Chinese—once again making Europe more "competitive" by allowing less competition in Europe. These ideas are not just confused; history shows us that they can be dangerous. As Germany's monopolies commission warned in 2004, efforts to nurture national banking champions in 1931, using similar arguments, contributed to economic crisis and the conditions that led to the rise of the Nazis.[41]

But Europe's leaders have doubled down on these confused policies, trying to deaden the pain with "solidarity mechanisms" and subsidies.[42] Extremism is now rising in many European countries, which is hardly a surprise, since this "competitiveness" in Euro-speak means extracting wealth from poorer, smaller, less mobile elements of the economy and handing it to bigger, more mobile global players, to compete on a world stage. So it is, from first principles, an inequality machine. It is also a machine for generating crime and abusive behavior. Dig behind pretty much any large modern economic scandal—the LIBOR scandal, LuxLeaks, the Panama Papers, Apple's $250-odd billion untaxed offshore cash pile, the global financial crisis, you name it—and you'll find that the competitiveness agenda lurks behind the headline, deregulating, de-policing, and de-taxing global financial markets. It is globalization's most potent ideological battering ram, cowing governments and populations across the world with a belief that they have no choice but to submit. In an important sense, the Third Way has been the handmaiden for these changes, by making them palatable through redistribution and an inclusive social agenda. What seems to have been lost is the understanding that it would have been possible to achieve these valuable social advances without throwing the working classes to the global wolves.

Dodgy ideologies are fed by potent myths and stories, which the Clintons, Blair, and many others were happy to exploit. One of the most potent of these myths was generated in the seas between Britain and the United States, on an ancient emerald isle of American ancestors that came to be ruled by a politician with a rather similar outlook: the indefatigable, irrepressible Charles Haughey, an evangelist for the need to "unleash the wealth creators" with a "competitive" economy and to spend the bountiful proceeds. Haughey was like Blair and Clinton—but with a difference. While Blair and Clinton mostly waited until they had left office to take on lucrative consultancies and get rich, Haughey was delighted to enrich himself while still in office. And the Irish Celtic Tiger economy that he helped usher in would become the shining poster child for the competitiveness agenda.

CHAPTER SIX

The Celtic Tiger

The tale of the Celtic Tiger, the Irish economic growth miracle of the 1990s and early 2000s, has become one of the most influential morality tales in the economic history of the modern world. The Irish model of low corporate taxes offered the ultimate free lunch: painless tax cuts leading to economic growth and, ultimately, larger tax revenues from the flood of new investment generated by those cuts. "The Irish formula [became] the new universal truth of economics, society and development," wrote Fintan O'Toole, a commentator for the *Irish Times* and author of *Ship of Fools*, a firecracker of a book about the Celtic Tiger. "It transcended history and geography and ... worked irrespective of time and place."[1]

Though the boom contained a lot of froth, and the global financial crisis hit Ireland worse than most countries, the Irish growth miracle wasn't just a bubble—it had some underlying substance—and the beast remains alive: foreign investment is strong, cranes decorate the skyline again, cafés groan with banker-talk, and there is a sense of life and purpose in Dublin. The story of the Celtic Tiger seems like a thunderbolt of evidence aimed squarely at one of the key arguments of this book: that if you want to build a prosperous and inclusive economy, you don't need to "compete" on things like cutting corporate tax rates or relaxing financial regulations.

The Celtic Tiger story goes back to the 1940s, when DC-3s and other propeller aircraft crossing the Atlantic from Europe needed to refuel at Shannon Airport on Ireland's west coast, near Europe's most westward landfall. To sugar the pill for aviators, in 1947 Shannon carved out from Ireland's tax system the world's first duty-free shop. But within five years commercial airlines began using jets, which could now fly directly to New York from London or Paris without having to refuel at Shannon. Brendan O'Regan, an ebullient local entrepreneur, warned that Shannon would have to "pull aircraft out of the sky" if it wasn't to sink back into green-pastured obscurity. So he proposed a new, more expansive tax-free zone just outside Shannon Airport, modeled on an emerging zone in Puerto Rico. In this new zone, established in 1959, foreign investors could escape normal Irish taxes and regulations. It grew rapidly, and O'Regan happily used his position as the airport's comptroller of catering and services to give the key contracts to a company he controlled.[2]

In the Shannon archives there's a photo from 1980 of a Chinese delegation sent to report on this Irish experiment, just as new president Deng Xiaoping was setting China out on a big modernization drive. In the lineup there's a junior Chinese customs official with thick black spectacles standing in a heavy coat. After a tour of the tax-free zone the delegation was treated to a songfest at Durty Nelly's pub—a fact that perhaps helps explain the remarkable warmth with which Bertie Ahern, the Irish taoiseach (prime minister), was received in Beijing in 1998 by the same bespectacled official, Jiang Zemin, who by then had risen to become president. Shannon had helped inspire China to set up the special economic zones that would prove key to propelling its own subsequent economic growth miracle,[3] and it is now regarded with such historical veneration that Xi Jinping and a succession of other top Chinese officials have made the pilgrimage to Ireland since then. "The Chinese embassy in London was constantly bringing guys to Shannon, it was a kind of Lourdes to them," said Tom Kelleher, a veteran consultant for the Shannon zone. "Visit Shannon and you get an indulgence." This backstory " . . . reinforces the widely-believed myth about how dirt-poor Ireland got rich: that its magic elixir of growth was radical corporate tax-cutting and financial deregulation."[4]

But there is a wrinkle in this happy tale, and it is a big one. Ireland's historical economic growth surge with the Celtic Tiger shows no correlation—no correlation *at all*—to the country's much longer history as a corporate tax haven. In fact, Ireland's population would almost certainly have been better off without its corporate tax cuts and its Wild West financial center. For the real story of the Celtic Tiger lies elsewhere.

Ireland's tax haven strategy was never really about offering secrecy to foreign money, as in some tax havens; it was, above all, about corporate tax cuts. The strategy properly began in 1956 with a measure called export profits tax relief (EPTR), an aggressive corporate tax haven strategy by the standards of the day that, once tweaked and embedded, meant zero taxes on export sales of manufactured goods. There was a bit of a pickup in exports and growth soon after that, and this has led many to conclude that it was the corporate tax cuts that did it. But in truth, growth rates were no higher than what was happening across western Europe during the Golden Age of Capitalism. Employment in manufacturing in Ireland would rise modestly for the foreseeable future, and by the early 1970s less than 3 percent of the Irish workforce was employed in foreign-owned industry, mostly in low-wage employment.[5]

Then, in the early 1970s, an odd thing happened. Foreign direct investment (FDI) into Ireland suddenly exploded: a *fifteenfold* jump in just seven years, from $25 million in 1971 to $376 million by 1978, according to one measure.[6] Many economists regard FDI as the great magic potion of growth for countries playing catch-up; not only do those foreign investors build factories and pay taxes and create jobs, but they also deliver a world of know-how and skills into the countries that receive it.

Irish corporate tax policies were tweaked over this period, but there was only one event that could explain this sudden FDI explosion: Ireland's accession to the European Economic Community (EEC) in

1973. Previously, a firm based in Ireland could sell freely to the tiny Irish market and, to a certain degree, Britain, but faced tariffs and difficulties if it wanted to sell farther afield. Accession to the EEC, two years before Britain joined, transformed investors' calculations. And a more convenient, friendly, English-speaking platform for American firms and investors—especially to those CEOs who had Irish ancestry—was hard to imagine. "Multinational firms locating here could use the country as a platform for exports to a European market of 250 million people," wrote Ray Mac Sharry, a former deputy prime minister, and Padraic White, a former head of the Irish Industrial Development Authority, in their jointly authored book *The Making of the Celtic Tiger.* "Above all, joining the EEC allowed Ireland to step out of the shadow of British influence."[7]

But Europe's impact on Ireland went far beyond market access. It helped usher in deep-rooted social reforms, not least a remarkable emancipation of women. Until 1973, would you believe it, female civil servants and other public employees in Ireland had to resign their jobs when they got married on the grounds that they were taking jobs from men. "Marital rape" was in law a contradiction, because Irish husbands had the right to have sex with their wives whenever they felt so inclined. Women had almost no access to contraceptives; child benefits could be collected only by the father; and women couldn't own their homes outright. Many pubs wouldn't admit women unless accompanied by a man. Europe forced Ireland to get rid of these archaic forms of discrimination, and in fairly short order. In the words of the Irish journalist Justine McCarthy, joining Europe "rescued us from slavery."[8]

But Europe also didn't like the "discriminatory" rules of the fledgling Irish corporate tax haven. The EEC cut the poverty-stricken country, which wasn't that much more than half as rich as the European average, some slack for a while, but by 1980 Ireland had to phase out its 0 percent rate for manufacturing and replace it with a 10 percent tax on profits for "manufacturing and internationally traded services." By then, the new foreign investment surge had created seventy thousand jobs, a decent but still only modest 5 percent of the workforce. Yet something was still amiss.

For an economy trying to develop, foreign investment is only a means to an end. What matters ultimately is how the economy as a whole performs. For one thing, if you have to take wealth or skilled workers out of other parts of the economy to subsidize FDI, that may not necessarily increase growth overall. The best way to measure Irish economic performance for our purposes is to look at gross national income (GNI) per person compared with the European average. On this measure, Irish incomes had flatlined at 60 percent of the European average since 1956 and had actually dipped modestly during the early 1970s even amid the rising tide of foreign investment. By the end of the 1980s Irish GNI per capita still hadn't budged above around 60 percent of the European average; unemployment was well over 15 percent, and one in every hundred Irish people was emigrating each year. For well over a quarter of a century Ireland's aggressive corporate tax haven strategy had worked for a minority, but not for the country as a whole.[9] Then suddenly, in about 1992, something new happened. Economic growth exploded.

The Celtic Tiger had been born. To understand the nature of this beast, it's necessary first to understand the biggest beast in Irish politics at the time: Charles Haughey.

Haughey was a practitioner of Vatican-level crookery who, on his death in 2006, had amassed a mansion and a 280-acre estate near Dublin, a string of racehorses, a yacht, an island retreat off the south coast, lavish gifts from Saudi princes, and a complex financial web of personal accounts and assets scattered across several tax havens. Staff at the exclusive Charvet outfitters in Paris, where Haughey paid thousands for bespoke silk shirts and dressing gowns, called him "Your Excellency," but to close associates he was simply "the Boss." Born in rural County Mayo in 1925, Haughey qualified as an accountant and trained as a lawyer but was always destined for politics. In 1951 he married the daughter of a grandee in the mainstream Fianna Fáil party, a centrist, populist, but conservative grouping that, alongside the more right-wing Fine Gael, had dominated Irish politics for half a century.

Haughey's thirst for influence was something to behold. "Friends and enemies alike were mesmerized by his relentless pursuit of power," explained Joe Joyce and Peter Murtagh in their 1983 biography, *The Boss.* "He was living proof of the dictum that, in politics, one should never resign."[10] By 1961, at age thirty-six, he was minister of justice; five years later he was made finance minister; and eventually he would become Ireland's taoiseach, winning power three times, in 1979, 1982, and 1987. He introduced, among other things, the 1968 Finance Act, which would for the rest of his life essentially exempt his fortune and that of many of his friends from tax. In 1970, a year after getting caught speculating with 100 million Deutschmarks of public funds, he was finally dismissed from government after being found to have helped gunrunners for the Irish Republican Army, which was fighting the British army in Northern Ireland (he was arrested and tried but found not guilty).[11]

Ireland's economy in the 1970s was still dominated by big agricultural interests and a loose group of high-society bankers and accountants. They operated in a system that was still economically subservient to London and rigged against the rural poor in favor of wealthy middlemen, who collected and exported the fruits of their labor, mostly to Britain. Haughey wore the story of his shaky working-class roots as a badge of honor, and he positioned himself as the antiestablishment candidate. But this ducking-and-diving interloper, dogged by endless rumors about his profitable shenanigans in Irish real estate, was about as welcome among the establishment as flatulence in a packed hotel elevator. They'd call Haughey and his associates "men in mohair suits" or "gombeen men." The nearest English equivalent is perhaps "shyster," explained the political historian Conor McCabe. "The fucking gombeens, you know? The spivs."[12]

This treatment seems to have inspired terrible insecurity in Haughey. He designed a family coat of arms to bolster a fake claim to being a direct descendant of the ancient high kings of Ireland. Amid applause from guests at a luncheon in Washington, DC, in 1982, he turned plaintively to Irish journalists: "Listen. They love me." This insecurity "would eat at him all his life," wrote the journalist Colm Keena in his book *Haughey's Millions*, adding that Haughey "would never gain acceptance, but for some reason always seemed to care."[13]

Subsequent public tribunals, long after he left power for the last time, in 1992, found that the biggest flows of dubious money into Haughey's personal accounts had tended to come within days of his assuming his latest ministerial post or other position of power. And this was a long, steady pattern throughout his political life. "When Haughey was in power the money tended to flow in," says Keena, "and when he was out of power the money tended to dry up." After getting sacked in 1970 he simply overdrew his accounts at the bank, on the correct assumption that the banks would write off his debts once he got back in, and by the eve of his re-election as taoiseach in 1979, his personal overdraft was seventy-seven times his annual salary.[14] It was a shameless kind of political wealth that he pursued too. "Haughey would have had the attitude that he was completely entitled to the money," says O'Toole, "as in 'I ought to have a stud farm and fly around in a helicopter. It's important, if I'm representing the nation, to be on the same level as these wealth creators.'"[15] And this attitude gives a clue to the deep connections between Haughey's corruption, the corporate tax haven that Ireland aspired to become, and the Third Way attitude of cutting corporate taxes, letting the financial sector rip, and not looking too closely under the hood or redistributing the proceeds.[16]

The basic ideological technique, O'Toole explains, is to separate the creation of wealth from its distribution, "so you don't have to ask questions about what kind of wealth is being created, or if it has any corruption at its heart. The moral side happens at the distributional level." That analysis could be applied to Juncker, Blair, Clinton, and any of the other Third Way leaders and hangers-on. The Irish musician Bono reflected this vision when he was asked to justify his band U2's decision to shift a chunk of its business affairs from low-tax Ireland to the Netherlands, another corporate tax haven, enabling it to pay even less tax. He described his financial moves as "smart" business, slamming the critics as non-Irish people who "wouldn't understand" that the country got rich by being a corporate tax haven.[17]

It's a funny thing, but a taint of corruption can even help politicians sometimes. To the man in the pub, Haughey was either a crook or the workers' savior. Centuries of British domination had fixed the Irish state in people's minds as something alien and British, explains Elaine Byrne, author of *Political Corruption in Ireland, 1922–2010: A Crooked Harp?* "There is a sense that Dublin is a different country," she said, adding that when Haughey was taking money out, people didn't make the connection—"That's my money." In a wider context this helps explain, among other things, voters' remarkable willingness in many countries to support ethically challenged candidates like Silvio Berlusconi or Donald Trump. "As a reaction to the idea of faceless, fluid forces shaping one's destiny, an extreme of local loyalty and of personal intimacy," says O'Toole, "is an act of defiance against Them—whoever They are. Doing the last thing you're supposed to do may be the final assertion of power against a feeling of powerlessness." O'Toole concludes, "The real wonder was not that fraudsters got elected but that more politicians did not claim to be crooks in order to get elected."[18]

Prioritizing the local, the familial, and the personal at the expense of the wider nation is a basis for corruption the world over—heroic corruption, you might call it. And this can be expanded to a global level. It wasn't a stretch for Haughey and his successors to harness this mentality to gain support for Ireland's tax haven policies, prioritizing the interests of Ireland—or, to be more exact, a section of Irish society—at the expense of large taxpaying populations in other countries whose multinationals used Ireland as a financial brothel to cut their taxes and other regulations.

Yet Haughey left office for the last time in February 1992, just as Ireland was about to enjoy its astonishing surge of economic growth and foreign investment. Irish GNP per person would rise from 60 percent of the European average in 1990, to parity by the year 2000, to a fabulous, undreamed-of 130 percent by 2007. This explosion, which became known as the Celtic Tiger economy, was made up of two booms. There was a real one based on job-creating foreign investment, which soared from 2.2 percent of GDP in 1990 to an astonishing 25 percent by 2000.[19] Then, in 2001, when a global recession hit and global FDI flows fell back sharply, the foreign investment machine gave way to a fake boom led by financial services and what O'Toole called "a demented property cult" mixed with "a lethal cocktail of global ideology and Irish habits."[20] This second boom would bring the reckless tiger back to earth with a teeth-cracking crunch. But despite all the excesses, this was still one of the biggest growth spurts in world economic history. And herein lies the big question. What was the secret ingredient that generated this sudden burst of growth?

The corporate tax-cut story doesn't seem convincing: all those tax haven facilities since 1956 had failed to ignite the economic growth engine, as Ireland barely kept pace with the rest of Europe for the next thirty-five years. No, the first sudden surge of foreign investment in the early 1970s was triggered above all by Ireland's accession to the EEC. In fact, Ireland's iconic 12.5 percent corporate tax rate was first applied in 2003, long *after* the sudden growth explosion began—and that involved a tax rate *increase* from 10 percent, which was itself an increase on the previous 0 percent rate for exporting firms. The comparable French and British corporate tax rates in the 1990s were between 30 and 35 percent and had been at that level or higher for years. And in any case, the main tax attraction for multinationals wasn't so much the corporate tax rate; it was the tax loopholes, which enabled multinationals to end up paying close to zero in Ireland. One of Apple's Irish subsidiaries, for example, typically paid less than 0.1 percent. Irish loopholes for multinationals had been available since the 1950s too.[21]

If it wasn't corporate tax that fathered the tiger, then what was it? The shortest answer to this big question really does come down to the luck of the Irish. A perfect storm of seven or eight extraordinary factors came together all at once to propel Ireland's explosive growth. As will become clear, no country has a hope of replicating even a fraction of this. Ireland is no growth model for anyone.

The biggest factor by far, once again, came from Europe and Ireland's accession to the European single market in 1992. The EEC had already created a spike in foreign investment into Ireland, but its member countries still had in place endless hurdles to protect their national businesses. The single market, a grand big-bang removal of those hurdles to the free flow of capital and investment across Europe, washed that all away. Ireland's accession was described by Padraic Fallon, the chair of *Euromoney*, as being akin to "Guderian's tanks breaking through the Maginot Line."[22] Peter Sutherland, the Irish former director general of the World Trade Organization and the EU's competition commissioner ahead of the single market opening, summarized the importance of accession by saying, "The completion of the single market was the vital moment for us. Suddenly, Ireland became as good a location for access to the French market as was France."[23]

This event coincided with a remarkable, related trend: at the same time a stupendous global investment boom was getting under way. FDI flowing from rich countries nearly *quintupled* from 1991 to 1999—from $230 billion to $1 trillion—while from the United States the global total rose more than sixfold, and those from the United Kingdom, Ireland's closest trading partner, rose by a factor of twelve.[24]

This investment explosion was bolstered and channeled into Ireland by another crucial actor: Ireland's heroic, indefatigable Industrial Development Authority (IDA), a body that was so successful in enticing foreign investors that it's probably fair to say the world has seen nothing quite like it. Long before the 1990s, IDA teams had been fanning out across the developed world. In 1973 alone, the year when Ireland became an EEC member, the IDA made an astonishing 2,600 presentations to companies in different countries, mostly tailored to each client. The logic, explained Padraic White, a former IDA head, "was to target with rifle-shot precision individual companies that met specific criteria, then go directly to them and make the case for locating in Ireland."[25] IDA officials dangled low corporate taxes, of course, and more—a *lot* more. They paid for advertising blitzes in the global business press. They invited journalists for all-expenses-paid trips to Ireland to meet the great and the good. They carefully planned routes from the airport to avoid eyesores and traffic snarls. They organized networks of top-notch hotels, restaurants, and entertainment for visitors. "From sheer necessity, [we] carved out another Ireland," says White. But, he adds, there was no doubt about the trump card. "Ireland's membership of the EEC, with access to its large market, was the bedrock business rationale for investing in Ireland."[26]

The IDA used "flagship marketing," aggressively targeting the big global names, whose vote of confidence would then make it easier to attract others. It got Apple to invest in 1980, then leveraged that to persuade Intel to move in. And then it went for Microsoft. It seemed to work every time. "I'm normally the sales guy," says Steve Ballmer, the CEO of Microsoft, recalling the extraordinary job the IDA did on him. "That is the first lunch I've been to where the government was selling to me!"[27]

The IDA chiseled Ireland's quirky international image into appealing new forms. The traditional American view of Ireland was "a romantic misty isle peopled by characters straight out of *The Quiet Man* and full of bog roads and stray donkeys," says White.[28] But the IDA's message tilted Ireland's charms in new directions. It still made plenty of Ireland's unspoiled rolling scenery, clean air, and open spaces; its multiple attractions for family life; and its disproportionately large share of the world's history, literature, song, humor, and general cultural charm. But it successfully harnessed these as offering a haven away from London's high-cost urban-commuter rat race, the Caymans' ghastly palm-fringed zero-tax soullessness, or Luxembourg's or Geneva's creepy, foreign-language Euro-sterility. Here was a genuinely new and appealing offering for the world's corporate bosses—and their families.

The agency did surveys that found one of the biggest attractions for companies was highly qualified graduate staff, which was where the next element feeding the boom came in: massive education reforms and investment in the 1960s, which by the 1980s were sluicing waves of bright, well-educated Irish secondary school and college graduates into the job market. Simultaneously, the European-led emancipation of Irish women was increasing female participation in the workforce, smartly boosting Irish productivity and growth. Over a quarter of the Irish women who worked within the home in 1994—activity that generally isn't measured in economic growth figures—had taken outside jobs by 1999, just six years later. The measured economic benefits were immense.[29] Adding further to the workforce was a flood of Irish job-seekers who had fled the country in previous bad economic times, been educated and trained at other countries' schools and universities, and were now returning home to join the boom. All this helped transform the Irish economy from a position where in 1986 every ten workers supported twenty-two dependents (people too young, old, or sick to work), to a ratio of ten workers to just five dependents by 2005. Here was a revolutionary demographic dividend to add to the fizzing mixture.[30]

The IDA designed a dazzling new marketing campaign to capitalize on this shift, with the slogan "Ireland—We're the Young Europeans." It ran flashy ads in the *Economist*, the *Wall Street Journal*, and *BusinessWeek*. "People are to Ireland as oil is to Texas," one advertisement went, accompanied by a photo of smiling male and female graduates on campus. Another image showed a mixed group of optimistic-looking students, representing the flower of Irish youth, ranged up a Trinity College, Dublin, stairway, against the simple caption "Hire them—before they hire you." Top US executives still remember those campaigns. The Irish advertising executive John Fanning described the strategies in military terms, with advertising providing the air cover and the IDA's "troops on the ground" engaging in the combat, fighting for investment.[31]

The IDA's approach was not to embrace the pure laissez-faire free-market orthodoxy of cutting taxes and waiting for the investors to come;

rather it pursued an unashamed and aggressive strategy of government intervention, surgically targeting sectors and businesses, then going after them, howitzers and all.[32] The particular choices it made—especially in pharmaceuticals, information, and medical technologies—were well researched and exquisitely timed: the Celtic Tiger coincided with a golden era of productivity for Big Pharma in the 1980s and 1990s and with the dot-com boom of the 1990s. A splurge of government spending on modern telecommunications infrastructure for Ireland iced the cake.

Yet there was still more.

The peace process in Northern Ireland across the border was bearing fruit, culminating in a cease-fire by the Irish Republican Army in 1994. "For the first time in decades," says Olivia O'Leary, a prominent Irish political analyst, "you had Ireland as a good news story just at the time when the IDA was trying to get American investment into Ireland. . . . This helped the IDA enormously [just as] a whole generation of Irish-American business people were beginning to surface in corporate America." Everyone wanted a piece of this country. There was also an outbreak of industrial peace, the result of a set of social partnerships negotiated between employers, unions, and farmers from 1987, an initiative considered so successful that the government of Sweden, itself a pioneer in social partnership, later turned to Ireland for advice. These deals, says former deputy prime minister Ray Mac Sharry, "laid secure foundations for . . . the Irish economic miracle of the 1990s."[33]

Yet *more* factors contributed to the perfect storm. Not only was Ireland becoming a sales platform into Europe, but by the late 1980s it was also receiving large European agricultural transfers and billions in European structural funds, which doubled in 1988 and then doubled again in 1993. "The funds helped finance a major investment in infrastructure that, in turn, has facilitated rapid economic expansion," explains White. "The foreign investment benefits to Ireland of EU membership are incalculable and enduring." A country that had just one stretch of two-lane highway in 1972 was soon transformed into a modern investment hub, crisscrossed with shiny new roads, railways, ports, and airports.[34]

With all these pieces falling into place within just a few years, nothing short of putting the heads of Bill Gates and Steve Jobs on spikes at Dublin Airport would have stopped a surge in US multinational investment, whatever the corporate tax incentives.

And yet all this raises a question. The bosses of multinationals, the big accounting firms, and many others all say that corporate tax cutting was Ireland's secret ingredient. But how so? The answer is that they would say that, wouldn't they? There's nothing quite like an Irish tax loophole to boost a CEO's stock options. And talk is cheap. They constantly bellyache that they *need* more tax cuts: of course they do, in the same way that my children say they *need* more ice cream. It's only on rare occasions—such as when Boeing in 2014 effectively threatened not to perform safety tests on its new planes if it didn't get tax breaks for doing so—that it becomes patently obvious how empty their threats are.[35] In survey after survey around the world, in fact, tax rates typically come fifth or sixth in genuine investors' lists of priorities. What they consistently want is the rule of law, a healthy and educated workforce, access to markets, good infrastructure, and ideally an English-speaking environment. "I never made an investment decision based on the tax code," said Paul O'Neill, chair of the US aluminum giant Alcoa and subsequently US Treasury secretary under George W. Bush. "If you are giving money away I will take it. If you want to give me inducements for something I am going to do anyway, I will take it. But good business people do not do things because of inducements."[36]

It wasn't corporate taxes but all these other factors *plus* the powerful, natural tailwind of catch-up growth that was inevitably going to happen someday—that is the *real* story of the Celtic Tiger. Corporate tax cutting contributed to the Irish *investment* boom for sure, but whether it boosted the Irish *economic* boom is quite another matter. Had Ireland had a more normal corporate tax system, most of this investment would have happened anyway; in fact Ireland would quite likely have earned higher tax revenues from the investment surge, helping support other parts of the economy such as an even better-educated workforce or infrastructure, which would have made the boom more profound and longer-lasting and with stronger tax-financed foundations.

Yet even this isn't the full story, for alongside the corporate tax tale there's another fiction—more financial and less salubrious—that is often credited with having fed the tiger. Like the tax-cut story, it's another example of Irish mythmaking.

On Custom House Quay on the north bank of the River Liffey in Dublin stands a group of yellowing rusty-bronze statues, a moving testament to the ships that sailed from here during the Great Famine of 1845–9, when Ireland was part of the United Kingdom and an economic vassal of London. Irish peasants toiled on tiny, precarious farms, while a mostly Protestant Anglo-Irish hereditary ruling class of landlords and middlemen gathered the peasants' produce to send for processing or slaughter in Britain. When the blight struck, London provided little assistance, believing that Ireland should rely on its own resources and the free market. Crop failure led to mass farm evictions, then a great hunger, which killed over a million people, an eighth of the Irish population. Over a million more emigrated.

Next to the monument, though, stands a hulking modernist seven-story building fronted by greenish-blue glass, called IFSC House.[37] The contrast with the commemoration of historic Irish misery could not be greater. IFSC stands for International Financial Services Centre, a reference to Ireland's low-tax, low-regulation offshore financial industry, whose futuristic buildings now straddle the Liffey up and down this part of Custom House Quay and beyond. Stand on one of the bridges here in the sunshine, and you'll see enough reflected light coming off those many large, shiny buildings to lift the spirits of even the grumpiest traveler.

The IFSC is, to an extent, a shadow banking center—where stuff goes on outside the walls of traditionally regulated banks, involving hedge funds and other exotic financial creatures and activities with names that will be familiar to connoisseurs of the global financial crisis: securitization, derivatives, conduits, special purpose vehicles, credit default swaps, and more.

The IFSC represents a second, smaller component of the Celtic Tiger. The offering wasn't corporate tax cuts this time but lax financial regulation and oversight for entities that came here. Yet the mythmaking has essentially been the same: Ireland relaxed its financial laws, persuaded global financial players to relocate there, and, in the process, transformed a run-down smokestack wasteland into a zinging new financial center, creating tens of thousands of jobs in the process.

The origins of the IFSC go back to 1985, to a meeting of businesspeople and public officials at the Shelbourne Hotel, a grand old redbrick Renaissance building in central Dublin, just down the road from the Oireachtas, the Irish parliament. At the time, living standards were falling, unemployment and inflation were high, and young Irish were emigrating. Finance Secretary Maurice Doyle bitterly recalled writing to the *London Times* to challenge a suggestion that "international bankers were about to pull the shutters down on Ireland."[38] At the meeting at the Shelbourne Hotel everyone was looking for new ideas. A flamboyant former Citibank and PwC official, Dermot Desmond, spoke up. How about, he wondered, setting up a financial center?[39]

His idea wasn't new, in fact. In the 1970s a Wall Street lawyer and expert on offshore banking, Bob Slater, had written a brief for the IDA urging Ireland to set up an offshore banking center modeled on the secrecy haven of Bermuda, and he had even gotten a couple of Wall Street banks interested. But the Central Bank of Ireland had blocked it. "The project smacked of a banana republic," as the IDA's Padraic White puts it.[40] A similar offshore proposal was floated in 1984 but also never took off.

But at the Shelbourne meeting Desmond at last detected a flicker of interest. As he recalled it, he quickly wrote a short concept note, presented it to the government, and agreed that his own stockbroking

firm would pay half the costs of a £150,000 feasibility study by Price
Waterhouse. It took a bit of time, but by 1987 he had garnered heavy-
weight political support, most notably from Haughey, who had long
ago emerged from gunrunning disgrace and was now facing elections
as leader of the opposition. Haughey gave Desmond forty-eight hours
to write a brief to put into his election manifesto. So Desmond and a
couple of colleagues wrote the policy section overnight—a plan to create
a financial center with Irish characteristics. Haughey inserted the "big
hairy idea," as one of his manifesto writers put it, almost verbatim into a
glossy party document launched at a preelection press conference. This
was all about Ireland joining in a "competition" with other countries,
Haughey declared. "Let them off and let the best horse win."[41]

Though the proposal had been inspired most directly by the tax
havens of Luxembourg, Singapore, and Hong Kong, London was at
the back of everyone's mind. "We are certainly seeking to draw business
away from London," White said, "but we want a satellite relationship,
rather than try to take London on in a head-on conflict that we cannot win." How the bankers in London must have chuckled at the idea
of a success story in Dublin's beaten-up docklands. Yet Haughey was
determined to push the project forward.[42] He was elected taoiseach for
the third time in March 1987, and on his first day in office he set his
chief political fixer, a bulldog of a man called Pádraig Ó hUigínn, onto
the case. Between them they conjured up a legally charmed zone at the
Custom House Docks, inside which qualifying financial firms would
be taken out of the normal Irish regulatory system and guaranteed a
10 percent corporate tax rate. They set up an all-powerful committee
of financiers and civil servants to bulldoze the project forward. "No
one is going to stop us," Haughey declared at the inaugural meeting.[43]
When egos clashed, Ó hUigínn wrangled everyone onto the true path.
The Clearing House Group, as the committee became known, evolved
into a fearsome, unaccountable, and secretive body, a classic tool of the
financially captured offshore state. Far from public scrutiny, the world's
shadow bankers could sit down with Irish lawmakers and present their

deregulatory wish lists, protected from such irritants as local democracy. A parliamentarian called Nessa Childers, who got hold of the minutes of Clearing House Group meetings in the wake of the global financial crisis, described lobbying "in secret, behind closed doors. . . . The bankers and hedge fund industry got virtually everything they asked for while the public got hit with a number of austerity measures."[44] Any critics of the project were pilloried as traitors to the national interest, and everyone in Ireland was urged to get behind the patriotic green jersey agenda.

The Finance Act of 1987 that ushered in the IFSC targeted global money managers and dealers in foreign currencies, futures, options, bonds, equities, insurance, clearing, information storage, and miscellaneous trading. Its provisions were drafted broadly because no one was quite sure who might turn up. "We engaged in dynamic research," said Brendan Logue, a top IDA official, which was "just another way of saying 'we made it up as we went along.'"[45] The special corporate tax rates available to companies located in the IFSC were attractive, but the major juice was light-touch financial regulation. This wasn't quite a brass-plate operation; there was usually some requirement that market entrants provide at least a bit of substance, generally meaning local jobs, but this wasn't onerous.

Two themes in the legislation stand out, which for those familiar with offshore tax havens marked it down as an all-guns-blazing tax haven model. First, it specified that the IFSC's players should be "persons not ordinarily resident in the State," an unambiguous bid for "elsewhere" tax haven status. Officials didn't want Irish residents playing the game because they knew that operations like these harm countries whose residents use the facilities. (If the IFSC undermined the tax systems and regulatory regimes of other countries, well, that was just fine.) Second, regulators were required by law to promote the IFSC. That is a quintessentially offshore rule, because the standard way to promote and develop a financial sector based on nonresident business is to lure foreign money by creating loopholes, relaxing regulations, and removing standard democratic controls on business—in other words, to not regulate foreign-owned businesses setting up shop there. That is a classic tax haven strategy.[46]

Cheerleaders among the Irish media served up helpful dog-whistle phrases and terms like "stifling businesses with burdensome regulations," "bonfire of red tape," "tax efficiency," and "pro-business" (and the obligatory "internationally competitive") regulatory environment. And under this unholy umbrella the world's banks, shadow banks, and accountancy firms began to show up: first a trickle, and then in strength. By 1993 the IFSC had created a thousand jobs or so, and already foreign regulators were getting worried. The Swedes began an investigation, and German officials said angrily that their banks were using the IFSC to escape paying their share of reunification costs.[47] But creating escape routes for large banks that would annoy other countries was kind of the point all along, as it always is with the tax haven model, so nothing was done.

The overall benefits to Ireland were never obvious, however. Over half of those arriving inside the charmed IFSC perimeter were simply shifting their existing nonresident operations into the IFSC to get the special treatment. "Irish Life across the road have their filing cabinets lined up to move fifty yards across to the site," a Labour Party official complained, "to go from a 50 percent tax regime down to 10 percent."[48] Multinational companies already in Ireland dived in too, as the IFSC's low-regulation, blind-eyed, low-tax offering turned out to be a great place to put the operations managing their global cash flows.

Vast global sums started wheeling in and out of Dublin, barely touching the sides. This offshore turntable lured fly-by-night operators and many big names too, allowing Ireland to cream off some fees and taxes. By 2001, "investment" in the IFSC was officially equivalent to six times the size of the Irish economy, and by 2005 bank assets in Ireland had nearly trebled again.[49] Charlie McCreevy, an Irish former EU commissioner, gushed about the "great entrepreneurial energies that a 'light touch' regulatory system can unleash," yet jobs and tax revenues were a whisper—less than 1 percent of the Irish labor force participated—compared to the frightening sums involved.[50]

Access to Europe had also provoked an influx of credit into Ireland, spreading warm tingly feelings into places that the FDI boom hadn't yet reached, puffing up house prices and helping the middle classes to feel rich, and encouraging them to spend, borrow, spend, borrow, and build. Through the early 2000s this property-fed bubble kept growing. By 2006 Bertie Ahern, then taoiseach, was exulting that "the boom times are getting even more boomier,"[51] and by the following year Ireland was building half as many houses as property-crazed Britain, despite having a fourteenth of its population.

Caught up in this insane urban construction frenzy, hardly anyone noticed that manufacturing was actually shrinking, that there were classic symptoms of the crowding-out effect of the finance curse.[52] Credit was roaring ahead, pumping up prices and eroding the cost-competitiveness advantages companies had found so attractive in Ireland. And now a volcano was beginning to tremble under everyone's feet.

When the global financial crisis hit, it turned out that the IFSC had been a key node in the global mischief. The collapse of four German banks—Sachsen LandesBank, IKB, WestLB, and HypoVereinsbank—can all be traced to activities in the IFSC. Under the benign eye of Irish regulators, Hypo's Dublin-based subsidiary, Depfa, had been operating profitably under an insanely risky leverage ratio of 80:1, meaning that a decline in the value of its assets by a couple of percentage points could have bankrupted the whole operation. The crisis quickly tipped it into insolvency; the German government had to put up €134 billion in an emergency bailout, and Germany's leading business daily, *Handelsblatt*, called Depfa "the source of all evil." Sachsen LB also fell apart after meddling in US subprime mortgages through its IFSC vehicle Ormond Quay (named after a section of the northern bank of the Liffey, just along from Custom House Quay). The Irish financial regulator had stated in the boom times, "It is not required to police the activities of vehicles such as Ormond Quay." You could submit your hundreds of pages of documents in a funds prospectus at three P.M. and have the authorization to start business the next day. Nobody in Ireland, it turned out, had been checking anything.

When the US investment banking giant Bear Stearns collapsed in 2008, it turned out to have had several dodgy investment vehicles listed on the Irish Stock Exchange and three subsidiaries located in the IFSC, owned by an Irish holding company, Bear Stearns Ireland Limited. Professor Jim Stewart of Trinity College, Dublin, among the only people in Ireland to have exposed the IFSC's shenanigans, found that by 2007 Bear Stearns Ireland Limited was operating with gargantuan leverage, where each dollar of equity was propping up $119 of gross assets. A deterioration in value of those assets of less than 1 percent could wipe it out. And it did.[53]

The Bear Stearns case illustrates a profound truth about offshore, race-to-the-bottom finance and regulation. The trick is so often to drape your company across several jurisdictions and then to get each place to say, "This thing is regulated elsewhere." US company accounts said Bear Stearns Ireland Limited and its subsidiaries were regulated by the Irish regulator, yet the Irish regulator said its remit extended only to banks *headquartered* in Ireland. So this ultra-high-risk entity was regulated elsewhere, which effectively meant nowhere.[54] And the "elsewhere, nowhere" concept has close parallels in tax avoidance. Apple Operations International (AOI), the subsidiary of the technology giant that owns most of Apple's offshore subsidiaries, played this game too. Under US law, AOI is incorporated in Ireland and isn't a tax resident in the United States. But Ireland uses a different test for tax residence: what matters is where the company is "functionally managed and controlled from," which in AOI's case is the United States. This was, as US senator Carl Levin put it, a "ghost company. . . . Magically, it is neither here nor there." So AOI was taxed by nobody, and this helped Apple generate a mighty chunk of the $215 billion that it was estimated to have stashed offshore by the end of 2017—out of reach, effectively nowhere.[55]

Has the IFSC benefited Ireland? On the face of it, yes. Visitors to Dublin can marvel at the acres of shiny glass, chrome, and concrete; the expensive coats and tea shops; the upmarket beer festivals; and the general bustle that you'll find these days along the banks of the River Liffey where the IFSC sprawls. At the last count, firms in the IFSC had paid over €500 million a year in taxes to Ireland since the global financial crisis, and it hosted over thirty-eight thousand jobs, according to official figures. Ireland deregulated, the story goes; it slashed red tape, and a new economic engine was born.

Yet this simple tale doesn't add up either. Those thirty-eight thousand jobs amount to less than 2 percent of Irish jobs, and those tax revenues are equivalent to just 0.2 percent of gross national income. That's not nothing, but it's not so special. And since the government won't publish a breakdown of employment in the IFSC, there's no way to know if those job figures are accurate. Two people I spoke to in Ireland said they believed the true numbers were significantly smaller. The IFSC certainly creates few jobs when the trillions of dollars and euros that come reeling through it each year are considered. In 2013 Jim Stewart studied a sample of eighty-two special purpose vehicles—companies owned and controlled from other large financial centers but incorporated in Ireland. These exotic, unregulated vehicles held assets averaging $350 million each and were perched on a tiny, rickety capital base averaging just $40,000—a leverage ratio of $1 of capital to a staggering $8,200 of assets. And, as Stewart stated, median corporate tax payments were zero for all years: "SPVs pay more in tax advice than in tax payments."[56] The big banks may not be much better. It is expected, for instance, that Allied Irish, one of Ireland's biggest banks, will pay no corporation tax for the next twenty years because of tax losses generated during the crisis.[57]

Did the IFSC create jobs in Ireland overall? All those factors mentioned above—the European single market, European subsidies, the IDA's efforts, the education reforms producing waves of skilled graduates, the emancipation of women, the social partnership, the peace process, and more—helped the IFSC to grow. Amid this golden environment, those highly educated Irish graduates who went to work in the IFSC would have, in its absence, gone instead into other professions that would surely have been more socially useful and probably more genuinely productive. But the IFSC, by boosting Ireland's reckless banking system, helped inflict much larger damage. The European Commission's 2012 official investigation into the global financial crisis, known as the Liikanen Report, shows how much state aid each country provided to its banking system during the crisis. Eight member states gave no support. France provided the equivalent of 4 percent of its gross domestic product, while Germany provided 10 percent and the UK nearly 20 percent. For Ireland, the figure was 269 percent. Those economic, democratic, and social costs utterly swamp any tax or employment benefits. It's hard to accept that the IFSC has created jobs or tax revenues for Ireland; the opposite is surely true.

On top of this damage to Ireland, consider the unquantifiable global damage caused by the IFSC's role in undermining other countries' tax and regulatory systems and in helping to transmit giant global pulses of risk and fear out into the mayhem of international markets during the crisis, while collapsing Irish banks wreaked similar carnage at home. Then there is the question of the international damage from tax losses facilitated by Ireland's corporate tax system. It's hard to put numbers on this, because so many of these tax games involve multiple countries, but the figure is in the tens of billions each year.[58] The story of Ireland's role in the global financial crisis and its aftermath is a truly blood-curdling tale of greed, corruption, hubris, ignorance, arrogance, austerity, secrecy, and competitiveness fetishism—the finance curse at its finest and most loathsome.

Until his death in 2006, Haughey, like many wealthy Irish people, used the libel courts to keep his scandalous acts hidden. But in December 2006, six months after he died, the Moriarty Tribunal, a government probe into political corruption in Ireland, produced a staggering array of damning facts. Not only was Haughey an Olympic-level tax evader, but he and his associates had built an enormous financial empire offshore. The Moriarty report mentions the Cayman Islands over 400 times and the Isle of Man over 130 times, plus several honorable mentions for Jersey, Zurich, and Geneva. There was, for instance, the Ansbacher scam, involving a bank within a bank set up in the Caymans by Haughey's friend, bagman, and fund-raiser, Des Traynor. The Central Bank of Ireland knew all about it but did nothing. "In view of the delicate nature of these matters, we did not pursue the matter further," a bank memorandum states, adding, "The bank would be placed in a very embarrassing position should the Revenue Authorities ever become aware of the situation."[59] A Central Bank director took large loans from Ansbacher and chaired a secret Haughey committee. The bank even doctored its own records, changing "evasion," which is illegal, to "avoidance," which is not.

There was a scheme called DIRT (deposit interest retention tax). Nonresidents didn't have to pay the tax, and anyone could walk into a bank and declare him- or herself a nonresident. Even Irish farmers, who are about as locally rooted as you can get, were hard at it. "Half the non-resident accounts are thought to be bogus," said one official memo. "We were broadly aware . . . everybody agreed it was wrong. 'For God's sake, don't rock the boat' . . . that was the culture; that was the necessity that drove us all forward."[60]

Moriarty reckoned Haughey had pocketed at least €45 million in 2006 money—171 times his gross salary from 1979 to 1996. He even diverted money raised for his best friend's liver transplant for his personal use. He ran his lavish lifestyle out of an account flush with political donations and built an incestuous network of complicity across the political spectrum, along with an intelligence-gathering operation that gave him material for blackmail and useful dirt on a hefty chunk of Ireland's political and business class. There was, as the author Elaine Byrne puts it, "an extraordinary degree of deference by regulatory authorities towards the Irish banking system and, similarly, absolute deference by banking authorities towards politicians."[61]

Visiting Ireland and talking to public figures, I am struck by the level of nervousness—although for some there seems no word quite as appropriate as "fear"—that greets any mention of Ireland's financial setup. Two particular taboos stand out: calling the country a tax haven, and doubting the importance of the corporate tax rate in Ireland's success. Ireland offers the usual theater of probity that all tax havens engage in, which involves endlessly repeating the same message—"We are not a tax haven but a clean, well-regulated, transparent, and cooperative jurisdiction"—burnished with cherry-picked statistics and violently out-of-context statements from august international bodies like the IMF. There's a comical report by PwC, for instance, that claims to show the effective corporate tax rate is higher in Ireland, at 12.3 percent, than in France, at just 8.3 percent. This statistic has been all over the Irish media. What the articles usually fail to add is that these numbers come from a PwC model of a company in Ireland that makes ceramic flowerpots, has no foreign owners, and does not trade overseas.[62] That it was the corporate tax offering that unleashed the Celtic Tiger is now a belief embedded in the Irish soul; anyone who talks of messing with the corporate tax regime is shouted down by a chorus of voices from across Irish politics, society, and media. When the troika of the IMF, the European Commission, and the European Central Bank imposed savage spending cuts and outrageous conditions on Ireland in a bailout deal in 2010, the corporate tax was the one thing that could not be put on the table, costing Ireland enormous negotiating capital. "They are wedded to it, like a spiritual totem pole," said Andrew Baker of Sheffield University, who worked in Northern Ireland for many years and closely analyzed the tax policies of north and south. "It has become part of the national psyche."[63]

Across the border, certain tax-raising powers are being devolved to the Northern Irish Assembly, and there has been a clamor for a corporate tax cut to Ireland's 12.5 percent, something that also chimes with nationalist politicians' aspirations for a united Ireland, according to Baker. Yet behind this push, if you look closely enough, are other interest groups. Delving into the nearly two-hundred-page UK legislation devolving powers to Northern Ireland, Baker encountered a minefield: "impenetrable legalese, with qualifications and sub-points all over the place, specifying who would qualify to pay 12.5 percent, what they would have to do to qualify," and so on. Who would benefit most from all this complexity? Why, the large corporate law and accounting firms, the same firms that have been the most vocal cheerleaders for Ireland's corporate tax offering.[64]

The reality behind the Celtic Tiger is not corporate tax cuts and financial deregulation as tonics for growth; they have produced short-term bubbles at best, with deadly hangovers. In the words of Kenneth Thomas, a US economist who has studied Ireland's experience extensively, "low taxes are not what makes the Irish economy tick."[65] I'd bet that if Ireland's corporate tax rate had been twice the 12.5 percent rate it would still have gotten a huge investment boom—with a less extreme upswing, perhaps, but a more sustainable one, with less focus on wealth extraction, stronger labor protections, and smaller inequalities of wealth and power. The real contribution of foreign investment to Ireland's economy has fallen steadily since the 1990s.[66] People do sometimes point to other low-tax countries instead of Ireland (or Luxembourg) as their poster children to demonstrate the virtues of corporate tax cuts: Hong Kong, the eastern European countries that enjoyed high growth rates after being released from the Soviet orbit, or China's economic zones, modeled on Shannon. But their stories are, like Ireland's, unique and impossible for others to replicate, and not based on low corporate taxes. The eastern European countries' growth, for instance, is largely based on the fact that they abolished Soviet Communist central planning, while Hong Kong's is based above all on the fact that it is the favored gateway to gigantic markets in China.[67]

Ireland used to be one of those very few countries that everyone condescended to love: the ancestral home, the cheeky, impoverished urchin in ragged trousers who livened up the world with music, whiskey, green fields, leprechauns, and the *craic*, never hurting anyone. Now, as Ireland swings wrecking balls into the tax and regulatory systems of countries around the globe, that image is in tatters. None of this was necessary, even for Ireland's sake. The ever-penetrating Fintan O'Toole summarizes Ireland's predicament today. "They blew it," he said.

> They practiced the economics of utter idiocy, watching a controlled explosion of growth turn into a mad conflagration and aiming petrol-filled pressure hoses at the raging flames. They amused themselves with fantasy lifestyles and pet projects while the opportunity to break cycles of deprivation and child poverty was frittered away. They turned self-confidence into arrogance, optimism into swagger, aspiration into self-delusion.[68]

Irish self-delusion, unfortunately, went on to conquer the world.

The global financial crisis had terrible consequences in Ireland, and Ireland transmitted those effects around the globe, but at the end of the day it was a small player compared to the beast across the Irish Sea, three hundred miles to the east, in London. And here lies one of the greatest untold stories of that crisis.

CHAPTER SEVEN

The London Loophole

In 2012 and 2013 Gary Gensler, a top US financial regulator, made a couple of speeches surveying the wreckage left by the global financial crisis. It was, he said, financial institutions operating complex "business in offshore entities that nearly toppled the US economy." He reeled off the well-known disaster stories from the crash. There was American International Group (AIG), which was felled by a freewheeling unit called AIG Financial Products, run out of an office in London, leading to a $180 billion bailout in 2008, the biggest in history. There was Bear Stearns, which two Cayman investment funds helped destroy. There was Lehman Brothers, whose operations in London were also central to that firm's demise. Then there was Citigroup, whose investment vehicles, launched in the Caymans and incorporated in London, enjoyed two multibillion-dollar bailouts. A decade earlier, there had been Long-Term Capital Management (LTCM), the Connecticut-based hedge fund whose risky bets almost triggered a gigantic bailout. "We had no idea what the ramifications would be," Gensler said, "because these trades were booked in the Cayman Islands. It was a terrible feeling." He mentioned JPMorgan Chase's multibillion-dollar trading losses from contracts executed in its UK branch by a trader known as the London Whale.[1] He could have, but didn't, mention Enron, the financialized

US energy company whose collapse in 2001 was the largest bankruptcy in history at the time and which turned out to have parked assets out of view in hundreds of financial vehicles in the Caymans and in the even murkier Turks and Caicos, both British overseas territories. He could have mentioned that global octopus of crime and financial engineering, BCCI, also headquartered in London and festooned across the Caymans and other tax havens. In each case, Britain and its satellite havens had taken the cream from the trading activity while the going was good, then when the risks eventually crystallized into disaster, "it comes right back here, crashing to our shores," according to Gensler. "If the American taxpayer bails out JP Morgan, they'd be bailing out that London entity too." Carolyn Maloney, a US Democrat, summarized the situation: there was "a disturbing pattern," she said, "of London literally becoming the centre of financial trading disasters."[2]

Back in London, analysts railed furiously against Gensler's allegations. "The Americans are full of shit," the head of a London-based fund management firm told me in 2012 after Gensler's first outburst: Wall Street was just as chock-full of bad actors as London was.[3] And in the United States, people watching the bat cave of horrors spewing steadily out of Wall Street generally weren't ready to swallow the idea that the country of the Beatles, Princess Diana, and tea with the Queen could be so appalling. This did not compute. The accusations sank back out of sight.

But Gensler's point is important. Were Britain and the City of London somehow "worse" than Wall Street in terms of financial regulation, and at least as much to blame for the global financial meltdown? If you've gotten this far in this book you'll understand that London and its offshore satellites had already played a central role in turning global markets into a hothouse for organized crime, corruption, tax evasion, and the cross-border stashing of looted wealth. This chapter will now advance this claim by showing two related things. First, London wasn't a side-show to an American meltdown but a central cause of a North Atlantic meltdown. Second, Britain's role in helping Colombian drug barons and North Korean nuclear smugglers, and otherwise fostering global financial crime, violence, and activities that threaten national security, cannot be understood separately from its role in generating the recklessness that led to the crash. These were two sides of the very same "competitive" offshore economic coin, and they must be understood together.

First of all, Britain is—would you believe it—even *more* deeply captured and penetrated and corrupted by Big Finance than the United States is. And this should hardly be a surprise. While the City of London and Wall Street are financial centers of comparable size, Wall Street is diluted in a much larger democracy, which still contains some checks and balances that restrain some of the worst excesses. In Britain, as I'll show, senior financiers are effectively above the law. Furthermore, Wall Street doesn't have the deep, centuries-old historical roots and encrusted layers of influence that the City of London enjoys, which have penetrated into every aspect of political and economic life since the days of empire. Britain used to deploy soldiers and gunboats to bully half the world's money into London; now it seeks to tempt it simply by letting laws and rules fall away.

By the time the global financial crisis hit, New York financiers were calling London the "Guantanamo Bay" of global finance, where they could do things forbidden at home.[4] And this Great London Loophole infected America in two main ways ahead of the crisis. First, it offered an escape route from regulations designed to protect the US public. Second, and perhaps more important, it was the perfect "competitive" battering ram that Wall Street lobbyists could wield to justify further degradation of laws and regulations at home, under the threat that if they didn't get what they wanted they would decamp to London (or Zurich or Luxembourg or the Caymans) and do those things anyway. (Then, when American regulators made a deregulating move, London made a point of carefully undercutting them.) "By God, London won the competition in regulatory laxity with the United States," said William

Black, a financial criminologist and former US bank regulator, "which is why it became the financial cesspool of the world."[5]

The origins of the global financial crisis go back as far as you like, but a good place to begin is with the waves of financial deregulation that hit the United States and UK from the 1980s. One wave fed the other, in a great transatlantic feedback loop, and these changes happened *inside* the fast-growing financial world and had nothing much to do with the needs of the real economy in either country. Finance didn't start servicing its customers better; if anything, service deteriorated.

In Britain, the most dramatic event after the collapse of Bretton Woods was Thatcher's big bang of sudden, massive financial deregulation in 1986. This was all about American investment banks, which came swaggering into London, laden with dollars. The flat-footed British players, who had grown complacent in their encrusted old boys' networks, were competitive roadkill. The Americans brought risky new ways of doing things too. A lot of City of London business had until then been done by partnerships, whose members got rich when things went well but who faced collectively losing their shirts in a disaster. The real possibility of personal bankruptcy tended to focus minds and encourage prudence. The American banks were often listed on stock exchanges, however, so while their managers could get very rich indeed on bonuses in good times, they weren't personally liable for failure, as they could dump the costs onto bank shareholders or wider society. Under this "heads I win, tails they lose" formula, a gambling culture took hold, rooted in what is called the "OPM attitude"—OPM being other people's money, and the attitude being that you should put as little of your money at risk as possible, while milking other people for theirs. The OPM attitude is arguably the biggest problem in financial markets today, and it can encourage spectacular recklessness.

All this was supposed to be held in check by regulators and the banks' risk and compliance officers, who were supposed to restrain the dangerous excesses and the money laundering. But those dogs didn't bark. When the UK's Financial Services Authority (FSA) challenged a British bank over a wealthy client from a(n unnamed) highly corrupt oil-rich country, the bank said it had been unable to find incriminating evidence on the client. The ensuing FSA report stated that "the first result of a simple Google search on the client's name linked the customer to serious and credible allegations of corruption." Company cultures made it clear who was in charge: the traders were the wolves, the tigers, the "rock stars, rainmakers, the dark side, movers and shakers, the big swinging dicks," as one anthropological study of the City found. The hapless compliance officers were the "business blockers, deal killers, show stoppers, box tickers." One compliance officer described himself as "a dog that likes to be kicked," while another compared himself and his colleagues to football linesmen, the "losers running back and forth along a line, stopping players from scoring or doing great things."[6]

The compliance officer's role in a bank wasn't so different between New York and London, but the Americans at least had another important set of backstops to curb excesses: some strong laws and the application of those laws. For instance, the Glass-Steagall Act of 1933, which separated investment banking from commercial banking, prohibited some of the riskier, more lucrative aspects of this from happening in the United States.[7] Yet in the UK, regulators were in thrall to a groupthink about financial risks that was similar to the ultra-libertarian attitudes of tax havens like the Caymans: sophisticated investors could look after themselves, and markets would sniff out trouble before it could happen, so clod-hopping regulators really should not try to second-guess what the clever, gentlemanly bankers were up to. Instead, regulators should simply promulgate "principles" of good behavior, then stand well back. The contrast between this "principles-based" regulation and the United States' potentially more stringent rules-based approach freed the UK to participate much more aggressively in the global race to the bottom. The rules of the European single market, which were launched in 1993, also meant that banks from around the world could set up financial instruments in London and sell them across Europe without interference from national regulators. German, French, Swiss, and Dutch banks, faced with rules at home that they didn't like, flocked to freewheeling London to join their American counterparts.

All these changes inevitably attracted another American import to London. Rowan Bosworth-Davies, a financial criminologist and former British fraud detective, describes a zoo of criminals arriving on his beat along with Wall Street culture: "a tidal wave of fraudsters, con men, financial snake-oil salesmen, and assorted ne'er-do-wells, all masquerading under the title of 'financial advisers,'" as he put it. "Get off the plane at Heathrow at 10 a.m. and you could be in business at 3 p.m.," he remembers.[8] "We started to see allegations of fraud coming through that we had never seen before . . . fraud in the derivatives markets, futures, options, that kind of thing. We started to see businesses set up in the City that were being run by mainstream US Mafiosi. Heavy American organized criminals." He continues, reeling off names: Arnold Kimmes, Tommy Quinn. "They were here to take advantage of the new relaxed atmosphere. We were talking to our friends in the US, particularly in the Manhattan District Attorney's office, and they'd say, 'So is *that* where he turned up? We wondered what happened to him.'"

Taking on these challenges, Bosworth-Davies says, made him feel like a salmon trying to swim upstream against a flash flood. On a work trip to America a regulator took him aside. "He said, 'The problem with you Brits is that you assume that everyone who handles other people's money is a gentleman. You are then shocked when you find out the converse is true. Here in America we assume everyone who handles other people's money has the potential to be a criminal. And we legislate for the possibility.'"[9]

Law and order was beneath the City of London grandees, and Bosworth-Davies's working-class accent and police background didn't help: in City of London circles, he says, he was treated with contempt, as a "nasty little Mr. Plod." He remembers giving a speech about money laundering in the City of London, then sitting down next to a top banker who said, "I listened with great interest to what you had to say, but I can assure you if you think Her Majesty's Government is ever going to prosecute people of my class, you are utterly mistaken. We are a protected species."[10] Compare this attitude in London to what had happened in the United States after the savings and loan crisis of 1989, the fruit of Reagan-era deregulation, which felled more than one thousand US "thrift" financial institutions and was the biggest series of bank collapses in the United States since 1929. Within six years of the crisis, more than 3,700 high-profile senior executives and owners of collapsed thrifts had gone to jail for fraud; the US Department of Justice secured convictions for over 95 percent of chief executives or presidents of their institutions who were charged. Prison terms added up to many thousands of years.[11] The comparison with Britain could not be more jarring.

The varieties of dangerous finance that were cooked up under the Queen's nose in this lawless atmosphere were inevitably numerous. But to understand London's central role in generating the global crisis, it is important to understand a couple of basic principles about how banks and bankers make money.

For centuries, banks had lent money out to companies or homeowners, who repaid these loans with interest, and they also borrowed money from depositors. Bankers used to speak of "3-6-3 banking," which meant paying 3 percent on deposits, lending money out at 6 percent, and being on the golf course by 3:00 P.M. If you can pay 3 and lend at 6, you can earn the difference—3 percent—for providing these useful services. Not quite, though, because you have to pay staff salaries, the costs of bank buildings, computers and other overheads—and take into account the fact that borrowers sometimes go bust and can't repay. Managing and understanding those latter risks traditionally involved quaint things like examining the company's balance sheet properly, researching the competitive environment it operated in, or taking a company's bosses to the golf course and looking into their eyes for signs of shifty thoughts. With all these overheads, a bank borrowing at 3 percent and lending at 6 percent might find its eventual returns wouldn't be 3 percent but 1 percent. That may not sound like much, but 1 percent of $10 billion lent out to companies is good money.

Banks are so important to the plumbing of our economies that government regulators also insist that they have safety cushions. They ought to have more assets (things of value that they own) than liabilities (what they owe to others); the safety cushion is basically the difference between the two—assets minus liabilities.[12] A bank's assets include things like cash, shares, property, computer equipment, and perhaps your mortgage (which entitles the bank to receive a long-term stream of payments from you, so it's a valuable thing). Bonds, which also promise a future repayment stream to those who have bought them, are also assets. Liabilities, on the other hand, include deposits and other things the bank owes to those who have lent to it. So if you deposit a $100 bill into your bank account, the bank physically has it but it is still your money, so it owes you that $100 and must give it back to you when you ask for it. Your deposit is counted as part of the bank's liabilities. The balance sheet of a bank is simply a document laying out assets and liabilities and the safety cushion between them. One side balances the other.

The safety cushion is called the bank's capital, and this—assets minus liabilities—should also be roughly what the bank's owners or shareholders think it is worth. If a company that has borrowed money from the bank collapses and that loan is written off, then the value of the bank's assets falls by that amount, all other things being equal; the difference between assets and liabilities falls, and the bank's shareholders absorb that loss. The bank's share price falls, but nobody other than its shareholders is harmed—yet. That's the safety cushion, working as it should. The trouble begins when the bank's capital falls to zero or, worse, the bank owes more than it expects to be able to pay back. Such a bank might collapse, potentially wreaking havoc across the financial system. Nobody wants that, so regulators insist banks have a big enough capital cushion, expressed as a share of their total assets, to prevent such a catastrophe. Of course many assets (like derivatives) are hard to value, which is why the balance sheets of banks have been called "the blackest of black holes," and in a market panic, assets can evaporate in minutes and, with them, all confidence in the bank. If a bank had a cushion worth just 2 percent of its assets, then a 3 percent fall in the value of those assets could wipe out the bank. That's what happened, on a global scale, during the financial crisis. So in any well-run economy, the safety cushions ought to be pretty large.

But modern bankers often hate such safety cushions, because they crimp the short-term profits that feed their bonuses. Imagine your bank has made $10 billion in loans (assets) and is earning a net 1 percent on them, or $100 million, this year. If your bank is forced to hold a cushion (shareholders' equity) worth 10 percent of its assets—$1 billion—then the shareholders earn $100 million on their billion, a lovely 10 percent annual return. But now imagine a different bank, also earning 1 percent on $10 billion in assets, but in a more lax jurisdiction where now the capital requirement is only 5 percent—so $500 million. A 1 percent return on $10 billion still earns $100 million, but this is now worth a much sexier 20 percent annual return on the shareholders' $500 million equity. Cut capital requirements to 2 percent ($200 million) and your returns jump to 50 percent. Just think: a 1 percent return on assets gets transmogrified into a 50 percent annual return for shareholders! This is a banking version of what they call "leverage"—think of a lever or crowbar, where a mild pull on the long end can create an immense force at the short end.

The key point here is this: the lower the capital that regulators require you to have, the bigger your profits—and your bonus. Cutting capital requirements from 10 to 2 percent could theoretically multiply your profits fivefold. And this inevitably leads to two great temptations. First, banks desperately try to reduce capital requirements, lobbying to water them down and dreaming up whizzy new techniques to sidestep the rules. Second, countries may try to lure greedy bankers with more "competitive" (or lax) capital requirements, then others may try to outdo them in laxity, and this can lead to a race to the bottom, driving down safety standards everywhere.[13]

And this is exactly what happened. Like the giant fish in Ernest Hemingway's classic novel *The Old Man and the Sea*, the safety buffers were relentlessly attacked by sharks and stripped of their meat until there was nothing left but a skeleton. And in each attack, lax London, urged on by hungry bankers, played a crucial role.

An early attack came in the 1980s, when worried US regulators sought to bash enough global heads together to tackle the race to the bottom on bank capital standards. The original global agreement on this was the so-called Basel Accord, the first of which was signed in 1988. The hard-nosed Paul Volcker of the Federal Reserve had insisted that international banks should have a capital cushion equivalent to 8 percent of their assets—so banks should not lend more than 12.5 times the value of their equity capital. Yet when Volcker went to Basel to discuss the accords with other central bankers, he found that European regulators, predominantly the British and the Swiss, were pushing a concept called risk-weighted capital.[14] Their argument was that some bank assets, like cash or US Treasury bonds, were safer than others, so it should be possible to set risk weights below 8 percent for them. It was agreed, therefore, that corporate loans would get a 100 percent risk weighting and residential mortgages a 50 percent risk weight, so a $100 mortgage loan required only a $4 capital cushion, 50 percent of the full $8. Loans to banks in other countries were considered even safer, under the gentlemanly assumption that counterpart regulators were doing a wonderful job, so these loans got a 25 percent risk weighting, meaning just $2 in bank capital for every $100 lent out. The general principle was reasonable, but it increased complexity and, with it, the possibility of mischief—and huge bank profits. It also had horrible side effects, encouraging banks to curb their lending to nonfinancial corporations— one of the most important functions of any useful financial system—in favor of homeowners and other banks and cross-border loans, which gobbled up less capital and thus generated more profits. These Basel risk weights unleashed enormous volumes of credit into housing markets, paving the way for the crisis.

Yet banks weren't content with cheeseparing down their safety cushions like this: they wanted more. So they deployed those two great financializing innovations, derivatives and securitization, to get around the remaining obstacles. At each stage, London and the British spider's web were delighted to help them.

Securitization emerged in its modern form in the United States in the 1970s. This happens when a bank takes income-generating assets like mortgages or government bonds, bundles them all together, and sells them to a special purpose vehicle, which is typically a company set up for a particular function—in this case, to buy and own these assets, and then parcel out all the payments and other financial flows associated with them. SPVs, usually located in an offshore jurisdiction like the Cayman Islands, are precisely tuned machines to determine exactly who gets how much and when. In contrast to a normal company, with its board of directors, annual general meeting, corporate governance codes, and managers' foibles and mistakes, the SPV is like a robot company, as the financial journalist Nicholas Dunbar explains:

> In the brave new world of securitization, that human element gets replaced with an engineered financial machine or structure, and for that reason it gets called *structured finance*. Unlike in a real company, where assets, revenues, and debt payments all involve real people and endless debate, the SPV doppelgänger is an android, programmed by a lawyer-crafted set of rules to mechanically transfer cash between various Cayman Islands mailboxes. In this world, the taxman is just another unpredictable creditor, best kept at bay by using a tax haven.[15]

Imagine one of these Cayman androids owns 1,000 residential mortgages, each worth an average $300,000 and each spitting out an average $1,500 in regular monthly mortgage payments, adding up to $1.5 million a month, or $18 million a year. To pay for the mortgages, the SPV borrows money by creating its own securities (valuable electronic pieces of paper, each promising a series of future payments) and selling them in tempting chunks to outside investors at a profit. In this example the bank keeps 10 percent of the SPV for itself.

Crucially, those mortgages don't belong to the bank anymore, because it has sold them to that Cayman SPV instead. So they are off the bank's balance sheet, for capital purposes. Had the bank instead gone old school and held on to the full $300 million worth of mortgages, with a 4 percent capital requirement it would have needed $12 million in capital tied up against those home loans, dragging on its profits. But with the SPV, the only thing it holds on its balance sheet now is the 10 percent of the SPV that it owns, so it must set aside only $1.2 million. By parceling up and selling off these mortgages to the SPV, the bank has (hopefully) made at least as much profit as if it had dealt with those mortgages the old-school way—but it now has used only a fraction of the capital. So it can crank the handle and do it again for a new round of profits. And again. It could, at least in theory, repeat the profitable trick ten times before it reached $12 million in capital under the old-school approach. Magically, bigger bonuses for everyone, along with (whisper it quietly) bigger risks in the financial system.

With securitization, banks could slalom around the bank capital rules. It wasn't just mortgages either; they securitized bonds, credit card repayments, vehicle finance payments, student loans, and all sorts of stuff. And it wasn't hard to find people to invest in these SPVs either. Financial deregulation was tipping a flood of money and credit into world markets, creating growing armies of cash-rich investors looking for places to put it all.[16] And here Europe—and especially British and other European banks in London—played another central role.

One of the traditional stories about the financial crisis goes like this. Chinese exports to the United States have been far greater than Chinese imports from the United States, and the resulting trade surplus generated a huge overhang of dollars in Chinese hands. So the Chinese invested these dollars in US financial assets, particularly government bonds and bills, and this was the main source of the global fount of money sluicing into the American securitization machine ahead of the crash. People paid less attention to Europe because it didn't have a big trade surplus to invest; net flows of financial capital between Europe and the United States were fairly modest. But behind this serene picture lay the fact that the *gross* flows each way were immense. Banks in Europe, and especially in London, were borrowing massive amounts of dollars from the United States then lending them back again into the US, often via tax havens like Ireland, in what the historian Adam Tooze calls "a transatlantic financial circulatory system quite independent of the trade connections between the two." US finance was no more reducible to Wall Street than the manufacture of iPhones, with Apple's world-spanning supply chains, was reducible to Silicon Valley. Transatlantic finance was a bigger deal than the Chinese trade surplus. Tooze continued: "the central axis of world finance was not Asian-American but Euro-American." The two great nodes of this financial circulator were New York and London. By the time the crisis hit, London would be turning over a trillion dollars' worth of foreign exchange deals—equivalent to a third of Britain's annual GDP—*every day*, and London was home to twice as many foreign banks as New York. The lack of a large transatlantic trade surplus was deceptive: like the balance of two adult elephants sitting at either end of a circus seesaw. Beneath the apparent calm lay massive latent tensions.[17]

To sweeten the attractions for these investors, the financial whizzes created some new water-into-wine mathematics to make the securities more attractive, and they browbeat, bullied, and corrupted the credit ratings agencies to get them the top rating, as low-risk vehicles. Their valuations invoked safety in numbers, the idea being that even if some loans defaulted, others wouldn't. The head of a Wall Street investment firm explained this idea to the finance writer John Cassidy: "You take hundreds of drunks staggering down the street, and you make them put their arms around each other's shoulders and lock hands. Then you rely on the fact that they are all falling in different directions to keep the entire group upright. Oh, and you call it a Triple A security."[18]

Parking SPVs offshore in places like the Cayman Islands made them even more enticing to cash-rich investors. Tax was crucial, of course; a layer of tax at the level of the SPV could wipe out the whole margin of profit. So the Caymans' zero-tax status was a huge plus. And the Caymans could often help the investors themselves escape tax too. What is more, nobody in the Caymans was going to ask any questions if wealthy organized criminals invested in your securities. At a more fundamental level, there was another reason to go offshore: because these offshore spaces are regulation-free. The Cayman Islands' entire model of financial legislation had always been to attract as much hot money as possible, while shaking off any associated risks. In the words of Anthony Travers, a stridently antigovernment British libertarian who helped construct the Cayman Islands' modern financial center, "the responsibility of the Cayman government was managed by avoiding the concept of prudential regulation."[19]

At the last count, the Cayman Islands' shadow banking sector held assets worth $5.8 trillion—equivalent to 170,000 percent of Cayman's GDP and over twice as big as the UK's GDP.[20] And anyone in the Caymans who challenges the dirty-money machine—a major feeder for the securitization business—comes up against terrifying mechanisms of administrative control in this financially captured British overseas territory. I heard about these control mechanisms when I interviewed a well-known local personality at his house in the Caymans in 2009. While talking, I heard a knock on the door, and a stocky, dark-skinned man walked in, wearing a polo shirt and sunglasses. He introduced himself as "the Devil" and declined to give me his real name; I still don't know it, but my host vouched for him. He had a background in international law enforcement and said his pseudonym reflected how he was viewed locally, due to his having investigated global crimes that should never have been touched. He spoke of arms dealers, international terrorists, and Cayman-based hedge funds, mutual funds, and SPVs, which he said were all thoroughly riddled with criminal money. He would not go into much detail but instead gave me a health warning: "If we discuss this with you, you will end up like Salman Rushdie. There are things here not to be discussed. I mean it—this is a wicked, vicious place." Transgressing the unwritten rules of the Caymans, he said, results in "economic isolation. They destroy your credibility and your integrity. They will strip you of your dignity. We operate here under a code of silence—*omertà*." He spoke of a local cabal of foreign financial interests, at which point our host interjected, saying this cabal was "spoken of in terms you'd speak of a ghost." Back in the United States, hedge funds and other investment vehicles have successfully beaten back efforts to get them to tackle money laundering. They are, as one money launder-ing expert said, "a black box to everyone involved."[21]

Fueled by shady money and various other gushers of global credit, and protected by the tax havens' anti-regulators, the London–New York securitization machine grew spectacularly.

Bank profits were growing spectacularly—but there was still a major hurdle holding them back: a shortage of raw materials in the form of mortgages and other streams of income that could be packaged up and fed into the securitization machine. Bankers were increasingly scraping the bottom to get hold of these things, as the Hollywood film *The Big Short* showed when the character played by Steve Carell encounters a young stripper who owns five houses and a condo. In the real world, an American bank whistle-blower, Michael Winston, recalls asking a colleague why his boss's car had a personalized license plate that read FUND-EM.

"We fund all loans," his colleague explained.
"What if the borrower has no job?" Winston asked.
"Fund 'em."
"What if they have no assets?"

"Fund 'em."

"No income?"

"If they can fog a mirror, we'll give them a loan."[22]

Banks had another problem too: their long-standing clients in the mainstream economy didn't much like being told that their loans had been sold off to an opaque SPV in the Cayman Islands. The banks wanted to find a way to keep these loans on their balance sheets, so they could say to their clients, "We're still your bank. We've kept your loans in house, so can you please do your next M&A [mergers and acquisitions] transactions with us?" yet *still* be able to dance around the capital requirements. In other words, to have their cake and eat it.

They solved that problem with one of the most dangerous strains of global finance ever invented. This scheme germinated in the summer of 1994, at a weekend get-together for JP Morgan staffers mostly from London, Tokyo, and New York at a luxurious hotel in Boca Raton, Florida. The usual drinking games went on; they hijacked golf carts and raced, giggling, around the lawns. Peter Voicke, a straitlaced German who was the most senior trader present, tried to calm them down; they pushed him into the pool. (His deputy got pushed in too and broke his nose.) Gillian Tett, a senior *Financial Times* journalist whose book *Fool's Gold* describes the episode in detail, said it wasn't possible to get a full account of the meeting because so many interviewees had "only the haziest, alcohol-fuddled memories."[23] Yet it was on this weekend that a new form of financial derivative was dreamed up, which would explode into the world's financial markets and later plunge the world economy into catastrophe.

A derivative is, in essence, a contract between two players whose value is *derived* from an underlying asset—maybe a barrel of oil, a government bond, or a bushel of wheat. Modern derivatives emerged around the 1850s in Chicago, a major center for storing and trading grain. Ahead of the harvest, a wheat farmer might agree to a contract with a speculator, which effectively locked in a future price for his wheat. For the farmer, this was like insurance, and for the speculator, it was like gambling. The idea proved popular and the market expanded steadily. By the 1970s it had branched far beyond wheat, eggs, and butter to include financial derivatives based on prices in foreign exchanges, interest rates, and other markets. By the 1990s, a kind of derivative called swaps was all the rage, in which you could swap one set of financial obligations for another. Let's say you've got a twenty-year fixed-rate mortgage, and your friend has a twenty-year floating-rate one. You think rates will fall, and she thinks they will rise. With a swap, you can agree to exchange your repayments: you will pay the floating rate for twenty years, and she will pay the fixed rate. Crucially, you don't actually exchange the mortgages; this is a purely financial arrangement overlaying the real economic activity, which is why these are called synthetic derivatives. And in fact, you can gamble by exchanging the swap payments without owning the underlying mortgages at all.

By the time the JP Morgan team met in Boca Raton in 1994, there were already an estimated $12 trillion in swaps outstanding, equivalent to the size of the US GDP. Concerns were being raised: a veteran banker had recently warned that such derivatives were "financial hydrogen bombs." The derivative concept that the JP Morgan team invented, the credit default swap (CDS), enabled market players to bet (or insure themselves) not against movements in the *price* of something, but against the possibility that a bond or a loan would *default*. And this unlocked a new world of profits. If a bank could keep loans on its balance sheet, then use CDSs to insure those loans against default, it would have a good case to take to the regulators. "These loans are fully insured," they could say. "They are much less risky, so we should get much more lenient capital requirements."

The JP Morgan whizzes hatched up a way to insure balance-sheet loans on a large scale, using a scheme they called Bistro. They would still use securitization—not to get the assets off their balance sheet this time, but instead to use those offshore androids to industrialize the process, transforming CDSs into new and more appetizing morsels precisely tweaked and tailored to the desires of global investors. And those investors, by buying those income-generating morsels, would effectively be insuring those loans still on JP Morgan's balance sheet. These new SPVs weren't filled with real-world mortgages but with credit default swaps—bets. Traditional securitization had begun to evolve into synthetic securitization.

Unlike traditional securitizations, which needed a constant supply of new underlying mortgages, these synthetic bets could be replicated without limit. This is because CDSs are just bets. If you bet on a horse in a race, that doesn't stop you from placing a second, bigger bet on the same horse in the same race; you don't need to find another horse or another race. Traders began to joke that Bistro stood for "BIS total rip-off"—referring to the Bank for International Settlements, which oversaw the Basel Accords. By the time the crisis hit, JPMorgan's exposure to CDSs and other credit derivatives would be more than five times the size of its balance sheet.[24]

But before their full power could be unleashed, a hurdle remained: regulators hadn't blessed the concept yet. Here, once again, the banks found help in the usual place, light-touch London. In 1997, the year that JP Morgan finally launched Bistro, the International Swaps and Derivatives Association (ISDA), a lobbying group for large financial players, was looking for someone to write a formal legal opinion about CDSs. Legal opinions of this kind are extremely important in regulatory terms: they act as a kind of semiformal blessing for the things that the players want to do. The opinion that ISDA wanted hinged on a simple but important question: Were CDSs bets, in which case they should be regulated and taxed under gambling laws, or were they insurance, in which case insurance regulators should get involved? Any sensible person could see that they were, of course, both bets *and* insurance, depending on which side of the trade you were on. In fact, some kinds of speculative CDSs are so dangerous that, as one commentator put it, regulation isn't enough: "the case for banning them is about as strong as the case for banning bank robberies."[25] But this wasn't the answer the ISDA was looking for. It knew that it wasn't just bankers in London who were infected with the Wild West, offshore-diving mentality: the legal profession was littered with such types too.

ISDA settled on a venerable British lawyer named Robin Potts, a well-known seller of his legal soul for money who was at home in the British tax havens. The chief justice of the Cayman Islands called Potts an "outstanding advocate."[26] David Marchant, a journalist who investigates tax haven scams and shenanigans with his Miami-based company, OffshoreAlert, took a different view. He recalled Potts trying unsuccessfully to have him jailed for contempt of court in the British overseas territory of Bermuda in 1999, after Marchant refused to identify sources for an article he had written. As Marchant put it, "[Potts] wasn't likeable, coming across as a weasel—the sort of guy you wanted to punch in the face. Generally, the pomposity that Potts and the other English barristers brought to the Bermuda courtroom was insufferable. Not much in terms of collective ability but an abundance of sneering arrogance and a comical sense of superiority."[27] In 1997 Potts helpfully provided ISDA with precisely the answer it wanted: CDSs weren't insurance *or* bets. This rubber-stamp for the nonregulation of CDSs in London opened the gates to unlimited, unregulated betting on credit defaults—the life and death of companies. "The business opportunities created by credit derivatives," purred Blythe Masters, a top member of the JP Morgan team, "are frankly staggering."[28]

Having obtained an effective exemption from regulation for these thrilling new instruments in Britain, the banks, wielding the London crowbar, then set about beating down US regulators. By then, banks not only could use derivatives or go offshore to find their escape routes, but they also had a third way, involving a different "competitive" game. The US financial system is overseen by a patchwork of regulators, each the fruit of some past financial crisis, and "regulator shopping" was all the rage, encouraging a "competitive" race to the bottom among US regulators, and with offshore jurisdictions, to degrade standards to attract "clients."

An ideological shift was under way too. Volcker had been replaced as the top US regulator by Alan Greenspan, an extremist libertarian who had said, channeling the wisdom of British tax havens, that laws against fraud weren't necessary because people would simply stop doing business with bad actors, and they'd soon be driven from the market. (It was a lesson he may have originally imbibed from the Bank of England, which had long held such views.)[29]

Greenspan joined deregulatory forces with President Clinton's Treasury secretary, the former Goldman Sachs banker Robert Rubin, and with Rubin's deputy Lawrence Summers, to form a Third Way–ish trio that cheered on the frenzy of financial innovation now exploding across the world's trading rooms.

In November 1999, a few months after Rubin had left his post to become the head of Citicorp, the new breed of American anti-regulators brought down their biggest trophy kill, the repeal of the Glass-Steagall Act, a singularly effective piece of antitrust legislation that had for six and a half decades prevented banks from gambling with depositors' money. If they did not pass this, Democratic senator Chuck Schumer thundered, London or other financial centers would surpass New York as the center of global finance. Summers gushed at the repeal ceremony that "this historic legislation will better enable American companies to compete in the new economy." Indeed it did, and the biggest beneficiary of the deregulation was Citicorp, which was allowed to merge with Travelers Group to create the global giant Citigroup. Indeed, the deregulation was designed to allow just that merger.[30] The losers would include smaller US banks—and America's population.

Regulation of derivatives was still a gray area, however, so an army of lobbyists, armed with the example of London and the offshore centers, mounted a blitzkrieg in Washington to bring it all aboveboard. The Commodity Futures Modernization Act of 2000 did the trick, explicitly removing the US government's right to regulate over-the-counter derivatives such as CDSs and other exotic financial instruments. This had been hurried along by a "president's working group," which asserted that deregulation was necessary to ensure that "US firms and markets are not at a competitive disadvantage relative to their foreign counterparties" and warned that any restraints "could discourage innovation and growth of these important markets and damage US leadership in these arenas by driving transactions off-shore."[31]

As ever, one "competitor" in particular was on everyone's mind: the City of London. As the US financial criminologist Bill Black said, in general terms "London is vital to Wall Street's ability to argue that it needs weak regulation. The City is the bogey man."[32]

Back across the Atlantic, also in 2000, Britain's regulator began approving aggressive risk models for Deutsche Bank and JP Morgan's London affiliates, which let them build up dangerous levels of borrowing that US regulators would never have given—yet. Other US banks soon piled in. Not long afterward, Goldman Sachs reached a deal with embattled US regulators for an arrangement that matched what London was offering. The next American domino had fallen, courtesy of the crowbar of the City.[33]

By the early 2000s, Greenspan's see-no-evil influence was all over Washington. But not all US regulators had fallen under his sway, and in 2004 a group of them flew to London to join international discussions on shoring up the Basel rules on banks' capital levels—rules that were by then already looking like a Swiss cheese. They arrived to discover that their top concerns weren't even on the agenda. In the end, the regulators effectively capitulated and agreed to what was, in effect, a privatization of bank regulation: the regulators would no longer calculate risk weightings but would let banks do their own calculations according to their own models, then tell regulators. They had moved from telling banks what to do to asking banks what they were doing. A member of the Fed team recalled pleading fruitlessly at the London meeting, "Look how little capital there is here. By any measure, you can't look at 800:1 leverage and say it's OK. I know it's not a true measure of risk. It just can't be true." But it was no good. In that committee room the international regulators "blew the last big chance to prevent a catastrophic financial disaster," explains derivatives expert Nicholas Dunbar. "Assailed by arbitrage from all sides, the erosion of Basel began to resemble a time-lapse movie of an elephant being consumed by maggots."[34]

The following year, in 2005, Britain's prime minister, Tony Blair, forcefully underlined the British anti-regulation approach in a widely noted speech. He slammed Britain's Financial Services Authority (FSA), which had been created by amalgamating nine specialized regulators, for being "hugely inhibiting of efficient business by perfectly respectable companies that have never defrauded anyone." The FSA's first chairman responded cringingly—though truthfully—that it applied "only a fraction of the resource applied by US regulators," and the FSA's *official* duties included "maintaining the competitive position of the United Kingdom" in financial services. The FSA chairman added, for good measure, "The philosophy of the FSA from when I first set it up has been to say, 'Consenting adults in private? That's their problem.'" At the same time, the contempt in the London banking community for American enforcement efforts against criminal and national security risks was as strong as ever. The year after Blair's speech, when the New York branch of UK-headquartered Standard Chartered Bank expressed concern about possible reputational damage from the London branch helping to cloak at least $250 billion in transactions violating sanctions against Iran, the reply from London was: "You f......g Americans. Who are you to tell us, the rest of the world, that we're not going to deal with Iranians?"

As the UK continued to lead the way down the slope of private recklessness and depravity, American banks gave steadily more global responsibility to their London offices, and American regulators scrambled to "compete" to stay abreast with London. Financial innovation proceeded apace across the Western world.[35]

In 1996, the year before Robin Potts wrote his eye-watering legal opinion on CDSs in London, there had been an estimated $150–$200 billion worth of CDSs out there, already a vast number. Ten years later, as the financial crisis began to bite, that number had risen three hundredfold, to over $60 *trillion*—roughly equivalent to the gross domestic product of planet Earth.[36]

This story, it turns out, is just one part of a far wider picture in which London served as the corrupting, deregulating, criminalizing crowbar that helped financial players jimmy open American public-interest regulation of finance. There's no space to mention all the many others, but a couple of big ones are worth explaining very briefly.

Another obstacle that faced the derivatives players was not with regulators but with the market itself. It was extremely hard to sell the ultra-safe super-senior tranches that the synthetic SPVs were issuing in large quantities, because they offered such tiny returns, so banks were struggling to get those parts of their balance sheets insured, and this meant they weren't getting the all-important capital relief. Who could solve this problem? Step forward a firm called AIG Financial Products (AIGFP), a buccaneering unit of the venerable insurance giant AIG based in London's hedge fund district of Mayfair. This unit was led by Joe Cassano, a former employee of Drexel Burnham Lambert, the collapsed US junk bond firm at the center of the savings and loan crisis in the 1980s. AIGFP agreed to earn just 0.02 cents for every dollar it insured each year, a tactic that has been compared to picking up pennies just in front of an advancing steamroller. (Cassano would take home 30 percent of those pennies for himself, netting $280 million between 2000 and 2008.)[37] This deadly unit was located in London because of its offshore approach of limited oversight and, Dunbar explains, as part of a complex transatlantic corporate structure to hide from the rules: "Each country thought others were dealing with it, and thought, 'What a relief we don't have to look at this thing.' And of course that was what AIG wanted."[38] When the crisis struck, AIG couldn't pay up on all the diseased financial instruments it had insured through its London affiliate, and the ensuing financial vortex would suck down the parent company with 115,000 employees in 130 countries and lead to the biggest government bailout in US history.

The other giant domino of the crisis was Lehman Brothers, which came to grief through a mechanism called repo, which is now central to the plumbing of global finance. Repo is an arrangement where one player deposits cash with a counterparty, and in exchange it gets collateral, like a government bond (or a securitized product from one of those Cayman androids), alongside a contract that says the bank will repurchase (repo) that collateral from the corporation very soon, often the next day or the next week, at a tiny premium equivalent to a day or a week's interest. To cut a very long and very squirrelly story very short, repo is another way for financial players to increase their profitable borrowing and lending to danger levels. And it is everywhere now. It interconnects most financial markets in trillion-dollar webs of tightly coupled relationships, linking government and corporate bond markets with central banking, securitization, taxes and spending, and more. It is so systemically important, in fact, that some people now call repo "shadow money." In times of crisis, all this interconnection makes repo a transmission mechanism for shocks, and wonks have described large parts of the global financial crisis as "a run on repo." It will underpin and amplify the next big crisis too.[39]

For a long time, US authorities could see the massive risks and refused to bless repo as a way to increase leverage without falling foul of capital requirements. But Lehman Brothers badly wanted to use it in this way. The company approached a few American law firms to get a legal opinion to support its case. None would oblige. By now it shouldn't be hard to guess where Lehman then went to get what it wanted. The London law firm Linklaters helpfully wrote the necessary opinion in 2001 and carefully mapped out a legal pathway for Lehman to make these trades through its affiliate in London.[40] Among other things, it used a technique called "Repo 105" to hide assets from investors, using the trades fraudulently to flatter their balance sheet just before they issued a quarterly report, then unwinding them again just afterward. A senior Lehman official said that Repo 105 was just "another drug we are on." When the crisis hit, it emerged that Lehman had used Repo 105 to remove some $50 billion of bad assets from its balance sheet. Lehman's auditors in London, Ernst & Young, earned a reported $150 million in fees for signing off on Lehman accounts between 2001 and 2008, which didn't mention repo. Jon Moulton, a venture capitalist, sums up Lehman's subterfuge: "They were jurisdiction shopping. They were trying to find the answer they wanted. They got it." They got it in London.[41]

And London played a second, bigger role in the repo market. When one player receives a government bond, say, in exchange for cash in a repo transaction, it can immediately pass that bond on to others in a second repo transaction. (This is called rehypothecation.) The receiver of that bond can then repledge it again, and so on. This is not like buying a car or a sofa, then selling it to someone else; when you sell someone a car, you can forget about it: it's now their problem. But with repo the cash and the collateral are still umbilically connected by those repurchase contracts, so as this collateral is passed onward from one player to the next, you create new daisy chains of leverage snaking across the system, with market players taking spreads and fees at each juncture and new risks building up all around the block, out of sight.[42] US rules restricted this practice tightly, but in London you could do this without limit. The longer the chain, the greater the risks. And any chain is only as strong as its weakest link. When the crisis hit, these hidden chains of rehypothecation across the financial system made it impossible for anyone—regulators or market players—to have any idea how much of this stuff was really out there. According to the IMF, the shadow banking system (that is, the parts of the financial system that fall outside traditional banking regulation) turned out to be a full 50 percent bigger—nearly $5 trillion bigger, that is—than the regulators had thought.[43]

When the crisis hit, regulatory capture and deregulation had become so deep and powerful in the United States that a casual observer might conclude that America had finally caught up with Britain in the deregulatory race. Not so—not even close. My exhibit A here is a remarkable lobbying document issued by New York City mayor Michael Bloomberg and Senator Chuck Schumer in January 2007, just months ahead of the first shocks of the crisis. Entitled *Sustaining New York's and the US' Global Financial Services Leadership*, its core argument rested on two words. One was "London," which it mentioned 135 times in as many pages, and the second was "competitive" (or variations of that word), with more than two hundred mentions.[44] New York was losing out in a great global race with the City of London and other financial centers, and it was urgent to keep up with London's "more amenable and collaborative regulatory environment" through massive further financial deregulation. "While our regulatory bodies are often competing to be the toughest cop on the street," the authors urged in an article complementing the document, "the British regulatory body seems to be more collaborative and solutions-oriented." New York was still "in the lead" in terms of size, the anxiety-inducing summary said, but London was "ahead" of the United States in many areas, like derivatives. America risked being "marginalized" in this "ultra-competitive global marketplace." The solution: relax regulations, stop policing financial markets, and chase London down into the vortex.[45]

Two months later the City of London issued its Global Financial Centres Index, announcing that, according to its own analysis, London had "a narrow lead over New York." It mentioned the home of Wall Street ninety-two times and the same C-words more than two hundred times: the UK government had to act urgently to ensure that a "'tipping point' was not reached."[46] The answer was even more deregulation in London. In June, Gordon Brown, Blair's chancellor, joined the financial lovefest, congratulating a group of City financial and political bigwigs on "an era that history will record as the beginning of a new golden age for the City of London." He crowed about having resisted pressure to tighten financial regulations in the wake of the Enron and WorldCom disasters, praising himself and his audience with messianic zeal:

> Your success is critical to that of Britain's overall, and consider-
> ing together the things that we must do—and, just as important,
> things we should not do—to maintain our competitiveness . . . I

believe it will be said of this age, the first decades of the twenty-first century, that out of the greatest restructuring of the global economy, perhaps even greater than the Industrial Revolution, a new world order was created.[47]

Within weeks the British bank Northern Rock had collapsed. The global financial crisis had finally arrived.

I won't spend much time picking through the rubble strewn across the global economy since the crisis—that's another story entirely. The response from regulators in Britain and the United States has been a complex, messy patchwork of missteps and failures under an overarching strategy on both sides of the Atlantic, under Democrats and Republicans, Labour and the Conservatives, to protect the financial system and to shovel the pain onto ordinary people. The fallout highlights a crucial aspect of the finance curse: it has had powerful geographical, racial, and gender dimensions. Between 2007 and 2010, for example, the average net worth of American households fell by nearly 20 percent, to around $460,000. But these numbers are skewed by extreme wealth concentration at the top, and behind this all-America average lies a very different story. The median household—that is, the household that sits at the center of the national wealth distribution, which is less likely than the average to be urban, less likely to be white, and more likely to be headed by a woman—saw its net worth nearly halved, from $108,000 to $57,000. The median white household saw its wealth fall by 35 percent, the median African American household suffered a fall of 50 percent, and the median Hispanic household lost over 85 percent.[48] The winners from the boom and bust—those mostly in the financial sector who made huge fortunes during the go-go years and got poorer taxpayers to bail them out—were mostly white men based in urban areas. Third Way Democrats had, in pursuit of the big money, jettisoned large parts of the American working class, hoping to make this up by appealing to these other constituencies. Those very constituencies ended up being the biggest losers.

It's fair to say that Britain's broad population generally has a more progressive and egalitarian outlook than America's, so popular outrage there has been larger, which has helped counteract the fact that Britain's political system and establishment have been even more deeply corrupted by finance than America's has. The messy result is that neither country has clearly done a worse job than the other of cleaning up finance and its regulation after the crisis. But there is one all-important area where Britain remains a clear, undisputed winner: when it comes to dirty and criminal money. It's impossible to wrap your mind around the scale of this; I must resort to a few statistics, quotes, and anecdotes to illustrate how bad things have been.

At the time of this writing, US authorities had levied over $150 billion in fines just for activities related to the financial crisis out of a world total of over $320 billion for all activities. In comparison, the UK's financial regulatory authorities had imposed $3.5 billion in fines on financial institutions between 2007 and 2018—yet that was *all* fines, including for run-of-the-mill misreporting or bad governance practices by small-fry brokers, payment protection frauds, insurance companies, the LIBOR scandal, and the like. I cannot find *any* fines, anywhere, clearly related to the causes of the global financial crisis. Zero. When British banks have had to pay big fines, it's nearly always been the American authorities doing the fining. In the United States more than 350 people had been criminally convicted and more than 250 sent to prison by July 2018 just for misusing bailout money. In Britain there had been five convictions with prison sentences—yet those were for rigging the LIBOR markets, not for financial crisis–related activities.[49]

US authorities have engaged in immense and detailed public grillings and inquiries in the wake of the crisis, while the UK government has washed its hands, at best setting up secretive inquiries that end up going nowhere. A probe into AIG in 2009 was dropped on the grounds of insufficient evidence, and its passing caused hardly a ripple in the

UK media or anywhere else. And when the United States has tried to prosecute British banks, it has met fierce resistance from London. Take HSBC, for instance, which took money from Russian gangsters, organizations linked to al-Qaeda and Hezbollah, and sanctions-busting North Koreans, and helped launder at least $880 million for Mexico's Sinaloa drug cartel[50]—people so evil, joked former New York attorney general Eliot Spitzer, "they make the guys on Wall Street look good."[51] A congressional inquiry into the US Department of Justice's decision in 2012 not to prosecute HSBC found that British chancellor George Osborne and the Financial Services Authority had actively interfered at the highest levels of the US government and justice system, threatening "global financial disaster" if "their" bankers were prosecuted. London's intervention, the report said, "hampered the US government's investigations and influenced DOJ's decision not to prosecute HSBC."[52]

Americans worry about the influence of crooked Russian money on their financial system: this is nothing when compared to what has been happening in London, where oceans of money from the former Soviet Union, cycled through British tax havens like the British Virgin Islands, flooded into high-end real estate, top football clubs, think tanks, universities, and the pockets of many government officials. A PwC report on Russian initial public offerings (IPOs)—companies being floated on the stock market—found that between 2005 and 2014 there were two listings on the New York Stock Exchange, thirty-seven in Moscow, and sixty-seven on the London Stock Exchange. Bernd Finger, a German former policeman specializing in mafia and organized crime, told me in 2017 that in his experience of trying to trace criminal assets, the German authorities usually got good cooperation from other countries, including the United States, with two notable exceptions: Russia and Britain. Treaties require the Brits to provide information when asked, he said, "but they simply do not answer." When French authorities investigating major money laundering and tax fraud in a large telecom firm asked the UK tax authorities for assistance, they received an *official* letter stating that the firm was "a large multinational company" with "vast assets at their disposal" and would be "extremely unlikely to agree to having their premises searched. . . . It is of note that they are the biggest corporate donor to the Conservative Party."[53]

Britain is the country of first choice for every kleptocrat and dictator in the world. People and institutions operate "as though they are beyond the reach of the criminal law," said Britain's former top prosecutor. "If you mug someone in the street and you are caught, the chances are that you will go to prison. In recent years mugging someone out of their savings or their pension would probably earn you a yacht."[54]

And so, it seems, would mugging a whole country—and indeed half the world.

CHAPTER EIGHT

Wealth and Its Armor

If you've got money sitting in a checking or savings account in the United States, the chances are that it's backed by the Federal Deposit Insurance Corporation (FDIC), a body set up to protect customers after the crash of 1929, and if your bank or banks go bust, the government will make sure you get up to $250,000 of your money back. The FDIC's website, though, contains some curious statistics. Financial institutions headquartered in America's four most populous states—New York, California, Texas, and Florida—held about $2.5 trillion of FDIC-insured assets among them in 2018, or around $25,000 per inhabitant. But there is a bigger player in this game, a state that hosts more than all these giant states combined. That state is South Dakota, whose population of fewer than a million people boasts $3.2 trillion in FDIC-insured assets.

Sioux Falls, South Dakota, which many financial institutions officially record as their home, is an unassuming Midwest town of fewer than 200,000 people.[1] Within a half hour or so you can walk a circuit of its tiny downtown, which has none of the glitz or scale of big metropolitan areas within a few hours' driving distance: Minneapolis, Kansas City, Des Moines, or Omaha. Tourist guides strain to squeeze out the superlatives: they highlight a 1,600-year-old Native American cemetery; some falls on the Big Sioux River in the center of town, which are only just too dangerous to kayak over; an eighteen-foot replica of Michelangelo's *David*; the butterfly house and aquarium; the airport (where frankly there isn't that much to see); and, perhaps, the birthplace of January Jones, the actress who plays Betty Draper in the television series *Mad Men*. The most exciting attraction is probably a plaque on a bank building celebrating a robbery there by the Dillinger gang in 1934, where Baby Face Nelson shot an approaching motorcycle cop and the gang members forced five bank employees to stand on the running boards of their car as human shields, as they escaped with $49,500 in swag. Today, the biggest bank buildings are a workaday six or seven stories high: grand enough by local standards, but still less impressive than the Minnehaha County courthouse down the road. The thirty-thousand-odd financial jobs across the state make up less than 7 percent of non-farm employment.

The contrast between Sioux Falls' giant banking statistics and its rather down-at-the-heels character can be explained with a single word: "offshore." To be precise, South Dakota has since the 1980s deregulated and tailored its laws to attract out-of-state financial business, and that's why there aren't any chrome-and-glass skyscrapers here: most of what has emerged here is a result of this letterbox activity for much bigger business that really happens elsewhere. Those banking customers don't visit in person but virtually, via interbank payment systems and accountants' spreadsheets. A lot of what happens here is low-level secretarial activity. Peering in the side windows of some of the bank buildings, I was reminded of Ugland House in the Cayman Islands, an unimpressive five-story block nominally housing around twenty thousand global shell companies (which Barack Obama once famously called "either the biggest building in the world, or the biggest tax scam"), or of the (even seedier-looking) low-rise at 1209 North Orange Street in Wilmington, Delaware, which is the legally registered office of more than 250,000 companies, including Coca-Cola, Kentucky Fried Chicken, Apple, Deutsche Bank, American Airlines, and many belonging to both President Trump and his former opponent Hillary Clinton. Companies can pay tiny fees to register here, then operate across the United States while qualifying to be treated under Cayman's or Delaware's low-tax, low-scrutiny, low-regulation, high-secrecy laws.

South Dakota's game of bank deposits got off the ground in 1980, when the state passed a statute removing interest rate caps: until then, interest rates had been carefully regulated to prevent usurious interest rates for borrowers and predatory lending. The new statute was, in the words of one of the central players in the drama, "basically written by Citibank," and in short order Citibank, Wells Fargo, and several others had set up shop here, bringing thousands of local jobs (including for the state governor's chief of staff, who left to become president and CEO of Citibank South Dakota). Like Delaware or the Cayman Islands, South Dakota's small size made it an ideal candidate for "state capture," where cross-border financial interests are easily able to overwhelm standard democratic checks and balances to get these places to write or rubber-stamp laws in their favor. In South Dakota's case (as in Delaware, which followed suit in removing interest rate caps the following year), the banking statute got bipartisan support and faced almost no opposition, and the end result was the classic offshore pattern: some local benefits in exchange for harm to certain people elsewhere. "We didn't do any favors for borrowers around the country, but it has been good for South Dakota," Bernie Hunhoff, a former legislator, explained. "It is [a bit] like opening a casino. . . . [I]f it's legal then you probably should try to get the benefits, because if you don't the town down the road will do it."[2]

While the FDIC insures huge sums in bank deposits in Sioux Falls, there is another financial game in town that provides protection of a very different, more indiscriminate, and, in many ways, more powerful kind: protection of the assets and secrets of some of America's richest families. The offices that provide these services are far more discreet, yet you can find them if you know where to look. The biggest and brassiest of them sits on South Phillips Avenue in downtown Sioux Falls, opposite the Vishnu Bunny Tattoo & Piercing parlor, next to a three-story concrete car park. This is the home of the South Dakota Trust Company LLC, which sets up and handles private trusts and trust companies, including those of a branch of Chicago's Pritzker family; the descendants of the banker Clarence Dillon, who cofounded the Wall Street juggernaut Dillon, Read & Co.; the heirs of William Wrigley, of chewing-gum fame; and the Minnesota-based Carlson family, which controls the Radisson hotel chain. You wouldn't guess it from looking at this building, but at the time of this writing its website declared that trust accounts held in these offices handle over $50 billion worth of assets connected to some four hundred billionaires and centimillionaires. There's almost no useful centralized data stored on trusts anywhere in the United States or anywhere else, but there are known to be many trillions of dollars' worth of wealth sitting in them worldwide, serving an array of functions such as helping banks keep assets off their balance sheets for regulatory purposes and helping the world's richest people avoid paying tax. The benefits to South Dakota from this sector are extremely modest: at the last count, this industry earned just 0.06 percent of state tax revenues and saw just 0.02 percent of its workforce directly employed in the trusts business;[3] and although there may have been some further trickle-down effects, it isn't much: one of South Dakota's selling points is that you don't need to live or operate there to benefit from its trust laws. The harms that South Dakota has inflicted on its people by undermining the federal tax system may well more than counteract these small local gains from jobs or employment.

To understand why South Dakota has become a magnet for trusts, it is necessary to go down a mazelike financial rabbit hole, which gets weirder the further you go down into its inner workings and back into its historic depths. The basic idea of the trust emerged in the Middle Ages, when English knights and nobles went off to fight in the Crusades. They often left their lands and properties in the hands of trusted stewards, who were supposed to manage them for the benefit of the knights' families until they returned. Sometimes, though, a knight would come home to find that his steward didn't want to hand his property back after all, and maybe had also screwed the knight's wife or daughters (or sons) while he was off risking his neck for the pope.[4] So the departing fighters took to making their stewards swear oaths of loyalty to these arrangements under threat of fire and brimstone, sometimes in the presence of sacred relics. The prospect of spending eternity surrounded by demons and pitchforks tended to focus stewards' minds, but it was still a messy business, and over time a body of enforceable trust law grew up, which endures today.

A classic trust is a three-way relationship. First, there's the original grantor of the assets—in the old days a knight, but today it's maybe a billionaire grandfather who bequeaths or places assets into a trust before he dies. Second, there's the trustee, the person who looks after those assets—historically it would usually have been a trusted family member, though today the trustee is likely a skilled lawyer. The third group comprises the beneficiaries—typically the knight's (or the grandfather's) family, who benefit from the trust assets. This is all tied together with a trust deed, a detailed agreement that regulates who is to get what, when, how, and under what conditions. This deed can be enforced in court. So a trust isn't really an entity like a company; it's a legal arrangement, more like a contract. The assets in a trust can be anything: a couple of Swiss bank accounts, ten gold bars, a castle in France or luxury apartments in Manhattan, a portfolio of tech shares, a valuable patent, half a commercial porn empire, a bunch of SPVs registered in the Cayman Islands, the rights to a terrible pop song, or several Delaware and British Virgin Islands shell companies that in turn own all of these things or own other shell companies that own these things. Anything really. This basic structure—grantor, trustee, beneficiaries, assets, trust deed—is the first level of the rabbit hole.

The alchemy of trusts—the next level down—begins when the grantor gives those assets away, and the very concept of ownership begins to separate out into different components: technical legal ownership versus the right to consume, enjoy, or control the assets. Usually the trustee is the legal owner, which enables him to sign documents, make transfers, and so on, following the terms of the trust deed. But this is a narrow slice of ownership; the trustee cannot legally run off with the assets or earn from them beyond carefully agreed management fees. (If he tries, other parties to the trust can sue in court to get them back.) The beneficiaries have other rights over the assets. Maybe the trust gives the old man's grandson the legal right to live in that castle, and Grandpa's second daughter to get half the income from the royalties on that terrible pop song when she is twenty-one, while an ex-wife gets the legal right to use the old man's yacht any time (except Thursdays, when Grandpa uses it to entertain his mistress) and is entitled to receive income from a portfolio of Facebook shares, but she can't sell the shares themselves. It's like pouring liquid assets into a cup: favored people may be allowed to sip from it, but they can't take away the cup itself. Maybe the trustee gets discretion to dole things out as he sees fit under more general, cozy guidelines from Grandpa. But in general terms, Grandpa has given the assets away, other people get to manage them, and others get to use or benefit from them.

Once Grandpa has given those assets to the trust, they are literally, legally, no longer his, and if he has set the trust up properly, he has created an all but impenetrable legal barrier. His tax authorities or creditors can huff and puff, but they can't get at those assets or the associated income. They're gone. This legal separation can be far more powerful than just the fact of having hidden the assets in a tax haven. And when Grandpa dies there couldn't be any inheritance or estate tax on the assets, because they weren't his and there isn't anyone to inherit them immediately either; the assets may just carry on, unmolested, safe inside the trust, not really "owned" by anyone. You've maybe seen that Patek Philippe watch advertisement in the glossy magazines, where a handsome father stands with his well-groomed young son in a vineyard or at the helm of an oak-paneled speedboat. The caption is "You never actually own a Patek Philippe, you merely look after it for the next generation." If that watch is held in a trust, then the caption is literally true. Trusts, especially offshore trusts, can be used to shield assets and income from tax authorities, from the forces of law and order, from divorced spouses, from Grandpa's irate creditors—from all sorts of people who might otherwise have a reasonable claim on them.

A lot of people who aren't familiar with trusts find this all rather odd; it seems like serious overkill if Grandpa has to *give away* his assets just in order to, for example, escape paying tax on them. As an English wealth manager in Hong Kong once put it,

> When you propose to an elderly Chinese gentleman, "Look, I'll tell you what, how about you give me control of your assets and I'll hold on to them for you and your kids until you need them, at which point I may or may not give the assets to you? And by the way, you'll be paying me a hefty fee all the while," the elderly Chinese gentleman laughs very hard for a long time.[5]

To understand why trusts are so attractive, one needs to get an idea of their extraordinary power and flexibility. Grandpa, or the elderly Chinese gent, may be able to have his cake and eat it by only *appearing* to give away the assets, erecting that essential legal fortress wall between himself and them, but then, with the help of a lawyer, creating discreet legal passageways, guards, permissions, and code words to allow him back into the castle, to carry on with the feasting and the bacchanalia, and retain a high degree of control, letting family members and others get a piece of the action, in carefully controlled ways.

Governments, of course, fret endlessly about how trusts can help a small, wealthy section of society escape many of the most important rules and laws that bind the rest of us. So they try to put in place defenses against some of the abuses that trusts facilitate. The IRS, for instance, can reach into some trusts and tax some assets and associated income, and it tries to put limits on how much any one individual can contribute. This all becomes very tricky very fast, depending on how the trust was set up and for what purpose; where the grantor, the trustee, the trust, or the beneficiaries are located; and a host of other factors. And all this complexity is good news for the South Dakota Trust Company LLC, because its job is to help clients craft careful pathways around the laws, without actually breaking the laws—and also to help influence and mold the laws themselves, which can be rather easy to do in a small state like South Dakota. And this ongoing game of chess between government and the top 0.1 percent of US society brings us to a third, deeper level of the rabbit hole of trusts.

The person who may have done more than anyone else to build up the trusts sector in South Dakota is Pierce McDowell III, president of the South Dakota Trust Company, who spoke to me at his offices in Sioux Falls in October 2018. A sprightly and infectiously cheerful sixty-year-old with graying curly hair and twinkly eyes, McDowell clearly gets a kick out of his job, confessing impishly that "I still don't know what I want to do when I grow up." His office wall contains a framed yellowing newspaper front page describing the Dillinger gang's 1934 robbery at the Security National Bank down the road, when Baby Face Nelson stuck a tommy gun in the belly of McDowell's grandfather, then a trust officer at the bank.

The trusts game in South Dakota kicked off in 1993 when McDowell wrote an article for *Trusts & Estates* magazine entitled "The Dynasty Trust: Protective Armor for Generations to Come." This word "armor" is, in fact, often found in the literature of trusts and wealth management. An advertisement from the world's most influential wealth-protection body, the Society of Trust and Estate Practitioners (STEP), shows an armed knight in chain mail standing before a couple of large bags of money, his hand raised defiantly. The caption reads, "Armor for your Assets." This image effectively conveys what trusts do, though the terms commonly used by trust lawyers—"firewall," "protection from attack," "impregnable," "shelter," "shield," and so on—suggest a slightly different medieval image: the castle or fortress. And these castles have guards. STEP is, depending on your perspective, a vast repository of top-class professional expertise or, as a jaded offshore lawyer put it to me in 2017, "a snake with many heads."

McDowell's article in 1993 concerned the rule against perpetuities, an arcane but powerful democratic curb to stop large concentrations of wealth from passing down family bloodlines from generation to generation inside trusts. This rule, which had strong and enduring bipartisan support, generally limited a trust's existence to the lifetime of a living heir, plus twenty-one years—after which time the trust would die and the assets would be ejected from it and suffer, among other things, the indignity of the estate tax, historically often above 50 percent. McDowell informed readers of what was then a little-known fact: South Dakota had recently abolished the rule against perpetuities, so its trusts could endure for a thousand years—or forever. Wisconsin and Idaho had also repealed their rules, but South Dakota had no state, corporate, or income tax and no tax on investment earnings either. South Dakota's colorful Republican state governor Bill Janklow had delivered the repeal after commissioning a study laying out the offshore possibilities of attracting out-of-state trusts business, with the bonus that the out-of-towners wouldn't be actually coming to live in South Dakota, so the state wouldn't need to pay for their kids' schooling or improved roads. The rule had been repealed quietly in the early 1980s, with pretty much no opposition from Democrats or Republicans, but it wasn't until McDowell's 1993 article that people started paying proper attention. Citibank, with its network of private bankers and wealth-management networks across the country, quickly hired McDowell in its trusts division—and in short order South Dakota was on the map.

Mark Meierhenry, a veteran Sioux Falls lawyer, former state attorney general, and a Republican who still believes in quaint old traditions of fair opportunities and a level playing field in the markets, was aghast. "I think it's a horrible idea for mankind, perpetual trusts," he said. "My party used to believe that the free enterprise system needs government to ensure equality of opportunity. You can't have that if you allow all this inherited wealth. Take the Trump children. Do we really want people like them to be our rulers? We looked at Europe, we said that part of the problem was all these kings and principalities, and we put in our constitution that we wouldn't have that."[6]

But in South Dakota, the simple offshore calculation put dollar signs in legislators' eyes and won the day. And, as with most offshore facilities, a race to the bottom got under way, as other states abandoned or curbed their rules against perpetuities (When I say "curbed" I am being generous—states like Alaska, Colorado, Utah, and Wyoming now limit the life of a trust to one thousand years). And to stay ahead, South Dakota has made constant "competitive" tweaks to its trusts legislation ever since, steadily shaping it into ever purer, stronger, and more billionaire-friendly forms. "Every year, we go through and analyze what other states are doing and what we can do better [to stay ahead] of the curve of a fast-moving landscape," said Bret Afdahl, director of the South Dakota Division of Banking. "We're always looking for subtle differences."[7] Within twenty years of McDowell's article, more than half of US states had followed suit, abandoning or curbing the rule against perpetuities. "The argument in this race to the bottom was 'Delaware is doing it; we just don't want those son of a bitches from Delaware getting all the dough,'" said Meierhenry. "Why should I be good if they're not? This is how morals break apart. We lost our minds."

Adam Hofri-Winogradow, a lecturer at the Hebrew University in Jerusalem, says this race to the bottom, which pits US states against offshore jurisdictions like the British Virgin Islands, is leading to a "stripping of the trust"—where legal provisions that are supposed to protect society from the most damaging asset-protection mechanisms are being whittled away, at each step sending America further along the road toward plutocracy.[8] By 2018, just three families—the richest seven Waltons of Walmart, the two Koch brothers of Koch Industries, and the six Mars family members from the Mars candy empire—owned around $350 billion in wealth, more than four million times the wealth of the median American household. A good chunk of this is tied up in trusts, foundations, tax havens, and other wealth-protection mechanisms.

And as these mechanisms have proliferated to help billionaires dodge taxes, the IRS itself has been under attack from another angle. This attack really got going in the late 1990s, when Senator William Roth of Delaware led a series of public hearings on the IRS in the Senate that were like show trials. IRS officials testified behind black curtains with their voices electronically distorted, as if they were mobsters afraid of being whacked. There was false testimony that IRS agents had forced girls at a slumber party to change their clothes at gunpoint "under the watchful eyes of male agents" and lurid tales of an agency generally run amok. The newspapers lapped it up—"Witnesses Accuse IRS Investigators of 'Gestapo-like' Raids" was one headline, and many of the raciest stories were only later revealed to be lies, long after everyone had lost interest. Today the IRS is down to fewer than ten thousand revenue agents, fewer than it had in 1953, when the economy was one-seventh of its current size and the wealth-management industry was a friendly minnow compared to today's kraken. These days the IRS often doesn't go after rich clients who they know are likely breaking the law, because resources are so tight. "It's like in the fall when you bob for apples," said Pam Reicks, a former manager at the IRS who, until she retired in 2017, oversaw a program to audit wealthy taxpayers with offshore bank accounts. "You've got a tub of apples and can't use your hands to grab them. You can see all this abuse and fraud, and people not paying their taxes, but can't use your hands to get it." As a result, all sorts of aggressive shenanigans that go on in trusts now get overlooked. These trends in trusts, and the way they are used to siphon money out of local economies for the benefit of wealthy folk in places like New York or Silicon Valley, go a fair way toward explaining why states like Mississippi have a life expectancy comparable to that in Saudi Arabia or Morocco.[9]

The tricks and alchemy that offshore jurisdictions and the wealth-management industry use to get what they want for their clients can seem simple, but the more you investigate, the more bewildering they can become.

One of the most straightforward offerings is secrecy. There are many flavors of this, especially if you can combine trust secrecy with tax haven secrecy. South Dakota's most unusual offering here is a "total seal forever" law, meaning that when disputes over billionaire South Dakota trusts erupt in the courts, lawyers can move to keep all the proceedings secret forever—an "unbelievable" perk, as Meierhenry put it: such secrecy is only otherwise invoked to protect juveniles or in highly inflammatory marital disputes where it's *really* nobody else's business. (Delaware, the main other state to do this, allows only a three-year seal.) A slightly more mystifying feature of the trusts game concerns the fact that individuals and families have been subjected to a lifetime limit of how much they can put into trusts. This limit was $600,000 for an individual and $1.2 million for a married couple when McDowell wrote his 1993 article—a limit that was steadily raised, then doubled under the Trump tax cuts to $11.2 million for an individual and $22 million for a couple.

Yet if billionaires may contribute only these relatively modest sums, how come some of their trusts contain many billions of dollars? (At the end of 2016, South Dakota's trusts sector alone held over $230 billion in assets.) Some of the most important answers to this are fairly straightforward. One is the simple mathematics of compound interest applied to long periods of time: an asset that grows at 10 percent a year, for instance, will have grown nearly 120 times as large after fifty years. Another reason is that some of these trusts are held by foreigners, who aren't subject to a gift limit. But a third reason is sneakier. The trick here is to put in a volatile, speculative asset (like a dot-com stock ahead of an IPO) that's got a very low value now, so it easily skips past the contribution limit, but then grows massively once it's safely inside the trust, where there are no restrictions on how much value it can accrue. (This is similar to a trick the Republican presidential candidate Mitt Romney appears to have used to get over $100 million into his individual retirement account, many multiples above the contribution limits.)[10] McDowell describes this practice as "getting the asset through the eye of a needle," then watching its value explode. A common version of this is the Walton GRAT (grantor retained annuity trust), named after Audrey Walton, whose wealth derives from Walmart. With these vehicles, you put money or assets into the trust but arrange to receive an agreed rate of interest and to get the amount you originally contributed returned to you at a fixed later time. Since you will definitely get out exactly what you put in, including interest, there's no overall gift, so no gift tax. But any excess profits those volatile investments may make above the interest rate can stay in the trust, untaxed, and pass to heirs. The casino mogul Sheldon Adelson used at least fourteen GRATs to pass at least $7.9 billion to his children, avoiding $2.8 billion in gift and estate taxes. In the 2018 midterms, he broke spending records with over $100 million in campaign donations. Facebook's Mark Zuckerberg and the lesser billionaire Lloyd Blankfein, the outgoing head of Goldman Sachs, are both known to have used GRATs.[11]

South Dakota specializes in another kind of vehicle, the directed trust, which takes us a little deeper into the rabbit hole. McDowell remembers that when he worked in Citibank's trusts division, the bank was keen to manage as many aspects of the trust as possible and promoted its own management services and investment advice alongside the trust structure, so the bank could milk all sorts of additional service fees from the users of the trust. But McDowell and colleagues began pushing the idea of the directed trust, which was first developed in offshore tax havens, then came to Delaware in 1986, then to South Dakota in 1997. In this arrangement, the decisions about asset allocations, investment management, and distributions are taken out of the bank's hands and passed back to the "trust protector" (effectively controlled by Grandpa or his family). "I did not endear myself to the bank's management," said McDowell—and indeed, his job was terminated soon afterward. The South Dakota Trust Company that he cofounded would be merely the "administrative trustee," to make sure tax laws were complied with, to do the accounting properly, to manage bank accounts correctly and make distributions, but to otherwise leave the real decision-making and investment strategies to the family. McDowell's crucial role is to ensure the trust has a "real" trustee, independent from the family, without which it couldn't be called a trust and would fall apart into a set of assets simply owned by some rich folk, back in society.

Giving the wealthy family more control over the assets in a trust can confer huge advantages, including the ability to manipulate matters to inject more low-balled assets through that all-important eye of the needle. Playing this game recklessly and aggressively could easily get you into trouble with the courts or the IRS, if you're not careful, and McDowell said his outfit is conservative ("We've turned down a lot of business, we want to be on the high road," he said), but there are shadier outfits in South Dakota and elsewhere that are happy to stretch the law—up to the breaking point and beyond. The less government regulation and oversight, the more this will happen.

These examples show the cat-and-mouse nature of trusts and their regulation and some of the sly pathways around things like the estate tax. But to get a still deeper sense of their mystery and power, it helps to go offshore—properly offshore, to some of the world's small islands that have forged furthest ahead in the race to the bottom.

Nobody has ever calculated how much wealth is held in trusts worldwide—endless trust deeds are hidden in desk drawers in tax havens so that it is impossible to find out—but there are clues. One tax haven alone, the British crown dependency of Jersey, has published an official estimate that its trusts alone hold about $1.3 trillion worth of assets, equivalent to the annual GDP of Spain. Several other island tax havens like the Caymans or Panama are believed to be as big as Jersey in the trusts game; the global total may be comparable to the amount of money in tax havens, whose estimates range between $9 and $36 trillion, with the higher number likely being the more accurate one.[12] There are considerable similarities between trusts and tax havens, of course. In a sense, trusts are like personalized tax havens, mechanisms that help wealthy people or institutions shield their assets from the rules that bind the rest of us. Trusts can also create amazingly complex layers of secrecy that can be tougher than anything a plain-vanilla Swiss bank account offers, where bankers simply promise to take their clients' secrets to the grave. (Threats of jail can change their minds, but with a trust the secrecy walls can be made of stronger stuff.) When the World Bank carried out a survey of how criminals use legal structures to hide stolen assets, it said trusts were rarely investigated, prosecuted, or prioritized in corruption investigations, because they were so hard to crack open.[13]

Trusts can create iron secrecy in a couple of ways, beyond what I've already described. Most important, when billionaire Grandpa gives away his assets, he not only creates a legal barrier between himself and those assets, but he also potentially creates a secrecy barrier. If he doesn't own the assets, how can they be linked to him? An ex-husband can use a trust to escape paying off a divorced wife; once safely inside a trust, those assets aren't his to distribute. A politician could give a fat contract to a company held in a trust, then truthfully declare that she doesn't own that company, even though she can benefit personally (this is just what Wilbur Ross, Donald Trump's secretary of commerce, did, helping him keep an estimated $2 billion worth of assets off financial disclosure forms[14]). A Muslim could profit from underlying assets that violate sharia laws but truthfully say that he doesn't own those assets. Even if a Mafioso gets hold of Grandpa and demands at gunpoint that he hand over the assets in a (properly constructed) trust, Grandpa literally doesn't have the power to do so, even to save his life. Deepening the secrecy is the fact that there is this trust deed—the agreement outlining how the trust works, who benefits, and so on—which may exist only as a piece of paper somewhere in a notary's office drawer, perhaps in a sleazy tax haven like Belize or Panama. It could even be a purely verbal agreement, made in front of witnesses. How could Interpol crack *that* open to find out what's inside?

The varieties of trust subterfuges get wilder and weirder, often constructed to defend against onshore tax and regulation. Many offshore jurisdictions specialize in helping Grandpa get all the benefits of a trust, while creating the easiest pathways for him to get back into the castle: the nest egg might be put into an offshore trust with a pliable trustee who can be persuaded or relied on to get one of the companies owned by the trust to lend money back to him, along with a quiet understanding (nudge, wink) that the loan won't ever be repaid. Or the trust could pay Grandpa consulting fees or invest trust money in his dodgy shell company, which sits outside the trust and can be milked at leisure. Or, even more crudely, Grandpa could put his assets in an offshore revocable trust while he's feeling the heat of a tax probe or criminal investigation, but once the smoke has cleared he just revokes the trust and gets the assets back. This is a sham, not really a trust at all, but for tax authorities or crime fighters to penetrate this financial vehicle's legal armor, they must prove it's a sham, and if the deed is locked away in a notary's desk drawer in Panama, that can be very hard indeed. There are letters of wishes—invisible little side deals that complement the trust deed—that can guide the trustee in umpteen shifty ways.

In theory, the IRS could try to tax income and assets in a trust by saying, "Ah, now the granddaughter, a US taxpayer, may not have received any assets from the trust yet, but she is ultimately *entitled* to them, so we'll call them hers and tax her accordingly." Well, English trust lawyers found an answer to that one over four centuries ago, with an arrangement called the discretionary trust, which is so effective that now it is probably the commonest of all general trust types. In this case, there are no firm rules in the trust deed about who will get what, when, where, how, and why; the trustee has *discretion* to decide. Maybe the granddaughter will get her hands on the family stables only if she passes all her exams, or a troubled son must satisfy the trustee that he has not used heroin in five years before he can get his hands on the lakefront property in the Hamptons. But here's the crucial bit: until the trustee uses her discretion to decide who gets what, none of the beneficiaries is entitled to anything at all. So how can the IRS touch it? Whose is it, anyway? The answer is: it's nobody's. It's probably fair to say that most asset-protection trusts are discretionary ones.[15]

Discretionary trusts have been put to some peculiar uses. When the British bank Northern Rock collapsed in 2007 at the leading edge of the global financial crisis, it turned out that it had been playing the securitization game hard, using snazzy SPVs based in Jersey, which held over $50 billion in assets under a "discretionary trust for the benefit of one or more charities." The named beneficiary was Down's Syndrome North East (DSNE), a charity run by volunteers to help children with Down's syndrome that operated out of a semidetached house in a modest suburb of the northeastern English town of Newcastle. DSNE volunteers raised funds from sponsored swimathons, ladies' luncheons, theater tickets, and even a helpful fellow who had earned them £125 cycling across the United States. Nobody at the charity had a clue that they were sitting under £40 billion in offshore mortgage androids plugged into their semidetached house, churning huge amounts of money through the financial ether. Apart from a contribution from the bank's office staff in 2001, DSNE hadn't received a bean from the bank. The trust meant that the assets were *controlled* by the bank but not *owned* by it. So it could remain economically connected to them, with the pipework of Jersey androids spitting profits out of the fortress and into the bank's bottom line, while the trust structures helped it claim the assets were off its balance sheet, thus freeing up capital.[16] Northern Rock, like billionaire Grandpa, got to have its cake and eat it—until the financial crisis.

The "discretionary" part helped reinforce that distance between the assets and the bank. Yet you may still ask: What's with the *charitable* trust? Well, this is another extensive part of the rabbit warren. There are many legitimate and excellent charitable trusts or foundations out there doing fine things, sitting on fortresses of endowed capital and paying out regular amounts to worthy causes. Some are less excellent, such as the foundation set up in California in 1989 to funnel millions to terror groups.[17] Because of the good stuff they often do, charitable

trusts or foundations get favorable legal and tax treatment. But many
so-called charitable trusts have far less benevolent purposes; their real
goal is not to pay money out to beneficiaries but to create a legal fortress
that enjoys this super-favorable treatment, inside which all the misrule
can take place, safe from scrutiny and from the laws of society. These
structures *must* have nominated beneficiaries—otherwise the structure
isn't legally a charitable trust—and if Northern Rock hadn't collapsed,
DSNE might have gotten a few thousand pounds after all the securitization vehicles had been wound down and the loose ends tied up. But
these would have been like scraps from the feast thrown over the castle
walls to the peasants below.

All this gives us a better sense of how slippery and yet powerful
trusts can be. Plain, crude ownership is for the little people. The flexibility of trusts to create the legal fortress is as varied as the imagination
of trust lawyers, and some of the names they come up with hint at their
deviousness: "beneficiary defective trusts" or "intentionally defective
grantor trusts" (don't ask), "sprinkling trusts" (which spread benefits
to lots of beneficiaries), "flee clauses" (the trust relocates to another
trust jurisdiction as soon as the cops or the IRS come sniffing around),
"duress clauses" (which are like steel portcullises that lock down the
moment there's an external threat to a trust beneficiary, preventing any
payments to any parties who come under "duress," such as receiving
a large tax bill, thus protecting the core trust assets). The strength of
these arrangements usually depends on interpretations, questions about
degrees of control, intentions, discretion, influence, and the very meaning of ownership. Even writing about trusts requires extreme care to
avoid the many pitfalls and hidden traps.

Tax havens boast "firewall" laws to make it harder for foreign courts
to get their legal crowbars into trusts. Take the Cook Islands, fifteen
isolated microdots in the Pacific Ocean with a population of twenty
thousand, which have made a tidy business out of some of the world's
most outrageous asset-protection laws. Once someone has placed their
assets into a Cook Islands trust, you can sue them all you like in American

or British courts, but if the trust has been set up the right way, you won't get them back. Well, you can try, but you'll have to fly out there, maybe changing planes in New Zealand for the five-hour flight to Rarotonga, then have the case tried in crooked Cook Islands courts under crooked Cook Islands laws, with crooked Cook Islands lawyers, and then often have to prove your case beyond reasonable doubt—as in a murder trial. The users of Cook Islands trusts include a monkey house of fraudsters, billionaire Ponzi schemers, hedge fund swindlers, spiteful patriarchs in vicious divorce battles, snake-oil salesmen peddling weight-loss nirvanas, and many others. One was Richard Edison, a Florida-based plastic surgeon nicknamed "Dr. Dread," who was sued after five of his patients died and he left a sponge in a woman's breast. His assets, in a Cook Islands trust, were immune from the full might of US law enforcement. But it isn't just the Cook Islands or offshore havens that allow this. Imagine an heir to the Rockefeller fortune, McDowell explains, who runs over someone in the street. His father has created a trust for him in the United States: he can sip from this financial vessel, but "someone seeking redress couldn't get into that cup." So trusts protect these charmed members of society from far more than tax; in important ways they elevate them above accountability. It is the strength of the fortress walls, and the almost infinite flexibility of the trust concept, that explains why so many of the world's greatest private fortunes, and many of the world's biggest commercial financing arrangements, sit inside these ancient structures. "Most people think that outright ownership of assets is preferable [to ownership via a trust] because of the control it gives," said McDowell. "Such control is illusory, however, in a world where asset value may be eroded by litigation from creditors or divorce settlements and, most certainly of all, taxes."

Trusts are just a part of a bigger financial game called "wealth management," where a specialist industry has emerged. People like McDowell and those in the Swiss-based "family offices" cater to truly vast global fortunes and help rich folk accumulate, protect, manage, and hide their wealth. These secretive family offices manage some

$4 trillion globally, more than all hedge funds. According to Credit Suisse, which tracks these things, in 2018 around 45 percent of all the world's wealth, or $142 trillion, was held by just 42 million people with a personal net worth above $1 million: that's the top 0.8 percent of the world's population, who are known as HNWIs (pronounced *Hen-Wees*), or high net worth individuals, each with assets worth more than $1 million. HNWI numbers have been growing six times faster than the world population. A good chunk of that is offshore, a good chunk is in trusts, and most is in both. Trusts, like tax havens, are vital mechanisms in the financialization of our economies, separating the wealthy further from the rest of us—and deepening the finance curse. In general terms, wealth managers who use trusts aren't that much interested in the 36 million HNWIs: the real prize is the 1.6 million people worth over $10 million each and *especially* the ultra-HNWIs—those 150,000-odd people worth $50 million or more (nearly half of whom are in the United States). That last group has been soaring by 10 percent a year, helped along by financialization, tax havens, megamergers, privatization, technology, and the rise of supranational criminal organizations. These numbers are likely to be underestimates, because national accounts can't usually penetrate trusts. After all, if billionaire Grandpa has given assets away into a trust, and the beneficiaries haven't received them yet, then the assets must sit in some kind of "ownerless" limbo, which can't be attached to any particular person or country, obscuring the true picture of global wealth.[18]

All this raises a couple of questions. Why do people with so much money fight so much harder than everyone else to get even richer, sometimes stooping to bestial levels of greed and cruelty to get what they want? How much is enough? And why is the world of great wealth suffused with a general spirit of heightened lawlessness? (One 2017 study found that tax evasion rates, at around 3 percent for the general population, rose to 25–30 percent for the richest 0.01 percent.)[19] And how do wealth managers feel about what they're doing in a world that seems headed steadily toward plutocracy?

Often when you confront wealth managers or tax haven operators with these questions, the responses come back as glib talking points, most of which we've all heard before. McDowell's main answer was that everything he does is legal—in fact, his job is to make sure his clients stay on the right side of the law—and that escaping tax was okay because "we need government, no question about it, but they are not going to spend or save my dollar as well as I can spend or save it." (I didn't press him on whether private spending on yachts or paintings is "better" than government spending on roads or schools.) Others resort to easy phrases like "the politics of envy" or "punitive taxation" or the evils of "welfare queens" to decry redistribution or fairness toward poorer people, and those shorthands also serve as personal screens against thinking these issues through more deeply. All these views are, of course, greatly amplified by the use of money to protect money: the funding of think tanks, academics, journalists, and politicians to propagate these ideas.

A different cookie-cutter answer came from Ely Calil, a fabulously wealthy London-based oil trader and financier, who was asked by a journalist friend of mine why he fought so hard to get *even* richer. He said simply, "If you have to ask, you won't understand." Calil elaborated a bit, talking about the thrill of winning and outwitting others, but gave little more. A related answer is a version of what is known as Gresham's law: bad money drives out good. The most ruthless, like Calil, will rise to the top, and the honorable, honest brokers will be left by the wayside. In 2004, Calil joined with Margaret Thatcher's son, Mark, in a failed plot to fly in a planeload of mercenaries to overthrow the president of oil-rich Equatorial Guinea (a crazy story that, as it happens, I helped uncover).[20]

Extreme wealth does often seem to generate unusual cruelty and vindictiveness. Traders in the City of London or on Wall Street like to speak in violent terms: successful deals are "rape and pillage" or "slash and burn," and traders are proud to "rip the client's face off." Greg Smith, a former Goldman Sachs partner who published an open letter in the *New York Times* outlining his company's culture, said, "It makes me ill how callously people talk about ripping their clients off." Some of the strategies the superrich adopt and the policies they advocate generate tiny rewards for them but astonishing pain for others. A proposed Trump tax-cut package in 2017, which wasn't passed, was projected to boost the average annual incomes of the wealthiest by just 2 percent, while causing, among other human catastrophes, an estimated two hundred thousand preventable deaths.[21] Which brings us back to the same question: Why?

The journalist Alex Cuadros remembers getting an insight into one answer in 2012, ahead of the publication of the Bloomberg Billionaires Index, to which he had contributed. A press person called him on behalf of Eike Batista, a Brazilian energy and logistics magnate. They'd sent through a detailed list of Batista's assets, including photos of his Gulfstream and Embraer jets; his $42 million Pershing yacht, the *Spirit of Brazil VII*; and even a Mercedes-Benz McLaren sports car parked in the living room of his mansion. Batista had heard that *Bloomberg* was estimating him to be the world's tenth-richest man, worth $30 billion. This wasn't enough, the PR man said—then patched through Batista himself. *Bloomberg* was underestimating the value of one of his gold mines, Batista fumed. His business empire was generating more and more cash, running "like Usain Bolt," and when the next set of numbers came out, he promised, *Bloomberg* would look "very foolish. I'm going to tweet it, actually." Batista grew so agitated that he started tripping over his words. Media reports had recently revealed that at a secretive meeting of Latin American billionaires and their heirs, Batista had called out from the stage to the Mexican billionaire Carlos Slim, then the world's richest man, *"Te voy a pasar!"* (I am going to overtake you!). As people get richer, they increasingly define themselves by their wealth, and this intensifies their desperation to get their hands on even more of it, to be seen by their peers as doing so, and to be seen as richer than them.[22]

Batista gave another reason, or self-justification, for his pursuit of extreme wealth, which connects more closely to the competitiveness agenda and the finance curse. His money was productive capital helping Brazil move forward, he said. He liked to picture the lives of his workers: where they lived, what they ate, their children at school, happy faces around the dinner table—the self-image of the billionaire as wealth creator, job creator. "Brazilians have always admired the American dream," he said. "What is happening in Brazil is the Brazilian dream, and I am the example." He peppered his rant with the word "honest"—a counter to the widespread suspicion in Brazil that the super-wealthy are all *malandros*, sleazy wealth-extractors who get rich through unfair, dirty, or criminal means. The heroic, honest wealth-creator meme that Veblen gave such short shrift to is indispensable to such people. It implies that whatever improves the fortunes of the business or the billionaire—including favorable tax treatment or smashing workers' rights—ultimately advances the fortunes of the nation as a whole in some sort of great global race. "I want my country to compete openly with the international companies," Batista said, confusing two very different forms of competition. "It's Brazil's time to be number one." Batista's heavily indebted empire later collapsed, and by 2014 his net worth was negative: he was jailed in 2017 for corruption.

The concept of the finance curse is anathema to many billionaires because it transforms them from wealth creators to wealth extractors, no longer patriotically advancing the cause of their nations but dragging them backward. If you look at the Bloomberg Billionaires Index, nearly all of those at the top are wealth extractors and, more specifically, monopolists (whose corporate and sometimes personal financial affairs are typically spread across tax havens too). At the top of the 2018 list sits Jeff Bezos, the head of Amazon, the everything-monopoly. Next comes Bill Gates, who created the Windows quasi-monopoly, followed by Warren Buffett, the portfolio monopolist who openly admits that he tends to invest only in businesses that have little competition. There's Mark Zuckerberg, the social network monopolist of Facebook, in fifth position, and Mexico's über-monopolist Carlos Slim, now pushed down to seventh place by the new giants of technology. All made their fortunes following the evisceration or lack of anti-monopoly laws or enforcement, the rise of offshore finance, the financialization of Western and other economies, and the general retreat of government. Rigged markets, in other words.

And here lies another reason for the relentless and almost thoughtless pursuit of ever more wealth: the heroic myth of the wealth creator is tied up intimately with a libertarian, antigovernment, anti-society ideology that pervades tax havens, the world of global finance, upper income brackets, and especially the superrich.[23] Spend time talking to people offshore, in parts of the City of London, or in the world of trusts and wealth management, and you'll crash into these attitudes again and again. I got a forceful verbal blast of them—typical of what I have encountered in tax haven after haven—from Adolfo Linares, a prominent Panamanian lawyer, who vented to me in a bar in Panama in 2016. High-tax countries like Germany or even the United States were "tax hells," he fumed. The problem was not tax evasion by the rich but overspending by the government. I repeatedly asked Linares about a number of near-empty residential skyscrapers in Panama, whose apartments are almost all dark at night and which anyone you talk to in Panama City will tell you are substantially owned by big players in the Colombian drug industry. Each time he angrily demanded why I wanted to know this, then finally relented, saying, "Our only tragedy is to be between the largest exporter and producer of drugs and the largest consumer. That is our curse." Which is a fair comment, but only up to a point: Panama deliberately courts dirty money. Linares continued, arguing that the Organisation for Economic Co-operation and Development, part of whose remit is to oversee international systems to boost transparency in global finance and crack down on tax havens, was "infested with socialists," and its initiatives represented "tax imperialism, fiscal predation—in order to support welfare states that are collapsing under their own bureaucratic weight." The notion that welfare systems might be collapsing partly due to tax dodging or wealth extraction by the rich didn't register. Offshore havens, by contrast, offered freedom. "My funds are mine, only mine," he continued. "I believe in freedom as the most important thing in life." When I hear such opinions, I often conjure a mental image of a fox outside a henhouse, brandishing a placard saying "Freedom for the chickens!"

And it is remarkable how much freedom from the law money can buy. Brooke Harrington, a researcher who took a top-level wealth-management qualification in order to study private wealth, remembers a wealth manager telling her about when she flew out of Zurich Airport with her boss to meet a client outside Europe. On the way to the airport she realized she'd left her passport at home, but her boss told her not to worry: sure enough, they were waved through customs both in and out of Zurich *and* at the other end, where a limousine was waiting to take them to the meeting. "The CEO was right," the wealth manager said. "These people, our wealthiest clients, are above the law."[24] In 2005 Arkady Gaydamak, a billionaire Moscow-based financier and middle-man, told me a similar story when I asked if he had visited France, Britain, or the United States, even though he was under an international arrest warrant. He would not confirm or deny reports that he had traveled to the UK, but added, "Have you watched the movies? Don't you think I am able to go where I want to?"[25] Harrington remembers an instance of this mentality during her training course, when learning how trusts can be used to shield assets from legitimate creditors. "People can get sued and lose or incur debts they can't cover, but if their assets are in a Cook Islands trust, they can say, 'Meh, I don't feel like paying. Come and get me,'" she explained. "I was horrified—horrified and fascinated. I'd ask things like 'Can't they sue for fraud?' 'I would never dream of trying something like this because I would imagine I would lose.' They said: 'No, no, this is how you do it.'"[26]

If there is one theme that unites tax havens, trusts, and the wealth-management industry, it is the pursuit of ways around the law—or, in the case of criminal activity, straight through it. They have created one set of rules for the rich and powerful and another set for the rest of us, which poses evident dangers for our democracies. Eva Joly, the Norwegian-born crusading French investigative magistrate who broke open the Elf affair, Europe's biggest corruption investigation since World War II, explained how the real money is so often not created *in* countries, but extracted *between* them, in an elsewhere land, offshore, nowhere, where the rules fall away. "Laws are made inside states. Money flows across borders," she wrote. "The magistrates are like sheriffs in the spaghetti westerns who watch the bandits celebrate on the other side of the Rio Grande. They taunt us, and there is nothing we can do." During her investigations a friend introduced her to a man called Franz, who took her aside one evening. "Madame, 98 per cent of felonies can be judged, but 2 per cent cannot. These are the state secrets. There are many powerful interests around you. Beware: the state secrets have their guardians, and they are not tender. Be reasonable." Joly got armed police protection and a Kevlar jacket. "I felt like I was penetrating into an unknown world, with its own laws." A card was stuck to her office door with a list of all the French magistrates killed since World War II. All the names were crossed out except hers. "I have seen so many resemblances, in France and abroad, between the corruption of the state and all the mafias. The same networks, the same henchmen, the same banks, the same marble villas," she wrote. "We think crime lurks in the shadows of our societies. But we find it linked intimately to our great companies and to our most honorable politicians."[27]

Perhaps the most peculiar thing about all this frenzied wealth protection is not the harm that it inflicts on other parts of society through lost taxes, rigged markets, undermined democracy, and so on, but the fact that it *also* doesn't seem to be making the super-wealthy any happier either. In fact, the reverse can be true, particularly when that wealth is inherited rather than earned. "The vast majority of the sons of rich men are unable to resist the temptations to which wealth subjects them, and sink to unworthy lives," wrote the nineteenth-century industrialist Andrew Carnegie. "I would almost as soon leave a young man a curse, as burden him with the almighty dollar." A 2010 study by the Israeli American psychologist Daniel Kahneman and the British American economist Angus Deaton found that happiness increases with income—but only up to around $75,000 per year, after which the rise stops. Another study of four thousand millionaires from 2018 concluded that people with wealth above $8 million were happier than millionaires with less wealth—but only very marginally so, and only when that wealth wasn't inherited. Over half of respondents said that for them to become happy, their wealth would have to be five to ten times greater.[28] Competition between family members to access a fixed pot of inherited money automatically pits them against each other, like the members of a band squabbling over who should get what. And money distances people from their loved ones for another reason: so many of those they meet are trying to wheedle or scam something out of them, and they begin to get paranoid about everyone's motives.

Charles Davidson, a Washington, DC–based publisher who inherited family wealth from an oil and engineering fortune, has seen money destroy families. "In my experience," he says, "wealth usually does hurt." He has been told by wealth managers that most of the rich people they deal with are burdened by their money. The fact that they generally don't need to work to make ends meet is a big problem, and there is also often perceived illegitimacy to inherited wealth. "Here in the US it's socially unacceptable to live from inherited wealth; everyone is supposed to be self-made," he told me—although some are shameless about inheriting money, like Donald Trump's children, and it can be easier in places like Europe, where cultural codes and intermarriage between wealthy families has legitimized the passing down of capital from generation to generation. But even in Europe, Davidson says, you only really hear about the success stories. "You don't hear about the people whose lives have been trashed by this. This is not fuel for self-esteem." The Society of Trusts and Estate Practitioners has an entire "Contentious Trusts and Estates" division to deal with intra-family conflicts, and one *STEP Journal* article selling Bahamas-based offshore trust services to "protect family wealth through the generations" explained that the "enemy within needs to be considered. Putting it bluntly: how can you stop the family from pushing the self-destruct button?"[29]

And Davidson points to a problem specific to trusts: they allow patriarchs to control their families' finances from beyond the grave. The beneficiaries must sit around waiting for their wealth to be doled out by trustees, bit by bit, sometimes with humiliating conditions attached, so they don't even have the psychological responsibility for that wealth; they are permanent supplicants. Some trusts specialize in helping rich people, usually older men, provide for their former spouses, not as a cast-iron entitlement but at the discretion of puppet trustees. Just think how much power that can give a rich old man over his unhappy children or ex-wife after a nasty divorce—control that can endure long after his death. And all *these* problems can be compounded when inherited fortunes were obtained or have been hidden using nefarious, criminal, or objectionable means, which is all too common. When someone hacked the phone of a daughter of Donald Trump's adviser Paul Manafort, the leaked details revealed deep unease. Their father had "no moral or legal compass," one sister wrote to another. "That money we have is blood money."[30] Nobody is winning in a lot of these situations, says Davidson. "Lawyers want to lock this up so they can continue to feed off it, colluding against the interests of the client. Though I'd call them the victim." It might be more accurate to describe wealth management as the unhappiness industry.

The wealth managers who handle these fortunes tend to justify their jobs to themselves, above all, by narrowing their focus and ignoring the big picture. Harrington reckoned that a quarter or so of the wealth managers she interviewed had "really hardcore neoliberal attitudes" like that of Panama's Adolfo Linares, where "socialists" lurk under every bed and where the world's ills stem from grasping big government (one American wealth manager said he got a kick out of the "intellectual challenge of playing cat and mouse with tax authorities around the world," while Richard Covey, the lawyer who set up the Walton GRAT scheme, used the words "romantic" and "beautiful" when talking about clever ways to help billionaires escape tax). Some of these people, Harrington said, seemed "completely unreflective about what they were saying. I don't think they realize how outrageous some of the statements are."[31] There are many others with at least some moral scruples who cope, as a former Bahamas private banker once told me, by simply "managing not to check in with your conscience" and clinging to the idea that you were at least helping *someone*—someone you know well—and their damaged, vulnerable families. The wealth manager is, as one put it, "like a confidant, a family physician who is unaware of practically none of the fortunes and misfortunes of the family group."[32] This made it a truly fascinating profession, as its practitioners need to probe into intimate areas. One told Harrington it was like being a voyeur: "the client has to undress in front of you." Another said clients "have to pick someone they want to know everything about them: about mother's lesbian affairs, brother's drug addition, the spurned lovers bursting into the room."[33]

To make their clients feel comfortable, the wealth managers ideally come from the same social class, having imbibed the same manners and customs from childhood: down-at-the-heels aristocrats from old European money or sophisticated, opera-loving smoothies for the more refined types. And for really rich people, they must be *good*: they need to construct and manage large, complex international structures involving banks, tax havens, trusts and foundations, wills, shell companies, hedge funds, share and bond portfolios, and insurance products, while funding pet think tanks and lobbyists and plenty more—putting them right at the heart of the machinery of global finance. They must keep their clients' assets dancing freely between different legal systems, taking advantage of accounting and legal loopholes while avoiding getting snagged by the rules and responsibilities of each place, and staying permanently abreast of shifting legal and political tides in each country. They may provide savvy investment advice; navigate family fights and foibles; organize bodyguards; pay gardeners and servants; and serve as friends, shoulders to cry on, psychologists, butlers, and guardians of mistresses, misdemeanors, and family secrets. Really good wealth managers have enormous patience, diplomacy, humility, the ability to multitask, and, above all, discretion. The very best are often women. These people provide a service that protects wealth far, far beyond the cover that the FDIC provides to your bank account or even the limited liability that corporations enjoy. Trusts conjure up another world entirely, where the rich and their money can obtain almost indiscriminate and wholesale protection from the rule of law.

The world of trusts and estate management is a rather genteel, discreet, rarefied one, where wealth and income is exempted from accountability and rules with as little public kerfuffle as possible. Yet there is another wealth-extracting sector that works alongside it, which is rougher, noisier, more reckless and grasping, and even more dangerous to the American economy and democracy. The world of private equity.

CHAPTER NINE

Private Octopus

The *Trentonian*, a gritty, scrappy tabloid newspaper serving Trenton, New Jersey, is a bit of an anomaly in local news. Born in 1946 as a strike newspaper during bitter industrial action at the *Trenton Times*, it is one of the rare exceptions to the conventional wisdom that towns and small cities can't support two competing newspapers. The *Washington Post*, which in 1974 bought the *Trenton Times*, had vowed in the new post-antitrust era to turn Trenton into a one-paper town, but by the early 1980s the *Trentonian*'s circulation of sixty-five thousand was beating the *Times*'s by three thousand readers. In the 1980s the *Trentonian* ratcheted up the pressure by setting out on a new path: less serious stuff and more sizzle. Headlines appeared like "Teen Slays Marauding Squirrel" or "Stud Snowman," about a snowman featured on a state tourism pamphlet that was, as the paper put it, "anatomically correct." In 1989, when a severed human head was found near the seventh fairway at a country club near Trenton, editors knew exactly what to do: splash it across the front page. "Those idiots [at the *Times*] put it on Page 3," said H. L. "Sandy" Schwartz, the paper's general manager. "If [they] want to be the paper of record, we don't care. We're going to play a different game." When they learned that the severed head's owner had contracted the HIV virus, the headline read simply, "Head Had AIDS"—and sales jumped again.

Alongside the sizzle, however, the paper still watched for the embezzle, digging for corruption and waste and keeping elected representatives on their toes. Today both papers still exist, but although the *Trentonian* still runs a regular Page Six, sporting what one editor called "attractive, healthy young people" (meaning, it seems, scantily clad young women), its sales have been in free fall.[1]

Local news is, of course, a shrinking sector, as internet platforms like Facebook and Google slaughter newspapers' business models by piggybacking on the journalists' graft and shoe leather to attract the clicks and eyeballs, then using their dominant positions to make off with most of the ensuing advertising revenues. But the *Trentonian* has been slashing jobs far faster than the national average, and its circulation in 2018 of just under twenty thousand on Sundays and almost ten thousand on weekdays is less than a sixth of what it once was, and far below the *Times*'s. The real story behind these savage losses lies in the financial sector.

Since 2011 the *Trentonian* has been owned by Alden Global Capital, a hedge fund and private equity investor specializing in "distressed newspaper companies." Alden is so secretive that its website, at the time of this writing, showed the company name emblazoned on a sunlit pine forest, but without any other information and no discernible way to click through to another page. An extensive search for a photo of its founder, Randall Smith, yields just one proper hit, from the *New York Post* in 2012, of a bespectacled, balding seventy-something obviously caught by surprise. Media reports say he has not given a press interview in three decades—an odd stance for one of America's biggest press barons. Cartoons of Smith, mostly modeled on that photo, show him as a grinning vampire or as a vulture eating up a newspaper. In the 1990s, the *Village Voice* reported, a painting of a vulture was hung proudly in the lobby of Smith's investment firm BDS Securities (the initials stood for "bankruptcy, distressed, and special situations").

The basic idea of private equity is that the owners of a firm invite outside investors to contribute large amounts of money to a small pool of capital they've set up. The firm then invests this pooled money on buying up or making large, concentrated bets on other companies—a chain of pizza restaurants, say. They'll then get the pizza chain to borrow a lot more money, shake it up, pay themselves large dividends, and hopefully sell the pizza chain on for a profit. The big shots who run the private equity firm, the outsiders who invest alongside them, and the financiers who lend to them then share out any gains from the pool under the agreed terms. The heroic story that private equity officials like to tell is one where they take sickly, tottering firms, throw out the lazy bums in charge, make painful choices, and reengineer the companies into healthy, roaring new engines of capitalism, making everyone rich in the process. Investors call both private equity and hedge funds "alternative investments," and they are similar but also different, mainly because of what they invest in. With hedge funds it's generally shorter-term stuff: flitting in and out of bonds, derivatives, commodities, shares, or exotic debt instruments; betting on price differentials across markets and changes over time, sometimes selling only days or even microseconds after buying. Private equity, by contrast, tends to get involved in the heavy lifting of taking control of and restructuring companies wholesale, processes that can take years. There's some overlap: hedge funds can take control of companies by buying up firms' debts, and this control can get them into more of a private-equity role. But in both cases the titans running the show take annual fees, typically 2 percent of the value invested, plus a cut, say 20 percent, of any profits, before returning the rest of the pool to the outside investors (this basic formula is sometimes known as 2 and 20). Private equity firms aren't generally listed on public stock exchanges (which is why they are private), and this frees managers from short-term shareholder pressures to show high performance every quarter-year. That's the heroic story, at any rate, and as with most areas of finance there's a solid kernel of useful stuff in what the players in do. But behind this, there's a much darker tale.

To understand better how Alden works I met Penny Ray, the *Trentonian*'s crime reporter, a gregarious, animated African American man with thick black-rimmed glasses, a graying beard and ponytail, and an earthy laugh. Ray, forty-two when I met him in October 2018, has a master's in screenwriting and has had a variety of jobs, including being a popular radio DJ in the Florida Panhandle a few years back, a stint in the military that he left after a noncombat injury, and time managing a Borders bookstore. He has won awards for stories in the *Trentonian*, most notably for a series on inmates in nearby Burlington County jail who died as a result of staff negligence. "Inmates just started dying and nobody cared," said Ray. "The Burlington County paper wasn't taking it seriously." Watching him operate in the *Trentonian*'s depleted newsroom, I got the impression that he's rather indispensable to the operation, and this may have given him the confidence to talk frankly to me. Amid all the layoffs there is a lot of fear among employees of Digital First Media (DFM), the umbrella group that Alden owns and which, in turn, owns all the newspapers, and it's hard to find people who will talk. Penny admits that talking to me could get him fired, but the pay isn't good and he's confident he could get another job easily enough—and he also doesn't have family nearby depending on his income: his is in the District of Columbia. "I'm not motivated by money or by the company; I mostly go by pride in myself and my reputation. I work my butt off. I'm not really scared of losing my shitty-ass job; if I do I'll just go back to DC." The cuts mean he has to multitask all over the place and work very hard to try to shore up the functions that have been sliced away in the cost cuts.

Penny Ray (a pen name: his real name is Anthony Ray Everette Jr.) took me to the far corner of a Mexican restaurant downtown, a place where he likes to come and interview cops. He talked a mile a minute. "This is murder city: we get a murder every couple of weeks," he said (published statistics show an annual murder rate of 0.25 per 1,000 people in Trenton, five times the national average and higher than nearby New York). "It is down to poverty, as simple as that. A lot of this stuff is drug-related, street beefs over girls, stupid robberies that go awry—'I wasn't going to pull the trigger but he fought back'—that kind of stuff." Though Smith, his ultimate boss, has donated to Republican causes, Alden doesn't seem to give the *Trentonian* journalists ideological steers. "We do what we do. I've never even heard a whisper of that," said Ray. "The closest thing is the sales team saying, 'OMG, you just killed my client'—that's happened maybe twice in five years. But it's just a complaint, not the company saying, 'Don't do this.' We put Chris Christie [New Jersey governor until 2018] with a cone on his head in the Bridgegate scandal; we've done all kinds of stuff." Ray was "pissed" at what he saw as a relative lack of editorial direction at the paper and added that, under Alden, cost cutting has led to almighty screwups, such as "double printing"—where "you'd open the paper and find they've run exactly the same article and the same picture twice." But it's when we get back after lunch to the *Trentonian* offices that the real savagery of the cuts becomes apparent. The building is a sprawling, light brown low-rise office block next to the police station that could, aside from the *Trentonian* name in big letters on the front wall, be mistaken for any industrial warehouse or distribution center. In the cavernous newsroom it looks like the three A.M. night shift: there are four or five reporters chatting and calling, but the rest of the desks are unused. On one side of this large open area are two doorways hung with plastic sheets to keep the dust out; that side of the building has been rented to a construction firm. Down one corridor is another room with part of what was once a busy marketing department: there's a desk covered with files, books, and papers that looks as if its occupant just stepped out for a few minutes. "She's been gone for a long time." Upstairs, the whole floor is completely deserted. I counted eleven rooms, including two large ones in the center, that are bare, with grim office carpeting. There's no hot water in the building and there hasn't been for a long time, including in winter: "I never checked the thermostat but it's always been freezing cold," said Ray. Large rats have been spotted. The building is "a piece of crap," he said, though it's been like that since he got here in 2013. The main theme under Alden's ownership, he said, has been layoffs, "like clockwork, every six months. We're down to bare bones."

The health of the Alden-owned newspapers seems to be shockingly poor, even given the overall difficulties in the sector. One of its biggest titles, the *Denver Post*, lost over 60 percent of its 185 staff from 2012 to 2018, with 30 culled in one mass firing in March 2018 alone. Staffing at the *Times Herald* (in the Philadelphia region) fell 73 percent over the same period, and Alden's subsidiary DFM closed its building, forcing staff to work from home or at the offices of the *Pottstown Mercury*, another DFM paper also near Philly, a building plagued by an "aggressive" mildew stink from a damp area under what a reporter called "a ghastly hole" in the roof. The *Mercury*, meanwhile, saw staffing fall by 83 percent. Union-covered staff at the *Daily Times* of Delaware County, also in the Philadelphia region, were slashed by 78 percent to twenty-five employees; its building was sold off too, and its newsroom relocated to a former bicycle shop. By comparison to DFM, the Philadelphia Media Network, a private organization that owns rival local newspapers in the Philadelphia area, cut staff by 26 percent over the same period, according to the NewsGuild, a labor union. On the West Coast the DFM-owned San Jose *Mercury News*, which had 440 reporters in the 1990s, had forty by 2018, despite being the paper of record in Silicon Valley. "Just short of setting the place on fire, being bought by Digital First was about the worst outcome possible," said Joshua Benton, the director of Harvard's Nieman Journalism Lab, who has studied the company in depth. The company's practices were, he said, "the newspaper equivalent of strip mining."[2] Julie Reynolds, an indefatigable reporter who has worked at Alden-controlled papers and has also investigated DFM in depth, reminds us that this is not just another business sector we're dealing with, but the lifeblood of local communities all across America. "This might be okay with some industries that are not so essential," she said, "but we are talking about a cornerstone of democracy."[3]

For those who don't know how hedge funds and private equity firms work, all this might seem not just unsettling but odd. If rival newspaper

firms judge that it makes best business sense to retreat steadily but gradually in the face of the internet giants' onslaught, why has DFM put such
a violent wrecking ball to its operations, demoralizing staff, leaching
newsrooms of their best talent, hemorrhaging readers, damaging its
papers' reputations, alienating advertisers, and risking total collapse? A
March 2018 *Denver Post* editorial predicted that under Alden's strategy its
newsroom would soon be "rotting bones." How could driving perfectly
good businesses into the grave help its owners?

The shortest answer to this question—how can a wrecking ball
create such a gusher of profits—lies in that familiar word: financialization. And it turns out that DFM is wildly profitable: a "non-stop cash
register," according to Ken Doctor, a media analyst who runs the Newsonomics website. He discovered that DFM showed profits of nearly
$160 million on revenues of nearly $1 billion in the 2017 fiscal year, a
17 percent operating margin that is around double that of comparable
news groups. Profit margins in the Philadelphia region were 30 percent.[4]
He added that, given how DFM operates, it was "an outlaw company
that just horrifies anyone who sees what they're doing": "there is no
long-term strategy other than milking and continuing to cut."[5]

To go deeper, it's necessary to understand how hedge funds and
private equity firms work. Alden usually gets called a hedge fund, but
as owner and controller of the *Trentonian* and a stable of nearly one
hundred other local newspapers—including the *Denver Post*, the *Boston
Herald*, the *Colorado Daily*, and the *Los Angeles Daily News*—it also operates like a private equity firm, and it is the history of private equity that
probably helps us understand the firm best.

The private equity industry properly got going in the 1960s, when
Jerome Kohlberg Jr., a senior official at the US investment bank Bear
Stearns, began urging his employers to stop merely advising companies
and helping them raise money and to start buying and selling them for
profit. And he proposed some interesting ways to juice up the numbers.
He persuaded the bank to set up a new division that would focus on buying up good, strong companies with healthy cash flows and then—here's

the first trick—to get the companies it had just acquired (called port-folio companies) to *themselves* borrow something like 90 percent of the purchase price, then channel most if not all of the proceeds back to the new owner. Bear Stearns could then take the profits from that portfolio company if things went well and offset the interest-payment costs on the new borrowing against the portfolio company's tax bill. But if the portfolio company went bankrupt, Bear Stearns wasn't on the hook for its debts. That is because of the magic of "limited liability" laws. If a limited liability company goes bust, the owners are liable to lose only as much money as they originally put in, but no more. So they make sure to put in as little of their own money as possible and get others—coinvestors or lenders, say—to inject the rest. It's a bit like if I set up a business with Joe Bloggs, he puts in most of the money, and, if the business goes well, we share a chunk of the proceeds—but if it goes bust I walk away and Joe shoulders the debts.

Why would a company accept being bought under such horrible terms? There are a couple of reasons: either the investor engages in a "hostile" takeover against management's wishes or sweetens the deal with appropriate "incentive structures" for the bosses of the portfolio company, so they too can get rich. It's the *other* stakeholders in the portfolio company—like its other employees or its trade creditors or pensioners—who are, like Joe Bloggs, effectively on the hook for its debts. This "heads I win, tails you lose" formula—taking the profits while shifting losses onto other people—is another version of the age-old game of other people's money, or OPM, that I described in chapter seven in the context of the global financial crisis. The more OPM that Bear Stearns could get into the pool of capital, the more regular fees and profit shares it could then milk from the expanded pool. And if Bear Stearns's traders have a good story to tell and are plausible people with good references and backers, they will get their OPM. One of the other successful traders, who joined Bear Stearns in 1974, was Randall Smith.

This leveraged buyout (LBO) game, Kohlberg had discovered, could be insanely profitable. So he left Bear Stearns in 1976 and, with

Henry Kravis and Kravis's cousin George Roberts, set up a new company, Kohlberg Kravis Roberts, or KKR. This was the first proper private equity firm, though in those days they and the others that soon emerged were known as LBO firms. Yet these corporate raiders faced a problem: persuading bankers to lend the funds they needed to make the game work. Fortunately for them, a new player had entered the scene, the investment bank Drexel Burnham Lambert, under the buccaneering junk bond king Michael Milken. Drexel played a different OPM game: it lent the money for LBO deals but then sold the loans (which became known as junk bonds because of their riskiness) to other, less clued-in players, like insurance companies or dowdy savings and loan organizations, tempting them with high interest rates and persuading them that the reward was worth the risk. And during the market upswing of the "Roaring 1980s," there seemed to be a near-bottomless pit of optimistic investors willing to buy these junk bonds. At this time, LBO deals were surging, from just $3 billion in 1981 to $74 billion by 1989. With fees often adding up to more than 6 percent of a company's purchase price, Milken became the highest-paid financier in history.

Smith had joined the LBO game too, reportedly using money he'd originally won in the game show *Dream House* as start-up capital to set up his own investment firm, R.D. Smith & Company, which he spun off from Bear Stearns in 1985. However, in 1989 a US federal grand jury indicted Milken in the biggest-ever criminal and racketeering action against a Wall Street figure. "A serious criminal problem has infected Wall Street," the acting US attorney in Manhattan put it. LBOs came to a shuddering halt, debt markets dried up, market conditions changed, and swathes of heavily indebted companies acquired in leveraged buyout deals collapsed. And this opened up whole new fields of opportunity for Smith, a voracious deployer of OPM, to buy up distressed debt. Smith specialized not in buying up whole companies with healthy cash flows, like KKR did, but in trading in the stocks and debt of "distressed" companies, playing "games of chicken" with coinvestors and creditors in debt restructuring deals to squeeze out the juiciest terms, muscling into creditor committees in bankruptcy cases to get maximum advantage and up-front information, and generally "profiting from other people's misery," in the words of a *New York Times* profile of him, entitled "Bottom Fishing with R.D. Smith."[6]

Some might have thought that the recriminations and fury that stemmed from the Milken scandal should have killed the whole LBO world, but this was only a pause for breath: KKR, Smith, and other emerging titans were determined to keep going. So they rebranded the sector with a fancy new name: private equity.[7] And a new intellectual savior appeared in the form of a Harvard Business School professor called Michael Jensen, who had trained at the University of Chicago and had some exciting new ideas about business strategy. Normal public companies—your General Motors or your General Electrics, say—are owned by a diverse group of shareholders but run by a different group, their managers. And these two groups' interests, Jensen argued in a couple of seminal papers in the *Harvard Business Review* in 1989 and 1990, weren't necessarily aligned. Managers didn't have strong enough incentives to look after shareholders' money, and this led to "widespread waste and inefficiency." Corporate America, he urged, needed a new breed of superstar owner-managers in a financial "market for corporate control" that would boost efficiency across the system. In pursuit of profits for themselves, they would fight like tigers to buy out bloated corporate has-beens and turn them into nimble, hyperefficient profit machines. Second, he said, these firms should borrow heavily, because the "discipline of debt" would make the owner-managers focus even more intensely on profits. And third, if you tied executives' pay to performance, that would make those already laser-focused executives work even harder and concentrate still more single-mindedly on generating those profits. The general idea, explains Peter Morris, a veteran banker and commentator on private equity, was "capitalism on steroids."[8]

Jensen's ideas rest on the concept of shareholder value or, to be more accurate, shareholder primacy. This was a radical departure from previous eras, when corporations were run with many goals in mind.

Corporations didn't just create profits; they also produced good jobs, good products, taxes, and healthy communities. Shareholders were just one among several interest groups. Peter Drucker's classic 1946 study, *The Concept of the Corporation*, argued that big business was "America's representative social institution. . . . [I]ts social function as a community is as important as its economic function as an efficient producer."[9] This was the corporate thinking that underpinned the high-growth Golden Age of Capitalism, and was still the received wisdom at the end of the 1960s.

Milton Friedman had already thrown a firebomb into this consensus with a violent article in the *New York Times Magazine* in 1970 entitled "The Social Responsibility of Business Is to Increase Its Profits." Business leaders had but one duty, he wrote: to their shareholders. Namby-pamby ideas like social responsibility, paying taxes, paying employees, or setting safety standards higher than the minimum were, in his view, "collectivist" and "fundamentally subversive." Business leaders who weren't nakedly pursuing profit alone were "unwitting puppets of the intellectual forces that have been undermining the basis of a free society." The money these wealth creators made, Friedman argued, would be reinvested somewhere else, and at the end of the day everyone would end up happy. His freedom-laden arguments caught the zeitgeist, following soon after the invasion of Czechoslovakia by Soviet and Warsaw Pact forces. Jensen took these ideas but elevated financiers to the apex of this system, as "rainmakers [who] draw from the people and institutions around them the dollars that are needed to build the nation's factories." All this combined to spark profound changes as Wall Street replaced the management-controlled firm with the finance-controlled firm. This was financialization, deliberate, pure, and ruthless.[10]

When the Harvard Business School embraced Jensen's ideas, explains the business journalist Duff McDonald, it transformed itself from an institution seeking to create a body of enlightened business-people into a cheerleader for Wall Street. "They basically threw in the towel and said, 'Fuck it, let's go for the money.'" (Not coincidentally, fund-raising improved spectacularly.) Clayton Christensen, a dissenting professor at the school who specializes in business innovation, explained more recently how destructive the new thinking has been. "The professors of finance in the main business schools, the professors of economics, have over the last forty years created a church. I call it the New Church of Finance. The doctrines are taught with the same force as the Catholic Church preaches their catechism."[11] And he describes a zealotry for financial ratios or fractions, which generate an obsession with maximizing financial returns. These ratios include return on net assets (RONA), internal rate of return (IRR), return on invested capital (ROIC), earnings per share (EPS), and a few others: in essence, the profits or income divided by capital or assets employed, and they bind businesses into insanely powerful—and vicious—mathematics. To see this, take any ratio or fraction. You can boost the fraction in two ways: you can either increase the numerator (the top bit), which here represents profits, earnings, or returns—what you get out from your investment. Or you can reduce the denominator, which is what you put in, usually something like investment. So take a firm that earns $20 million this year on an investment of $200 million. Its annual ratio of 1:10 is only half as successful by this financial yardstick as one that earns $2 million on an investment of $10 million, for a ratio of 1:5. If you can reduce your net assets to zero, then RONA will theoretically give you infinite returns! This is better for you, the investor—but for the economy as a whole it's generally far better to have a firm that employs five thousand people and invests a lot but makes small profits, than a private equity firm that borrows heavily and makes ten times the profits, while only employing a hundred people.

"As long as they can get more capital out than they put in, and the faster they can get it out, the higher the IRR," Christensen said. "So they invest in stripping things." These ratios airbrush out and even work against the all-important world of employment, innovation, supply chains, and livelihoods inside the company. Instead, businesses like Penny Ray's direct employer, the *Trentonian*, just become data points in this financial market for corporate control. Such ratios help drive financialization and the finance curse, as companies cut investment or outsource activities in order to get capital-intensive factories off their balance sheets. They borrow more, reducing the capital they invest themselves and shrinking the denominator. And it often turns out to be less profitable to focus on operational engineering—fixing up badly run companies to create wealth—and more profitable to focus on financial engineering—that is to say, on good old wealth extraction. This is the "buy, flip, and sell" mentality that Alden's Randall Smith understood very well, having learned this from his time as a trader at Bear Stearns. Private equity firms often do the fixing-up part simultaneously with the milking, but they are *always* incentivized to do the stripping and the milking—and they have a lavish smorgasbord of tricks to achieve this.[12]

The main event in this game is borrowing. Taking on debt provides a range of benefits—none of which focus managers' minds on building better and longer-lasting companies. The first joy of debt is that it magnifies returns. To take a simplified example, imagine you spend $100,000 of your own money to buy a house and its value rises by 20 percent, or $20,000. You've increased your capital by 20 percent. But if you instead borrow $900,000 to add to your own $100,000 and buy ten such houses, which each rise by 20 percent, you could sell off the lot for $1.2 million, pay back the $900,000 loan, and keep $300,000. You've tripled your money. This is, once again, the principle of leverage: a relatively small movement at one end translates to a much larger movement elsewhere.

But there is a snag: if house prices fall 20 percent, the debt magnifies your losses: your houses are worth $800,000 and you owe $900,000, deep in negative territory. So private equity titans engineer that risk away with the next trick, the one that Kohlberg learned. They don't take on the debts themselves but instead load them onto the shoulders of the companies they buy. If the bet goes badly it's the company's other stakeholders—employees, suppliers, and lenders—who take the hit. So imagine you put down $100,000 of your own money and take out a $900,000 loan from the bank to buy those same ten houses, then rent them out, and each house is now owned by a limited liability company that you own. Now it is the business, not you, that is legally required to pay back the loan, and your liability is limited to the amount of money you've invested yourself—in this case $100,000. If the business goes bankrupt, then it's the bankers who are on the hook, and you can walk away scot-free—and maybe even with a profit.

But wait! You, the investor, have still lost your original $100,000, haven't you? Not necessarily. Let's say that, after you set up the house business, you take shortcuts on repairs and insurance costs. You also do cheap paint jobs, mow the lawns inexpensively, and produce some glossy, doctored photos. You now raise the rents by 30 percent, increasing regular new cash flows. Investors will lend multiples of annual cash flows, so if you can produce an additional $30,000 a year in rental income, you might be able to borrow another $250,000, say, maybe even $350,000, if house prices and rental rates are generally rising and the lenders are feeling flush. Next, you tell the house business, which you control, to funnel all this borrowed money back to you in a special dividend. You have now got your full $100,000 back and then some.

But now the economy tanks and some tenants lose their jobs and fall behind on rent. The over-indebted house business goes bust, but since the business is a limited liability company, your losses are limited to what you've injected, that original $100,000. Beyond that, the debts are on other people's shoulders: the bankers or investors, who will salvage what they can. You lost $100,000 but got that $350,000 special dividend, so you've still pocketed $250,000 overall. And especially if you set up the company or partnership in a tax haven like the Caymans, you might be able to escape tax on that too. From this slash-and-burn operation, you've more than doubled your money. And if you can find more people crazy enough to lend to you, you can then take that $250,000 to repeat the trick, only on a larger scale.

The next happy thing for you is that those crazy people aren't hard to find. And they aren't crazy either, because there is a financial logic to what they do. There are oceans of global hot money out there, trillions of it, the product of immense changes in the global economy—capital looted out of poor countries, vast Chinese savings spilling over into world markets, new credit constantly created out of thin air by private banks and Western central banks, and so on. This money is looking for somewhere, anywhere, to invest—anywhere offering higher rates of return than low-interest German government bonds or US T-bills. And the lenders—maybe hedge funds or other specialist lenders—can get the debts off *their* backs via the great financial pass-the-parcel of securitization, packaging these income-generating loans up into new income-generating collateralized loan obligations (CLOs) and selling them to other cash-rich investors. CLOs are now a $500 billion industry globally and growing fast, another powerful vested interest demanding ever more private equity deals and mergers—and ever more debt: something that the IMF warned in 2018 was so large that it now poses risks to global financial stability.[13] And the players in these debt markets who are holding the baby when things fall apart usually aren't personally on the hook either: they have probably already earned their bonus, and their wealth is now protected by trusts and limited liability structures. It's OPM as far as the eye can see. The ultimate victim is the sucker at the end of the chain—which may be you, if your pension fund has invested in this stuff.

So this is one of private equity's great games: buy up a company, shake out new cash flows, use those to borrow more, then funnel the borrowings back to the company's owners, hopefully in large enough sums to pay them back for the original purchase of the company. When Alden bought its majority stake in the DFM media group, it turned a largely debt-free company into an indebted one.[14]

There are myriad ways to free up new cash flows from a successful business. The most obvious is to cut costs: slash employee numbers, cut wages, reduce pension entitlements, skimp on investment. The private equity mogul Wilbur Ross, who became Donald Trump's commerce secretary, did this after winning control of a big chunk of the US steel industry. In 2005 he walked out with a $4.5 billion gain, pretty much the same amount as steelworkers and retirees lost in health and pension plans.[15]

If your mind is repelled by the brazenness and simplicity of this extraction device, you're not alone. In 2005, for example, the private equity giants Texas Pacific Group and Apax Partners of London launched Project Troy, a €1.4 billion buyout of TIM Hellas, Greece's third-largest mobile operator, then a healthy company. Within a year its new owners had jacked up the company's debt nearly twenty-fold, from €166 million to over €3 billion, funneling payments from this new borrowing to themselves via some complex tax-minimizing securities and a chain of Hellas companies. Had the Goldilocks era continued, Hellas might have survived. "It was a free ride that took advantage of buoyant markets," a private equity official said. "In 2006 the world was beautiful and we thought we could walk on water." They tried to flip the company to another investor for a profit, but when that failed they ramped up their withdrawals, milking the underlying company like a cash machine and eventually selling the creaking, debt-laden shell to an Egyptian investor in 2007, who in turn moved the company's domicile from Luxembourg to London, where the firm's debts could be wiped out through more lenient British bankruptcy laws. When it all went into administration in 2009, the liquidators said the company had been "systematically pillaged."[16]

Another common extraction technique is the Opco-Propco shuffle. In these cases a private equity firm buys up a company with lots of real estate and divides it into two parts: a "Propco" to own all the property and real estate, and a separate operating company, or Opco, to run the business. Next, Opco signs a long-term contract to lease those properties back from Propco at exorbitant rates. This sale and leaseback makes Opco more fragile and Propco more valuable. The private equity firm might then sell this newly valuable Propco and use the proceeds to pay itself a giant special dividend, which in turn can pay, especially in rising real estate markets, for the whole deal and then some, almost risk-free. If Opco can't cope with its expensive leases and goes bankrupt—well, the moguls have got their payoff; the debts and losses are somebody else's problem. When Sun Capital bought the iconic and profitable Friendly's ice-cream parlor and family restaurant chain for $337 million in 2007, it sold off the real estate, then leased it back to the restaurants, which immediately started to struggle now that they had to pay those leases on top of their other costs. It closed more than sixty restaurants and laid off over 1,200 workers, but the company still went bankrupt in 2011. Then the next phase began. Another unit of Sun Capital lent the bankrupt shell the money to keep the operations running, and Sun Capital used those fresh loans it had made to Friendly's as leverage to gain control of the company again when it came out of bankruptcy, having shaken off debts and the pension obligations for its six thousand or so employees onto the government-run Pension Benefit Guaranty Corporation (PBGC)—effectively, onto the shoulders of US taxpayers. The PBGC alleged fraud in the way Sun Capital had done this, but the parties settled out of court. Alden too has separated and sold off the real estate of most of its media properties, though it has as yet failed to sell off the *Trentonian*'s building: a deal to sell it to Dunkin' Donuts in 2016 fell apart, and when I visited; its grungy building was up for sale on a realtor's website at a forlorn $495,000.[17]

It is hard to make out the exact structure of the corporate pipework that lies behind these kinds of deals, not just because private equity firms and hedge funds are so secretive but also because it's hard to use US public records to trace precise corporate ownership structures, especially when the companies are in a secrecy state like Delaware. But overseas records can sometimes make this possible—and the results are often bizarre. Using public records in the UK and European tax havens, I traced most of the structure for one profitable KKR property, a company called Trainline, which is the most popular platform for buying rail tickets in Britain. Trainline raked in nearly $190 million in UK revenues in 2017, mostly through charging a standard booking fee of 75 pence (a bit less than a dollar) for each ticket sold. Trainline.com Limited, the London-based company that runs the service, is owned by another company called Trainline Holdings Limited. That company is owned by another, which is owned by another, and so on. Five companies above Trainline.com, that little booking fee skips out across the English Channel to the tax haven of Jersey. Then it comes back again to London, where it passes through five more companies, then hops back out to Jersey once more, before migrating over to the European mainland, where it enters the accounts of two companies in Luxembourg, another tax and secrecy haven. Along the way, all sorts of other rivulets join in and leave the tinkling, rustling flows of money, as different companies in this hierarchy borrow money from banks or from each other, or inject and lend cash back and forth, sometimes at eye-wateringly high interest rates. Once in Luxembourg, our brave little 75 pence enters a financial tunnel, where it becomes a little harder to track. But it soon pops up again, this time in the Cayman Islands, where it wriggles up through three or four more mysterious companies until finally, having already passed through twenty or so companies after leaving a train traveler's bank account, it joins a multitude of other financial streams and rivers from around the world and flows into the maw of KKR—and thence onward to KKR's shareholders, including its two surviving founders, the billionaires George Roberts and Henry Kravis.

At the last count, KKR still owned more than 180 real companies. I say "real" because KKR actually owns or controls well over 4,000 corporate entities, including over 20 in Jersey, over 200 in Luxembourg, and over 800 in the Cayman Islands, most of which are detached from the lives of real people and exist only in the accountants' virtual reality world. Each solid underlying company in the KKR empire, like Trainline or the Sonos electronics company, has one of these convoluted corporate structures perched on top of it, snaking chains of entities often with peculiar names drawn from finance's arcane lingo, like (in Trainline's case) "Trainline Junior Mezz Limited" or "Victoria Investments Intermediate Holdco Limited."[18] None of what I have described so far is remotely illegal; in fact, this is increasingly the way business is done.

But what *on earth* is all this snaking complexity for? Most of the answers to this question boil down to OPM again. A private equity official described one reason: to split companies and their cash flows into a spectrum, so as to create niches to attract all the different kinds of specialist lenders out there, each with different risk appetites and sectoral preferences. They may, for instance, want to invest at the level of either the whole company, a subholding company, or a particular subsidiary. Alongside straight bank lending and equity finance there are also senior and junior debt, mezzanine finance, preference shares, warrants, varieties of hybrid debt, and more. Different companies in this stack may be located in different places, including tax havens, depending on their role. It's a bit like cutting a $10 multi-topping pizza into ten slices, then rearranging the toppings to suit customers' tastes better—this piece has lots of salami, that has olives and capers, that has olives and artichokes—so you can now sell each piece for $1.50. The more lenders you can find, the more OPM you have to play with, and the bigger the pool of money from which to extract fees. So alongside all that OPM invested into the main funds, you also get other streams of OPM coming in through these complex corporate towers.

Another reason for the complexity goes back to those all-important limited liability companies: you can isolate pockets of risk in a range of different companies, earning strong returns when times are good, but using the barrier of limited liability to stop any losses hitting other parts of the empire. Private equity firms have done this in the care sector, for example, incorporating each nursing home in a chain in a separate limited liability company. In the event of negligence or medical errors leading to massive claims, the damage to the moguls' bottom line is limited to what the moguls put in: limited liability shields them from the debts. Successful firms in this complex structure feed nice profits through to the moguls, but with the unsuccessful ones, limited liability protects the moguls against losses (and the victims of medical malpractice get stiffed). For the moguls, it's almost a one-way bet, and the more pockets you can create, the more potential for profit. "The private equity business is like sex," says Howard Anderson, a professor at MIT. "When it's good, it's really good. And when it's bad, it's still pretty good."[19] That statement directly contradicts Jensen's claims about the "discipline of debt" and the private equity model sharpening managers' focus to build better companies. Instead of sharpening focus and improving the process, baroque internal financial flows, risk shifting, tax games, debt darting in and out of corporate stacks, and the overall OPM principle only obfuscate, dilute, and diminish responsibility and accountability.

There's a third reason for all the snaking chains of corporate complexity, which brings that other large stakeholder into view: the shambling, unloved, grouchy giant that invests in the roads, the courts, the education of workers, the sewage pipes under homes and office buildings, and the other essential things that underpin all of the titans' profits. Government. After it has picked up the human flotsam from the lacerated pension pots and the layoffs, be they burned-out journalists or the victims of rogue doctors, the government is at least supposed to get a payback in the form of tax levied on corporate profits. But the private equity titans want a free ride here too. "The key to this is getting the cash out at the end," a private equity tax official told me. Everyone tries to avoid what he called "trapped cash—cash that is hard to get out of a subsidiary without triggering tax"—and banks and the Big Four accounting firms are on hand to help find the right pathways through the tax laws. This is a big, complex area, but again debt plays a key role. You borrow money, and the interest payments on that debt can be offset against your tax bill, and the tax code inexplicably encourages firms to do this. All that borrowing is OPM, and the tax benefits are icing on the cake.

Another tax trick with debt involves "shareholder loans," where one part of the corporate empire lends money to another part using an old tax haven trick, "transfer pricing," to shift profits into tax havens. In short, if XYZco's entity in a tax haven lends $100 million to XYZco's onshore entity at high interest rates, then the onshore company can deduct those interest payments from its tax bill, while the tax haven company receives those high interest payments as income, but because it's in a tax haven it pays no tax there. The IRS fights against this kind of thing, but it's a sieve, and other countries have laxer rules. These kinds of games aren't limited to private equity firms or hedge funds: they are found across the business world. But the titans get an especially large helping of this cream because they tend to use so much more debt. One study estimates that up to 40 percent of the value of companies bought by private equity firms comes from tax deductions on interest payments alone.[20]

Most of the tax games these firms play are legal. But are they legitimate? One of my favorite answers comes from the Scottish comedian Frankie Boyle, who pointed out on Twitter that the economic and political effects of this are just as important as their legality. "If you're rich, don't look at it as tax avoidance," he said. "Look at it as a children's hospital buying you a pool table." This isn't a frivolous comparison: effective tax subsidies to a single private equity firm have in the past exceeded the costs of building a major new hospital.

The tax havens provide another, possibly bigger benefit: they are conduits for sucking up questionable and criminal money—more OPM for the funds—from around the world, while using their secrecy laws to block the information that would allow us to know whether Alden Global Capital, for instance, was being funded by criminals. All we can see, in Alden's case, is that it has several funds based in tax havens: at least one in the British tax haven of Jersey, which in 2015 listed two front companies as its owners, Ralgo Nominees (Jersey) Limited and Ogier Nominees (Jersey) Limited, two local law firms. There is an Alden firm, now dissolved, based in Dubai—which is, for my money, probably the world's most crime-tolerant tax haven.[21] There is the Alden Global CRE Opportunities Master Fund LP, based in the Cayman Islands, a vehicle that has invested in, among other things, a Mexican slumlord called Homex, which an article in the *Los Angeles Times* described as "one of the country's most despised companies."[22] Alden invested $83 million in the residue of Homex after the firm went bankrupt amid rolling scandal, and it appears to have been the controversy that attracted the bottom-feeding Alden, as part of a strategy of what the investigative journalist Julie Reynolds called "buying into ethically sketchy companies dogged by claims of illegal pollution, corruption or fraud."[23] The US Securities and Exchange Commission in 2017 accused Homex of having committed the biggest fraud in Mexico's history, and although Alden was not one of the parties to the suit, Mexican commentators were dismayed that Alden and its coinvestors kept the disgraced firm's executive team in place. Alden has also invested in companies operating in Russia, Brazil, and Angola, all of which have been investigated or prosecuted for various offenses.[24]

The foundation also lists Alden DFM SPV, Ltd., also registered in the secretive Cayman Islands. The DFM stands for Digital First Media, which ultimately sends Penny Ray his paychecks, but no other useful information on it could be found—until March 2018, when Solus, another hedge fund with a minority stake in DFM alongside Alden, filed a lawsuit in Delaware accusing Alden of improperly milking its newspaper empire to shore up other loss-making Alden investments elsewhere: in Greek government bonds, the ailing drugstore Fred's, and other investments "entirely unrelated to the company's core business." Alden's financial reporting since 2017 had been "nearly useless," it said, keeping Solus in the dark. All this, of course, would help explain Penny Ray's description of his "shitty-ass job."[25]

So what is Alden DFM SPV, Ltd., up to? Well, you won't get much useful public information on it, except that it was formed in 2014 and its local agent is Ogier Fiduciary Services (Cayman) Ltd., an affiliate of one of the "offshore magic circle" law firms. But hedge funds and private equity firms have a long record in the Caymans setting up what they call "blocker corporations" to help foreign investors and tax-exempt investors escape tax and scrutiny. To cut a long story short, if foreigners were to invest *directly* into a private equity fund, they may well be deemed to be involved in a trade or business in the United States and get tangled up in the US tax system. They'd have to—horrors!—file a US tax return. But if they invest *indirectly* in the same fund via a blocker corporation in the Cayman Islands, their link to the US tax system gets severed (or blocked) in the Caribbean. No US tax return, no taxes paid in the United States, no taxes in the Cayman Islands—and deep secrecy. These are ideal lures for OPM from overseas. But we can't know who Alden's foreign coinvestors are.[26] According to Julie Reynolds, in June 2018 Alden's SEC filings suggested it had fewer than ten investors, mostly from unspecified "overseas" locations. "But who most of those few souls are, and how much of the hundreds of millions skimmed from DFM papers they've received remains a deep, dark mystery."[27] What is sure is that, as Professor Michael Hudson explained in chapter three, it has been American policy to encourage such inflows of shady money since the Vietnam War.

Mapped out across the whole economy, what is going on in the world of private equity and hedge funds is a *harvest*. These players operate as giant bidding companies that hunt for and buy up mostly healthy firms, then put them through the financialization wringer. They festoon their financial affairs through tax havens, milk other taxpayers, and magnify their OPM through limited liability tricks that also protect them from losses. They buy up competing firms to create monopolizing market power in the market niches where they operate, to milk customers. They load them up with debt—stiffing employees, creditors, suppliers, or victims of medical malpractice—often by driving them into bankruptcy. This harvest is all about wealth extraction, not wealth creation, and it has created immense concentrations of money. One private equity official, who didn't want to be identified by name, compared the remarkable growth of his sector to a cancer: "a good idea gone bad, like a normal healthy process that has grown wildly in ways that were never envisaged." Matt Stoller, one of America's most astute commentators on corporate power, calls private equity "the disease factor for monopolization." The recently collapsed Toys 'R' Us might eventually have been killed by competition from Amazon and Walmart, but its demise was massively hastened by the $400 million annual debt payments hanging over from a 2005 private equity buyout and aggressive moves by hedge funds holding its debt that forced it abruptly into liquidation. This is an example of how private equity has made a large portion of corporate America fragile, Stoller said, "and that opens the doors to companies that are not vulnerable"—in this case, Amazon or Walmart. This is a second way that private equity and hedge funds contribute further to monopoly power.[28]

To be fair, private equity firms and hedge funds do sometimes use their business skills to also create genuine value, improving operational efficiencies alongside the financial engineering. But it's a minority sport, simply because the hard work of patient investing isn't so insanely profitable. One of the most careful in-depth independent studies of private equity is a quietly devastating 2014 book, *Private Equity at Work*, by US academics Eileen Appelbaum and Rosemary Batt. "What is striking," they found, "is how little of the earnings of the PE funds depended on business strategy or improvements in operations." Firms bought out by private equity tended to have been more productive and faster-growing than their peers *before* the buyouts; afterward, jobs and earnings tended to fall, and significantly so.[29] The authors of a 2018 study surveying 390 deals worth $700 billion said that "most private equity firms are cutting long-term investments, not increasing them, resulting in slower growth, not faster growth. If PE firms are not growing businesses faster, investing more in growth, or gaining much operational efficiency, just what are they doing?"[30]

German leftists use the term *Heuschrecken*—locusts—to describe private equity firms, which is often apt. Tamara Mellon, cofounder of the Jimmy Choo luxury shoe company, who worked with private equity for a decade, said that in her experience private equity attracted "vultures and parasites. . . . [N]one of these private equity firms have actually put capital in the business for growth. They have been more of a burden." More unusually, she also said she had never met a woman in a senior private equity role. According to two studies, only 6 percent of senior private equity officials and 3 percent of hedge fund officials are women—and if you exclude investor relations, legal work, operations, and human resources—the softer side—private equity's 6 percent falls to 3 percent. These figures compare to an average of 30 percent or so for firms in the S&P 500. Theresa Whitmarsh, executive director of the Washington State Investment Board, remembers a private equity official telling her that women simply aren't cut out for their kind of deal-making because private equity is "a blood sport."[31]

All this is troubling enough. But the most tragic part of this sorry tale is still to come.

In 2005 the billionaire investor Warren Buffett offered $500,000 to any investor who could select at least five hedge funds that outperformed a simple fund tracking the S&P 500 index over ten years. A brave asset manager called Ted Seides accepted. He chose a fund of funds, which invested in more than one hundred hedge funds—and the results are now in. A million dollars invested with Seides would have gained $220,000 in ten years, a 2 percent annual return. The average passive, boring index fund gained $854,000, nearly four times as much. Seides would have done better pinning a list of popular stocks to a board, then incentivizing a chimpanzee with peanuts to throw darts at it and investing directly in the ones it hit. The law of averages says the chimp would have been closer to the bigger number and, because its fees were peanuts, probably above it.

So, you may ask: How come so many private equity players and hedge funds have gotten so stupendously rich if they are collectively so rubbish at generating profits for investors? The answer is simple. The titans who run the mother ship—the general partners, or GPs in the parlance—write the rules for who gets what, when, and how. They get their hands on nearly all the profits before the limited partners (or LPs)—those hapless, trusting outsiders like your pension fund manager who innocently pour your money into the pool of investable capital without properly reading those hundred-page prospectuses—get their cut. Simon Lack, a former JP Morgan banker who advises on alternative investments, wrote a book, *The Hedge Fund Mirage*, which concluded that returns to investors in hedge funds are just as feeble as those from private equity.[32] He found that from 1998 to 2010 the titans took a total of $440 billion from the deals he studied—that is, *98 percent* of all the internal returns generated—while the credulous outside investors took $9 billion, or 2 percent. The results for private equity are at least as bad.

How do these rules work? Well, let's say a private equity firm buys a successful pharma company and generates huge internal profits, whether from creating an even better pharma company or from debt-fueled looting. The GPs' first trick is the famous 2 and 20 formula: they take 2 percent of the value of invested funds annually as management fees, plus 20 percent of any internal profits generated (after the fund has attained a "hurdle rate" of profit). That formula may seem reasonable, but in the real world the mathematics of it rips surprisingly large chunks of the profits away from the outside investors and channels them into the moguls' pockets. "The thing I love about this business is the fee structure," the hedge fund multi-billionaire John Paulson gushed in 2019. "The more money you have, the greater the fees." With his fund managing $30 billion, he added, "the fees just pour out of the sky."[33] Below the obvious fees exists another world of chicanery of hidden fees and small print, which your pension fund manager probably hasn't read. Let's say PE Capital, a private equity firm, buys up VictimCo, which owns lots of office buildings. PE then sends in its affiliate PE Properties to run, maintain, and service those buildings, charging VictimCo exorbitant hidden fees for not much work. Or PE Capital owns a consultancy business that charges outrageous prices for its (mandatory) services to VictimCo. Listed company or mutual funds aren't allowed to pull this kind of stunt, but private equity and hedge funds are lightly regulated, so the titans get a free pass here. And the powerless LPs get the scraps.[34]

This is like Hollywood accounting, which David Prowse, the actor who played Darth Vader in the original *Star Wars* trilogy, now understands well. "I get these occasional letters from Lucasfilm saying that we regret to inform you that as *Return of the Jedi* has never gone into profit, we've got nothing to send you," says Prowse, even though it is one of the highest-grossing films of all time. "I don't want to look like I'm bitching about it [but] if there's a pot of gold somewhere . . . I would like to see it."[35] The aging actor now runs a rather low-grade website selling signed photos of Darth Vader for £35 each, and in 2010 he said he had been banned from Lucasfilm events because he had "burned too many bridges." Hollywood accounting—milking assets before they hit the balance sheet—turns profits into losses, eliminating pesky royalty checks and tax bills. And funds are also often invested via structures such as blocker corporations in secrecy havens like the Caymans or Luxembourg, making it harder for investors or tax authorities to see what's going on. A standard index tracker fund that you or I might invest in typically charges its investors between 0.1 and 1 percent of the value of the assets in management fees each year. By contrast, private equity fees, all told, add up to between 6 and 13 percent of the value of the investment *annually*. "Investors continue to regard private equity fund managers as trusted business colleagues, even as they continue to pick investors' pockets," says Yves Smith, an expert on private equity who runs the influential financial website Naked Capitalism. Private equity and hedge funds are utterly hopeless at the *one thing* they are supposed to be good at: generating good returns for investors.[36]

So why are sophisticated money managers throwing money at this sector? At the time of this writing, waterfalls of money are pouring into private equity and hedge funds. Alden's investors include the California Public Employees' Retirement System, Citigroup's and Coca-Cola's pension funds, a few European banks, some charities such as the Circle of Service Foundation and the Alfred University endowment. (More surprising, perhaps, is the John S. and James L. Knight Foundation, which has a long and honorable history of supporting local news.) Private equity alone raised over $3 trillion from investors between 2013 and 2017, and a survey of institutional investors in 2017 found that on

average they expected private equity to outperform markets by 4 percent a year, even after it underperformed in the S&P 500 index by 1.5
percent a year for the past five years.[37] In 2018, total hedge fund assets
stood at $3.6 trillion and rising.

The reasons are many, and they get steadily more piteous further
down the list. A first, dull reason is the rich stew of studies claiming
wonderful returns to investors—usually by authors who are beneficiaries
of the industry in some way. They cherry-pick time periods and funds
to make the firms look good, exclude the bad stuff or use the wrong
benchmarks for comparison. Many tout the aforementioned metric
called internal rate of return (IRR), a financial ratio that cheerleaders
can easily manipulate to make pedestrian returns to investors seem
stratospheric.[38] Good independent studies of private equity returns
do exist, though. The most positive suggest that the median PE fund
outperforms normal stock indices by around 1 percent per year, but that
shrinks to zero when it's benchmarked against more appropriate indices
of smaller companies, like the kinds of companies private equity firms
buy out. Others are less rosy: "The average private equity fund return is
comparable or inferior to that of public equity," stated Ludovic Phalippou of Oxford University, "in sharp contrast to what industry associations
report." And almost everyone agrees that returns to private equity are
likely to only decline, and faster than other sectors.[39]

It's worse than this. An iron rule of investing is that higher risks
should correlate with higher returns (and with investor control and good
liquidity, which means investors can easily find a buyer when they want
to sell). But private equity turns this around: the poor LPs must lock
their capital away, inaccessible, often for years, and they get pedestrian
returns. The GPs, by contrast, take very little risk while potentially reap-
ing enormous returns. Which is why the titans are better paid—much
better paid—than the CEOs of big banks. These billionaires are living
proof of that old adage in finance: "Where are the customers' yachts?"
Recently at a dinner party I sat next to a former private equity general
partner, a smart, witty, and engaging man. I ran these complaints past

him and he replied by drawing for me on a napkin a simple picture of the typical capital structure of a private equity acquisition—those Bidcos, Holdcos, and so on—to explain why the GPs *needed this* structure. What about society's perspective? I asked. So he drew a graph of risk against return. But, I pressed, how much of the money put at risk actually belongs to the GPs? One percent, he replied sheepishly. And that's in line with the private equity norm: between *1 and 2 percent* of the investment pool tends to come from the titans' own funds. He stopped drawing. Within minutes he had gathered up his family and left without saying good-bye.[40]

There are a couple more dull but important reasons people invest in these sectors. First, that ocean of money sloshing around the world has to go somewhere; and second, accounting and tax factors encourage people to invest. Some funds also do genuinely and consistently outperform for investors, so everyone wants a piece of them, but the queues are so long that only the Goldman Sachses and Harvard endowments of this world will get in. As one researcher caustically put it, those funds "will never manage *your* money." If the sector has underwhelming returns overall, and if you're not Goldman Sachs, then mathematically your pension funds are more than likely to end up investing in a fee-eating donkey. Many pension fund managers also think like gamblers: that they are so brilliant that they can beat the odds.

The reasons get sadder. When a scarily underfunded pension deficit can't be filled with normal market returns, many managers—with a duty of care over our private pensions, for goodness' sake—think the answer is to gamble by flinging money at these high-risk creatures, assuming that returns should correlate with risk. These investors may well understand the predation that's going on at Penny Ray's end, but they fail to appreciate that they are unlikely to share in its fruits. There are even less wholesome reasons people invest in private equity and hedge funds. One is bribery. In 2009 the Carlyle Group agreed to pay a $20 million fine after a New York State official took a bribe in exchange for channeling a portion of the state's pension fund to Carlyle for it to manage—and cream fees from. And, one report found, the episode "did not prove to be isolated."[41] Less illegally, some big university endowment fund-raisers chasing donations from wealthy private equity alumni will offer to return the favor. Backscratching and favors for friends are rife.

But now here's the most tragic part of this sorry mess. Get this: many fund managers invest our money into private equity and hedge funds because they want to be cool. I'm not kidding. Every single person I asked about this agreed it was a factor.

Phalippou says investors often tell him how dull it is to invest in plain-vanilla stuff. "They say, 'I work in this bank. I am bored to death. I just have to invest in these equities and bonds. You can only invest passively; you don't trade, you don't turn over your portfolio; you try to minimize costs and taxes. How boring is that? If I don't invest in private equity and hedge funds then I am the biggest loser ever.'" Simon Lack said he looked at 3,500 hedge fund proposals when he worked at JP Morgan and remembered that "there were no boring meetings. You meet some of the most talented people in investing. That is pretty cool." A Swiss bank employee with years of experience choosing how and where to invest clients' money scoffed at how many people were dazzled by the "halo effect" of the moguls' mega-riches. "With some investors, there is nothing you can say to them that will ever persuade them they aren't going to make tons of money," he told me. "They want status. They open the *Financial Times* in the morning and read about KKR doing billion-dollar deals. They want to be at the table with the big boys."[42] He described a steady stream of opportunists in hedge funds and private equity trooping through his office, pitching marvelous tales of why his bank should invest with them. They smacked of desperation. They *had* to operate out of ultra-swanky offices. They played mind games, making his bank wait for six months to get an "exclusive" meeting with their sales people. They would shroud their proprietary trading strategies in mystery, a modern version of the eighteenth-century South Sea Bubble, where the company behind the scam offered a once-in-a-lifetime chance to invest in "a company for carrying out an undertaking of great advantage, but nobody to know what it is." The banker put on a painfully upper-class British accent to imitate a recent private equity visitor, saying the guy had taken himself so seriously that he had to double-check to make sure the whole thing wasn't a spoof. He almost never recommended that his bank invest with private equity.

Private equity firms and hedge funds sometimes get called locusts, vultures, or parasites, but I prefer to think of a different creature: the octopus. These companies take control of firms, then reach their tentacles out to every stakeholder group they can think of: employees, pensioners, taxpayers, elderly and vulnerable recipients of home care, creditors, consumers, people living nearby breathing in the company's factory fumes—and also those "sophisticated" coinvestors and lenders. The octopus-like entity will grasp each group, turn it upside down and shake out new cash flows from its pockets, then use those cash flows to borrow more, expanding the pool and expanding its fees.

Do these sectors serve *any* useful purpose?

Well, they make several points in their own defense. First, they attract large amounts of foreign investment into our countries. This is true, but if much of that inward investment is in the form of crowbars to tear the wealth and soul out of our newspapers and communities and siphon that wealth offshore, is that a national benefit? A second defense is that these sectors contain some, and perhaps most, of the most experienced, brilliant corporate minds, experts in fixing up failing companies. This is also true, but it's a *bad* thing, because those people—who include a couple of friends of mine—have been lured away from true wealth creation and helping build great companies and incentivized to engage in reckless financial engineering. They are a classic example of the finance curse brain drain out of useful sectors that I described in the introduction.

A third, related defense is that private equity firms have often built good, strong companies, either by fixing up failing firms or by squeezing out efficiencies through the buy-and-build model: buying up lots of companies and joining them together, centralizing functions, and creating economies of scale. There are indeed many examples of this.

But without these aggressive players the corporate fixers would have done their job anyway, as they used to, without the insane pay incentives to slash and burn. And while "buy and build" does often unlock value, much of it comes from monopolization rather than from building better products. A final defense argues that even if there is predation at one end, at least there are deserving beneficiaries at the other—private pension funds, for example, or the tax authorities. This is the old Chicago School story of shareholder value again, the quasi-religious belief held by many in the financial markets that if you focus on profits and profits alone, those will get reinvested, and it all washes out in the end, making everyone happy. But this defense doesn't hold water either, not just because the victims are generally poorer than the potential beneficiaries but also because the pension funds and tax authorities are usually getting screwed over too, and a lot of the profits flow offshore.[43]

Randall Smith's son, Caleb, once asked his father why he worked. "He said, 'It's a game and I love it. It's competition.' I said, 'How do you know who wins?' He told me it was whoever dies with the most money. I thought to myself, 'That's foolish.'"[44]

This game may or may not have been good for Randall Smith or for his family. What is certain is that it is good neither for Penny Ray nor for the country. Private equity and hedge funds are among the purest examples of financialization at work. The techniques these sectors have pioneered have spread to other business sectors, egged on by the law and the accounting firms and banks that set up so many of these schemes. The question now is: How do these techniques and financial flows play out across a whole country, and what other risks might they be storing up?

CHAPTER TEN

Big Hog

About an hour north along I-35 from Des Moines, Iowa, there was an old truck stop called the Boondocks that, until the day I visited it on October 19, 2018, sold gas and souvenirs. A former oil company engineer and entrepreneur named Bob Welch opened it in 1973, because this was where the highway ended. "You either had to go left, right—or come see me," he said. With its disheveled red-and-white exterior and its diner selling pork chops, fish sticks, and chicken-fried steaks and fries, it was a bit of a legend among midwestern travelers. During a blizzard in the 1970s it housed six hundred people for two days, with state troopers taking turns at the grill and washing dishes. At least three people who first met here have gotten married, and staff members remembered breaking up fights in the parking lot during divorce custody exchanges. Over the years, truckers had told staff not to change a thing, and so it remained, a historical relic in a changing world. Until the money finally ran out.[1]

I'd come to the Boondocks to meet Nick Schutt, a small corn and soybean farmer in his forties who had decided to run for the position of county supervisor in Hardin County, almost dead center in the middle of Iowa. Schutt (pronounced *shoot*), a beefy and imposing man with a gentle manner, wore jeans, a checked shirt, and a baseball cap, and he carried an air of quiet melancholy. "All I ever wanted to be was a farmer," he said.

"Small people have been kicked around so hard here that I decided to run for office. Ten years ago, you couldn't get me to introduce myself to you, I was so shy and timid. But if the dog gets kicked enough, it's going to bite." We left the Boondocks and he took me on a tour of the nearby town of Williams, near his farm.

Williams is a pretty, tree-filled lattice of four by twelve streets, with painted wooden houses, freshly cut lawns, and two churches: one Lutheran, one Catholic. Schutt grew up in a house next to the town's meat locker and remembers, as a child, watching workers butcher cattle. The locker had closed a few weeks before my visit. He showed me an antiques and craft shop on the corner, which had failed a year earlier but still had merchandise in the window. There was a bar, where he used to play pool, which had closed three or four years ago. Farther back, there'd been three grocery stores, two dealers in farm implements, and four gas stations: two on the highway, and two in town, all competing for business. There'd been a creamery, a chicken hatchery, a stockyard, and a sale barn taking in cattle and hogs from the surrounding area for delivery to the packing plants nearby. They were also gone. Williams had once had a car wash, a hobby shop, and a doctor's office: all closed. Schutt pointed sadly to a building, now shuttered and dark, where his mother used to run a restaurant. I visited her in an old farmhouse nearby, where she lives with her wheelchair-bound husband, Tom, who could remember how things used to be. "They'd have a band in summertime, every Wednesday night. It would be so full of cars, you couldn't park," he reminisced. "They had a big walk-in screen outdoors; you'd pay a dime for a movie." He paused for a while. "Then the shops began to close down. One by one, they just closed. And," he added as an afterthought, "the morals and the values are gone."

When I visited Williams on a Friday afternoon in October 2018, the only signs of movement I could see in the town center were two men chatting and the Stars and Stripes fluttering in a light breeze. There's still a post office, open four hours a day; a small, nondescript café; a library; a local bank; and a building housing a collection of classic cars mostly from the '40s and '50s, put together by a wealthy local enthusiast, who had died recently, which Schutt expected to close soon. People still live here, but it's morphed from an agricultural town into a dormitory town for retired folk and people who mostly work in urban centers elsewhere. When I visited I'd just watched *Back to the Future* on my hotel television, in which the time-traveling action mostly happens in 1955 in a thriving rural town square abuzz with shops, theaters, and a classic diner throbbing with hormone-fueled teenagers. The contrast with Williams in 2018 shocked me.

Williams's slow-motion decline is just a version of a story that has played out across rural America. While the US population has risen by 75 million since 1990, rural populations have fallen by 3 million, and the country has seen a "ruralization of distress," as one study put it, with a loss of jobs and businesses, more empty houses, and a rise in the average age of residents. In metropolitan areas, especially "superstar cities," the trends have been in the other direction. Rural decline is linked to many factors: falling birth rates and demographic changes, the removal of government agricultural supports, deindustrialization and the shift to services sectors, globalization and foreign competition in manufacturing, the global financial crisis and its aftermath, drug addiction, and increased economic inequalities. Deregulation has also hammered rural areas by allowing airlines, banks, and telecom providers to raise the price of infrastructure and services to high-cost, sparsely populated regions.[2]

Maybe the most commonly held idea about rural decline hinges on the rise of capital-intensive farming and big agribusinesses, as large farms employ ever-bigger machines and fewer workers. Iowa's mostly flat topography is especially amenable to this, allowing for enormous fields where you can deploy monsters like the John Deere forty-eight-row corn planter, 120 feet wide at the business end, steered by satellite. People harbor a sense of inevitability, even fatalism, about all this: machines get bigger and more efficient, and jobs get displaced. But, many believe, higher profits from mechanization also get reinvested, creating new jobs elsewhere, and in Iowa's case this has meant people shifting their workplace from farms to urban centers. This, they shrug, is just the inevitable price of progress.

There's certainly something to this. But if that's as far as your understanding goes, you're missing half the story. The other half concerns the financialization of agriculture, which has had a devastating impact on towns like Williams across America and helped persuade millions of disempowered rural voters to march for Donald Trump. This part of the story is anything but inevitable; in fact, it's quite reversible. And this is tremendously good news, for it means it's possible to breathe life back into rural America.

Iowa is one of the best places to see the finance curse in action. That's because the essence of farming—the sustainable conjuring of crops and animals from rain, soil, and old-fashioned hard work—is pure wealth creation. Mechanization and technology, among other things, have unleashed immense efficiencies and created oceans of new wealth. The problem is the invisible infrastructure of financial engineers perched atop these farms and communities, using market power, tax "optimization," and many other techniques. Mechanization has created great wealth in rural America—and financialization has then extracted it and shipped it out to where the rich folk live. This returns us to the paradox at the heart of the finance curse: as more money has flooded into the farming system, the rural farming economy has grown dramatically poorer.

In an earlier age the federal government provided American farmers with remarkable multilayered support. Faced with the finance-driven Great Depression and the legendary Dust Bowl of the 1930s, Roosevelt's New Deal directed large public infrastructural investment to rural communities. The first Farm Bill in 1933 supported farm economies by discouraging overproduction and establishing a link between the price of farm goods and their costs of production, so farmers could be confident of making a good living. A price floor was set for agricultural products (a bit like setting minimum wages for jobs), and a nationally coordinated grain reserve was created to soak up excess production from bumper harvests and release it back into markets when supplies tightened up, smoothing price swings. The government provided cheap loans and subsidized cutting-edge agricultural research. There were multiplier effects all over: healthy farms formed the backbone of local economies, providing good livings not just for farmers and their employees but also for the local purveyors of feed, seeds, veterinary services, and agricultural implements and for the meat lockers, sale barns, doctors, diners, cinemas, car washes, dealerships, gas stations, local banks, and insurance firms. When millions of increasingly prosperous urban and coastal consumers bought their Iowa-raised pork loins or milled flour, cash cascaded back into towns like Williams. All these people and businesses paid taxes, which helped support the whole system. Mechanization multiplied farm yields, and while some farm jobs were lost, much if not most of the new wealth stayed circulating locally.

Alongside this healthy economic system ran another circulatory system, just as important, involving farming itself. Typical farms were widely diversified: corn, soybeans, hay, oats, alfalfa, fruit, hogs and cattle in pasture, and often chickens, turkeys, and geese. Diversification served as an economic shock absorber: if prices fell in one market, the farm would be cushioned by its other output (and lower grain prices, for instance, meant lower feed costs for animals). This, plus government supply-management systems to smooth commodity price swings, reduced the need for financial insurance. And farm diversification served as an *ecological* shock absorber too. Manure fell in open pasture, earthworms and dung beetles helped it fertilize the soil directly, and regular crop and pasture rotations exchanged nutrients back and forth. Plants like alfalfa reinforced the soil with deep perennial roots, and cover crops stopped hard rains from causing erosion, helping farmland regenerate. "The first law of ecology is that everything is interconnected," said John Ikerd, professor emeritus at the University of Missouri and a well-known agricultural economist based in Fairfield in eastern Iowa.

"The industrial approach comes out of a mechanistic way of looking at the world: if a part doesn't work, you take it apart and fix it. The other is a living system: if you take care of it, it regenerates and renews."[3] Farming back then was a skilled, creative, and innovative profession, requiring constant attention and deep expertise not only about the soil, the vegetation, the animals, the inputs, the machinery, and all the other elements in the interlinked system, but also about how the parts fit together—and how they fit into different produce markets, the government's support system, and the community. My father, who specialized in tropical soil management during my childhood in Malawi, India, and Brazil, said his career was significantly inspired by the principles of skilled land management developed in the US Midwest, which he imbibed at Cornell University in the 1950s. Farming was a source of immense pride, even superiority, and as a highly skilled job it commanded good incomes, comparable to those of—believe it or not—bankers.

From the 1950s, libertarians and big business began to push back against government regulations. Ezra Taft Benson, secretary of agriculture, urged farmers to "get big or get out." The farm payments system began to get whittled down, and the system of supply and demand management was weakened but also got a third pillar: international trade was opened up as an outlet or inlet for farm surpluses or deficits. A gargantuan deal to export grain to the Soviet Union in 1972 soaked up all of America's excess grain supplies within two years; in short order, wheat prices had doubled and corn prices tripled. The rise of the global Euromarkets and the financial loosening as the Bretton Woods system collapsed were opening vast credit taps, so farmers could borrow plenty to invest more. Ikerd remembers being part of what was then an idealistic movement pushing for the rapid high-tech changes. "We were going to improve the efficiency of agriculture, bring down the costs of production, and deliver food security by making food affordable for everyone," he said. "The basic approach, which had been adopted in industry after industry, was to industrialize, specialize, and standardize [each component] and consolidate into larger operations. We moved away from the traditional idea of the family farm as a way of life, and it became a business."[4] In 1980, as the "Volcker shock" of high interest rates flayed newly indebted American farmers, the instability in the new farming system became clear. Soviet tanks rolled into Afghanistan, President Carter halted the grain deal in protest, and grain prices collapsed. A severe drought in 1983 tipped many over the edge. By the following year the nation's farm debt was fifteen times what it had been in 1950. Output was higher, yet net farm income was less than a third of what it had been then. Iowa was at the epicenter of the ruin.

For many Iowans, farming was much more than a business: it was part of their identity, their soul, their heritage, their status, their family, and their community. One was Norma Fetter, who lived with her husband, Phil, and their ten children on his third-generation family farm near Chelsea, Iowa, raising hogs, cattle, and chickens. She remembers the day when debt destroyed her family. Phil had borrowed heavily to replace his hog herd, which had been wiped out by swine disease, but could no longer pay, and his depression got bad. "The little one, Joe, was five years old. He said that Daddy was out in the barn, out in the machine shed with a rifle," Norma recalled. She got some neighbors in to try to talk him out of it. "He kept saying things like 'Mom would be so disappointed in me,'" she said, adding, "He couldn't hear anything. . . . His mind was just too far gone. He just couldn't grasp anything anymore. And finally, I did stand back, otherwise I could have been gone too." The farm and house were sold back to the bank at a loss, and she and the children "had no place to go." She took a string of different jobs: "You get up every day and you do what you have to do."[5] Across the Midwest, white crosses were driven into courthouse lawns, each memorializing a farm that had gone under. Lenders were taking family pets as collateral.

Meanwhile, another development was emerging: a process some call the "Great Chickenization." This was pioneered by John Tyson, a truck owner who started out transporting poultry from farmers in Arkansas to Chicago and St. Louis, then began to assemble a chicken meat empire. He reached exclusive supply agreements with farmers and supplied them with his own vitamin-enriched feed and chicks from local hatcheries. He offered or arranged credit for the farmers and got them to build bigger chicken houses. He bought feed mills and hatcheries and, in 1947, incorporated his company, Tyson Feed & Hatchery, to run it all. By the 1950s, as his son Don took over, the Tysons started to borrow large sums. They built slaughterhouses and negotiated special deals with supermarkets and fast-food outlets. They invested in advanced chicken-rearing technologies to make bigger, meatier, faster-growing birds. They also took on a brilliant accountant, who provided a lesson that had already been learned by Britain's monopolizing, tax-cheating Vestey brothers (see chapter one): if you can build a vertically integrated company, from farmer to processor to transporter to consumer, there's a lot more money to be made in the twists and turns of the supply chain. The Tysons set up a shell company operation to help them shift profits around inside their empire, saving them $27 million in tax in 1985 alone.[6] And the firm's size helped it mine another large seam of profit: during cycles of boom and bust, its fortress balance sheet allowed it to buy up the flotsam from bankrupt competitors very cheaply.

And there was one further trick that the accountant insisted on: Tyson should own as many parts of the supply chain as possible—all except for the chicken houses. Buying these would have required large, risky capital investments and a massive expansion of the company balance sheets. Under the New Church of Finance (described in chapter nine), more capital outlay meant a lower return on assets: a less impressive financial ratio to show to Wall Street investors and analysts. Better to shunt these risks off to small chicken farmers, then simply send chicks to the farmers, pay them a fee per chicken once they were fully grown, then absorb the birds back into Tyson's processing, transport, and logistics operations. But for the farmers there was an almighty catch: they couldn't buy their chicks or inputs from, or sell the slaughter-ready chickens to, anyone else. And this gave Tyson what all monopolists crave: power. If farmers dared join a union, Tyson just stopped buying their chickens, and with a Tyson-linked mortgage over their heads, their large debts would tip them into bankruptcy—then Tyson could buy up the pieces on the cheap, or find someone else to take over. The company started to shackle these captive farmers with ever more restrictive contracts, cheeseparing their profits in countless ways. In *The Meat Racket*, a landmark book about the Great Chickenization, the author and investigator Christopher Leonard describes hearing from a field technician how a Tyson manager gave them one explicit instruction: "Go out there and piss the farmer off!" They needed to show the farmer who was boss, and "if anything went wrong, they were told to blame the farmer for it. . . . [M]istakes could never be admitted."[7] Leonard followed the story of Jerry and Kanita Yandell, chicken farmers who lost their home after chicks that Tyson delivered began inexplicably falling sick in large numbers, and they had to soak up the losses. They borrowed more to invest in better heating and hygiene systems, but to no avail; they went bankrupt and had future paychecks docked to pay off their debts. Laotian immigrants took over their operations, rather like the fictional immigrant family in Upton Sinclair's classic novel *The Jungle* (1904), full of hope and visceral optimism, confident that they could succeed by withstanding extreme hardship and bone-bending hard work. Tyson helped them borrow large sums like the farmers who preceded them, got the Farm Service Agency to guarantee the loans, and tied them into even more onerous terms than those that had bankrupted the Yandells. Tyson also created a secretive internal competitive "tournament" that set farmer against farmer, constantly telling them they were in danger of falling behind, manipulating the prices paid, and shifting more risk onto their shoulders. "An invisible force hung over their farms, steadily driving down their paycheck each month," Leonard explained, which created "a new breed of high-tech sharecroppers who live on the ragged edge of bankruptcy."[8] Eventually even these frugal, overworked farmers were driven into bankruptcy too.

This profitable Tyson-led model of farming began to spread across America and into the beef industry. Hogs took longer to chickenize, largely because they were much more susceptible to disease when cooped up together closely. By the late 1980s, though, they had cracked the problem with massive doses of antibiotics, ushering in a staggering rush of consolidation. The number of hog farms in Iowa has fallen from 105,000 in the mid-1960s to few more than 5,000 today, while the number of hogs has risen from 13 to 20 million.[9]

In purely financial terms, that's an unvarnished success. I heard this story from Dave Miller, director of research at the Iowa Farm Bureau (IFB), one of America's most potent lobbyists for agribusiness. From a farming family himself, Miller still produces crops not far from the IFB's headquarters in Des Moines. He's old enough to remember cleaning out the dairy farm by hand, mucking out manure with a pitchfork every Saturday, and hand-carrying water to twelve sows in a lean-to shed. An affable, talkative man, Miller kept referring to a large tapestry on the wall behind his office desk showing a bucolic farm scene: a cow, a pig, chickens and sheep, and a small tractor and trailer harvesting on a lazy summer afternoon. "They want to take us back to that," he said, responding to the critics of the IFB's support of agribusiness. "Setting out on an open-station tractor, bouncing across the field on a hard steel seat? Now I'm in air-conditioned comfort. I plant half at night because of lighting and GPS, and now I'm at least twenty times more productive."

Miller described how the big money came in alongside the machines. As agricultural supply management and price controls fizzled out and credit was unleashed, hog farming had become a boom-and-bust business. "You could go from $15 hogs to $45 hogs in a year, then back to $15—a 300 percent swing." With breakeven in the $20s, $45 hogs were terrific. "But $15 killed you." Bankers didn't like lending into this seesaw world—but they also knew there was a ton of money in the system. It was chickenization that showed them the way in.

The new idea was that the small farmers would borrow to build large hog barns, and the large integrator firms would supply them with piglets and take away the hogs when they'd grown to slaughter weight. The barn owners would receive a fixed processing fee, say $8 per pig, to raise them from "farrow to finish" (piglet to adult). Now, with a fixed margin per hog and fairly predictable costs, this was at last a no-brainer for the banks to finance. The loans were made more secure for the banks by being bundled as part of the contracts the small barn owners had to sign with the large agribusinesses. "I call it New York money: this was Wall Street money, corporate money," Miller said. "This wasn't your small community bank anymore." This transformation of hog farming really got going in the 1990s, just when a new law deregulated banks' abilities to operate across state lines: within a decade from 1994, the number of out-of-state bank branches rose from 62 to almost 25,000. Banks bulked up, amid a merger frenzy. Denise O'Brien, an organic farmer near Atlantic, west of Des Moines, remembers the local effects. Local bankers who had once gone to church with their communities and shared in their pain were replaced by bigger players from out of town. "Regional banks started buying small banks, and their boards moved to urban areas; they could make these cold decisions about communities—they were no longer part of the community."[10] Money poured into Iowa—and it was soon flowing out again in rivers of interest payments and corporate dividends.

Though the agribusiness firms and increasingly confident finance houses took on the price risk from raising hogs, they could easily handle it, not least because large profits cushioned their balance sheets, their scale sometimes allowed them to massage market prices up and down to suit them, and they could also afford skilled risk teams to hedge prices with commodity derivatives in Chicago. Independent family hog farmers outside this system who carried the price risks themselves couldn't compete, and as they went bankrupt, the big firms, alongside financial investors, could then buy their assets at distressed prices. As small farmers lost ground, the number of hogs freely on sale in independent markets began to shrink rapidly. Old Iowa farmers all remember the meat lockers, auction markets, buying stations, and sale barns winking out of existence, one by one, as the large integrated agricultural firms took these operations in-house, owning and controlling more and more of the pipeline from rural piglet to slaughterhouse to even, in some cases, urban dinner plate.

Until these changes came along, "the packers had to go out and beg for pigs and pay a fair price," remembers Chris Petersen, one of Iowa's few remaining small-time hog farmers. "The packer had to run around the countryside looking for pigs to keep their plant running. Some days you got more money because they wanted those pigs real bad."[11]

As late as 1992, less than a third of American hogs were raised on farms with more than two thousand animals, and nearly 90 percent were sold on the open market. Today, perhaps 98 percent are raised on large farms, and only 5 percent are sold at open auction. Now, said Ikerd, "you have those large corporations making the decisions. They can stabilize the supply of product into the market at a level that is profitable" in a market that is, he continued, concentrated and centrally controlled. "People brag about the free-market economy, but we have central planning here—just not by government. It's central planning by corporations." While mechanization undoubtedly delivered one narrow kind of efficiency, he said, it stripped out others, notably the *market* efficiency that comes from competition generating the right price signals. "With the competitive situation you had accurate information and you could be sure the prices reflect what the markets want and value," he said. "Now we have an economy that is producing a lot of cheap stuff—but we don't know if it's producing the *right* stuff." For an example of this industry producing the wrong stuff, look at America's obesity statistics. But obesity has also been accompanied by hunger. "We now have more people food-insecure than back in the 1960s," Ikerd continued. "One in eight people in general, meaning they're not sure they'll have enough food to get them to their next paycheck. All that industrialization didn't feed hungry people."

Drive around Iowa's countryside today, and you'll soon see the large hog barns: long, low, straight buildings with mildly slanted corrugated roofs, large ventilation fans at the ends, and small grain silos attached— often with a large, murky lagoon next door. They call them CAFOs (concentrated animal feeding operations), confinements, or, in the words of Petersen and many others who oppose them, "corporate hog factories." The standard barn these days fits just under 2,500 hogs (any larger, and they are subject to more onerous supervision), and they often come in pairs or clusters. The ones I saw were generally deserted: once they've been built to the integrator's specifications and filled with pigs, they can be left alone and serviced maybe once a day, often by a low-paid laborer who comes in to check the machines, maybe top up the feed silos, and haul out any dead pigs. "Hog house janitors," some call them: this is not the high-skilled farming of an earlier age. There are about ten thousand CAFOs in Iowa.

Petersen has a small herd of high-quality Berkshire hogs—darker and hairier and more valuable than your standard bright pink pig in the hog barn—and he farms with his wife, Kristi, near Clear Lake in northern Iowa. He was radicalized as a young boy in the 1960s after he found the body of his mother, who had shot herself after getting a foreclosure letter. He's a well-known but divisive figure in Iowa farming: a former president of the Iowa Farmers Union and a card-carrying Democrat who has shared platforms with Hillary Clinton, John Kerry, Senator Cory Booker, and several other big names. Petersen drove me around some of the dirt roads crisscrossing the landscape near his home to look at the CAFOs. I'd asked some of the larger hog firms and some independent farmers if they could help me get inside one, but it was a "no" each time. Petersen took me up to the gate of one of them, but no farther. "If you go past that fence and someone comes, we're in jail," he said. It's often hard to figure out who owns these places, because they are frequently held by limited liability entities in complex and impenetrable corporate structures; usually the best way to find out who owns one is to follow one of the heavy trailers back to the packing plant. These limited liability structures, as one academic study explained, "deflect responsibility and liability from producers and shift risk to rural communities."[12]

Others have been inside the CAFOs, though, and it's well known that conditions for the animals are terrible. The pigs stand in large, densely packed pens, rarely seeing sunlight, touching real ground, or smelling fresh air, and their waste falls through a slatted floor to a huge concrete-lined pit underneath. They are often fed with special mixtures, including heavy-duty antibiotics, which bulk up the animals' muscles and speed their growth but also have helped build up antibiotic resistance in such delightful disease strains as the hospital "superbug" MRSA. Many animals are also fed ractopamine or Paylean, steroidal additives banned in more than one hundred countries, which give the pigs diarrhea and make them bite and fight: their tails are routinely cut off to minimize the damage.[13] The freaky diarrhea that falls down into the giant pits under the barns doesn't undergo the healthy, oxygenated organic processes that would happen in open pasture or in your garden compost heap; this is *anerobic* decomposition, which produces a farrago of toxic and noxious biochemicals and gases: hydrogen sulfide, ammonium bisulfate, and dimethyl sulfide, along with methane and nitrous oxide—potent greenhouse gases. It's not manure, Petersen said, it's "raw sewage." (And there's a lot of it: a 2,400-hog CAFO produces as much waste as a town of 8-10,000 people.) Visitors to CAFOs have described "an astringent chemical burn that sears your nostrils" and a choking haze from dried waste that's turned to powder. Fall into one of the bubbling pits when it's got a good brew going, and you won't come out alive. (Methane explosions happen: one explosion reportedly lifted a whole hog barn off the ground and threw an employee twenty feet from the building.) CAFOs spray this foaming mix on surrounding fields as fertilizer, and the rain washes it into the rivers. A Department for Natural Resources map of Iowa's "Impaired Waterbodies," with the worst rivers marked in red, looks like a slice of Iowa-shaped skin covered from top to bottom in red varicose veins. Agricultural toxins flow from Iowa rivers all the way to the Atlantic Ocean and are largely responsible for a "dead zone" the size of New Jersey in the Gulf of Mexico, depleted of aquatic life. Studies show all sorts of nasty medical effects on people living near CAFOs: asthma, bronchitis, watering eyes, tension, depression, and fatigue, to name a few.[14]

It wasn't until I met Marjorie Van Winkle, a feisty eighty-year-old grandmother from Brighton, in eastern Iowa, that I got a proper sense of how unpleasant these places can be for their neighbors. Marj, who drove a school bus for thirty-eight years, got active in opposing the CAFOs just after she retired in 2013, when she got a call from Kim Andersen, a woman she barely knew. "She said, 'Dave Eichelberger [a big local CAFO owner] is going to build a hog house, will you help me stop it?' I said, 'I sure will.' We've been fast friends ever since."

It's fair to say that Marj, as people call her, is hopping mad. She had voted solidly Republican for most of her life, but "boy, not anymore." She said, "Both sides are crazy. You have to hold your nose and vote." And it seems that holding noses—literally—has become a way of life in Big Hog country. As Marj drove me around Jefferson and Washington counties in her battered car, she'd stop at intervals and urge me to roll my window down. They weren't spraying the waste when I visited, but the smell was unpleasant in places and on one occasion, seventy-five or so yards from a CAFO waste lagoon, it made me gag.

But what really grossed me out wasn't the hog waste. Marj pointed to a structure across a field, an "animal mortality facility" that resembled an open aircraft hangar, with two long lines of what looked like pink sausage meat. "Piles of dead pigs," she said. They were too far away to count—a hundred? In a plastic file, Marj has a macabre collection of images of dead hogs: Dumpsters overflowing with them, heads lolling over the side; pink bloated bodies with legs sticking up; and even a pair of photos she calls "melted pig": one of a pig lying on the ground, taken in June, and another of the same pig looking flatter, taken a month later. "This pig made its own gravy," she added darkly. Outside each hog barn there's a pen or two where workers dump the dead animals; in a couple I could see trotters or ears or just a line of pink under a solid gate. The bodies go to rendering facilities, where they are crushed and tipped, bones, trotters, and all, into superhot cookers and turned into a range of products, including medicines, biofuels, cosmetics—and ingredients for animal feed.[15]

The stench and the pollution are large factors driving people off the land here, compounding the economic forces. Build a CAFO, and house prices nearby will slump, starting a domino effect. And once the hog barns made people move away, said Marj, "then the outlaws moved in. People making drugs, meth labs. They smell like hogshit; put them in a hog area, and they won't be noticed." She showed me a house near her own with a yard full of rusting machinery, which she said she and the local sheriff suspected was a meth lab. "Then there are the sex offenders. They aren't allowed to live near a school. So when the local school closes, guess who moves in?"

The CAFOs have, unsurprisingly, created enormous community tensions, as Petersen explained. "In the good old days, farmers waved at each other," he said. "Now they just stare at each other. One guy, he gives us the finger when we pass him on the roads."[16]

Kim Andersen, the woman who first brought Marj into anti-CAFO activism, lives on a gorgeous, tree-filled, four-hundred-acre family farm not far from Brighton. A college teacher, she moved here twelve years earlier with her husband, both doing off-farm jobs, and only fairly recently decided to make a go of organic farming. Along with the usual corn and beans, they grow oats, pumpkins, peas, and pick-your-own blueberries, and there's a large orchard with nut trees, pawpaws, and persimmon. (She has no animals: "We have a puppy, I can't even handle that, it's like a baby.") Prices for organic food can be good, but she has to work hard, emailing and calling to find buyers—there's a small feed mill in Wisconsin that has bought her oats, for instance, and a firm fifteen miles away that purchases corn and beans, and even a large Maharishi community in the pretty town of Fairfield, nearby, whose members consume a lot of organic produce. She reckoned there were 7,500 hogs within two miles to the south, and she doesn't drink from her taps now because "it tastes funny." A visiting granddaughter had recently asked her, "Why does it smell like piggies here?" and she's not sure she wants her grandchildren to come and be exposed to the fumes again. Community life hasn't turned out as she'd hoped. "People drive forty to fifty miles to work every day; they don't have time to talk to their neighbors. I had hoped that there would be a real sense of community around here: I would get eggs from the neighbor, and people would get their blueberries from me. Butcher a cow, and we all take a quarter. I described this to somebody and they said, 'You want to live in a commune?'"

She soon discovered where power lies in rural Iowa. A new CAFO operator nearby, whom she didn't want me to name in print, threatened new hog barns on the other side of her fence unless she bought his land at way above the market price. "He terrorized me: he called me, texted me, gave me ultimatums and deadlines," she said. He and other CAFO operators "walk around with this air, 'I am invincible; I can do whatever I want to you people.' He said this stuff with a shit-eating grin. He turns up, and sometimes I am alone." She got a dog and a pistol for protection and went with old Marj to take an NRA class on how to shoot. Lawyers have told her to keep a "smell calendar" as evidence but say it's unlikely to help much; the best solution, they said, is to move away. But who, in such stench, would buy? "I have had cancer twice. I say, 'Who was here first, folks?' Last winter I was so depressed, I wouldn't open the blinds anymore. Some days I think, 'Screw him, I'm going to do this blueberry thing. I am passionate about it. I want to grow food.' Other days I want to move, but I don't know where to go. Everywhere there's something going on; if it's not hogs, it's chickens or fracking."

With Kim Andersen, Marj Van Winkle, Chris Petersen, and pretty much every one of the twenty-five or so people I spoke to for my Iowa research, one name kept cropping up: the Iowa Farm Bureau. Set up in 1918 to represent farmers' interests, it describes itself today as a democratic, grassroots member organization and a voice of rural farmers and communities. But that doesn't paint an accurate picture. By far the most powerful member of the American Farm Bureau Federation, the IFB is a master of slick, snarky advertising and is the foremost protector and promoter of the financialized CAFO agricultural system. Anyone who confronts the system immediately bumps up against what feels like an electrified force field of power and money in the form of the IFB.

In its corporate structure, the IFB is a peculiar, tax-exempt creature.[17] Essentially its core function, alongside lobbying, is insurance. At the last count, the Iowa Farm Bureau Federation owned 59.3 percent of an NYSE-listed company called FBL Financial Group, Inc., its main operating subsidiary, alongside a range of other shareholders including BlackRock, Vanguard, Deutsche Bank, Goldman Sachs, Wells Fargo, Morgan Stanley, Citigroup, Bank of America, UBS, Barclays, and a bunch of hedge funds and other investment funds. FBL Financial Group in turn owns various other entities, including FBL Wealth Management, LLC; FBL Financial Services, Inc.; FBL Financial Group Capital Trust; FBL Leasing Services, Inc.; and, most impressively, the Farm Bureau Life Insurance Company. This last entity held $8.8 billion in assets in 2016 and earned $1.1 billion in revenues, mostly from life insurance premiums and investment income from its diversified holdings (bonds, stocks, derivatives, mortgage loans, and mortgage-backed securities). This "voice for Iowa's farmers" is a thoroughly financialized body that represents out-of-state finance and has long lobbied for causes close to Wall Street concerns: it opposed the Voting Rights Act of 1965 outlawing racial discrimination in voting, it has opposed raising the minimum wage, and it has supported drilling offshore for oil.[18] What this has to do with Iowa agriculture is a good question.

One group that regularly confronts the IFB is a scrappy nonprofit in Des Moines called Iowa Citizens for Community Improvement (CCI), which campaigns on behalf of local communities. (Iowa CCI won national fame in August 2011 when its members provoked Mitt Romney on the campaign trail by urging big corporations be taxed, prompting him to shoot back, "Corporations are people, my friend.") CCI's modest office walls are festooned with images of people brandishing placards at gas stations, outside town halls, and inside offices and courts. Jess Mazour, an organizer there, showed me a picture filled with

protesters, most holding up CLEAN WATER NOW! signs and one holding
up a jar of dirty water representing runoff from CAFOs. "I made up this
jar with dirt from the parking lot," Mazour said. "When we left, they
called in a hazmat team to have it taken away." Another poster shows
a cartoon Grim Reaper with HF 316 written on his scythe. This refers
to the extraordinary events that happened after the Des Moines Water
Works tried to sue three drainage districts in northwest Iowa over high
levels of nitrates running off from CAFO-heavy farming operations and
polluting Des Moines's sources of drinking water, costing the waterworks a fortune in cleaning costs. The IFB responded by sponsoring
a state bill called House File 316, which sought to *dismantle* the Des
Moines Water Works utility into bite-sized municipal fragments. "It
was revenge—absolutely," said Mazour. "And our own city council was
so weak that it came out in favor of the bill; they were scared that if
they didn't participate in the dismantling, they wouldn't have any say in
how it was being dismantled." A judge dismissed the Des Moines Water
Works' lawsuit. CCI helped blunt the IFB's attack on the waterworks,
but only after "tough, tough organizing, demanding public hearings at
the Capitol, getting hundreds to show up." And the IFB's bill was, when
I saw Mazour in October 2018, merely dormant, not dead. "Someone
could reintroduce it," she said. "It's this haunting little bill. If we pissed
anyone off, they'd advance it."[19]

New CAFOs are popping up all the time, and fighting against
them, Mazour said with a sigh, is like playing whack-a-mole with both
hands tied behind your back. There's a predictable pattern: a big firm
opens a slaughterhouse and needs new, steady supplies of animals to
keep its production lines running at full tilt. So it signs up new CAFO
farmers nearby, making easy credit available to set up hog barns. Mazour
reeled off the names of incoming slaughterhouses: a joint venture facility
between Seaboard Foods and Triumph Foods in Sioux City, in western
Iowa, to process six million hogs a year; another five-million-hog processing plant near Marshalltown, northeast of Des Moines, run by the
Brazilian meat giant JBS; and a robot-filled plant that Prestage Farms

of North Carolina was opening up in Wright County, just north of where Nick Schutt farms, which Mazour predicted would "see a massive expansion of factory farms."

The CCI activists go to community meetings, file complaints with the EPA, lobby the governor's office and the attorney general, and organize letters to news editors. They contact legislators and advise farmers and homeowners on tactics and tools to resist encroaching CAFOs. Everywhere, at every turn, they face a hard barrier of money, usually created by the IFB, which seems to have eyes and tentacles everywhere and a stable of powerful allies: the Iowa Cattlemen's Association, the Iowa Pork Producers Association, the Iowa Poultry Association, large multinationals like John Deere or the commodity traders Cargill or Archer Daniels Midland. There are fake front groups, often set up by the IFB, with appealing names: the Coalition to Support Iowa's Farmers, for instance, or the Iowa Partnership for Clean Water. The latter organization seeks to "inform all stakeholders" about "the consequences of frivolous legal action against farmers and the agriculture industry," and warns that "imposing harsh regulations would impede production."[20] Everyone profiting from this model of farming has teamed together to protect it, Mazour said: "We have run lots of campaigns to make minuscule changes to the system: air quality rules, manure, water quality. We tried passing a bill that said you can't spread manure on steep slopes or water-saturated ground. Something as commonsense as that, it still won't pass. We have met a brick wall, every step of the way."

Francis Thicke, a dairy farmer who ran for state secretary of agriculture in 2010, remembers encountering the IFB when serving on the Iowa Environmental Protection Commission. "With any controversial issue they were at every meeting," he said. "They would fight anything, any change, any rule. If the change gets through they would go to the legislature and fight it there. They can just knock out legislators." The IFB's political action committee finances friendly candidates—usually Republicans—arguably swinging the 2018 midterm results to Iowa's Republican governor Kim Reynolds, who won with 50.4 percent of the vote. It generally doesn't finance Democrats but hems them in, said Stephanie Mercier, an Iowan who worked on the Senate Agriculture Committee and is now senior fellow at the Farm Journal Foundation: "It is more like threats: 'We will spend against you.'" Tom Fiegen, a lawyer and state senator from 2001 to 2003, said the IFB's lobbying "has an Alice in Wonderland quality: when they say black they mean white, up means down, and family farmer means the big guys, corporations, integrators." The joke was, he said, that there were two types of officials: those who were owned by the IFB, and those who were scared of the IFB. Thicke summarized the situation in earthier terms: "The Republicans are fully on board with the Farm Bureau and the lobbyists—and the Democrats are chickenshit."[21]

Denise O'Brien, the organic farmer from Atlantic, had a more shocking encounter with the IFB in 2006, when she was the Democratic Party's nominee for Iowa secretary of agriculture. A few days before the election, she said, the Farm Bureau helped her Republican opponent by dredging up a $319.45 fine her husband had paid by check in 1987, because a hired worker had mistreated some of their cattle. They unleashed the "news" at a press conference. "They had a photo of the check," O'Brien remembered, "and they had this little old lady saying, 'Hi, Denise is an animal killer.'" Having been fifteen points ahead of her Republican rival in the polls, she said, she lost the vote, 51–49 percent. "In the last seventy-two hours they ran me under," she said. "The Farm Bureau owns the Iowa legislature."[22]

With the IFB's relentless urging, the integrated family-farming systems of an earlier age have been dismantled and put back together in new ways, with the long path from pig semen to adult hog to your dinner plate now partly or largely controlled by a single big actor. As competition has shriveled and been replaced by private central planning, the roundabout pipelines that once circulated wealth and food back and forth within and between rural and urban populations have been straightened out and turned into a one-directional set of financial pipelines (or, as academics put it, "value chains"), shipping wealth and farm produce steadily outward from rural America to the urban money centers, overseas, and offshore. Fresh hog meat leaves Iowa and returns wrapped in branded plastic. "It pisses me off," said Austin Frerick, a native Iowan and fellow at the Open Markets Institute, "that folks in DC or New York or San Francisco can get a better, healthier locally sourced meal than I can in most Iowa towns."[23]

Various players along these chains are engaged in a tug-of-war with each other to try to maximize their share of the immense streams of wealth flowing from Iowa. Alongside the various farming operations, there are the giant seed and agrochemical companies; the big integrator companies like Smithfield or JBS, which typically own the slaughterhouses and packing plants; the giant global commodity trading firms like Cargill that buy and sell animal protein; the distributors; the processors; the transporters; and the supermarkets and online delivery services that get the hog meat into American homes. The more of these functions that can be brought into one integrated operation, the more knowledge and control the players have. And at each node in these chains, private equity–like extraction from a range of stakeholders is going on.

One stakeholder is the land itself and the environment. With the loss of the old diversified, sustainable farming practices, with their inbuilt shock absorbers, and their replacement with vast, rolling monocultural fields of corn or soybeans, Iowa's "black gold" soil—long regarded as among the world's best—is now steadily degrading, losing an estimated five tons or so of healthy topsoil per acre per year, versus a natural regeneration rate one-tenth of that. At this rate, by some estimates, Iowa would have maybe sixty harvests left. "We have been deficit-spending our ecological capital," explains Thicke.[24] The poisoned rivers, the barren "dead zone" in the Gulf of Mexico, the pain inflicted on hogs fighting and biting for space in reeking hog barns, the bronchitis and depression among people inhaling air laden with CAFO toxins, and the obesity resulting from the availability of so much cheap, antibiotic-fed hog meat—all are outcomes of the guiding ideology of maximizing the wealth of shareholders at the expense of everyone, and everything, else.

As the natural shock absorbers have been removed, and as a dispersed ecosystem of American farming skills, expertise, and intellectual property has been brain-drained into the corporate offices of global giants in Chicago, New York, Shanghai, or São Paulo, farms growing only one or two crops rely more on financial markets to insure themselves, feeding finance. And some 60 percent of crop insurance is now covered by the biggest stakeholder of all: the American taxpayer. When crop prices fell in the 2014–15 season, for instance, American farmers received almost $25 billion in federal farm subsidies from three crop insurance programs routed through private for-profit providers—and nearly 80 percent of that went to the biggest ten recipients.[25]

The next set of stakeholders are the CAFO operators themselves. You might think, by the way they can mistreat their neighbors with such impunity, and by the protection the Farm Bureau affords them, that they'd be doing well. Not so. And that's mostly because these "hog janitors," like those poor poultry farmers, are hemmed in by restrictive contracts that leave them almost entirely at the big integrator firms' mercy. Here's how it works. A 2,500-hog barn costs perhaps $750,000 to build on a turnkey basis these days. If the farmer borrows that much at 5 percent over twenty years, the interest and amortization would come to some $75,000 per year. The Big Ag firm arranges all the financing through its connections in financial markets in New York or Chicago, and then it simply sets the price it pays per hog to give the CAFO operator just enough to service the loan and pay for running costs, with only a modest amount left over.

Why would a farmer sign such an unfair contract? Josh Flint, spokesman for The Maschhoffs, one of America's largest pork producers, explained one reason. "If you are independent, you can either make a fortune or lose a fortune. That's what we offer the partners: that revenue stabilization so they aren't at the whims of the market. The market risks, we assume. . . . We have a team that uses hedging and options, risk tools."[26] But owning the farms was too much for the big guys: "If we owned all these sites and held the equity to secure the land," he said, "it becomes a really massive proposition." This was, again, the New Church of Finance, with its obsession with returns to capital: the less capital on the balance sheet, the better the ratio. (This is the same general reason Uber doesn't own cars, Facebook doesn't create expensive in-house media content, and Airbnb doesn't own apartments: these platforms shovel the risks, costs, and debts onto the shoulders of others and make nice profits off the top of their hard work.) The CAFO operators are also attracted by the idea that after the twenty-year loan is paid off, they have equity in those barns, and they also like the hog waste, because it saves them from buying expensive chemical fertilizers for their corn and beans.

Yet these apparent attractions obscure just how little power the farmers have. The custom feeding contract the farmer signs with the big integrator is a complex document setting forth the farmer's role and responsibilities, alongside some incentives to maximize output. The lawyer Tom Fiegen, who has advised several CAFO farmers near his practice in Cedar Rapids on these contracts, describes them as "pages of things that shift the risk from the integrator to them." While there is wiggle room in a few places, there is basically "no choice, and everything is dictated," Fiegen said. There are countless ways for the large firm to cheesepare the hog-barn owner's income. Most important, while the loans for the hog buildings typically run over twenty years, the contracts are for shorter terms, usually ten years. At year eleven, the farmer still has ten years to pay on the loan and desperately needs a new contract to keep the pigs flowing through, to earn the per-hog fees and meet the bank payments. His anxiety is ratcheted up by the fact that the loan is often secured not just against the hog barn, but against the farmer's *entire* farm, including the cropland. This gives the integrator all the leverage to obtain much more onerous contract terms.

All sorts of other nasties lurk in the contracts. A farmer may have to reimburse the integrator for pigs that die above a percentage threshold, say 3 percent—yet if the integrator delivers an injured or limping pig to the farmer, "too bad," said Fiegen, "you have to keep it." If the integrator doesn't deliver enough piglets, or there are losses during transport or from extreme weather events, the farmer may have to take the lost revenues on the chin. Unionization is a no-no. Farmers may be required to pay for all repairs and upgrades to their facilities—pay to install new heaters, say—at the company's request. Liability for pollution damage can be pushed onto the CAFO operators too, even though they don't have anything like the capital required to settle such claims. They may even be charged for using the hog manure. The list of leverage points is long and varied. The Iowa attorney general's office has pushed back against some of the worst contractual abuses, but lobbying, especially by the IFB, ensures that the contracts are essentially unregulated.[27] "They got them over a barrel, they get turned into indentured servants," said Petersen. "It's a gotcha thing." The CAFO farmers are unwilling to pay to clean up environmental damage largely because they can't afford to. The big firms, delivering "value to shareholders," won't pay.

The power and influence of the large monopolizing firms spread far beyond CAFOs. Fiegen also remembers representing the owners of small-farm grain elevators and feed mills in 1990–2000, as their markets withered. "These integrators either have their own mill or an exclusive contract with one mill, and everybody is shut out. It got to the point where [my clients] were giving away assets: if you wanted their feed mill, or grain bins or a truck, make an offer, any offer. We were selling for pennies on the dollar, because all the farmers that used to buy feed every week or every other week from them were gone." The bank got paid first, and as revenues and profits fell apart, the small businesses were "out of luck, they were just out of luck."

But Fiegen added one more thing, which brings us back to the money-parched plight of the town of Williams. As these large firms have taken more and more functions in-house and railroaded CAFO farmers into using their proprietary piglets, their custom feed, their veterinary services, their financing channels, their transporters, and their machinery suppliers, the local economic infrastructures have been denuded of life as functions have moved out of town, out of state. "Everything is at a distance," Fiegen said, "none of that trade is in the small towns." He recounted how an eight-thousand-acre operation run by two brothers near Jefferson, in central western Iowa, was broken up. "Everybody in town assumed that when those brothers retired or went out of business," he said, "everyone would have the chance to compete to rent part of it and farm it. But the lender forced them to liquidate and to sell it lock, stock, and barrel to a corporation out of Missouri. They brought all the equipment from Kansas City or parts of Missouri on a semi, they put the crop in, it's planted, then taken back. They don't spend a penny, *not a penny*, in Jefferson farming this eight thousand acres. We are seeing that scene repeated across Iowa."

This giant coastward, cityward shift of wealth is, as much as the mechanization, why the Boondocks truck stop closed, why Williams, Iowa, is so deserted early on a Friday afternoon, and why so much of rural America is so bitter. What's going on is a bit like the repeal of the 1862 Homestead Act, which spurred the settlement of the West. "All of this can be traced back to the financial services industry," said Fiegen. "Everyone is getting their cut, except for the people who are doing the work. The people at the top of the pyramid are siphoning it off." In 1995 the top four pork packers slaughtered around 45 percent of all of America's hogs. Now, around 85 percent of US hog production is under the sway of just four giants, with combined revenues of some $120 billion in 2017: Tyson Foods, Hormel Foods Corp., Chinese-owned Smithfield, and Brazilian-owned JBS.[28] The remaining family farmers serve as the packing plants' suppliers of last resort, giving this "the characteristics of a salvage market," as one study put it. Several other studies have found evidence of what you might call a "Big Hog Curse" or a "Hog Finance Curse." A 2003 survey of 2,250 US counties, another study of 1,100 Illinois towns, and a subsequent University of Tennessee study of all 99 Iowa counties all found that those with more and larger hog confinements suffered from lower per capita economic growth; in hog-heavy counties in Iowa, incomes fell even as statewide income rose by 54 percent from 1982 to 2007. Others have found that the Big Hog counties have higher numbers of food stamp recipients, faster declines in small businesses, lower retail sales, lower real estate values, and slower job creation.[29] One study found that siting a large hog barn within half a mile will knock 40 percent off a home's value; another found that siting within a tenth of a mile tended to reduce it by 88 percent. Usually, such places would simply be unlivable. All this reduces property tax revenues and schools budgets, even as heavy vehicles visiting CAFOs every day put large new strains on road maintenance budgets.[30]

This is how wealth floods out of Iowa to the coastal money centers, overseas, and offshore. This is the finance curse in action. And it's nice work if you can get it.

Have American consumers, at least, benefited from the Great Chickenization of hogs? In a word, no. Studies show that raising pigs in open pasture or alternative systems can generate similar or better per-hog revenues than raising them in CAFOs, and Ikerd estimates that if alternative methods are applied and done right, retail prices would be barely higher than they are today. In fact, since the mid-1980s the inflation-adjusted cost of a basket of groceries has risen steadily, faster than inflation, while the farmers' share of that basket has fallen, from around a third to a sixth. The National Farmers Union reckons that hog farmers now get just 69 cents for every $5 that consumers spend on bacon. But that's the price in the markets that still exist; CAFO farmers, roped in their contracts, get a lot less. If farmers are getting less but consumers aren't paying less, then there's a large hidden surplus of wealth being extracted from the system.[31]

To understand where that surplus is going, consider again that long "value chain" of agricultural wealth, but this time as a series of links made of strong but stretchy rubber, each link containing a certain amount of value. The players ranged along the chain all pull against each other, to get as much for themselves as they can. As some firms merge or vertically integrate into bigger entities, they not only increase their reach along the chain, but bigger players have stronger muscles too, so they can grab even more. So monopoly will cascade through the chain: if one set of players merges into a bigger, stronger player, others will feel the need to do likewise—or get pulled over.

This is now happening apace. The 2018 approval of a $66 billion merger between the German chemical giant Bayer and the agricultural colossus Monsanto, following the even bigger merger of agricultural chemicals juggernauts Dow Chemical and DuPont Inc. in 2017 and the purchase of Syngenta by ChemChina in 2016, has generated massive new concentrations of market power in agriculture. Among other things, this has raised fears of a "Facebook of Farming," as the large firms amass troves of data to stay ahead of and kill smaller competitors. Antitrust economists use a CR4 measure of market concentration of the top four firms, and a figure above 40 percent is considered highly concentrated; after the recent agrochemical mergers, the CR4 ratio in this sector was estimated at 82 percent.[32] Vastly increased power may enable the giants to force farmers into accepting such delights as "suicide seeds" (or the "terminator gene"), herbicide- and pest-resistant seeds that are infertile, meaning farmers can't resow their crops and have to buy another expensive load each year. Each corporate giant is the fruit of many mergers, with historical family trees with numerous filigree parts converging to a single fat stump.

Similarly, four global trading firms now control three-quarters of the world grain market. Known as ABCD—Archer Daniels Midland (ADM), Bunge, Cargill, and (Louis) Dreyfus—they own extensive transport networks worldwide, and they own or control ports, grain silos and mills, biofuel refineries and food processing plants, trucks, ships, and farming relationships, giving them the privileged information they need to manipulate markets, often using complex financial instruments, and the ability to shift billions around to escape tax. Once, an ADM executive wearing an FBI wire recorded company executives in hotel rooms in Hawaii agreeing with competitors to fix prices and sales volumes, costing others hundreds of millions. Executives at ADM had a saying: "The competitor is our friend and the customer is our enemy."[33]

These firms, like the Iowa Farm Bureau, push a "feed the world" vision that favors deregulatory free-trade deals and prioritizes big agribusiness over family farming, ignoring the fact that thrusting low-cost US agricultural exports into foreign markets has thrown millions of small farmers in poor countries off the land, generating widespread rural hunger (and in Mexico's case, sending large numbers of people north to the United States, many to work in CAFOs). Denise O'Brien remembers the conversations under the Clinton trade department in the 1990s. "They were talking about 800 million hungry people in the world. They saw them as consumers, not as people in need. It hit me: we weren't talking the same language. What's wrong with people feeding themselves?"[34]

And following deregulation, much of the American hog farming industry is now foreign-owned. Smithfield Foods, America's largest pork producer, was bought in 2013 by Shuanghui (now WH Group), a Chinese conglomerate, in a deal brokered and encouraged by the Wall Street investment firm Morgan Stanley and with help from a $4 billion Chinese government loan. Smithfield, whose brands include Farmer John, Old Country Store, Kretschmar, and Nathan's Famous, owns one in every four pigs raised in the United States and is substantially controlled by the Chinese Communist Party, which is well aware of how to use market power to create political influence. The purchase has seen technology, profits, and higher-value jobs shift to China, leaving the low-margin, more menial tasks to people in the United States, like the "hog janitors" running the CAFOs. Here's one kind of central planning laid upon another. Although a backlash on Capitol Hill forced this Chinese-owned firm, in 2018, to withdraw a bid for direct US government subsidies from President Trump's $12 billion farm bailout, Shuanghui still captures lots of subsidies indirectly by using its awesome market power to milk the farmers who receive the subsidies, holding them like sharecroppers just solvent enough to stay afloat, with the power to cream off any subsidies or other new money that flows into the farmers' livelihoods.[35]

Meanwhile Brazil's JBS, with slaughterhouses across the United States, is the world's second-largest pork producer, selling its product under the Swift brand. It has received US government farm subsidies too, helping it report revenues of $51 billion and profits of $7.5 billion in 2017. It has also been involved in at least six Brazilian probes in the giant, freewheeling "Car Wash" scandal, and in 2017 members of the Batista family, which controls JBS, signed plea deals with Brazilian prosecutors in which they admitted to bribing scores of politicians, including former president Michel Temer, to get illicit favors and subsidies.[36]

The large agribusiness firms that dominate US pork production are typically privately held, so it is hard to find out how much they pay in tax. Smithfield's parent company, Hong Kong–based WH Group, reported worldwide tax payments of $182 million on profits of $1.5 billion in 2016, but it gave no clear indication how much US tax was paid, beyond describing a $314 million net tax windfall from Trump's tax cuts. (JBS's annual report gave no information.)[37]

Another large agricultural wealth pipeline involves speculation in commodities and farmland. The players include investment banks, real estate investment trusts (REITS), private equity and hedge funds, and pension funds. There are agricultural exchange-traded funds (ETFs) with catchy stock ticker names, like MOO, COW, and SOIL. There is a zoo of financial derivatives and hedging mechanisms, commodity swaps, options, futures contracts, and more. As with private equity, there are squirrelly corporate structures, layer on layer of limited liability entities and partnerships, and special purpose vehicles, with debts and payments darting in and out at different levels, carefully isolating risks and rewards in preferred places, either to minimize taxes or to tailor the most appetizing corporate parcels to attract the world's OPM chasing niche opportunities. There are those "blocker corporations" in places like the Cayman Islands, which funnel foreign investment into private equity–like agricultural interests, stripping out taxes for the foreign investors, veiling them in secrecy, and, in some cases, potentially serving as hidden crowbars for shady or mysterious foreign interests to get into the US political process. There is a world of agricultural patents and licenses, from seeds to pig genetics to machinery, which not only serve as legal walls keeping competitors off of lucrative economic turf, but are also ideal for those "transfer pricing" techniques I described in chapter one, sucking profits into the zero-tax havens where the patents sit collecting royalties, while also creating tax deductions in the United States.[38]

There are the farmland speculators that wait for times of rural distress to set up vehicles to buy swathes of cheap farmland, which some call "gold with a coupon," because of its status as a long-term store of value and a productive asset. In the words of Paul Pittman, chief executive of Farmland Partners and a former investment banker, "A little bit of pain in farm country makes our job easier."[39] And as the world's hot money sluices in and out of agricultural and commodity funds, it plays havoc with price signals that are supposed to make markets efficient, and whipsaws food consumers and producers with cycles of feast and famine. All through these ups and downs and twists and turns, mechanization has dramatically expanded the wealth being created in rural areas—then financialization has ripped it away, outwards and offshore, leaving the rural areas far poorer than they were, subject to a new system of central planning justified in the name of the "free market." Once again, it's like the paradox of poverty from plenty I experienced living in Africa's resource-cursed oil zones: more money, it seems, can make whole communities—and even an entire nation—poorer.

Something like this agricultural story has played out in other parts of the US economy. Take manufacturing, which now accounts for little more than 11 percent of US GDP, compared with 21 percent in

Germany.[40] This difference has several explanations, but probably the biggest is that Germany's companies still operate in a rich, collaborative industrial ecosystem supported by the state, with technical universities, apprenticeship training, research institutes, and local and regional banks, all hooked into large and small firms and their local supply chains, with spillovers all over the shop.[41] This is not unlike the economic ecosystems that once formed the backbone of rural America, or indeed the nation-wide industrial landscape that once undergirded the American dream. Financialization and "free-market" ideology have ripped it all up. The political dividends from fostering a new high-technology farming sector that takes wealth back from out-of-town shareholders and returns it to the rural areas where it was created would be immense.

Financialization hasn't just sucked money and power away from rural communities; it has extracted their dignity. "They are outsiders, coming to rural Iowa, the rural Midwest; they set up shop and split the neighborhood into two camps," said Petersen. "The big money saw that the Midwest hadn't been conquered, these itsy-bitsy farmers. They thought, 'Let's figure out how to get our hands on it.' And they did."

Conclusion

On February 13, 2018, the US Treasury's Financial Crimes Enforcement Network (FinCEN) issued one of its rare Section 311 notices against Latvia's ABLV Bank, which it said had serviced entities involved in North Korea's ballistic missile program and "institutionalized money laundering as a pillar of the bank's business practices." A Section 311 notice is a ferocious beast: essentially, it cuts off a bank's access to funding in dollars. ABLV was shut down within a week.

This pretty little Baltic state of around two million people, nestled against northern Europe's border with Russia, had become a major conduit for handling and laundering large murky flows of money from the former Soviet Union, washing and channeling it into real estate and securities markets in London, Paris, Berlin, New York, and around the globe. As a former Soviet puppet state that joined the European Union in 2004, it's hardly surprising that Latvia became a money-laundering hub and that it developed a large, crooked financial oligarchy hooked into the country's politics and main banks, many under Moscow's influence.

The United States began putting pressure on Latvia to crack down on these networks three years earlier, when a US Treasury official warned that around 1 percent of all dollar transactions in the world were passing through Latvian banks. The pressure was remarkably successful:

foreign deposits in Latvian banks fell by 75 percent between 2015 and 2018, and the country also put in place draconian prohibitions on local banks servicing shady shell companies in tax havens.[1] This willingness to cooperate was hardly surprising: Latvia has been invaded, fought over, and beaten up more times than its inhabitants care to remember, and they are hellishly nervous about their giant nuclear-armed neighbor to the east, which has developed a nasty reputation recently for invading bordering countries, like Ukraine and Georgia. So Latvians take the US-led NATO military alliance extremely seriously, and when Washington issues such warnings, they listen.

Over a quarter of the population is Russian-speaking, a fact that Vladimir Putin could easily use to stir up trouble. So, like the citizens of several other small nations up against the Russian border, Latvians also take the phenomenon of fake news and information warfare very seriously and harbor some of the most advanced thinking on this subject. On a visit to Riga in November 2018 I asked Jānis Bērziņš, director of the Center for Security and Strategic Research at the National Defense Academy, how a country can address and parry such information attacks. He worked through several answers on his way to the big one. Attackers will focus on exploiting "inner sociocultural decay," he said, in an "invisible occupation" that makes the civil and even military population support the attacker against their own country. They seek to "penetrate into the state's internal structure, into its governance system, as a virus does, surreptitiously and spontaneously." Shady offshore banking is one gateway to political influence, but carefully constructed falsehoods or distortions spread on social media can be highly effective too.

But why are so many people receptive to fake news? Essentially, he said, because of fear, and especially fear of what the American baseball legend Yogi Berra articulated: "The future ain't what it used to be." Fear that the opportunities older generations took for granted are evaporating. Fear for our safety and economic security and for that of our children. And how do we address these fears? The main task, Bērziņš continued, is to "decrease the gap between governments and societies, the notion that the political class broke the social contract, which is the main vulnerability that can be used as leverage by adversaries." How, then, do we decrease that gap? Ultimately, he said, the big answer is "to completely transform the financial model of our economic systems." Or, as I'd put it, to reverse the finance curse.

The finance curse constitutes one of the most significant, troubling, and complex national security threats the Western world has ever faced. Any engineer (or any child who has played with LEGO or wooden blocks) will tell you that if you concentrate too much weight at the top of a structure, it will topple. The finance curse, underpinned by endless wealth-extraction tools and techniques, is shifting wealth, and with it America's economic and political center of gravity, steadily upward. As private equity firms leach wealth out of productive enterprise, and as corporate share buybacks and dividends divert vast amounts more, the economy and society and political system become less stable. Meanwhile, mysterious foreign actors can use secret financial shell companies based in offshore tax havens to channel campaign finance payments to both main political parties and to support billionaire-friendly think tanks, which seem hell-bent on poisoning and corrupting the institutions of state, pulling hidden political levers we'll often never know about. Monopolies active in the United States don't only drain wealth from ordinary Americans; they are also formidable instruments of political power—and the Chinese Communist Party, and many more shadowy foreign actors, are well aware of this.

So here's the question. How do we reverse the finance curse?

First, and most obviously, get big money out of politics. It has corrupted both the Republicans and the Democrats. With the Trump administration, this is clear. But many Democrats don't appreciate how far their party has fallen. Barack Obama was thrilling and inspiring and progressive, in cultural and social terms. But his administration's steward-ship of the economy was, on balance, disastrous—and Democrats must face this if they are to move forward. Obama didn't cause the financial crisis; his predecessors George W. Bush and Bill Clinton must carry

much of *that* burden. But when Obama came into office in the thick of
the meltdown in 2008, he fluffed it. He could have gotten the financial
sector to share in the nation's pain and transformed the financial system
into something that serves America. Instead he oversaw an administration whose officials heaped the horror show largely onto the shoulders
of homeowners and ordinary folk, prioritizing the oversized financial
system, sweeping its crimes under the rug, and letting it reassert its
wealth and power. He appointed Timothy Geithner, a former private
equity titan, as Treasury secretary. Geithner pushed through a program
of millions of foreclosures that he said would "foam the runway" for
the crashing megabanks. Further aid to the perpetrators was provided
by a collapse in financial prosecutions, which let bank officials get away
with widespread fraud and money laundering. And the different bailout
programs, as one analysis put it, "mapped directly onto each of the key
elements of the shadow banking system" and bailed out foreign banks
at least as much as American ones, "remotely backstopping the City of
London." By the time Obama left office the big banks were bigger than
ever, and the globally interconnected shadow banking system—that is,
the part of finance that lies outside the normal regulatory net, the most
financialized part of finance—was in dangerously rude health.[2] It still is.

On the campaign trail in 2008, Obama decried "a building in the
Cayman Islands that supposedly houses 12,000 corporations: that's
either the biggest building, or the biggest tax scam, on record." He
would shut down this nonsense, he rightly promised. But on his watch
the Cayman Islands prospered, along with the private equity firms and
hedge funds that use them, and America consolidated its position as
arguably the world's biggest money-laundering tax haven in its own
right, attracting trillions of dollars of undeclared money from around
the globe, strengthening the finance curse. Obamacare, meanwhile,
while highly progressive in extending medical coverage to millions of
uninsured Americans, also left intact the giant medical monopolies that
help explain why America's healthcare costs per person are two and a half
times those of other rich countries.[3] It's true that Obama was hedged

in by vindictive Republicans, and it's also true that in most areas of economic policy Trump has been worse—often much, much worse. But this does not excuse the Obama-era failure to tackle or even properly examine the root causes of all the economic mayhem. In fact, Obama's administration openly embraced some of the biggest monopolies the world has seen, waved through a stream of gigantic mergers, and all but gave the keys to the White House to tech giants like Google. It is telling that the first thing Obama did after leaving office was to go kitesurfing in the British Virgin Islands, that offshore British overseas territory, with the British billionaire Richard Branson—a mogul who once declared that his empire would be half the size if it hadn't been substantially run through tax havens.

Trump has done a lot worse, pulling off the conjuring trick of harnessing culture wars and popular anger about the economy to enact giant tax cuts and deregulatory splurges that are directly against the economic interests of most of his voters. But in economic terms, this just represents a worsening of years, even decades, of bad, finance-led policy.

The real economic dividing line today isn't so much between Republican and Democrat as between those who favor rigged markets and the finance curse, and those who oppose them. Since Tony Coelho began corrupting the Democratic Party with floods of corporate money in the late 1970s, both parties have belonged mostly on the wrong side of this divide. If Democrats are to rescue America, as a first step they must decisively repudiate the pro-financialization policies embraced by the Clinton and Obama administrations. And if Republicans are to rescue America, they need to turn away from most of the economic policies of Donald Trump and return to old Republican traditions of equality of opportunity and genuinely competitive markets, and of justice and the rule of law: break up and effectively regulate the big banks, big tech firms, and other cartels and monopolies; empty out the tax havens; stop the orgy of share buybacks; target those actors that grow rich on OPM; prosecute financial crime and corruption; police and exclude dirty-money inflows from overseas; and in doing so generally look out for the national security of the United States and the well-being of the American people.

And here's a good place to start: crack down on fake news. I don't mean the kind of fake news that was generated by a handful of teenagers with laptops in the town of Veles, in the former Soviet republic Macedonia, whose hundred-plus Trump-supporting websites earned them large advertising fees (through fake headlines such as "Hillary's Illegal Email Just Killed Its First American Spy") and helped swing the 2016 election. I'm talking about a far more important category of fake news. It comes mostly from the economics profession, and it is presented as *evidence*.

There are a couple of fundamental reasons why so much of this evidence is wrong. One reason, of course, is the corrupting influence of Wall Street money on research. But a more interesting reason is this. When honest policy makers are considering whether or not to put in place a pro-corporate policy (like cutting corporate taxes, or gutting an environmental law) they usually look for evidence to see if it is a good idea. The big problem is that what gets called evidence usually involves measuring stuff—and it's nearly always easier to measure the benefits of a policy to banks or multinational corporations than it is to measure the costs that policy may inflict on others. So the very act of measurement tends to skew the evidence systematically in favor of big banks and multinationals and against everyone else.

I'll use corporate tax cuts to illustrate very briefly what I mean. Let's assume an honest policy maker commissions a clever academic without corporate conflicts of interest or axes to grind to study the effects of corporate tax cuts. The academic digs into the numbers, comparing the effects in different states and countries across a range of taxes and different types of investment, and makes allowances for the fact that a tax cut is unlikely to have the same effect in California as it does in Idaho, Germany, or Hong Kong. There's endless stuff to grapple with. Let's assume for the sake of argument that she finds that corporate tax cuts increase multinational investment rates, attract foreign investors, or create jobs. Quite often, that's all the honest policy maker thinks he needs. These tax cuts create jobs—so they are a good idea!

But any good academic knows that these results haven't yet said *anything* useful about whether the tax cuts are a good idea. That's because the policy maker looked at only the benefits of the tax cut; he didn't look at the costs. He fell for what is called the "fallacy of composition." What's good for Goldman Sachs or KKR isn't necessarily good for America. A tax isn't a *cost* to an economy; it's a *transfer* within it, from one interest group to another. The costs are usually inflicted on a much more diffuse range of stakeholders, and many of these costs will be hard or even impossible to measure. "Taxation, in reality, is life," said Sheldon Cohen, a former top IRS official. "If you know the position a person takes on taxes, you can tell their whole philosophy. The tax code, once you get to know it, embodies all the essence of life: greed, politics, power, goodness." And how do you assign a price to any of those things?

Here, for instance, are a couple of costs that don't get measured. The more you cut corporate tax rates, the more rich folk will convert their ordinary income to corporate income to pay the lower rate, and this cannibalizes the top part of the income tax system. This income shifting is hard to measure—but it's no less real for that. Or take the Trump tax cuts of 2017, which cut the headline corporate tax rate from 35 to 21 percent, to "make American business competitive again" and to grow jobs, as the White House put it. The Treasury Department estimates that the cuts will transfer some $100 billion annually to corporations, and independent experts estimate they will deliver a combined $10 billion windfall for Apple and Google, plus a combined $12 billion for Wells Fargo, Citigroup, Bank of America, and JP Morgan. Taken at face value, those tax cuts delivered $100 billion in clear, measurable benefits. Happy days! But the real question is this. Who got those benefits, and at what cost? In the year after the Trump tax cuts, American corporations said they gave their workers a combined $7 billion in pay hikes due to the tax cut—but they also spent over $850 billion, or 120 times as much, buying back their own stock, a gargantuan upward shift in wealth, encouraged by the tax cuts. These shifts of wealth, among many other things, damage American democracy in unmeasurable ways. Also hard to measure is the fact that this upward transfer will make big, rich, powerful corporations bigger, richer, and more powerful, strengthening their monopolistic and political powers and corrupting markets. How to account for those costs?[4]

Next, there's the fact that corporate tax cuts tend to reward the profit-gushing share flipper more favorably than the low-margin job-creating business, making the cuts like refined sugar in the human body—empty financial calories with adverse long-term health effects. How would you even start to try to measure the long-term costs of any of these things, over what timescale, and against what yardstick? You can't. You just can't. So they get airbrushed out.

Or try this. The estimated $100 billion in lost corporate tax revenues goes most of the way toward explaining the $113 billion increase in the federal deficit from 2017 to 2018. The administration has said it will tackle the rising deficit by cutting public services for working families, especially Social Security, Medicare, and Medicaid. So this $100 billion gain to multinationals entails a plethora of ills, like poverty, crime, suicides, opioid addiction, or racially tinged radicalization. These indirect impacts can't reasonably be plugged into a spreadsheet.

There are other ways to look at these lost revenues. With this much money you could send 1.4 million Americans to Harvard each year—at least if you could fit them all in. Or you could treble the annual budget of the Federal Highway Administration, which builds and runs the national highway system. Is this trade-off worth it? Do these transfers to large firms make America any more "competitive"? There is no way to answer these questions using numbers. To make matters even more complicated, the benefits from these tax cuts are felt *now*—over $100 billion injected by the tax cuts into corporate shareholders' pockets in 2018—while the costs of roads that aren't built or repaired, or of those children whose school budgets are being slashed, will play out over half a century. How do you weigh those long-term costs against the short-term benefits?

Once again, you can't. So the airbrush must come out here too. (In fact there are so many other unmeasurable costs associated with corporate tax cuts that I'll have to shovel them into this endnote.[5])

All this reminds me of what has been called the "McNamara fallacy," which refers to the use of enemy body counts in the Vietnam War as a precise and accurate measure of success, ignoring all the other less countable stuff that was going on:

> The first step is to measure whatever can be easily measured. This is OK as far as it goes. The second step is to disregard that which can't be easily measured or to give it an arbitrary quantitative value. This is artificial and misleading. The third step is to presume that what can't be measured easily really isn't important. This is blindness. The fourth step is to say that what can't be easily measured really doesn't exist. This is suicide.[6]

The evidence gets re-engineered, in stages. These sharks come in waves: the "competitive" consensus nudging academics toward certain conclusions; the wall of corporate money selecting the "right" academics in the research institutions; partisan players in the media cherry-picking numbers from a nuanced picture; and policy makers and politicians desperate to reach conclusions that will find favor with, say, Fox News or the Wall Street–Washington–Silicon Valley establishment. Honest civil servants and researchers have to fight their way through all that. This is how corporate subsidies get justified, through "evidence-based policy."

They've even got a machine for manufacturing this kind of fake news, called "dynamic scoring." As with the best tricks, dynamic scoring is based on a sound underlying idea. When a tax gets cut, economic agents respond by building or consuming more or less stuff. So you anticipate their responses and build them into your model, which is fine, in theory. The trillion-dollar question is: How do these models work, what evidence gets put into them, and, just as important, what gets left out? Well, with dynamic scoring you can only put in things that can be measured, and the machine gives you no choice but to airbrush out all the unmeasurable costs. Out pops a result—presto! Corporate tax cuts are great! And if your model is a black box, or its internal machinery is too complex for anyone but Einstein to understand, the possibilities for bamboozlement multiply. That's why US tax expert Edward Kleinbard calls dynamic scoring "a Republican ruse to make tax cuts look good."

There's a much broader point here. What goes for corporate tax cuts goes for pretty much any policy that touches multinational corporations or big banks. Relax pollution standards on Iowa's CAFOs, or remove curbs on cross-border swaps trading, or cut construction workers' pay, and the results will show up on the bottom lines of Big Ag, Big Banks, or Big Build. The costs, in terms of higher rates of bronchitis, rural depopulation, toxic algae in the Gulf of Mexico, global warming, leaky or collapsing buildings, or the buildup of hidden risks that will one day erupt in a new financial crisis—well, there's no good method for measuring any of these things in a usable way. Economic evidence is distorted and skewed systematically, generically, against the interests of the American people.

But this raises a new question. If the evidence isn't there to support a corporate tax cut—and I'm saying it's *impossible* to create useful numbers, no matter how clever or honest your academic economists are—then what is the poor policy maker to do? Well, in fact there's plenty they can do. Evidence matters, and there is a place for numbers. But bad evidence is worse than no evidence. And there are other forms of evidence that don't come from spreadsheets. One is called *analysis*: you make sensible arguments and judgments and discuss and debate those openly with colleagues or the public. You beef this up with what the pioneering US economist James Henry called "investigative economics": recognizing those uncertainties and judging where your spreadsheets might help and, crucially, where they won't; getting out of your armchair and *talking* to people; discovering the blood and guts of what's going on: Who's screwing whom, how, and why? It's a great way to find out how the world actually works. And policy makers who are forsaken by the data can also look to two reliable words to help them. One is "politics." The other is "democracy." In these two infuriating concepts lies the wisdom of centuries. And these, for me, are the most legitimate of all guides to how we should move forward. If voters don't like it, then it's probably a bad idea. Don't call this "populism," because this word is part of the fake-news problem. It not only sanitizes fascism and equates very different positions on the Left and the Right, but it also suggests that what's popular is wrong. And the financial crisis and its aftermath have revealed that it is the experts, not the voters, who have been wrong—and for a very long time.

Radical change is usually possible only after a big crisis. This didn't happen after the global financial crisis because of what former British prime minister Margaret Thatcher used to call TINA—There Is No Alternative. When the crisis hit, there weren't any radical ideas ready to challenge the "competitiveness" consensus about protecting and subsidizing oversized finance and financialized business. Now, though, following the earthquake of Trump's election, there are endless good ideas circulating. And radicalism is gaining traction fast—as it should.

Taming the megabanks is essential and urgent, but the bigger task is to fix financialization. This will involve reviving antitrust, curbing activities run out of tax havens, and generally looking for ways to dis- courage wealth extraction and to favor wealth creation. Focus especially on private equity and hedge funds, which have been at the leading edge of the efforts to craft the most voracious financial wealth-extraction techniques. Uncover the schemes that are the biggest money gushers for their titans and shut them down, while also being careful to leave intact the useful stuff that's going on in the real economy.

And think about what happens beyond America's borders. Some in Latvia decried the recent US pressure on their murky banks as imperial- ism, neocolonialism, and arrogance. Many in Switzerland took a similar view when the US Department of Justice, starting in 2008, began jail- ing Swiss bankers who had been helping rich Americans evade tax. It's certainly true that the United States has an ugly record of intervening militarily and covertly in foreign countries, from Vietnam to Iraq to Nicaragua. But there's an important difference of principle here, which concerns geography and inequality. The episodes involving Swiss or Latvian banks weren't battles pitting the United States against Switzerland or Latvia. They were local skirmishes in a global economic war that pits ordinary people around the world against a rootless, criminalized, financialized, oligarchical global billionaire class. In these skirmishes and many others, the Department of Justice and FinCEN, for all their many faults, were standing on the side of justice and democracy.

America's financial regulators need to move decisively to the right side of these fights too—and to pay special attention to the City of London financial center and its tax haven satellites. As a British citizen, I'm now selfishly calling on America's crime-fighting authorities and financial regulators to rein in the rogue actors in Britain's rotten financial system, from those high financiers whose risk-taking threatens global financial stability, to those shady bankers handling the proceeds of organized crime or terrorism. The City of London's grip on my country is too strong, too deep, and too dangerous for us to succeed on our own. We, the people of Britain, need your help, America. We, the people of Britain, need your help, America. (And when you do this, to avoid claims of favouritism, crack down on the excesses of Wall Street too.) All this is in America's interest, not least for reasons of national security. "I'd always say to colleagues, 'Don't assume the British are our friends in everything—especially for anything financing related,'" a US counterterrorism official told me in 2017. "That is where I think Britain in general is really playing with fire." He's right.

And here's another international policy to tame the finance curse. I call it "smart capital controls." The aim here is not so much to try to control *outward* flows of capital but to be selective and careful about what flows *in* from overseas. I'm not advocating barriers to flows of capital at the US border, but instead calling for explicitly recognizing the categories of financial inflow that are most dangerous—those billions looted from former Soviet republics or Latin American nations and stashed in

Miami real estate, for instance—then enacting policies—such as radical transparency requirements, strong environmental regulations, targeted taxes, strong worker protections, and so on—to keep this predatory money out. These reforms that democracy demands will tend to chase away the harmful, debt-loaded, finance-curse-deepening stuff, while leaving the useful investment firmly in place. This is the opposite of the competitiveness agenda that I outlined in chapter five, which underpinned the Third Way philosophy that Bill Clinton embraced and all his successors have followed. This misplaced fear that effectively regulating or taxing oversized finance will make it all run away to London or Hong Kong is one of the great blockages stopping people from seeing the possibility for change. The finance curse reveals this competitiveness agenda as a billionaire-friendly hoax, an intellectual house of cards ready to fall.

In the introduction I described a study estimating that oversized finance will have cost the US economy a cumulative $13–$23 trillion over the period 1990–2023. If democratic reforms shrunk the financial sector back toward its optimal size and function, economic growth would rise. There is no trade-off between effective financial regulation and economic growth. More democracy means more economic prosperity too—and a smaller, better financial system. Once this blockage is cleared, sweeping new vistas of political possibility open up. People who feel hopeless about prospects for change often forget that democracy is a mighty weapon and it remains very much alive. Here is a vast opportunity for any political party in America. Reversing the finance curse could prove immensely, election-winningly popular. So *The Finance Curse* contains some exceptionally good news.

Acknowledgments

Many people have helped me write this book. After my family, John Christensen takes top credit. We developed the finance curse concept together over several years, but his influence on my thinking is older. As Director of the Tax Justice Network he introduced me properly to the world of tax havens, which in my view is the best possible entry point for understanding modern global finance. Others who have been more than generous with their time and/or contacts include Andrew Baker, Elise Bean, James Boyce, Richard Brooks, the group at Manchester University formerly known as CRESC, Charles Davidson, Will Davies, the Enlighten project, Ian Fraser, Daniela Gabor, Andy Green, Martin Hellwig, James Henry, Abby Innes, Bill Lazonick, Adam Leaver, Benoit Majerus, David Marchant, Peter Morris, Ludovic Phalippou, Clair Quentin, John Singleton, Jim Stewart, Matt Stoller, Matthew Watson, Anna-Sophia Watts, Duncan Wigan, Angela Wigger, and others who wish to remain unrecognized. Beyond these people, I offer great thanks to the many others who generously offered their time and insights over the past few years.

Notes

INTRODUCTION

1. One measure of the size of finance is the ratio of credit to GDP. In Gerald Epstein and Juan Antonio Montecino, *Overcharged: The High Costs of High Finance*, Roosevelt Institute, July 2016, the average ratio of credit to GDP for the United States was 130 percent, well above the threshold of 90 percent estimated by the IMF and others. (Their conclusions are discussed later in this introduction.) Separately, the IMF has created its own index of financial development, ranging between 0 and 1, with the "optimal" growth-maximizing point lying between around 0.4 and 0.7, above which the growth-finance relationship becomes "significantly negative." It estimated the United States' ratio at 0.8. See Ratna Sahay et al., *Rethinking Financial Deepening: Stability and Growth in Emerging Markets*, IMF Staff Discussion Note, May 2015. For pointers to a range of other studies looking at financial depth/size and economic growth, see my website financecurse.net, especially "Academic Studies: Too Much Finance" under the "Research" page.

2. The "curing cancer" quote is from Stephen G. Cecchetti and Enisse Kharroubi, *Reassessing the Impact of Finance on Growth*, Bank for International Settlements Working Paper No. 381, July 2012. The authors looked at employment data and also used a different measure of credit to GDP and said, "Take the example of the United States, where private credit grew to more than 200% of GDP by the time of the financial crisis. Reducing this to a level closer to 100% would, by our estimates, yield a productivity growth gain of more than 150 basis points."

3. The Dutch Disease specifically afflicts sectors producing tradable goods and services. It is less salient in the United States than in smaller countries like Britain, where inflows can be far larger relative to the size of the economy.

4. On the finance share of GDP, which is widely reported, see for example figures 1 and 2 in Epstein and Montecino, *Overcharged*, which are constructed from data from

the Federal Reserve and national income and product accounts. On real hourly wages and other signs of worker stagnation, see Jay Shambaugh et al., *Thirteen Facts About Wage Growth*, Hamilton Project, Sept. 2017.

5. See Epstein and Montecino, *Overcharged*.

6. The "around $150 billion" is extrapolated from Richard Waters and Andrew Edgecliffe-Johnson, "Five US Tech Giants Spend Combined $115bn on Buying Back Stock," *Financial Times*, Nov. 13, 2018. They calculated the five had bought back $115 billion in the first three quarters of 2018. The education figure is from the 2018 budgets; the National Priorities Project has a website providing mandatory and discretionary federal spending. The 2018 military budget in the Trump spending bill of 2018 was for $892 billion. See Kimberly Amadeo, "US Military Budget, Its Components, Challenges, and Growth," The Balance, Nov. 12, 2018. On the S&P 500 buybacks, see "S&P 500 Q3 2018 Buybacks Surpass $200 Billion Mark for the First Time Ever," S&P Dow Jones Indices, Dec. 18, 2018. The accompanying table estimates buybacks at $720 billion plus dividends at $446 billion for the S&P 500 for the twelve months to September 2018. The Congressional Budget Office (CBO) estimated that the Obama stimulus, or "American Recovery and Reinvestment Act," would add up to $831 billion over 2009-2019. See CBO, "Estimated Impact of the American Recovery and Reinvestment Act," on Employment and Economic Output from October 2011 Through December 2011," Feb. 2012. On buybacks see also William Lazonick, *Stock Buybacks: From Retain-and-Reinvest to Downsize-and-Distribute*, Brookings Center for Effective Public Management, Apr. 2015, and William Lazonick, *The Functions of the Stock Market and the Fallacies of Shareholder Value*, Institute for New Economic Thinking Working Paper No. 58, June 3, 2017. The IBM share buyback data was from Daniel McCrum, "Lex in Depth: The Case against Share Buybacks," *Financial Times*, Jan. 29, 2018, by which the total was already $162 billion; the IBM market cap was from Yahoo data on Nov. 21, 2018. The Lazonick quotes come mostly from my interview with Lazonick via Skype, June 7, 2017. Over 2004–2013, he said, 454 companies in the S&P 500 Index did $3.4 trillion in stock buybacks, representing 51 percent of net income. These companies expended an additional 35 percent of net income on dividends. The "extraction" figure is $416 billion per year over 2007–2016; this figure refers to "net equity issuance"—that is, new corporate stock issues, minus outstanding stock retired through stock repurchases and through mergers and acquisitions activity. On the European data, see Mustafa Erdem Sakinç, *Share Repurchases in Europe: A Value Extraction Analysis*, Academic-Industry Research Network, May 2017, 10–11. The 150 percent figure for the UK came via email from Sakinç, Dec. 5, 2017, confirming a media report about his forthcoming research but giving no further details. On "eating themselves," see Andy Haldane, "Firms Are 'Almost Eating Themselves,'" interviewed by BBC Newsnight, July 25, 2015, available on YouTube.

7. The figure for concentration in stock ownership in the United States is from figure A3a (p. 63, the category is "Fin," which represents individuals' holdings of financial assets, grouped by percentile group) in Arthur B. Kennickell, *Ponds and Streams: Wealth and Income in the U.S., 1989 to 2007*, Divisions of Research & Statistics and Monetary Affairs, Federal Reserve Board, Jan. 2009. The figure for 2007 was that the top 5 percent

owned 60 percent of financial wealth (and the top 10 percent owned 73 percent), but given the large and well-publicized rise in wealth inequality since then, I have rounded upward. (A more recent paper estimates that the top 10 percent owns 80 percent of stocks; see Edward N. Wolff, *Household Wealth Trends in the United States, 1962 to 2016: Has Middle Class Wealth Recovered?* National Bureau of Economic Research Working Paper No. 24085, Nov. 2017.)

8. See Emin Dinlersoz, "Business Formation Statistics: A New Census Bureau Product That Takes the Pulse of Early-Stage U.S. Business Activity," *Census Blogs*, US Census Bureau, Feb. 8, 2018.

9. Robert Jenkins "Robert Jenkins' Partial List of Bank Misdeeds," Finance Watch, Oct. 26, 2016, finance-watch.org/robert-jenkins-partial-list-of-bank-misdeeds.

CHAPTER ONE: SABOTAGE

1. The "fabrication of vendible imponderables" quote is from Robert Heilbroner, *The Worldly Philosophers: The Lives, Times and Ideas of the Great Economic Thinkers* (New York: Simon & Shuster, 1986), 220. The other quotes in these paragraphs are from Heilbroner, 218–248, except for "emigrating to America," which is from George M. Fredrickson, "Thorstein Veblen: The Last Viking," *American Quarterly* 11, no. 3 (Autumn 1959): 403–415.

2. See Nils Gilman, "Thorstein Veblen's Neglected Feminism," *Journal of Economic Issues* 33, no. 3 (Sept. 1999): 689.

3. Qtd. in Sidney Plotkin and Rick Tilman, *The Political Ideas of Thorstein Veblen* (New Haven, CT: Yale University Press, 2011), 16. The friend was a professor called Jacob Warshaw.

4. The "lightning calculators" quote is from Thorstein Veblen, *The Place of Science in Modern Civilization and other Essays*, (New York: B.W. Huebsch, 1919), 73; the "Aleutian Islanders" is from Thorstein Veblen, *Professor Clark's Economics: In The Place of Science in Modern Civilisation and Other Essays*, (New York: Russell & Russell, 1908), 180–230.

5. As Matthew Watson of Warwick University put it, *The Theory of the Leisure Class* was in a sense merely a scene setter for *The Theory of Business Enterprise*: "It might very well be described as one of the subject field's most important forgotten books; it raises barely a stir in the collective consciousness of contemporary economists." Watson sent me these comments via email, 2016. See also Matthew Watson, "Thorstein Veblen: The Thinker Who Saw Through the Competitiveness Agenda," Fools' Gold, Feb. 29, 2016, foolsgold.international/thorstein-veblen-the-thinker-who-saw-through-the-competitiveness-agenda.

6. Rube Goldberg was a cartoonist and inventor famous for drawing ridiculously complicated machines for achieving simple goals.

7. As Watson put it, "A repeated theme throughout pretty much every chapter of the 900-page *Wealth of Nations* is that productive labor is good and should be encouraged, whereas unproductive labor is bad and should be discouraged. We wouldn't have a finance curse if we really did live in Adam Smith's world."

8. Nancy MacLean, *Democracy in Chains: The Deep History of the Radical Right's Stealth Plan for America* (New York: Viking, 2017), 10. It was the historian Richard Hofstadter who called Calhoun the "Marx of the Master Class."

9. The "toad" quote is from Heilbroner, *Worldly Philosophers*, 239. The "conscientious withdrawal" is from Thorstein Veblen, *The Engineers and the Price System* (New York: B. W. Huebsch, 1921.)

10. Qtd. in Steve Weinberg, *Taking on the Trust: The Epic Battle of Ida Tarbell and John D. Rockefeller* (New York: W. W. Norton, 2008), 219–20. Rockefeller defended himself by arguing that he had found a solution to the tragedy of the commons, where too many oilmen were drilling on the same bounteous oil field, leading to overproduction and mayhem in oil prices.

11. The Hancock episode is from Henry Demarest Lloyd, *Wealth against Commonwealth* (New York: Harper, 1899), 162–3.

12. Most of the quotes in the preceding three paragraphs are from Ida Tarbell, *The History of the Standard Oil Company* (New York: McClure, Phillips and Co., 1904). The "jew's harp" quote is from Weinberg *Taking on the Trust*, 83, and the "sovereign power" quote is from Ron Chernow, *Titan: The Life of John D. Rockefeller* (New York: Vintage, 2004). The death of Franklin Tarbell's business partner is recorded in several accounts, but none gives his name or date of death.

13. The Standard Oil Trust was created in 1882, and its assets transferred to a new company in 1899, after state laws on corporations were relaxed somewhat. See Eliot Jones, *The Trust Problem in the United States* (New York: Macmillan, 1929), 58, 60. Jones adds that beyond Standard Oil's control of 90 percent of the market, "not all of the remainder could properly be considered as independent" (58).

14. *Money Trust Investigations: Investigation of Financial and Monetary Conditions in the United States under House Resolutions Nos. 429 and 504*, US House Subcommittee on Banking and Currency, Dec. 18, 1912, esp. exhibit 134-B: "Table Showing Affiliations of J.P. Morgan & Company, Guaranty Trust Company, Bankers Trust Company, First National Bank and National City Bank with Other Corporations Through Interlocking Directorates."

15. Louis D. Brandeis, *Other People's Money, and How the Bankers Use It* (New York: Frederick A. Stokes, 1914), ch. 1.

16. Ovidio Diaz Espino, *How Wall Street Created a Nation: J. P. Morgan, Teddy Roosevelt, and the Panama Canal* (New York: Four Walls Eight Windows, 2001).

17. Thorstein Veblen, *The Theory of Business Enterprise* (New York: Charles Scribner's Sons, 1904).

18. I discovered this family connection to the Vesteys after a relative of mine read my book *Treasure Islands: Tax Havens and the Men Who Stole the World* (London: Vintage, 2012), which has a chapter on the Vesteys, and emailed me a summary of my great-great-uncle's history. The Vesteys' descendants still own interests in South America; I worked for six weeks as an assistant cowboy on a Vestey-owned farm in São Paulo state in Brazil in 1988.

19. Quoted in Phillip Knightley, "The Big Chill," *The Times* (UK), Nov. 16, 1991.

20. On crude oil, see Michael Greenberger, testimony on behalf of Americans for Financial Reform, Commodity Futures Trading Commission on Excessive Speculation: Position Limits and Exemptions, Aug. 5, 2009. On Metro, Goldman Sachs, and aluminum, see *Wall Street Bank Involvement with Physical Commodities*, Majority and

Minority Staff Report, US Senate Permanent Subcommittee on Investigations, Nov. 20–21, 2014. See also David Kocieniewski, "A Shuffle of Aluminum, but to Banks, Pure Gold," *New York Times*, July 20, 2013. To get a sense of how baffling the market was, see Matt Levine, "The Goldman Sachs Aluminum Conspiracy Was Pretty Silly," *Bloomberg*, Nov. 20, 2014.

21. See for instance the Tomlinson Report, originally released in 2013 but eventually published by the UK Treasury Select Committee on February 22, 2018. The Financial Conduct Authority appointed the City of London firm Promontory Group to lead an investigation into the scandal. Promontory has been called a "safe pair of hands" but has been accused by US regulators of helping banks cover up scandals it was supposed to unearth. See for example Ben Protess and Jessica Silver-Greenberg, "Promontory Financial Settles with New York Regulator," *New York Times*, Aug. 18, 2015. The ensuing report cleared RBS of the worst accusations, but the bank had to pay out hundreds of millions of pounds. Also see James Hurley, "Watchdog Kept RBS Scandal Report Secret for Fear Bosses Would Sue," *London Times*, Dec. 5, 2017, and Heidi Blake et al., "The Dash for Cash: Leaked Files Reveal RBS Systematically Crushed British Businesses for Profit," *Buzzfeed*, Oct. 10, 2016.

22. I use "know-nothing" to refer to people who are often highly educated and intelligent but nevertheless have a dangerously narrow understanding of the real world, viewed through the prism of finance. Many financial market players' knowledge is exceedingly restricted, even in their own fields. John Kay, one of the most astute observers of the financial system, describes this phenomenon: "Many senior executives talk privately with contempt of the analysts who follow their company. . . . Most of what is called 'research' in the financial sector would not be recognised as research by anyone who has completed an undergraduate thesis, far less a PhD." He adds, "Anyone who comes from outside the financial sector to the world of trading is likely to be shocked by the superficiality of the traders' general knowledge." John Kay, *Other People's Money: Masters of the Universe or Servants of the People?* (London: Profile Books, 2015), 86.

23. These quotes are from Weinberg, *Taking on the Trust*, 225–6, 227–30, 258.

CHAPTER TWO: NEOLIBERALISM WITHOUT BORDERS

1. Telephone interview with Lee Hansen, Nov. 21, 2016. The "communist" quote is from Charles Leven, "Discovering 'Voting with Your Feet,'" *Annals of Regional Science* 37, no. 2 (May 2003): 237.

2. McCarthy drank himself to death in 1957, which may have amused Tiebout, whose father, a psychiatrist, was a pioneer in the Alcoholics Anonymous movement.

3. Chicago neighborhood, next to Evanston.

4. This section is largely based on Leven, "Discovering 'Voting with Your Feet,'" and from John D. Singleton, *Sorting Charles Tiebout*, Center for the History of Political Economy Working Paper Series No. 2013–20, Jan. 8, 2014. Leven was at the lunch, and his seems to be the only firsthand account of this episode. Singleton expressed some skepticism over the precision of Leven's recollections. Tiebout seems to have had the germ of the idea for some time before this conversation, however. In terms of citations, Singleton's paper said, "Forty-five years on from Tiebout's passing, Tiebout (1956)

boasts nearly 11,500 citations, ranking it among the most cited articles in economics. By comparison, Samuelson (1954) claims under 6,000, while Musgrave (1959) and Buchanan and Tullock (1962) own approximately 5,400 and 8,000 citations respectively."

5. Tiebout wrote his 1956 paper as an explicit riposte to Samuelson. The name of his 1956 paper, "A Pure Theory of Local Expenditures," was almost identical to that of Samuelson's 1954 paper about the free-rider problem, "A Pure Theory of Public Expenditures." The "happy as a clam" quote is from Leven, "Discovering 'Voting with Your Feet.'"

6. As Professor William Fischel of Dartmouth College put it, "Tiebout thought of it that way, stop dissing your local government because this is the one you chose." From my telephone interview with Fischel, Nov. 22, 2016. As Tiebout put it, "Spatial mobility provides the local public-goods counterpart to the private market's shopping trip" (422). Charles Tiebout, "A Pure Theory of Local Expenditures," *Journal of Political Economy* 64, no. 5 [Oct. 1956].

7. Telephone interview with John D. Singleton, Nov. 3, 2016.

8. See for instance Walter Scheidel, "The Only Thing, Historically, That's Curbed Inequality: Catastrophe," *Atlantic*, Feb. 21, 2017.

9. Oliver Bullough, *Moneyland: Why Thieves and Crooks Now Rule the World and How to Take It Back* (London: Profile Books, 2018), 28–9.

10. For example, the iPhone and iPad were less the result of Steve Jobs's "foolish genius" than of massive state investment in the revolutionary technologies behind these objects of consumer desire: the internet, GPS, touch-screen displays, and communications technologies. On this see Mariana Mazzucato, *The Entrepreneurial State* (London: Anthem, 2013), particularly chapter five, "The State Behind the iPhone." For example, figure 12 on p. 92 shows that Apple spent the equivalent of just 2.8 percent of its sales on research and development between 2006 and 2011, compared with 13.8 percent for Microsoft. Jobs's genius was mainly in making these technologies consumer friendly (p. 93). Financiers talk of "Death Valleys"—stages in the design, investment, development, and marketing of technologies where private bankers rarely dare to venture and the entrepreneurial state has to step in.

11. For data and analysis comparing wage rates, see Thomas Philippon and Ariell Reshef, *Wages and Human Capital in the U.S. Financial Industry: 1909–2006*, National Bureau of Economic Research Working Paper No. 14644, Jan. 2009.

12. For growth rates, see for instance Andrew Glyn et al., "The Rise and Fall of the Golden Age: An Historical Analysis of Post-War Capitalism in the Developed Market Economies," United Nations University World Institute for Development Economics Research seminar, Helsinki, Aug. 1986, cited in Stephen A. Marglin and Juliet B. Schor (eds.), *The Golden Age of Capitalism: Reinterpreting the Postwar Experience* (Oxford: Clarendon Press; New York: Oxford University Press, 1990). Table 2.1 shows annual average GDP growth per capita for sixteen major advanced countries of 1 percent (1920–70), 1.4 percent (1870–1913), 1.2 percent (1913–50), 3.8 percent (1950–73), and 2 percent (1973–9). For developing countries, the growth rate was an unprecedented 3 percent. Golden Age growth was, moreover, more equitable than in other eras, benefiting the poor and middle classes disproportionately. Older growth

rates are much, much lower: according to Ha-Joon Chang, *Economics: The User's Guide* (London: Penguin, 2014), 54–68, per capita growth in western Europe averaged 0.12 percent between 1000 and 1500 and a mere 0.04 percent in Asia and eastern Europe, and between 1500 and 1820 in western Europe just 0.14 percent. Growth rates rose sharply to 1 percent in the Industrial Revolution (1820–70) and 1.3 percent in 1870–1913. The 4.1 percent statistic for western Europe comes from Chang, 79.

13. Harold Macmillan, speech to Conservative Party rally in Bedford, July 20, 1957. Widely reported.

14. The Metcalf quote is from Stephen Metcalf, "Neoliberalism: The Idea That Swallowed the World," *Guardian*, Aug. 18, 2017. The Davies quote is assembled from William Davies, *The Limits of Neoliberalism: Authority, Sovereignty and the Logic of Competition* (Los Angeles: Sage, 2014), 3, 8; William Davies, "How 'Competitiveness' Became One of the Great Unquestioned Virtues of Contemporary Culture," blog post, London School of Economics and Political Science, May 19, 2014; and William Davies, "What Is "Neo" About Neoliberalism?," *The New Republic*, July 13, 2017.

15. See Olivier Longchamp and Yves Steiner, "The Contribution of the *Schweizerisches Institut für Auslandforschung* to the International Restoration of Neoliberalism (1949–1966)," presentation, European Business History Association 11th Annual Conference, Geneva, Sept. 13–15, 2007.

16. The history of MPS is well known. On Hayek and corporate sponsors, see Metcalf, "Neoliberalism." For the "army of fighters for freedom" and for the financing of the Mont Pèlerin meeting, see Shaxson, *Treasure Islands*, 83–4, 301.

17. On Thatcher's "to which I have returned so often," see "Hayek and Thatcher," Ryan Bourne, Center for Policy Studies blog, Sept. 11, 2012.

18. Wallace E. Oates, "The Effects of Property Taxes and Local Public Spending on Property Values: An Empirical Study of Tax Capitalization and the Tiebout Hypothesis," *Journal of Political Economy* 77, no. 6 (Nov.–Dec. 1969): 957–71.

19. For example the economist Joseph Stiglitz said, "The so-called Tiebout hypothesis is one of the predominant rationales for decentralization." See Joseph Stiglitz, "Redefining the Role of the State: What Should It Do? How Should It Do It? And How Should These Decisions Be Made?" presentation, World Bank, Tokyo, Mar. 17, 1998, 19n. The Fischel quote is from William A. Fischel (ed.), *The Tiebout Model at Fifty: Essays in Public Economics in Honor of Wallace Oates* (Cambridge, MA: Lincoln Institute of Land Policy, 2006), 8.

20. Most of the Davies quote comes from William Davies, "There Is No Such Thing as 'UK PLC,'" Fools' Gold, Apr. 1 2015, republished as "'National Competitiveness': A Crowbar for Corporate and Financial Interests," Tax Justice Network, Apr. 2, 2015, taxjustice.net/2015/04/02/national-competitiveness-a-crowbar-for-corporate-and-financial-interests. I commissioned the blog from Davies.

21. The LeRoy quote is from Greg LeRoy, *The Great American Jobs Scam: Corporate Tax Dodging and the Myth of Job Creation* (San Francisco, CA: Berrett-Koehler, 2005), 2–3, 69, 70, 90. Good Jobs First has identified a total of 500,000 deals costing $250 billion in subsidies from more than 740 federal, state, and local incentive programs in all fifty states and the District of Columbia.

22. *Kansas County Profiles: Johnson County*, University of Kansas Institute for Policy & Social Research, 2017, 41, 43.

23. For data and quotes underlying these opinions, see Bryce Covert, "Cities Should Stop Playing the Amazon HQ2 Bidding Game," *New York Times*, Nov. 13, 2018; for a detailed study of US incentives, see Timothy J. Bartik, *A New Panel Database on Business Incentives for Economic Development Offered by State and Local Governments in the United States*, W.E. Upjohn Institute for Employment Research Project No. 34435, Feb. 2017. It finds that incentives in 2015 were on average worth around 1.5 times the business value-added—in other words, a pure waste of money—and that about two-thirds of incentives went to companies that knew where they were going to relocate, regardless of the incentives.

24. On corruption, see for instance Jon Swaine, "New Jersey Grants $1.25bn in Public Funds to Firms That Back Republicans," *Guardian*, June 26, 2014. Such donations are not necessarily illegal.

25. See *Basic Financial Statements and Supplementary Information*, Jackson County Community Mental Health Fund, 2016–17, jacksoncountycares.org/wp-content/uploads/2018/08/2017-Audit.pdf.

26. The Amazon race was widely reported. On the subsidy package, Amazon in its press release estimated that it would receive $2.1 billion in subsidies from Arlington and Long Island City, but an analysis by Good Jobs First revealed an array of subsidies not included in its estimate, including Long Island City's Relocation and Employment Assistance Program (REAP), the Industrial & Commercial Abatement Program (ICAP), and payment in lieu of taxes (PILOT) incentive schemes, plus the costs of a new tech campus in Virginia, which would yield $4.6 billion in subsidies. On top of that, Good Jobs First added that "the Long Island City project site is in an Opportunity Zone, so that high net-worth individuals who have large unrealized capital gains (e.g., long-term Amazon shareholders) can invest in the project and avoid federal capital gains tax." These costs "omit damage inflicted on retailers, employees, and consumers suffering from Amazon's monopolizing ways." See "Amazon HQ2, HQ3 Subsidy Awards Costly, Not Yet Fully Accounted For," Good Jobs First, Nov. 14, 2018, goodjobsfirst. org/news/releases/amazon-hq2-hq3-subsidy-awards-costly-not-yet-fully-accounted. For the Scott Galloway quote, see "Amazon Is Creating 'Hunger Games' Environment for HQ2," CNBC, Jan. 25, 2018, cnbc.com/video/2018/01/25/amazon-is-creating-hunger-games-environment-for-hq2-finalists-nyus-scott-galloway.html, and Dennis Green, "The Professor Who Predicted Amazon Would Buy Whole Foods Says Only Two Cities Have a Shot at HQ2," *Business Insider*, Feb. 12, 2018 (Galloway correctly predicted, long ahead of the announcement, that only the New York and DC areas had a chance, for exactly the reasons laid out by LeRoy).

27. See Thomas Cafcas and Greg LeRoy, "Smart Skills versus Mindless Mega-deals: Cost-Effective Workforce Development versus Costly 'Buffalo Hunting,'" with Proven Policy Solutions," Good Jobs First, Sept. 2016, goodjobsfirst.org/smartskills. As the report notes, it is usually legal to take the money and run—promise jobs, take the subsidies, and then either not create the jobs or enact layoffs. For the tech jobs, see

"Study: State and Local Governments Pay $2 Million per Job to Tech Giants for Data Centers," Good Jobs First, Oct. 11, 2016, goodjobsfirst.org/news/releases/study-state-and-local-governments-pay-2-million-job-tech-giants-data-centers. A 2012 *New York Times* investigation of 150,000 deals estimated that Kansas spent 17 percent of its state budget on incentive programs; West Virginia and Oklahoma each spent 37 percent, and Texas 51 percent, while the richest states of Maryland, California, New Jersey, and Connecticut spent between 2 and 5 percent. The subsidies figure comes from the *New York Times* series and database "United States of Subsidies," authored by Louise Story, Tiff Fehr, and Derek Watkins, Dec. 1–3, 2012. On Foxconn, see April Glaser, "The New Wisconsin Foxconn Plant Will Probably Be Staffed by Robots—if It Ever Gets Built," *Slate*, July 27, 2017, slate.com/technology/2017/07/the-wisconsin-foxconn-plant-will-be-staff-by-robots.html, and the Foxconn entry on Good Jobs First's Subsidy Tracker, which estimates the Foxconn subsidy from Wisconsin at $4.8 billion. The $600 job-training figure is from Steve Duscha and Wanda Lee Graves, "The Employer as the Client: State-Financed Customized Training 2006," US Department of Labor, Employment and Training Administration, 2007.

28. See also Albert O. Hirschmann, *Exit, Voice, and Loyalty: Responses to Decline in Firms, Organizations, and States* (Cambridge, MA: Harvard University Press, 1970), which argues that dissatisfied citizens can opt for either exit (relocate elsewhere), voice (get angry and fight for change), or loyalty (give up and accept it). He thought voice was particularly important, as it bred accountability, energized civil society, and provided useful information about what was going on. But Tiebout had already developed the exit option into a formal theoretical framework in *The Tiebout Model*.

29. The academic literature talks about the "California effect," a race to the top on standards, and the "Delaware effect," a race to the bottom in subsidies for big business.

30. The Maurer quote is from "Diversity, Competition and 'Resilient Dynamism,'" address by President Ueli Maurer at the World Economic Forum Annual Meeting 2013, Jan. 23, 2013, in Davos. (The quote has been mildly condensed from the original, to improve readability.) Fischel and Singleton said Tiebout first offered this "joke" idea during a Richard Musgrave seminar at the University of Michigan. Fishel told me, "Musgrave told me that he offered it as a joke." Singleton states in his report, "In a characterization fitting Tiebout's personality, Musgrave described the suggestion as offered jokingly." The "fuckers" quote is from Leven, "Discovering 'Voting with Your Feet.'"

31. Tiebout, "Local Expenditures," 424.

32. See "Peter Thiel on Tax Fairness," Big Think, Jan. 4, 2008, bigthink.com/videos/peter-thiel-on-tax-fairness, and Matt Drange, "Peter Thiel Obtained New Zealand Citizenship Possibly because of 'Exceptional Circumstances,'" *Forbes*, Jan. 25, 2017.

33. The Clinton quote comes from Paul Krugman, "Competitiveness: A Dangerous Obsession," *Foreign Affairs*, Mar./Apr. 1994. Trump's words come from his speech at Carrier Corporation, Indianapolis, IN, Dec. 1, 2016; he has made variants of this "competitive" promise many times. The Cameron quote comes from his speech to the Conservative Party Conference, Oct. 10, 2012.

CHAPTER THREE: BRITAIN'S SECOND EMPIRE

1. On East India, see for instance Shashi Tharoor, *Inglorious Empire: What the British Did to India* (London: Hurst, 2017), or a shorter account in Jason Hickel, "How Britain Stole $45 Trillion from India," *Al Jazeera*, Dec. 19, 2018, aljazeera.com/indepth/opinion/britain-stole-45-trillion-india-181206124830851.html. The "roads for the merchant" quote is from Lord Palmerston, quoted in "The Business of Diplomacy," a speech by UK Foreign Secretary William Hague to the Confederation of British Industry Annual Conference, Nov. 21, 2011. On "Jesus Christ," see Philip Bowring, *Free Trade's First Missionary: Sir John Bowring in Europe and Asia* (Hong Kong: Hong Kong University Press, 2014).

2. For the "Mahometan" quote see, for instance, my article "A Tale of Two Londons," *Vanity Fair*, Mar. 13, 2013. On "invisible financial empire," see P. J. Cain and A. G. Hopkins, *British Imperialism: Innovation and Expansion, 1688–1914* (London: Longman, 1993), 241.

3. On protectionism, see for instance Chang, *Economics*, especially the sections "Britain as the pioneer of protectionism" and "The US as the champion of protectionism," pp. 61–4. See also Dani Rodrik, *Straight Talk on Trade: Ideas for a Sane World Economy* (Princeton, NJ: Princeton University Press, 2017), esp. p. 210, which contrasts the two main arguments for trade: first, the British political economist David Ricardo's that trade encourages specialization and efficiency and delivers benefits through imports; and second, the mercantilist position that the benefits come from exports, creating jobs. Britain allocated an average 37 percent of all government spending on the military in 1860–1912, supporting its colonies—and by extension the City's freedom to trade profitably, at taxpayers' expense. Despite its oversized financial center, Britain *still* has nearly the lowest rate of investment among large industrial economies. See for instance *Time for Change: A New Vision for the British Economy*, Interim Report of the IPPR Commission on Economic Justice, Institute for Public Policy Research, 2017, 37–9. As the report put it, "The juxtaposition of a highly successful financial sector and weak investment might appear paradoxical, but it is not difficult to explain. Many of the UK's financial services serve the global market, not the domestic one: their purpose is not financing investment in the UK economy" (p. 39). See also "Who Are UK Banks Lending To?" Finance Curse, Sept. 14, 2018, financecurse.net/research/who-are-uk-banks-lending-to. It uses Bank of England data to show that just 3.5 percent of UK banks' business lending went to domestic manufacturing—compared to 77 percent to finance, insurance, pensions, and real estate.

4. On "sleeping elephant," see David Kynaston, *The City of London Volume IV: A Club No More, 1945-2000* (London: Pimlico, 2002), 54. See also Glyn et al., "The Rise and Fall of the Golden Age."

5. The "slushy Socialism" quote is from the last handwritten line of a letter from Macmillan to Sir George Bolton, then a governor of the Bank of England, June 23, 1952, which I obtained from the UK National Archives. (Unfortunately, I have mislaid the file reference.)

6. Nyasaland, a small British protectorate in Africa, where my father had served as a colonial officer, became Malawi, whose first president, Kamuzu Banda, appointed my mother head gardener at his presidential palace. I was born there in 1966, two years after independence.

7. See Catherine R. Schenk, "The Origins of the Eurodollar Market in London: 1955–1963," *Explorations in Economic History* 35: 225.

8. The New Deal regulations involved strong curbs on finance, which included, among other things, splitting investment banking from deposit-taking banking to stop bankers taking customers' deposits to the casino.

9. For the origins and history of Swiss banking secrecy, see in particular Sébastien Guex, "The Origins of the Swiss Banking Secrecy Law and Its Repercussions for Swiss Federal Policy," *Business History Review* 74, no. 2 (Summer 2000): 237–66.

10. This history is told more fully in the UK edition of my book *Treasure Islands*, in the chapter entitled "The Profitable Shield of Neutrality." The British sympathies with Swiss bankers are reported in still more detail in Tom Bower, *Blood Money: The Swiss, the Nazis and the Looted Billions* (London: Pan, 1997), 79–91.

11. The "very liberal company legislation" quote is from the UK national archives, "Problems for Bank Supervisory Authorities in the Group of Ten Countries and Switzerland Raised by the Existence of Offshore Banking Centres Elsewhere in the World," 1978, file in the National Archives marked BS/78/2. I got the cloud computing analogy from Harold Crooks's excellent film *The Price We Pay* (2015).

12. The Cohen quote is from my telephone interview with him on February 28, 2017. The Cohen report is mentioned in Gary Burn, *The Re-emergence of Global Finance* (Houndmills, Basingstoke; New York: Palgrave Macmillan, 2006), 158–64. "Transnational reservoir" is from Records of the Undersecretary for International Monetary Affairs, qtd. in Burn, 161. The remaining quotes in this section are from Burn, 135–161, 164.

13. A highly imprecise calculation. An inflation calculator would multiply this number by 10, but a comparison with house prices would multiply it by 100. In the early 1960s the average UK house price was around £2,000; today it is over £200,000. The tenfold increase is nominal; it would be roughly sevenfold in inflation-adjusted terms for 1960–70, and a roughly fivefold real increase for 1970–80.

14. Jeremy Green, "Anglo-American Development, the Euromarkets, and the Deeper Origins of Neoliberal Deregulation," *Review of International Studies* 42, no. 3 (July 2016): figs. 1.1, 1.2, citing *Bank of England Quarterly Bulletin Statistical Annex 1962–70* for "London banks, 1962–70 market share current account deposits of overseas residents (all currencies)." At the same time, British banks' share of the London market fell from 45 to 20 percent. See also Bank of England, *The International Banking Markets in 1980–81*, table A, which shows the gross size of the Eurocurrency markets as $1.6 trillion then. The figures in this paragraph aren't directly comparable with this. The "frighten the horses" quote is from Bullough, *Moneyland*.

15. The Thatcher quote comes from "Speech at Lunch for President of Mexico (Miguel de la Madrid Hurtado)," June 12, 1985, margaretthatcher.org/document/106071.

16. The quotes about de la Madrid, and on estimates of scale, and on "back out the door" are from James S. Henry, "The Debt Hoax," *New Republic*, Apr. 14, 1986. This was the first major article linking the cycle of Euromarket lending, debt, and offshore wealth. Years later, Henry would create the first credible in-depth estimates for the quantity of wealth stashed offshore: see James S. Henry, *The Price of Offshore Revisited: New Estimates for "Missing" Global Private Wealth, Income, Inequality, and Lost Taxes*, Tax Justice Network, July 2012, taxjustice.net/cms/upload/pdf/Price_of_Offshore_Revisited_120722.pdf. For a more recent account of the recycling of debts into flight capital, see Léonce Ndikumana and James K. Boyce, *Africa's Odious Debts: How Foreign Loans and Capital Flight Bled a Continent* (London: Zed Books, 2011). Tim Congdon, a City of London financier, summarized effectively: "Fly-by-night rascals . . . effectively stole the proceeds of syndicated loans [and] did not have to carry the burden of debt service. . . . It fell on the general body of taxpayers, not the jetsetting fraudsters, to meet the demands of the international bankers" (qtd. in Susan Strange, *States and Markets* [London: Bloomsbury, 2015], 124).

17. On the iPhone analogy, see Adam Tooze, *Crashed: How a Decade of Financial Crises Changed the World* (London: Allen Lane, 2018), 80; Burn, *Re-emergence of Global Finance*, 90–1; and Ferguson, *High Financier: The Lives and Time of Siegmund Warburg*, Niall Ferguson, Allen Lane, 2010, 216.

18. The Bank of England memo qtd. in Burn, p. 90. As Bank of England governor Rowland Baring, 3rd Earl of Cromer, put it, the Bank did not believe "the existence of risks provided any reasons for our seeking to restrict the development of this market" (161–6). The Keogh quote is reported in Caroline Binham, "Is the Financial System Broken?," *Financial Times*, Nov. 9, 2018.

19. Post-crisis, the Bank of England has admitted that "today's system has performed poorly against each of its three objectives [efficiency, stability, and internal balance], at least compared with the Bretton Woods System." See Oliver Bush, Katie Farrant, and Michelle Wright, *Reform of the International Monetary and Financial System*, Bank of England Financial Stability Paper No. 13, Dec. 12, 2011.

20. Other countries had offshore territories as well. There was the Tangier International Zone, which served as an offshore Gomorrah for years before it became part of independent Morocco in 1956. In 1962 *Le Monde* described "waves of capital" fleeing to Monaco, from Tangier and elsewhere: "the Indochina wave, the wave of old African colonies, the wave of the Congo, and others perhaps to follow." See Vanessa Ogle, "Archipelago Capitalism: Tax Havens, Offshore Money, and the State, 1950s–1970s," *American Historical Review* 122, no. 5 (Dec. 2017): 1431–58. For further discussion of developments in the Caribbean, see also Kristine Saevold, "Capital Entrepôts at the Margins of States: A British Dual Position to Tax Havens, 1961–1979," presentation, World Economic History Congress, Boston, Aug. 2018.

21. From a memo written by Stanley Payton, Bank of England, to A. D. Neale and O'Brien, Foreign and Commonwealth Office, Apr. 11, 1969, marked "West Indies—tax havens," obtained from the National Archives by Paul Sagar for *Treasure Islands*, funded by the Tax Justice Network.

22. The "brass plates" quotes are from a Bank of England document marked "West Indies—Tax Havens" and dated April 11, 1969 (archive file number not available).

It is available to view in Paul Sagar, John Christensen, Nicholas Shaxson, "British Government Attitudes to British Tax Havens: An Examination of Whitehall Responses to the Growth of Tax Havens in British Dependent Territories from 1967 to 1975," presentation to the Centre for the Study of International Governance, Loughborough University, Sept. 29, 2010.

23. See Saevold, "Capital Entrepôts."

24. For the quotes in this paragraph, see Ogle, "Archipelago Capitalism," 1443–5. She wrote, "The Cayman law was particularly perfidious, as it was based on a close reading of Britain's tax laws, with its own language carefully chosen so as to fall outside those laws." The Cayman council is called the Private Sector Consultative Committee, and you can find the official list of its members at gov.ky/portal/page/portal/cighome/find/organisations/azpublicbodies/pscc.

25. As one international banker, A. E. Moore, remarked in 1979, "The development of the concept of the Eurocurrency market . . . can be seen as leading directly to the phenomenon of offshore banking centres, based away from any country in which regulatory, monetary or fiscal controls might apply." See A. E. Moore, "The Phenomenon of the Offshore Centre," speech, International Conference of Banking Supervisors, London, July 5–6, 1979, National Archives. *Treasure Islands* popularized the idea of a British "spider's web" of tax havens, though I first saw the term in an email from James S. Henry, a senior adviser to the Tax Justice Network. There is now a film, *The Spider's Web: Britain's Second Empire* (2017), about this episode, coproduced by my close collaborator on *Treasure Islands*, John Christensen. (The Scythian philosopher Anacharsis offered a different, yet also appropriate, analogy using the spider's web. "Laws are like spiderwebs. They catch the little flies, but cannot hold the big ones.")

26. As David Quentin, a UK tax lawyer, puts it, "The UK uses the Cayman Islands and similar jurisdictions to create a tax-free space for rich people from everywhere else in the world to place their assets under UK-based management." While the UK cannot easily tax those foreigners or foreign assets directly, it can tax London-based managers receiving fees for managing those "swollen sacs of undertaxed capital" sitting offshore. So the UK takes a cut of the tax dodged elsewhere. See David Quentin, "Seventy-seven Nation Industrial Reserve Army," *New Socialist*, Jan. 6, 2018.

27. On Anthony Field, see *United States of America v. Anthony R. Field*, 532 F.2d 404 (5th Cir. 1976).

28. For Grundy, see Shaxson, *Treasure Islands*, 106.

29. See "Britain Is Most Corrupt Country on Earth, Says Mafia Expert Roberto Saviano," *Telegraph*, May 29, 2016, and for the Palan quote, see my article "A Tale of Two Londons," *Vanity Fair*, Apr. 2013.

30. On Britain's powers, see for example Nicholas Shaxson, "Britain Can Force Its Tax Havens to Curb Secrecy. But Will It?" Tax Justice Network, Nov. 13, 2015, taxjustice.net/2015/11/13/britain-can-force-its-tax-havens-to-curb-secrecy-but-will-it, and associated links. A veteran British Virgin Islands lawyer who wanted to remain anonymous told me by telephone in 2013 that the UK has "complete power of disallowance" over all its legislation. And it was always thus: a confidential letter of May 18, 1973, signed by N. B. J. Huijsman of the West Indian and Caribbean Department,

to Mr. Larmour, states clearly Britain's extensive powers over these territories. "[The Governor] can introduce appropriate legislation, and if the legislative assembly fails to pass it, he can declare it passed under his reserve powers, whether in original or in amended form." Furthermore, his instructions require him to reserve for royal approval "any bill establishing any banking association or altering the constitution, rights or duties of any banking association." He must also reserve any bill "of an extraordinary nature and importance whereby . . . *the rights or property of Our subjects not residing in the islands . . . may be adversely affected*" (my emphasis; this explicitly covers harms transmitted elsewhere). Finally, even in respect to bills to which the governor has given his assent, the secretary of state has a "back-stop power to disallow the legislation." In 2013 John Christensen of the Tax Justice Network wrote to the Queen, enclosing a copy of *Treasure Islands* and requesting that she use her influence to stop Britain's tax haven activities. Her offices replied, saying this was the government's job, not hers.

31. This quote has been amalgamated from two places: Hudson's interview in the documentary *The Spider's Web* (around forty minutes in) and my interview with Hudson in New York in 2008. The full memo is reproduced in R. T. Naylor, *Hot Money and the Politics of Debt*, 3rd ed. (Montreal: McGill-Queen's University Press, 2004), 33–4.

32. The quotes in this paragraph are from Eric Helleiner, *States and the Re-emergence of Global Finance: From Bretton Woods to the 1990s* (Ithaca, NY: Cornell University Press, 1994), 59–60.

33. This is covered in the US edition of my last book, *Treasure Islands*, 58–59, and also in Helleiner, esp. 55–60.

34. Qtd. in Charles P. Alexander, "America the Tax Haven," *Time*, Aug. 13, 1984.

35. Lee Sheppard, "Our Hypocrisy On Tax Havens," *Forbes*, July 22, 2010.

36. From "British Development Division in the Caribbean: Report on a Team Visit to the Cayman Islands," Apr. 14–17, 1969, FIN/CMS/1407/15, UK National Archives.

37. Fonseca qtd. in Martha M. Hamilton, "Panamanian Law Firm Is Gatekeeper to Vast Flow of Murky Offshore Secrets," International Consortium of Investigative Journalists, Apr. 3, 2016, icij.org/investigations/panama-papers/20160403-mossack-fonseca-offshore-secrets.

38. To see the documents and the analysis, see Nicholas Shaxson, "Guest Blog: How Switzerland Corrupted Its Courts to Nail Rudolf Elmer," Tax Justice Network, July 1, 2015, taxjustice.net/2015/07/01/guest-blog-how-switzerland-corrupted-its-courts-to-nail-rudolf-elmer, and associated links. (I worked with Elmer on the blog.) At the time of this writing, in October 2018, he was still being pursued by the Swiss legal system, more than ten years later.

39. The most widely used exposition of financialization comes from Epstein, who defined it as "the increasing role of financial motives, financial markets, financial actors and financial institutions in the operation of the domestic and international economies." See Gerald Epstein, *Financialization and the World Economy* (Northhampton, MA: Edward Elgar, 2005.) Greta Krippner, in her landmark book *Capitalizing on Crisis: The Political Origins of the Rise of Finance* (Cambridge, MA: Harvard University

Press, 2011), defines financialization as "the tendency for profit-making in the economy to occur increasingly through financial channels rather than through productive activities." Her core argument is that policy-makers turned to looser credit and finance as a way of avoiding difficult tax-and-spend distributional struggles, particularly from the 1960s and 1970s as economic growth began to slow. On the "transatlantic regulatory feedback loop," see Jan Fichtner, "Perpetual Decline or Persistent Dominance? Uncovering Anglo-America's True Structural Power in Global Finance," *Review of International Studies*, 43, no.1 (Jan. 2017): 3–28.

CHAPTER FOUR: THE INVISIBLE FIST

1. The "devil's bargain" sentence has been adapted from one of the few media articles that properly discussed monopoly in the Zuckerberg episode: David Dayen, "The Senate Is Afraid to Govern. That's Great News for Facebook," *Intercept*, Apr. 10, 2018, theintercept.com/2018/04/10/facebook-the-senate-is-afraid-to-govern-thats-great-news-for-facebook.

2. On Google and the Obama administration, for instance, see David Dayen, "The Android Administration: Google's Remarkably Close Relationship with the Obama White House, in Two Charts," *Intercept*, Apr. 22, 2016, theintercept.com/2016/04/22/googles-remarkably-close-relationship-with-the-obama-white-house-in-two-charts, showing at least 427 meetings with Google during Obama's two terms.

3. Director, Stigler, and Friedman had also been at the all-important Mont Pèlerin meeting in Switzerland in 1947. The Watson quotes are from a series of email exchanges I had with him over 2016–17.

4. See Edmund W. Kitch, "The Fire of Truth: A Remembrance of Law and Economics at Chicago, 1932–1970," *Journal of Law & Economics* 26, no. 1 (Apr. 1983): 163–234. Further testimony about Director's influence is on pp. 185–6. The "Christ" quote is on p. 192. On "obvious mistake," see Patrick J. Lyons, "Ronald H. Coase, 'Accidental' Economist Who Won a Nobel Prize, Dies at 102," *New York Times*, Sept. 3, 2013.

5. Kitch, "The Fire of Truth," 221. The list of attendees at Director's dinner is not available, but the group recalled Stigler, Friedman, Director, John McGee, H. Gregg Lewis, Reuben Kessel, Lloyd Mintz, Arnold Harberger, and Martin Bailey as being present.

6. Ibid, 196.

7. Quote from a paper Greenspan presented at the Antitrust Seminar of the National Association of Business Economists, Cleveland, OH, Sept. 25, 1961. This paper was the basis for Alan Greenspan's *Antitrust* (New York: Nathaniel Branden Institute, 1962). The ideas began moving out of academia and into policy when Stigler led a government task force in 1969 whose final report was a flimsy document slamming antitrust regulators and citing "nebulous fears" about corporate size and power, a report that one expert said "felt no need to cite either data or scholarly literature." See Kenneth Davidson, *Reality Ignored: How Milton Friedman and Chicago Economics Undermined American Institutions and Endangered the Global Economy* (Arlington, VA: s.p., 2011), 35–6.

8. From the Boston Tea Party section in a timeline published by the Open Markets Institute, undated, at openmarketsinstitute.org/timeline/.

9. Alexis de Tocqueville, *Democracy in America*, vol. 2 (New York: J. & H. G. Langley, 1840).

10. "Caesarism" is from Charles F. Adams Jr., "The Government and the Railroad Corporations," *North American Review* 112, no. 230 (Jan. 1871): 31–61. (Other quotes are from the Open Markets timeline.)

11. The Sherman quote is widely publicised. David Gerber, a law professor at Chicago-Kent College of Law, said the rise of antitrust law was spurred by "resentment towards the new super rich and their lavish and ostentatious lifestyles . . . located primarily in New York and other cities on the East Coast." Another catalyst, he said, was "rising anger among Midwestern farming communities at what they saw as rapacious and monopolistic conduct . . . manipulating prices paid to farmers for their grain and livestock." See David J. Gerber, "U.S. Antitrust: From Shot in the Dark to Global Leadership," in Lori Andrews and Sarah Harding (eds.), *Then & Now: Stories of Law and Progress* (Chicago: IIT; Chicago-Kent School of Law, 2013).

12. Brandeis's "inevitable friction" quote is widely cited. The 1931 analysis is from "Summary Competition Policy under Shadow of 'National Champions,'" Monopolkommission Fifteenth Biennial Report, 2002/2003, p. 581, no. 24. On monopolies and the rise of Nazism, also see Daniel A. Crane, "Antitrust and Democracy: A Case Study from German Fascism," University of Michigan Law & Econ Research Paper No. 18-009, No. 595, Apr. 17, 2018; and Diarmuid Jeffries, *Hell's Cartel: IG Farben and the Making of Hitler's War Machine*, (London: Bloomsbury, 2009). The Roosevelt quote is from Franklin D. Roosevelt, "Message to Congress on Curbing Monopolies," Apr. 29, 1938. As the US monopolies expert Barry Lynn puts it, monopoly power "means that [a corporation's] power to govern the political economic systems under its control is entirely despotic in nature" (Barry Lynn, *Cornered: The New Monopoly Capitalism and the Economics of Destruction* [Hoboken, NJ: John Wiley & Sons, 2010], 52). The Celler quote is in Kenneth Davidson, *Megamergers: Corporate America's Billion-Dollar Takeovers* (Washington, DC: Beard Books, 2003).

13. See for instance Brett Christophers, *The Great Leveler: Capitalism and Competition in the Court of Law* (Cambridge, MA: Harvard University Press), 171.

14. The Treaty of Rome, particularly Articles 85–88, enshrined classic antitrust laws. Its terms focused heavily on preemptive market regulation: "concerted practices that *are likely* to affect trade between member states and that *intend* or *effect* the prevention, restriction, or distortion of competition within the Common Market"—as opposed to the Chicago School's later approach: regulating only after the event, if then. See for instance Angela Wigger, "The Political Interface of Financialisation and the Regulation of Mergers and Acquisitions in the EU," *Journal of European Integration* 34, no. 6 (Aug. 2012): 623–41.

15. Telephone interview with Blum, May 5, 2017.

16. The section on "homosexuals, American Indians," etc., is from Bork's book *Slouching Towards Gomorrah: Modern Liberalism and American Decline* (New York: Regan Books, 1996), 5, 10.

17. This section on Bork brings together different time periods. For the Kennedy quote, see 133 Cong. Rec. S18519 (July 1, 1987). The "throw a book at you" quote is widely cited.

18. The Berk quote is from my telephone interview with Gerald Berk, July 28, 2017. Most of the quotes in the paragraph are from *The Antitrust Paradox: A Policy at War with Itself* (New York: Basic Books, 1978), esp. 154 and 234. Bork's idea that predatory pricing didn't exist was based on mathematical modeling that suggested predators would have to spend too much on loss-making strategies to make those losses worthwhile. He credited Director with some of these insights (see for instance Robert H. Bork and Ward S. Bowman Jr., "The Crisis in Antitrust," *Fortune*, Dec. 1963), which laid out some of the arguments that would emerge in the *Antitrust Paradox*. It includes the magical sentence: "Professor John McGee, an economist now at Duke University, reviewed the entire case record of the Standard Oil litigation and reported that there is not one clear episode of the successful use by Standard Oil of local price cutting or other predatory practices" (p. 368). (A counterexample to McGee would be Rockefeller's use of dynamite and cannon fire against the independents trying to lay pipe in Hancock, which I outlined in chapter two.) Also see Lina Khan, "Amazon's Antitrust Paradox," *Yale Law Journal*, 126, no. 3, (Jan. 2017).

19. "Timeline: Robert Bork & *The Antitrust Paradox*, 1978," Open Markets, openmarketsinstitute.org/timeline.

20. See MacLean, *Democracy in Chains*, esp. 122–5. On Manne and corporate funding, see Henry Manne, "How Law and Economics Was Marketed in a Hostile World: A Very Personal History," in *The Origins of Law and Economics: Essays by the Founding Fathers*, Francesco Parisi, Charles K. Rowley, (eds.,) 309-327, 2005 George Mason Law & Economics Research Paper No. 06-49, esp. 315, where he says, for instance, that "the program at Rochester was funded by ten or twelve large corporations, most of which were concerned about antitrust matters." He also highlights funding from the Olin Foundation during his career.

21. See for instance Spencer Weber Waller, review of *Competition Policy in America, 1888–1992: History, Rhetoric, Law*, by Rudolph J. R. Peritz, *Law & Social Inquiry* 22, no. 2 (Spring 1997): 447–8. Intellectual property rights were given new teeth too, on the similarly shaky justification that this would, by promoting big American high-technology champions, promote exports. See Christophers, *Great Leveler*, 237–8: Reagan-era lobbying to weaken antitrust was specifically "in order to promote better international 'competitiveness' for the United States."

22. See Davidson, *Megamergers*, 39. Other indirect quotes are from my interview with Davidson in March 2016. When the Federal Trade Commission in 2018 launched its biggest-ever inquiry into corporate concentration, it turned out that every economist who testified had taken money from large corporations. See Jesse Eisinger and Justin Elliott, "These Professors Make More Than a Thousand Bucks an Hour Peddling Mega-Mergers," *ProPublica*, Nov. 16, 2016. See also Matt Stoller and Austin Frerick, "Should We Break Up the Tech Giants? Not If You Ask the Economists Who Take Money from Them," *Fast Company*, Oct. 19, 2018. On banking, see also Brett Christophers, "Financialisation as Monopoly Profit: The Case of US Banking," *Antipode* 50, no. 4 (Jan. 2018): 864–90.

23. On March 16, 2017, the *Financial Times* printed a story entitled "Unilever Investors Favoured Talks with Kraft Heinz." Even entertaining the idea of this proposed $143 billion merger would have been inconceivable under classic antitrust. The "cornucopia" phrase is from Lynn, *Cornered*.

24. The Luxottica information is largely drawn from its 2017 annual report, showing €5.9 billion ($6.4 billion) in gross profits on sales of €9.2 billion ($9.9 billion). The Walmart data is from the gross profit rate in its 2018 annual report. The "forgive me" quote is from Sam Knight, "The Spectacular Power of Big Lens," *Guardian*, May 10, 2018. On Oakley, this was widely reported. One Luxottica-related example of financial profits being teased out of "snaking chains of corporate entities" is a document I obtained from the Irish corporate registry, *Luxottica Trading and Finance Limited*, Director's Report and Financial Statements, Oct. 24, 2013, registered at the Matsack Trust Limited in Dublin, and listing its bankers as Citibank Ireland, AIB Dublin, Bank of China (Guangdong), Yapi ve Kredi Bankasi A.S. Ataturk (Istanbul), Citibank Hong Kong, and Citibank Istanbul. (This particular Irish trading/treasury company no longer does business.)

25. See "2018 List of Global Systemically Important Banks (G-SIBs)," Financial Stability Board, Nov. 16, 2017, fsb.org/wp-content/uploads/P161118-1.pdf, and "Review of the List of Global Systemically Important Insurers (G-SIIs)," Financial Stability Board, Nov. 21, 2017, fsb.org/wp-content/uploads/P211117-2.pdf. The 1990 banking data is from Chris Vanderpool, "Five Banks Hold More Than 44% of US Industry's Assets," SNL Financial, Dec. 2, 2014, and the 2016 data comes from "5-Bank Asset Concentration for United States," Federal Reserve Bank of St. Louis, Sept. 21, 2018, fred.stlouisfed.org/series/DDOI06USA156NWDB. On a visual estimate from the graph, the figure was around 47 percent in 2016.

26. See "The British Experiment," *Economist*, Mar. 4, 2017. For the BlackRock statistic, see "Too Much of a Good Thing?" *Economist*, Mar. 26, 2016.

27. See Rana Foroohar, "Amazon's Pricing Tactic Is a Trap for Buyers and Sellers Alike," *Financial Times*, Sept. 2, 2018; Phillip Longman, "The Case for Small-Business Collusion," *Washington Monthly*, Nov./Dec. 2018; and Matt Stoller, "Democrats Can't Win until They Recognize How Bad Obama's Financial Policies Were," *Washington Post*, Jan. 12, 2017. The "relic of history" is from Jonathan Tepper with Denise Hearn, *The Myth of Capitalism: Monopolies and the Death of Competition* (Hoboken, NJ: John Wiley & Sons, 2019), 4. On Buffett and monopolies, see also David Dayen, "Special Investigation: The Dirty Secret Behind Warren Buffett's Billions," *The Nation*, Feb. 15, 2018.

28. This episode is from a telephone interview with Barry Lynn, Mar. 21, 2017, and *Boosting Resilience through Innovative Risk Governance*, OECD Reviews of Risk Management Policies, 2014, 37. See also Yossi Sheffi and Barry C. Lynn, "Systemic Supply Chain Risk," *Bridge* 44, no. 3 (Fall 2014): 22–9, and Barry C. Lynn, "Built to Break: The International System of Bottlenecks in the New Era of Monopoly," *Challenge* 55, no. 2 (2012): 87–107.

29. Gazprom has frequently cut off or threatened to cut off gas supplies to countries to further Russia's political and geostrategic ambitions. See for example Alan Riley, *Commission v. Gazprom: The Antitrust Clash of the Decade?* Centre for European

Policy Studies No. 285, Oct. 31, 2012, and European Commission competition case 39816: "Upstream Gas Supplies in Central and Eastern Europe."

30. The trader/manager spoke to me on condition of anonymity in an interview in London in March 2017.

31. On airline consolidation and price gouging, see the explainer published by the Open Markets Institute called "Airlines & Monopoly," openmarketsinstitute.org/explainer/airline-monopoly. On the $9,000 estimate for health insurance, see Paul S. Hewitt and Phillip Longman, "The Case for Single-Price Health Care," *Washington Monthly*, April/May/June 2018. The estimate comes from comparing Medicare prices to commercial health insurance, and cites a study by the Congressional Budget Office showing "the price for a one-day hospital stay is 89 percent higher when charged to commercial insurance plans and their customers than when a Medicare patient stays in the same bed for the same amount of time."

32. On LIBOR, US attorney general Loretta Lynch called the small group setting LIBOR rates "a cartel" engaging in "brazenly illegal behavior" and a "brazen display of collusion." Four banks, Citicorp, JPMorgan Chase & Co., Barclays PLC, and The Royal Bank of Scotland PLC, paid a combined $2.5 billion in antitrust fines. See "Attorney General Lynch Delivers Remarks at a Press Conference on Foreign Exchange Spot Market Manipulation, Washington, DC," justice.gov, May 20, 2015.

33. The thesis that patents currently stifle innovation is hardly controversial. For example, see Lynn, *Cornered*, particularly the chapter "Lightning Escapes the Bottle," and a series of articles linked to Joshua Gans, "Do Patents Stifle Cumulative Innovation," Economist's View, July 17, 2014, economistsview.typepad.com/economistsview/2014/07/do-patents-stifle-cumulative-innovation.html.

34. On Gilead, see *Gilead Sciences: Price Gouger, Tax Dodger*, Americans for Tax Fairness, July 2016, americansfortaxfairness.org/files/ATF-Gilead-Report-Finalv3-for-Web.pdf. On South Africa, see "HIV Drugs 'Boost South African Life Expectancy,'" BBC News, Aug. 1, 2004; Linda Nordling, "South Africa Ushers in New Era for HIV," *Nature*, July 13, 2016; Sarah Boseley, "Big Pharma's Worst Nightmare," *Guardian*, Jan. 26, 2016; and "SA Drops Price of ARVs, Saves R11bn in Six Years," *TimesLIVE*, Sept. 22, 2017, timeslive.co.za/news/south-africa/2017-09-22-sa-drops-price-of-arvs-saves-r11bn-in-six-years. The 'yachts' quote is from Matt Stoller on Twitter, June 22, 2017.

35. The changes included the Airline Deregulation Act of 1978, the Depository Institutions Deregulation and Monetary Control Act of 1980, the Staggers Railroad Act of 1980, and especially the 1982 Merger Guidelines under the Reagan administration, which explicitly cited "efficiency" and "consumer welfare" as the only legitimate goals of antitrust. The Lynn quote is from *Cornered*, 68.

36. The Harvie quote is from Deena Shanker, "Farmers' Beef with Trump over 'Big Meat,'" *Bloomberg*, Apr. 21, 2017. For a shocking exposé of monopolization in American agriculture, see Christopher Leonard, *The Meat Racket: The Secret Takeover of America's Food Business* (New York: Simon & Schuster, 2014). Leonard describes a "vast, hidden territory of finance, economics and power" (p. 3) that includes farms, processors, transporters, and consumers, helping Tyson to gain astonishing influence over significant parts of America's meat supply, reshaping US rural economies wholesale.

In Arkansas, Leonard's investigations revealed a company behaving "like an economic dark star that has drawn into itself all the independent businesses that used to define a small town like Waldron, the kinds of businesses that were once the economic pillars of rural America" (p. 2).

37. The Bartlett quote comes from Bruce Bartlett, "How Fox News Changed American Media and Political Dynamics," SSRN, May 11, 2015.

38. On the Trump rollback of local news broadcasting restrictions, see Tom Wheeler, "On Local Broadcasting, Trump Federal Communications Commission 'Can't Be Serious!'" Brookings, Apr. 12, 2018, brookings.edu/blog/techtank/2018/04/12/on-local-broadcasting-trump-federal-communications-commission-cant-be-serious.

39. On Amazon, see Lina M. Khan, "Amazon's Antitrust Paradox," *Yale Law Journal* 126, no. 3 (Jan. 2017): 564–907. On the Gazelle Project, see "A New Book Portrays Amazon as Bully," *New York Times*, Oct. 22, 2013). On Amazon admitting its strategy see, for example, Bezos's first letter to shareholders in 1997, widely available: "A fundamental measure of our success will be shareholder value [which] will be a direct result of our ability to extend and solidify our current market leadership position. . . . Market leadership can translate directly to higher revenue, higher profitability . . . and correspondingly stronger returns on invested capital."

40. For an overview of labor and profit shares worldwide, see *The Labour Share in G20 Economies*, International Labour Organisation and Organisation for Economic Co-operation and Development, 2015, and for the UK, the *Time for Change* report (fig. 2.6 shows a roughly 10 percent decline in the labor share of national income). See also Eric A. Posner, Glen Weyl, and Suresh Naidu, "Antitrust Remedies for Labor Market Power," *Harvard Law Review* 132, no. 2 (Dec. 2018): 536–601. Other reports include Matt Stoller, "Bigger Corporations Are Making You Poorer," *Vice*, Apr. 5, 2017, which found that wages would be $14,000 higher per year in the United States if the economy had the level of competition it had in 1985. See also David Autor et al., *Concentrating on the Fall of the Labor Share*, National Bureau of Economic Research Working Paper No. 23108, Jan. 2017; Peter Orszag (panel member), "Concentration, Market Power, and Inequality," Stigler Center Conference, Chicago, Mar. 27, 2017; and Jae Song et al., *Firming Up Inequality*, National Bureau of Economic Research Working Paper No. 21199, May 2015. Going further back in history, Christophers, *Great Leveler*, 165–6, 212, summarizes the research findings of Michal Kalecki, Josep Steindl, and others, suggesting that degrees of monopoly go a long way to explaining relative changes in the share of income going to labor versus capital.

41. Tepper and Hearn, *The Myth of Capitalism*, 10.

42. On variety and balance and resilience, see for instance Gerald Berk and Marc Schneiberg, "Varieties in Capitalism, Varieties of Association: Collaborative Learning in American Industry, 1900 to 1925," *Politics & Society* 33, no. 1 (Mar. 2005): 46–87. On monopolies reducing economic growth, productivity, investment, and innovation there is a large body of varied literature. A good collection is contained in Tepper and Hearn, especially pp. 45-61; and in Brink Lindsey and Steven M. Teles, *The Captured Economy: How the Powerful Enrich Themselves, Slow Down Growth, and Increase Inequality* (New York: Oxford University Press, 2017).

CHAPTER FIVE: THE THIRD WAY

1. Quotes are from Peter Truell and Larry Gurwin, *False Profits: Inside the Story of BCCI, the World's Most Corrupt Financial Empire* (Boston, MA: Houghton Mifflin, 1992), 11.

2. The BCCI Ponzi scheme is outlined on p. 51 of John Kerry and Hank Brown, *The BCCI Affair: A Report to the Committee on Foreign Relations, United States Senate* (Washington, DC: US Government Printing Office, Dec. 1992).

3. Telephone interview with Blum, May 5, 2017.

4. Maurice Punch, *Dirty Business: Exploring Corporate Misconduct: Analysis and Cases* (London: Sage, 1996), 12.

5. Morgenthau quotes are from my interview with him on May 4, 2009, in his office in New York, shortly before his retirement.

6. Kerry and Brown, *The BCCI Affair*. The senators obtained a heavily redacted copy of the Sandstorm report, Price Waterhouse's secret report to the Bank of England regarding fraud and money laundering at BCCI (Professor Prem Sikka of the University of Sheffield later obtained a less-redacted version in 2011, after a five-year Freedom of Information fight). The confidentiality quote is from p. 54; the shift to Abu Dhabi is on p. 13. The Senate report is shocking; it said US investigators "were hampered by examples of lack of cooperation by foreign governments, including most significantly the Serious Fraud Office in the United Kingdom" (p. 12).

7. The Kerry quotes are from Kerry and Brown, *The BCCI Affair*, and Conal Walsh, "Old Lady Won't Be Keen on President Kerry," *The Observer*, Feb. 15, 2004. For the Virani details, see Truell and Gurwin, *False Profits*, 87; also see Austin Mitchell et al., *The BCCI Cover-up*, Association for Accountancy and Business Affairs, 2001. The sections and quotes on Thatcher are from Mark Hollingsworth and Paul Halloran, *Thatcher's Fortunes: The Life and Times of Mark Thatcher* (London: Simon & Schuster, 1995), 273-276, and from my interview with Hollingsworth, Sept. 28, 2018. On Thatcher and Bakeland, this is from my interview with Hollingsworth, plus "Summary of Share Capital and Shares of Bakeland Property Company Limited," Jan. 1, 1992, obtained from Jersey Financial Services Commission. Alongside Leonard Day, with 2,497 shares, and Hugh Thurston, with 2,500 shares, it also lists Margery Rosita Day, with 3 shares. A registration document dated February 14, 1991, lists the founders as David Peter Huelin, Bryan John Dauny, and Natalie Veronica Faudemer, "wife of Ian Robert Cutter." Hollingsworth said that the trust companies were in Switzerland, and yet there were also a significant number of Panama companies involved too, which warranted further investigation.

8. For the *Financial Times* quote, see Matthew C. Klein, "More Evidence in the Case Against Luxembourg," *FT Alphaville*, Mar. 9, 2017.

9. The controversial Juncker quotes are from "Jean-Claude Juncker's Most Outrageous Quotations," *Telegraph*, July 15, 2014. Also see "Who Is Luxembourg's Most Popular Politician?" *Luxembourg Time*, Oct. 9, 2012, and Jeroen Dijsselbloem, "Farewell to Juncker," speech at the farewell dinner for Juncker, Feb. 11, 2013.

10. On Luxembourg sabotaging European efforts to counter financial secrecy, see "Austria's and Luxembourg's Anglo-German Fig Leaf," Tax Justice Network, Feb. 22, 2011,

taxjustice.blogspot.com/2011/02/uk-germany-connive-with-austria.html. On Luxembourg's history as a tax haven, see *Narrative Report on Luxembourg*, Financial Secrecy Index 2018, Tax Justice Network, Nov. 13, 2013, financialsecrecyindex.com/PDF/Luxembourg. pdf. Juncker's main role was to provide political protection to the financial center as it grew fast under its own steam. See Simon Bowers, "Jean-Claude Juncker Can't Shake Off Luxembourg's Tax Controversy," *Observer*, Dec. 14, 2014; Simon Bowers, "Jean-Claude Juncker Blocked EU Curbs on Tax Avoidance, Cables Show," *Guardian*, Jan. 1, 2017; and "Junckergate: When It Becomes Serious, You Have to Lie?" European United Left/ Nordic Green Left European parliamentary group, Sept. 28, 2015, guengl.eu/news/ article/junckergate-when-it-becomes-serious-you-have-to-lie. Until the late 1980s, most "profit-shifting" into tax havens is accounted for by the "Big Five" of Switzerland, the Netherlands, Ireland, Bermuda, and Singapore. Juncker became finance minister in 1989, and at this point Luxembourg's share started to grow sharply, accelerating as he became prime minister, and today Luxembourg is one of the "Big Six." For a visual illustration, see Nicholas Shaxson, "Jean-Claude Juncker and Tax Haven Luxembourg, in a Picture," Tax Justice Network, Jan. 30, 2015, taxjustice.net/2015/01/30/jean-claude-juncker-tax-haven-luxembourg-picture. The graph is drawn from Gabriel Zucman's *The Hidden Wealth of Nations: The Scourge of Tax Havens* (Chicago: University of Chicago Press, 2015), with Juncker timings added by David Walch of Attac-Austria. By 1992 the offshore mutual fund industry, which in Luxembourg's hands was a classic tax evasion play, was growing at rates of 60 percent annually. See Rupert Bruce, "Luxembourg Thrives as an Eden for Funds," *New York Times*, Nov. 13, 1993.

11. The trip was in October 2011. The writer of the email, whom I met later, declined to be identified by name.

12. In a rare outburst in October 2011, Luxembourg's state prosecutor-general Robert Biever said that of fifty thousand criminal cases in the previous year, two-thirds involved traffic violations and only seven involved the financial sector. See Alain Ducat, "Robert Biever dénonce," *Paperjam*, Oct. 14, 2011.

13. Bomans's comments come from my telephone interview with him on March 10, 2017, and subsequent emails. On conflicts of interest, for instance, in 2016 Belgian and German newspapers revealed that Claude Marx, head of the Commission de Surveillance du Secteur Financier (CSSF), the main finance regulator in Luxembourg, had been heavily involved in setting up offshore companies with Mossack Fonseca, the firm at the heart of the Panama Papers scandal. See "Claude Marx, directeur de la CSSF, très impliqué dans les Panama Papers," *Le Quotidien*, Mar. 15, 2017. Luc Frieden, Luxembourg's finance minister, said of the Madoff cases in June 2009, "The principle is very clear: the custodian bank has to indemnify investors." See Press Release Madoff—Luxalpha SICAV, Deminor.com, July 2, 2015, https://drs.deminor.com/en/ press-release-madoff-luxalpha-sicav. Yet Luxembourg's courts still did not hold the banks responsible. See Stephanie Bodoni, "Madoff's European Victims Still Waiting to Recover Losses," *Bloomberg Businessweek*, Feb. 6, 2014.

14. For more on Patman's history, see Alexander Cockburn and James Ridgeway, "Why They Sacked the Bane of the Banks," *Village Voice*, Feb. 3, 1975, and Matt Stoller,

"How Democrats Killed Their Populist Soul," *Atlantic*, Oct. 24, 2016. On "money is part of politics" see Gregg Easterbrook, "The Business of Politics," *Atlantic*, Oct. 1986.

15. The Coelho history is drawn from multiple sources, including the US House of Representatives bio of him at history.house.gov, as well as Gregg Easterbrook, "The Business of Politics," *Atlantic*, Oct. 1986; "The Tony Coelho Factor," *Washington Times*, Jan. 17, 2006; and several stories in the *New York Times* about Don Dixon. Coelho resigned in 1989 amid the savings and loan crisis but reappeared ten years later as general chairman of Al Gore's presidential campaign committee; he was brought in, as one senior Gore official put it, because they needed "an adult" to run it.

16. See David Sirota, "Presidents Obama and Clinton Failed to Defend the Middle Class: Robert Reich," *International Business Times*, Nov. 30, 2017.

17. On Hillary Clinton's speech, see Amanda Marcotte and Moe Tkacik, "Hillary Clinton Suggested Breaking Up the Big Banks Won't End Racism and Sexism. Is She Right?" *In These Times*, Mar. 11, 2016. For the sake of crystallizing her message, I edited the full quote down from "If we broke up the big banks tomorrow—and I will if they deserve it, if they pose a systemic risk, I will—would that end racism?" (The rest of her speech makes her position clear, as my main text shows.) On the Democratic National Committee sanctioning seven groups as official party caucuses, see Ronald Elving, "Debating Length, Language, Democrats Ponder Platform," *CQ Weekly Report 1583*, June 11, 1988, cited in Jon F. Hale, "The Making of the New Democrats," *Political Science Quarterly* 110, no. 2 (Summer 1995): 207–32. See also Michael Lind, "Trumpism and Clintonism Are the Future," *New York Times*, Apr. 16, 2016. On some history of identity politics and the working class, see Stoller, "How the Democratic Party."

18. Michael Porter, "How Competitive Forces Shape Strategy," *Harvard Business Review*, Mar. 1979. Porter built a lucrative consulting business out of these ideas. See Steve Denning, "What Killed Michael Porter's Monitor Group? The One Force That Really Matters," *Forbes*, Nov. 20, 2012.

19. Michael Porter, "The Competitive Advantage of Nations," *Harvard Business Review*, Mar.–Apr. 1990.

20. The details on Fisher and Atlas are from several sources, including Richard Cockett, *Thinking the Unthinkable: Think-Tanks and the Economic Counter-Revolution, 1931–1983* (London: HarperCollins, 1994); Gerald Frost, *Antony Fisher: Champion of Liberty* (London: Profile Books, 2002); MacLean, *Democracy in Chains*; Jane Mayer, *Dark Money: The Hidden History of the Billionaires Behind the Rise of the Radical Right* (New York: Doubleday, 2016); and Marie-Laure Djelic, "Spreading Ideas to Change the World: Inventing and Institutionalizing the Neoliberal Think Tank," SSRN, Sept. 2014, papers.ssrn.com/sol3/papers.cfm?abstract_id=2492010.

21. On "Magic Meeting Place," see "The Magic Meeting Place: Europe's corporate chiefs go to Davos for play and work," *Time*, Feb. 16, 1981.

22. See "The New Orleans Declaration: Statement Endorsed at the Fourth Annual DLC Conference," Democratic Leadership Committee, Mar. 1, 1990. Quotes are from Robin Toner, "Eyes to Left, Democrats Edge toward the Center," *New York Times*, Mar. 25, 1990.

23. The Clinton quote is from Krugman, "Competitiveness." The Davies quotes are from, *Limits of Neoliberalism*, 110.

24. Reich qtd. in Sirota, "Presidents Obama and Clinton Failed."

25. Jackson qtd. in Karen Ho, *Liquidated: An Ethnography of Wall Street* (Durham, NC: Duke University Press, 2009), 22–3.

26. The Watson quotes come from my Skype interview with him from March 2015.

27. On Blair's 2005 speech, see William Black, "New Labour Leaders Want to Go Back to Blair's Policies That Blew Up the UK," *New Economic Perspectives*, May 13, 2015, neweconomicperspectives.org/2015/05/new-labour-leaders-want-to-go-back-to-blairs-policies-that-blew-up-the-uk.html. Also see Atul K. Shah, *The Politics of Financial Risk, Audit and Regulation: A Case Study of HBOS* (London: Routledge, 2018).

28. James S. Henry, "The Curious World of Donald Trump's Private Russian Connections," *American Interest*, Dec. 19, 2016.

29. The Trump bankruptcies are widely documented. The Trump quotes are from Donald J. Trump with Kate Bohner, *Trump: The Art of the Comeback* (New York: Times Books, 1997), and from Henry, "Curious World."

30. Krugman, "Competitiveness." The "teach our undergraduates to wince" quote in fact comes from Krugman's book *Pop Internationalism* (Cambridge, MA: MIT Press, 1996), 125.

31. See for instance the work of Professor Bob Jessop of Lancaster University (bobjessop.wordpress.com/tag/competitiveness). In my interview with Jessop on June 24, 2015, he spoke of a "high road to competitiveness," which might be summarized as "upgrading," and a "low road" via deregulation. He opposes critiques by Krugman and others because, he says, their starting point is neoclassical economics, which airbrushes out a lot of messy institutional and other real-world factors. He adds, "My critique of competition is: be brutally clear about how competition works, and how competitiveness works, and don't just dismiss it as so much rhetoric because it is misused by politicians and ideologues." See also Eric Reinert, *Competitiveness and Its Predecessors: A 500-Year Cross-National Perspective*, paper, Business History Conference, Williamsburg, VA, Mar. 11–13, 1994. Martin Hellwig, director of the Max Planck Institute for Research on Collective Goods and former head of Germany's Monopolies Commission, is fiercer still. "The notion of competitiveness of an economy doesn't make sense. It is a semantically nonsensical use of the term," he said. See Nicholas Shaxson, "An Interview with Martin Hellwig: Competitiveness as Doublespeak," Fools' Gold, Mar. 14, 2015, foolsgold.international/interview-martin-hellwig-competitiveness-doublespeak, which was based on my telephone interview with Hellwig on June 29, 2015.

32. The Martin Wolf quote comes from Nicholas Shaxson, "Optimistic About the State: Martin Wolf's Searing Attack on the Competitiveness Agenda," Fools' Gold, May 7, 2015, foolsgold.international/optimistic-about-the-state-martin-wolfs-searing-attack-on-the-competitiveness-agenda.

33. For a deeper discussion of this, see for instance William Mitchell and Thomas Fazi, *Reclaiming the State: A Progressive Vision of Sovereignty for a Post-Neoliberal World*

(London: Pluto Press, 2017), or Dani Rodrik, *Straight Talk on Trade: Ideas for a Sane World Economy* (Princeton, NJ: Princeton University Press, 2018).

34. On the surge in profit shifting and tax avoidance, see Alex Cobham and Petr Jansky, *Global Distribution of Revenues Loss from Tax Avoidance: Re-estimation and Country Results*, UNU-WIDER Working Paper No. 55, 2017, and Ernesto Crivelli, Ruud A. de Mooij, and Michael Keen, *Base Erosion, Profit Shifting and Developing Countries*, IMF Working Paper No. 15/118, May 2015. Also see Alex Cobham, "New Book Examines Alternative Approach to Taxing Multinational Companies," International Centre for Tax and Development, Feb. 28, 2017, ictd.ac/blog/international-tax-rules-for-multinational-companies. Figure 3 shows that profit shifting by US multinationals grew from less than 10 percent of gross profits in 1994 to around 50 percent by 2012. Also see Annette Alstadsæter, Niels Johannesen, and Gabriel Zucman, *Who Owns the Wealth in Tax Havens? Macro Evidence and Implications for Global Inequality*, National Bureau of Economic Research Working Paper No. 23805, Sept. 2017. Long-standing research suggests that corporate tax cuts do attract portfolio flows and profits, with high or moderate "elasticities." However, new research has found a crucial qualifier: it is only once the tax rate is at serious tax haven levels—5 percent or lower—that companies start to take any interest. See Kimberly A. Clausing, "The Effect of Profit Shifting on the Corporate Tax Base in the United States and Beyond," *National Tax Journal* 69, no. 4 (Dec. 2016): 905–34, summarizing a paper from Tim Dowd, Paul Landefeld, and Anne Moore, "Profit Shifting of U.S. Multinationals," *Journal of Public Economics* 148 (Feb. 2017): 1–13. Her crucial summarizing line is this: "They find a nonlinear tax response, with far more responsiveness at lower tax rates than at higher ones. Findings indicate tax semi-elasticities of –4.7 at corporate tax rates of 5 percent and –0.6 at tax rates of 30 percent" (p. 909). Even at very low rates—and the race to the bottom is driving the bar ever lower—tax cuts may not help. For instance, individual US states charge corporate tax rates ranging between 0 and 6 percent, yet there's still a whole industry dedicated to helping corporations escape even this. A qualifier to the above: the Laffer Curve does sometimes work for tiny tax havens like Bermuda, where the business of handling corporate profit shifting can be the largest sector of the economy.

35. When income is received in corporate form, earnings can be retained in the corporation and deferred until a dividend is paid at the choice of the recipient. That corporate income could be deferred indefinitely or received in tax-exempt ways.

36. Piper is quoted from "The Kansas Experiment," *Planet Money*, NPR, episode 577, Jan. 11, 2017.

37. The 1.2 percent figure is from Robert G. Lynch, *Rethinking Growth Strategies: How State and Local Taxes and Services Affect Economic Development* (Washington, DC: Economic Policy Institute, 2004), 6n. A more striking example comes from Robert Ady, known to some as the godfather of US site relocation experts, who of all people might be expected to lobby hard for lower taxes and to overstate their impacts. He estimated cost factors for a manufacturing project and an office project were, respectively, labor (36 percent and 72 percent), transport (35 percent and 0 percent), utilities (17 percent and 8 percent), occupancy (8 percent and 15 percent), and taxes (4 percent and 5 percent). See LeRoy, *Jobs Scam*, 52, table 2.1.

38. Michael Mazerov, *Academic Research Lacks Consensus on the Impact of State Tax Cuts on Economic Growth: A Reply to the Tax Foundation*, Center on Budget and Policy Priorities, June 17, 2013, 1.

39. Neelie Kroes, "European Competition Policy in a Changing World and Globalised Economy: Fundamentals, New Objectives and Challenges Ahead," GCLC/College of Europe Conference, Brussels, June 5, 2007. In the speech she also said, "Competition is the key means to increase consumer welfare, to ensure an efficient allocation of resources, to keep market players on their toes," reflecting two Chicago School attitudes: the obsession with price rather than market structure, and the belief that market processes were the route to efficiency. The *WSJ* quote on Kroes came from Alexei Barrionuevo and Daniel Michaels, "EU Antitrust Nominee Didn't Disclose All Ties," *Wall Street Journal*, Oct. 21, 2004. Kroes was later exposed in a leak from the Bahamas corporate registry, showing she had illegally failed to declare her directorship of an offshore firm set up by a private equity boss from the United Arab Emirates, which had tried (but failed) to buy billions of dollars' worth of Enron assets. See also Corporate Europe Observatory's page on Kroes, outlining a series of possible conflicts of interest, and Belén Balanya et al., "Writing the Script: The European Roundtable of Industrialists," in *Europe Inc.: Regional & Global Restructuring and the Rise of Corporate Power* (London: Pluto Press with Corporate Europe Observatory, 2003).

40. The merger figures come from fig. 1.5: "Value of cross-border M&As in relation to the value of FDI flows," in *World Investment Report 2000: Cross-Border Mergers and Acquisitions and Development*, UNCTAD, 16. (An acquisition is a kind of merger.) On p. 14 it explains that the measured ratio can rise above 100 percent because of time lags, and notes that the data is imprecise. It defines M&A as "the acquisition of more than 10 per cent equity share," which is clearly a broad definition. According to Wigger, private equity was responsible for a full fifth of all global M&A activity in 2007.

41. In 1994 the *Economist* described UK policy to boost "competitiveness" by reducing competition as follows: "Mr Hesltine [Minister for Trade and Industry] has already expressed more interest in nurturing national industrial champions than in championing the interests of the nation's consumers" (Christophers, *Great Leveler*, 242). In addition, arguments were made that competition in banking generated reckless behavior; therefore an exception for banks should be made from antitrust laws. (The financial crisis, of course, revealed this as nonsense: the biggest banks caused the most havoc.) On Germany, see "Summary Competition Policy," esp. nos. 23, 24.

42. For example, the EU's "Lisbon Agenda" of 2000 had as its central aim to make Europe "the most competitive and dynamic knowledge-driven economy by 2010." Yet even European leaders have declared the Lisbon Agenda a failure. For example, see "Sweden Admits Lisbon Agenda 'Failure,'" EURACTIV, June 3, 2009, euractiv.com/section/eu-priorities-2020/news/sweden-admits-lisbon-agenda-failure.

CHAPTER SIX: THE CELTIC TIGER

1. Fintan O'Toole, *Ship of Fools: How Stupidity and Corruption Killed the Celtic Tiger* (London: Faber and Faber, 2010), 12. The sentence has been slightly abridged to remove a comment about Uruguay, but the sense is intact.

2. For more on O'Regan, see Patrick Neveling, "Export Processing Zones and Class Formation," in James G. Carrier and Don Kalb (eds.), *Anthropologies of Class: Power, Practice, and Inequality* (Cambridge: Cambridge University Press, 2015).

3. The main sources for this are Matt Kennard and Claire Provost, "Story of Cities #25: Shannon—A Tiny Irish Town Inspires China's Economic Boom," *Guardian*, Apr. 19, 2016; Paul Quigley, "Why Do China's Leaders Love Visiting Shannon?" *The-Journal.ie*, Feb. 23, 2012, thejournal.ie/why-do-chinas-leaders-love-visiting-shannon-363579-Feb2012; and "70 Years a-Glowing as Shannon Airport Celebrates Milestone with Launch of Photographic Exhibition," Shannon Chamber, Dec. 2, 2015. With thanks to Mic Moroney for the Shannon tip-off.

4. The Kelleher quote is from James Meek, "Somerdale to Skarbimierz," *London Review of Books* 39, no. 8 (Apr. 20, 2017).

5. Initially, the EPTR gave a 50 percent reduction on taxes on income from export sales, but this rose to 100 percent in 1960. See John Bradley, "The History of Economic Development in Ireland, North and South," *Proceedings of the British Academy* 98 (1999): 35–68, esp. p. 48, which shows employment in manufacturing rising from 175,000 in 1960 to 232,000 in 1990: a rate of around 1 percent annually. See also Frank Barry, "Foreign Investment and the Politics of Export Profits Tax Relief 1956," *Irish Economic and Social History* 38 (2011): 54–73, and Frank Barry, *Foreign Direct Investment and Institutional Co-Evolution in Ireland*, SSRN, Feb. 2006, papers.ssrn.com/sol3/papers.cfm?abstract_id=978764. See also Kenneth Thomas, "Ireland's Recent Success Not Built on Low Taxes," Middle Class Political Economist, Aug. 12, 2011, middleclasspolitica-leconomist.com/2011/08/irelands-recent-success-not-built-on.html, and associated links, for a broad summary.

6. For the FDI data, see appendix table 1 in Frank Barry and Clare O'Mahony, *Making Sense of the Data in Ireland's Inward FDI*, SSRN, Dec. 2006, papers.ssrn.com/sol3/papers.cfm?abstract_id=978768.

7. In 1973, 59 percent of Irish exports went to Britain; by 1987 this had fallen to 34 percent. See Ray Mac Sharry and Padraic White, *The Making of the Celtic Tiger: The Inside Story of Ireland's Boom Economy* (Cork: Mercier Press, 2001), 29, 149.

8. See for instance Jane Walsh, "Things That Irish Women Could Not Do in 1970s," *IrishCentral*, May 10, 2017, irishcentral.com/news/how-things-have-changed-ten-things-that-irish-women-could-not-do-in-1970s-183526621-237593131. The McCarthy quote comes from my interview with her in Dublin on Sept. 22, 2016.

9. For a graph showing this, see Nicholas Shaxson, "Did Ireland's 12.5 Percent Corporate Tax Rate Create the Celtic Tiger?" Fools' Gold, Mar. 12, 2015, foolsgold.international/did-irelands-12-5-percent-corporate-tax-rate-cause-the-celtic-tiger. The background data came from *Statistical Annex of the European Economy*, Director-ate General for Economic and Financial Affairs, European Commission, Autumn 2014, p. 24. This records gross domestic product per capita, as a share of the Euro-pean average. However, Ireland's GDP data is skewed by artificial profit flows from multinationals (which don't meaningfully connect with the Irish economy), so GDP data is converted to gross *national* product (GNP) to strip out much of this profit shuffling. (Irish GNI is around a third lower than Irish GDP.) For further details on

why even GNI or GNP overstates Irish performance, see for instance Cole Frank, "Tax Avoidance and the Irish Balance of Payments," Council on Foreign Relations, Apr. 25, 2018, cfr.org/blog/tax-avoidance-and-irish-balance-payments. The underlying tables show dramatic "catch-up" growth in other European low-income countries too; for instance, the Czech Republic's GDP per capita as a share of the EU average rose from 16 percent in 1990 to 43 percent by 2007, with an average corporate tax rate of around 30 percent; Estonia's grew sevenfold, from 1993 to 2007, with an average 23 percent corporate tax rate; and Portugal's nearly doubled, with an average 33 percent corporate tax rate and little FDI.

10. From Joe Joyce and Peter Murtagh, *The Boss: Charles J. Haughey in Government* (Dublin: Poolbeg, 1983), 48, 62, 100–2.

11. The Deutschmark gambit is described in Elaine Byrne, *Political Corruption in Ireland, 1922–2010: A Crooked Harp?* (Manchester: Manchester University Press, 2012), 96–7.

12. From my interview with McCabe at the Dáil Éireann in Dublin, Sept. 22, 2016.

13. "They love me" is from Joyce and Murtagh, *The Boss*, 100. The "never gain acceptance" quote is from Colm Keena, *Haughey's Millions: The Full Story of Charlie's Money Trail* (Dublin: Gill & Macmillan, 2001), 1.

14. For an analysis of Haughey's many different corrupt methods, see Byrne, *Crooked Harp*, esp. p. 148; the seventy-seven times salary statistic is on p. 156.

15. From my telephone interview with O'Toole, Oct. 4, 2016.

16. This attitude was summarized by Bertie Ahern in 2004, when he told the *Irish Times*, "If there are not the guys at the Galway Races in the tent who are earning wealth, who are creating wealth, then I can't redistribute that" ("Let Us All into the Tent, Bertie," *Irish Times*, Nov. 16, 2004).

17. See "Bono Rejects Criticism of U2 Tax Status," *Irish Times*, Feb. 27, 2009. The O'Toole quote comes from my October 2016 interview with him.

18. O'Toole, *Ship of Fools*, 38–9. The earlier "that's my money" quote is from my telephone interview with Elaine Byrne, Oct. 3, 2016.

19. From the Irish section of "Foreign direct investment, net inflows (% of GDP)," World Bank. For a brief summary of the two booms, see Jack Copley, "The Celtic Tiger: The Irish Banking Inquiry and a Tale of Two Booms," Fools' Gold, May 5, 2016, fools-gold.international/the-celtic-tiger-the-irish-banking-inquiry-and-a-tale-of-two-booms..

20. O'Toole, *Ship of Fools*, 2, 25.

21. The Apple Subsidiary was Apple Sales International. See "Offshore Profit Shifting and the U.S. Tax Code—Part 2 (Apple Inc.)," memorandum to the US Senate Homeland Security Permanent Subcommittee on Investigations, May 21, 2013. The action involved schemes to ensure that only a tiny portion of a company's profits get taxed at that 12.5 percent rate; the rest is kept outside the tax system. The tax loopholes were essentially due to historical omission: Ireland did not adopt significant transfer pricing legislation (to combat such abuses) until 2010.

22. "The Pitch to Attract Occupants into Financial Services Centre," *Irish Times*, Mar. 19, 1988.

23. Peter Sutherland said, "The Italians, the French—a lot of the European countries—used every conceivable barrier to stop goods being exported into their domestic markets, even from other EU countries. It was the 1992 project that really changed this." See the Sutherland interview in Paul Sweeney, *Ireland's Economic Success: Reasons and Lessons* (Dublin: New Island, 2008), 17, 19.

24. "World Investment Report 2016: Annex Tables: Annex Table 2, FDI Outflows, by Region and Economy," UNCTAD, June 2016. The table shows US and UK outward investment rising from $32.7 billion and $16.4 billion, respectively, in 1991 to $209.4 billion and $201.5 billion in 1999.

25. Mac Sharry and White, *Celtic Tiger*, 231–2.

26. Ibid., 243.

27. The Ballmer quote is from Sweeney, *Ireland's Economic Success*, 112.

28. Mac Sharry and White, 239.

29. For the economic data, see Helen Russell and Philip J. O'Connell, "Women Returning to Employment, Education and Training in Ireland: An Analysis of Transitions," *Economic and Social Review* 35, no. 1 (Spring 2004): 1–25.

30. As Sutherland put it in Sweeney, *Ireland's Economic Success* 14–5: "Our GDP per capita was distorted in the period up to the 1990s, because we had a much higher dependency ratio and a much lower labour participation rate—by women in particular. When our dependency ratio dropped (because there were fewer young children, because of birth control and everything that happened in the 1990s), this increased the GDP per capita." The worker-to-dependent ratio is from O'Toole, *Ship of Fools*, 17.

31. There is a good collection of these images at "What's the Big IDA then?" Broadsheet, Dec. 9, 2015, broadsheet.ie/2015/12/09/whats-the-big-ida-then. On education, as Mac Sharry and White put it, "The rate of economic recovery was . . . underpinned by another important and visionary political development from the sixties—the introduction of free second-level education. Its economic impact . . . ensured Ireland in the late eighties was well placed to exploit the employment opportunities created by the new knowledge-based industries" (*Celtic Tiger*, 47). On the IDA survey and marketing strategy, see especially Mac Sharry and White, 244–5. The Fanning analogy is from Mac Sharry and White, 240.

32. Part of the traditional story is one of virtuous Irish "fiscal consolidation," but the true picture is mixed: government spending rose steadily in absolute terms from 1980 until 2007, though it fell from around 40 percent to around 30 percent of GDP at the same time, as GDP boomed (though as a share of GNP, which in Ireland's case rose more slowly to become only around three-quarters the size of GDP, the fall was modest.) See for instance "Expenditure Strategy," *Expenditure Report*, Department of Public Expenditure and Reform, 2014, p. 9.

33. Mac Sharry and White, *Celtic Tiger*, 122.

34. Ibid., 29, 153–5. Mac Sharry and White report that Ireland's Economic and Social Research Institute later estimated that the structural funds from 1989 to 1999 had increased Irish GNP by 3–4 percent. Also see pp. 179, 193, and the chapters "The Evolution of the IDA" (pp. 183–97) and "The IDA Philosophy through the Decades" (pp. 198–226). European funds also financed carefully targeted IDA training grants,

helping the IDA further fine-tune its offering to the world's investors. For information on telecoms, see for example James B. Burnham, "Why Ireland Boomed," *Independent Review* 8, no. 4 (Spring 2003): 542–4.

35. On Boeing, see "Should It Bother Us That Boeing Says It Needs a Tax Incentive to Make Its Planes Safe?" Citizens for Tax Justice, Jan. 13, 2014, ctj.org/should-it-bother-us-that-boeing-says-it-needs-a-tax-incentive-to-make-its-planes-safe, referencing Boeing arguments submitted to an IRS hearing on Jan. 8, 2014. (I took the ice-cream analogy from *Waiting for Godot*, the blog of Jolyon Maugham, and the "refined sugar" analogy from David Quentin, another UK tax barrister.)

36. The O'Neill quote is quite widely reported. Crafting tax strategies made up most of the Big Four accounting firms' total $1.3 billion in fee income for PwC, Deloitte, KPMG, and Ernst & Young in Ireland in 2016 (see Fiona Reddan, "Brexit Boost for Ireland's 'Big Four' as Fee Income Jumps," *Irish Times*, May 2, 2017). The surveys cited are numerous, summarized by the Organisation for Economic Co-operation and Development (OECD) as such: "There is a consensus in the [academic] literature about the main factors affecting (foreign) investment location decisions. The most important ones are market size and real income levels, skill levels in the host economy, the availability of infrastructure and other resource that facilitates efficient specialisation of production, trade policies, and political and macroeconomic stability of the host country. Survey analysis shows that host country taxation and international investment incentives generally play only a limited role in determining the international pattern of FDI." From *Tax Incentives for Investment—A Global Perspective: Experiences in MENA and Non-MENA Countries*, OECD, 2008, doi.org/10.1787/9789264052826-11-en. See also LeRoy, *Jobs Scam*, 48–50, for an overview of what diverse businesses want. A longer list of such surveys and evidence is provided in the footnotes in Nicholas Shaxson and Ellie Mae O'Hagan, *Mythbusters: A Competitive Tax System Is a Better Tax System*, Tax Justice Network/New Economics Foundation, Apr. 2013.

37. Pedantic point: it's not exactly seven stories; different parts of the building are different heights.

38. "The Poorest of the Rich (Ireland Survey)," *Economist*, Jan. 16, 1988. Doyle qtd. in "Patriots Who Knew How to Play the Power Game," *Irish Independent*, Sept. 5, 1999.

39. For this history of how the IFSC emerged, the two main sources are Mac Sharry and White, *Celtic Tiger*, esp. 317–55, and Fiona Reddan, *Ireland's IFSC: A Story of Global Financial Success* (Cork: Mercier Press, 2008). Also see "An Irish Player on the Global Stage—Profile: Dermot Desmond," *Herald* (Scotland), Dec. 16, 2005.

40. Desmond was seemingly so proud of the IFSC that he later would sue a newspaper that reported a claim that the financial center wasn't his idea. See "Desmond Extracts an Apology from the *Sunday Times*," *Village*, Nov. 5, 2014. See also *Desmond v. Doyle and Others*, IESC 59, Dec. 17, 2013. White's quote is from Mac Sharry and White, *Celtic Tiger*, 324.

41. Reddan, *Ireland's IFSC*, 28.

42. See "Dermot Desmond on the IFSC Past and Future," Finance-magazine.com, finance-magazine.com/display_article.php?i=2300&pi=142. See also Reddan, *Ireland's IFSC*, 26–28; on London, 54. A careful marketing process examined which

aspects done in London could be done in Dublin instead, and an industrial policy for the IFSC was partly crafted around that. "The sector was really beginning to boom in New York and London," said Walter Brazil of Allied Irish banks. "It was a sophisticated world, and it just seemed too big a jump for us" (qtd. in Reddan, *Ireland's IFSC*, 29, 38–40).

43. Reddan, *Ireland's IFSC*, 42.

44. The Childers quote comes from Jamie Smyth, "Great Tax Race: Ireland's Policies Aid Business More Than Public," *Financial Times*, May 1, 2013. See also Fiona Reddan, "First Meeting for New IFSC Clearing House Group," *Irish Times*, June 22, 2015.

45. See "Reflections: '87-'02 - 15 Years of Finance," *Finance Magazine*, June 2002.

46. Finance Act, 1987, Section 30 (available at irishstatutebook.ie/eli/1987/act/10/section/30/enacted/en/html#sec30). Also see, for instance, Jim Stewart, "How the IFSC 'HQ' Became a Shadow of Its Intended Self," *Irish Times*, Sept. 6, 2010. In it, Stewart states, "By law, the financial regulator was required to promote the development of the financial services industry. Considerable resources were devoted by the regulator to 'meeting and greeting' prospective regulated entities—instead of to the overriding need for adequate regulation. Aspects of this policy have now changed, particularly in regard to regulation. But the broad thrust of economic policy remains the same."

47. One German official said that the IFSC and Shannon were little more than "tax havens for many big foreign investment companies," in particular for special purpose investment companies handling huge funds but with "no real trading function" (*Irish Times*, Nov. 14, 1992, qtd. in Conor McCabe, *Sins of the Father: Tracing the Decisions That Shaped the Irish Economy* [Dublin: History Press, 2011], 168). Statistics from McCabe, esp. 56, 166–8.

48. Reddan, *Ireland's IFSC*, 29–31.

49. Erkki Liikanen et al., *High-Level Expert Group on Reforming the Structure of the EU Banking Sector*, European Commission, 2012, p. 12 chart 2.3.2.

50. Stewart, "How the IFSC."

51. O'Toole, *Ship of Fools*, 45.

52. The US economist Barry Eichengreen noted the single market's role: "borrowing by property developers and aspiring homeowners was fueled by the decline in interest-rate spreads that flowed from the advent of the euro." "Claims on the Irish banking system peaked at some 400 per cent of GDP. . . . This was an exceptionally large, highly leveraged banking system atop a small island. . . . It reflected [among other things] the freedom with which Irish banks were permitted to establish and acquire subsidiaries in other EU countries" (*The Irish Crisis and the EU from a Distance*, International Monetary Fund, Oct. 2015, 1–2). O'Toole noted that the number of manufacturing jobs in Ireland fell by 20,000 between 2000 and 2006, and price levels in 2004 were 28 percent above the 1997 level, compared with an EU-wide increase of 14 percent (O'Toole, 21).

53. Most of this information is from Jim Stewart, *Low Tax Financial Centres and the Financial Crisis: The Case of the Irish Financial Services Centre*, IIIS Discussion Paper No. 420, 2013, pp. 13–6 for Depfa, and pp. 3–4 for "competitive" regulation and a brief exploration of the Ormond Quay debacle. Also Jim Stewart, *Shadow Regulation and the Shadow Banking System: The Role of the Dublin International Financial Services Centre," Tax*

Justice Focus, 4, no. 2, Jul. 18, 2008. The "source of all evil" quote is from Derek Scally, "Near-Collapse of German Bank and Its Irish Subsidiary Shrouded in Mystery," *Irish Times*, Aug. 30, 2013.

54. See Stewart, *Low Tax Financial Centres.*

55. See "Offshore Profit Shifting and the U.S. Tax Code—Part 2 (Apple Inc.)," especially the opening statement by Senator Levin, which explains the matters clearly.

56. Qtd. in Joe Brennan and Mark Paul, "Panama Papers Shine a Light on Ireland's SPVs," *Irish Times*, Apr. 15, 2016.

57. See Daniel McConnell, "AIB to Pay No Corporation Tax for 20 Years: CEO," *Irish Examiner*, Sept. 27, 2017.

58. For instance, a study in November 2015 estimated that in 2012, US multinationals alone shifted $500–$700 billion to low-tax countries, almost all of which went to Ireland, Luxembourg, the Netherlands, Bermuda, and Switzerland. Tax losses on those would have been well over $100 billion (Francis Weyzig, *Still Broken: Governments Must Do More to Fix the International Corporate Tax System*, Oxfam International/Tax Justice Network/Public Services International/Global Alliance for Tax Justice, Nov. 2015). Separately, Citizens for Tax Justice in the United States estimated that multinationals booked $2.5 trillion offshore in 2015 and, by stashing that amount overseas indefinitely, had avoided up to $717.8 billion in US taxes. Ireland plays a central (but unquantifiable) role in this. See "News Release: 367 Fortune 500 Companies Collectively Maintain 10,366 Tax Haven Subsidiaries," Citizens for Tax Justice, Oct. 4, 2015.

59. *Report of the Tribunal of Inquiry into Payments to Politicians and Related Matters*, Part 1, Government of Ireland, 2006, 513, 515. The Isle of Man mentions came mostly in part 2.

60. Quotes are from O'Toole, *Ship of Fools*, 51–60. See also "In the Event, the DIRT Tax Was a Brave Event," *Irish Times*, July 21, 1999; *Report of the Tribunal*, 513, 515, 520; and Byrne, *Crooked Harp*, esp. 156. O'Toole adds, "They knew that there was a system of networks and connections, with the ruler of the country at its center. . . . It was reinforced by the utter impunity from legal consequences of those who had engaged in flagrant fraud" (*Ship of Fools*, 72).

61. Byrne, *Crooked Harp*, 155.

62. For the ceramic flowerpot example and others, see Jim Stewart, *PwC/World Bank Report "Paying Taxes 2014": An Assessment*, IIIS Discussion Paper No. 442, Feb. 2014, and Nicholas Shaxson, "Now Brazil Puts Ireland on Its Tax Haven Blacklist," Tax Justice Network, Sept. 15, 2016, taxjustice.net/2016/09/15/now-brazil-says-ireland-tax-haven. Even Jim Stewart, one of the bravest and most outspoken "dissidents" against the financial and tax vortex that Ireland has become, hedges his words carefully: he tends to avoid calling Ireland a tax haven outright and instead says that Ireland's tax system has aspects of tax havens.

63. From my interview with Baker by telephone, Nov. 15, 2016.

64. At the time of writing, the most vocal lobby was the Northern Ireland Economic Reform Group (NIERG), run by the head of KPMG in Belfast but whose funding is unclear. NIERG stated on its website that it is "an independent group consisting of economists, accountants and businessmen based in Northern Ireland who wish to see

a more successful and competitive NI economy.... [T]he group take [*sic*] the view that reduced corporation tax is the best way to ensure a rapid acceleration in investment and productivity." I submitted a question about NIERG's funding on November 17, 2016, via its website but received no reply.

65. Kenneth Thomas, "That's What I'm Talkin' About! (Ireland)," Middle Class Political Economist, Sept. 16, 2016, middleclasspoliticaleconomist.com/2016/09/thats-what-im-talkin-about-ireland.html. David Begg, a former general secretary of the Irish Congress of Trade Unions, put this in context: "Ireland's great *economic* success could have generated a great *social* success if we had done things differently," he said. "If the government had not cut taxes so sharply on incomes and on companies, we would have had much more to spend on health, on education and on earlier investment" (qtd. in Sweeney, *Ireland's Economic Success*, 119).

66. See *Corporate tax policy in Ireland: Time for a Change?* Jim Stewart, paper in Economia & Lavoro, 2018, 179-186. Table 2 shows that in the mid-1990s local expenditures were equivalent to over 35 percent of sales; by 2014 that had fallen to well under 15 percent, as the international race to the bottom has progressed. (Stewart said, via email, that "perhaps that [trend] is why the IDA has stopped publishing data.") This has also accompanied a rise in data centres which, Stewart added, "have few economic linkages, apart from purchasing electricity and grass cutting." See also *Where's the Harm in Tax Competition? Lessons from US Multinationals in Ireland*, Critical Perspectives on Accounting, Vol. 17, 2006, by Sheila Killian. She outlines several costs to Ireland from its low-tax policies, including: loss of tax revenues from many investments that would have happened anyway; a more regressive Irish tax regime; huge power imbalances as multinationals wield the threat of relocation to squeeze out ever greater subsidies; adverse selection towards more predatory investors; the redirecting of state investments towards multinational-focused but socially inappropriate goals; democratic anger; heightened risk of corruption among local officials serving as gateways to subsidies; a steady loss of attractiveness as other nations engage in the race to the bottom; and unaffordable domestic real estate prices. (Table 1 provides a fuller list.)

67. As for China's economic zones, what the Chinese learned from Ireland was how to enact reforms in controlled, geographically restricted ways, which allowed the Communist Party to remain firmly in control. The reforms in the zones initially allowed farmers to sell excess production—after state quotas were fulfilled—at uncontrolled prices. For more on this, see for instance Rodrik, *Staight Talk*, esp. 57.

68. O'Toole, *Ship of Fools*, 21.

CHAPTER SEVEN: THE LONDON LOOPHOLE

1. See "Chairman Gary Gensler's Keynote Address on the Cross-Border Application of Swaps Market Reform," Sandler O'Neill Global Exchange and Brokerage Conference, New York, June 6, 2013 (available at cftc.gov/PressRoom/SpeechesTestimony/opagensler-141); "Statement of Support by Chairman Gary Gensler," US Commodity Futures Trading Commission, June 29, 2012, cftc.gov/PressRoom/SpeechesTestimony/genslerstatement062912b; and Rana Foroohar, "The Myth of Financial Reform," *Time*,

Sept. 23, 2012, reprinted in Rana Foroohar, *Makers and Takers: The Rise of Finance and the Fall of American Business* (New York: Crown Business, 2016), 189.

2. Maloney's statement (and part of the quote from Gensler) came from Tom Braithwaite, Shahien Nasiripour, and Brooke Masters, "US Watchdog Hits at 'Risky' London," *Financial Times*, June 19, 2012.

3. My interview was on October 1, 2012. The fund manager, who subsequently moved offshore, declined to be identified as the source of this quote.

4. See Ian Fraser, "Lehman Examiner's Report: London Was the 'Guantanamo Bay' of Finance," Ian Fraser, Mar. 12, 2010, ianfraser.org/lehman-brothers-what-next.

5. From my phone interview with Black, Sept. 30, 2012. See also Black, "New Labour Leaders." When he spoke to me, Black was telling me about mortgage frauds and other related crimes, but I've expanded the point.

6. Quotes from the superb Joris Luyendijk, *Swimming with Sharks: My Journey into the World of Bankers* (London: Guardian Faber, 2015), 71, 75, about the City of London. For the anthropology of finance with a more US focus, see also the more academic Ho, *Liquidated*. For the Google search, see *Moneyland*, 100-101.

7. See Gillian Tett, *Fool's Gold: How Unrestrained Greed Corrupted a Dream, Shattered Global Markets and Unleashed a Catastrophe* (London: Little, Brown, 2009), 18. London's role as a regulation-escaping platform had also been greatly enhanced by unfettered access to the European single market from the early 1990s, boosting its attraction in the same way that Ireland was now serving as a beachhead for US tax-escaping corporations wanting to operate across Europe. Hedge funds were fast getting into this exotic game, and again it was in London, not New York, where most of the new innovations gushed forth. As Tett put it, "Initially, the epicentre of experimentation was not J.P. Morgan's headquarters, but the London branch" (p. 18, referring to the general growth of swaps and derivatives from the 1970s). "While funds were springing up in New York and Connecticut, it was London where the evolution—and mutation—appeared to be most densely concentrated" (p. 107, referring to the 1990s onwards). On p. 116 she also identifies London as the key locale for SIVs, another kind of related vehicle that had been especially problematic.

8. Bosworth-Davies's more detailed comments on the arrival of criminal elements in London after the big bang are recorded in Rowan Bosworth-Davies, "Financial Crime—Staring Failure in the Face," Rowans-blog, Dec. 13, 2006, rowans-blog.blogspot.com/2006, and subsequent blog posts.

9. These quotes come from my telephone conversation with Bosworth-Davies on September 17, 2012, and subsequent emails with him.

10. Ian Fraser first related the "protected species" quote to me by email; I emailed this quote to Bosworth-Davies and he replied on December 18, saying it was "100% accurate." Also see Rowan Bosworth-Davies, "Has the UK Rediscovered Its Appetite for Prosecuting 'White Collar' Crime?" Ian Fraser, Mar. 16, 2012, ianfraser.org/has-the-uk-rediscovered-its-long-lost-appetite-for-prosecuting-white-collar-crime. Bosworth-Davies said a watershed was the collapse of the Blue Arrow case against rogue bankers in 1992, then Britain's costliest criminal trial. Afterward he said a friend in the Serious Fraud Office told him that "the message had come down from on high

that there would never again be any similar kind of prosecution of any City institution or its senior executives." The BBC had reported on Blue Arrow: "the Appeal Court ruled that due to the length of the trial and the complexity of the subject matter the jury could not have reached a fair verdict" (Sam Francis, "Did Blue Arrow Make Bank Fraud Untriable?" BBC News, Apr. 14, 2014). But Bosworth-Davies took a different view, saying the reason that Blue Arrow proved so terrifying for senior financiers "was that it demonstrated that ordinary juries *could* understand the ramifications of complex fraud cases, and that they *could* convict." This had to be prevented.

11. See Michelle Singletary, "Justice Dept. Hails Prosecutions at Banks, S&Ls," *Washington Post*, Nov. 14, 1995; Joshua Holland, "Hundreds of Wall Street Execs Went to Prison During the Last Fraud-Fueled Bank Crisis," Billmoyers.com, Sept. 7, 2013, billmoyers.com/2013/09/17/hundreds-of-wall-street-execs-went-to-prison-during-the-last-fraud-fueled-bank-crisis; and "S&L Fraud Sentences Average 3.2 Years: Thrifts: The Justice Department Says Federal Cases in General Typically Draw 2.5-Year Terms," Associated Press, Sept. 4, 1990.

12. The value of bank assets and liabilities is highly uncertain. See Matt Levine, "Bank of America Made $168 Million Last Quarter, More or Less," *Bloomberg*, Oct. 15, 2014.

13. For instance, see the testimony of Richard Berliand, managing director and global head of futures and options at JP Morgan Securities Limited, to the CFTC Global Markets Advisory Committee (GMAC), Jan. 12, 2005, https://www.cftc.gov/sites/default/files/files/ac/acgmac011205.pdf, esp. 85–86. He summarizes, "I don't think we want to see a wholesale exit of business to other jurisdictions."

14. See Nicholas Dunbar, *The Devil's Derivatives: The Untold Story of the Slick Traders and Hapless Regulators Who Almost Blew Up Wall Street . . . and Are Ready to Do It Again* (Boston: Harvard Business Review Press, 2011), esp. 116–7 for a discussion of this episode. In the book, Dunbar talks of "European regulators," but in a telephone interview on May 16, 2018, Dunbar said that he was referring to British and Swiss regulators in particular.

15. Ibid., p. 59.

16. Offshore SPVs had many attractions. For one thing, they gave investors financial exposure to residential mortgages without their having to go through the grubby kerfuffle of dealing directly with actual homeowners; the banks had already done all the hard work. SPVs were made more enticing by giving investors access to different tranches of their output—slices of the annual $18 million in the aforementioned example, each with a different mix of risk and reward. Those investing in the riskiest equity securities at the bottom would get the largest absolute returns in good times but would be the first to lose money if loans went bad. Above that there were progressively safer levels: junior debt, then mezzanine debt halfway up, then senior debt, and, finally, super-senior debt at the top—ultra-safe securities that paid tiny returns. Think of it like one of those cone-shaped towers of champagne glasses. Our SPV pours up to $18 million worth of champagne in at the top at regular intervals through the year; if there's plenty to go around, the champagne will sluice all the way down to the lowest levels, where there will be the most glasses to catch it and, hence, the most champagne

available. But if a lot of mortgages go sour, there's less champagne next time, so those at the bottom may go thirsty, while those at the higher levels should still be fine.

17. See Tooze, *Crashed*, esp. 73–90. The graph on p. 76 shows that gross capital flows from the UK were a lot larger than from the rest of Europe combined. I borrowed the metaphors of the iPhone and the elephant from Tooze.

18. John Cassidy, *How Markets Fail: An Atlas of Economic Irrationality* (New York: Farrar, Straus and Giroux, 2009), 270.

19. Travers qtd. in Alan Markoff, "The Cayman Islands: From Obscurity to Offshore Giant," *Cayman Financial Review*, Oct. 5, 2009. Travers was, in this instance, talking in the context of a regimen for attracting funds to Cayman, not specifically with respect to SPVs. As John Kay put it, "These offshore locations ('treasure islands') are often described as 'tax havens' but they are every bit as much regulatory havens" (Kay, *Other People's Money*, 122–3). (Travers has in the past publicly called me an "imbecile" for criticizing the Cayman Islands.)

20. See *Global Shadow Banking Monitoring Report 2016*, Financial Stability Board, May 2017, 18, 92. See also Thomas Rixen, "Why Reregulation After the Crisis Is Feeble: Shadow Banking, Offshore Financial Centers and Jurisdictional Competition," *Regulation & Governance* 7, no. 4 (Dec. 2013): 435–59, and Markoff, "Cayman Islands."

21. I described "the Devil" in slightly more detail in *Treasure Islands*. It is true that the Caymans are now, under international pressure, somewhat less tolerant of dirty money than they were back then, but that's not saying much. On hedge funds beating back money-laundering curbs in the United States, see Heather Vogell, "Why Aren't Hedge Funds Required to Fight Money Laundering?," ProPublica, Jan. 23, 2019.

22. See David Dayen, "Wall Street's Greatest Enemy: The Man Who Knows Too Much," *Salon*, Aug. 28, 2013, salon.com/2013/08/28/wall_streets_greatest_enemy_the_man_who_knows_too_much.

23. Tett, *Fool's Gold*, 4–5.

24. For JPMorgan's derivatives exposure, see "OCC's Quarterly Report on Bank Derivatives Activities, Second Quarter 2007," occ.gov, table 1. It showed JPMorgan had $1.2 trillion in total balance-sheet assets, and $6.52 trillion in OTC credit derivatives gross exposures. (Total derivatives exposure was $79 trillion.)

25. On CDSs being both insurance and gambling, a fundamental concept in insurance is called "insurable interest," where you are allowed to take out an insurance policy only if you have an identifiable insurable interest in the thing you are insuring. You'd be creeped out if you discovered that a stranger had taken out an insurance policy that would pay him a million dollars if you died this month or if your house were to burn down. Laws have grown up to embed some responsibility, so you are allowed to insure your own life, but not a stranger's. CDSs involved the same problem: you could use them to insure a loan against default (insurance against the death of a company, as it were), or you could gamble and be the one to insure that loan against the company's default. This dual nature meant they were simultaneously insurance and betting and should have been strongly regulated, crimping trading profits, for sure, but also protecting wider society. Using CDSs, for instance, you could easily and secretly build up huge incentives to destroy a perfectly healthy company—or destabilize a government.

(At the time, financial institutions were being investigated for their role in destabilizing Greece.) See Wolfgang Münchau, "Time to Outlaw Naked Credit Default Swaps," *Financial Times*, Feb. 28, 2010. (With naked CDSs you can take out insurance on the bonds without actually owning them.)

26. On Potts and insurable interest, see John Kay, "Of Cows, Communities and Credit Default Swaps: Why Gambling with CDS Should Be Banned," *Financial Times*, Apr. 6, 2010, and Kay, *Other People's Money*, 61–3, 72. An obituary of Potts, who died in 2009, said he was in great demand, particularly in Britain, Hong Kong, and Bermuda. See "Robin Potts, QC: Lawyer," *London Times*, Sept. 9, 2009.

27. David Marchant, via email, Mar. 8, 2018.

28. Tett, *Fool's Gold*, 58.

29. For Greenspan's views, see Manuel Roig-Franzia, "Brooksley Born, the Cassandra of the Derivatives Crisis," *Washington Post*, May 26, 2009. On the Bank of England, for example, Peter Cooke, the Bank of England's head of banking supervision, told *Institutional Investor* in 1980 that "when we judge the reputation and standing of an institution relative to giving it our 'seal of Good Housekeeping,' we like to think we have the opportunity to get the views of those within the marketplace to help us make a decision. . . . [A] banker who doesn't play according to the market's rules—which are essentially our own—will lose, because the market will reject him." See Kynaston, "A Club No More," 593.

30. The Summers quote is from "10-Year Anniversary of the Bill That Led to the Current Economic Crisis," allgov.com, Nov. 15, 2009. Banking analyst Kenneth H. Thomas said, "Citigroup is not the result of that act but the cause of it." Chris Suellentrop, "Sandy Weill: How Citigroup's CEO Rewrote the Rules so He Could Live Richly," *Slate*, Nov. 20, 2002, slate.com/news-and-politics/2002/11/citigroup-s-sandy-weill.html.

31. From *Over-the-Counter Derivatives Markets and the Commodity Exchange Act: Report of The President's Working Group on Financial Markets*, US Department of the Treasury/Board of Governors of the Federal Reserve System/Securities and Exchange Commission/Commodity Futures Trading Commission, Nov. 1999.

32. From my telephone interview with Black, Sept. 15, 2012.

33. As Dunbar described the process to me in an interview on May 16, 2018, the UK regulator, the Financial Services Authority, was seen as the light-touch regulator, so "US banks were then able to go back to the SEC or whoever it was in Washington and say, 'We are doing all our business over in London, because you are not being flexible enough.' I think they used that as a stick to beat US regulators with, and that created this race to the bottom."

34. The US regulator's quote and the "maggots" quote are from Dunbar, *Devil's Derivatives*, 131, 141. The number of risk-weight categories has grown from five in the original Basel accords to several thousand today; see Thomas M. Hoenig, "Back to Basics: A Better Alternative to Basel Capital Rules," speech, American Banker Regulatory Symposium, Washington, DC, Sept. 14, 2012.

35. On "hugely inhibiting," see "Full Text: Tony Blair's Speech on Compensation Culture," *Guardian*, May 26, 2005. The "consenting adults" quote is from Jesse Eisinger, "London Banks, Falling Down", Portfolio.com, Aug. 13, 2008. The quote on Iranians was widely reported. Britain made a very similar boast on corporate tax: for instance,

Ian Barlow, a top UK tax adviser, boasted that US corporations found the UK taxman's approach "refreshing" and that HMRC was "much easier to deal with than their own tax authorities." See Tom Bergin, "Special Report: How the UK Tax Authority Got Cozy with Big Business," Reuters, Dec. 27, 2012. Also see Shah, *Politics of Financial Risk*.

36. The $60 trillion number comes from *OTC Derivatives Market Activity in the Second Half of 2007*, Monetary and Economic Department, Bank for International Settlements, May 2008, p. 1. The market value of these swaps was assessed at about $2 trillion. See also Oskari Juurikkala, "Credit Default Swaps and Insurance: Against the Potts Opinion," *Journal of International Banking Law and Regulation* 26, no. 3 (2011): 132–9, and Cassidy, *How Markets Fail*, 282.

37. This amount is from testimony by Jackie Speier in *The Causes and Effects of the AIG Bailout*, US House Committee on Oversight and Government Reform, Oct. 7, 2008: "on every dollar he was receiving $0.30 back in terms of the products that were being sold."

38. Technically, AIGFP was registered in Delaware and theoretically overseen by the US Office of Thrift Supervision, while the London-based entity was the UK branch of an AIG subsidiary in France, called Banque AIG. This was all about playing international hopscotch with regulation. As Dunbar explained (from my interview with him on May 16, 2018), "It was better to do that in London, because in the US there was always the possibility that the Fed would find out and might ask more questions than the FSA [Financial Services Authority] would; it was a perception that they were going to get a better regulatory environment in London. . . . It was quite complicated, with AIGFP in London, the parent company in [the] US, and between all three of them could then get the lightest-possible-touch regime. They optimized it for the lowest possible regulation they could find." In his book *Devil's Derivatives*, he explained, "Banque AIG was really just a front for AIGFP . . . the bank was a shell where Cassano booked his default swap trades. But because it was a European bank it fell under the Basel umbrella and ensured the capital benefits from the super-senior default swap trades" (p. 159); see later in the chapter for an explanation of this. See also Richard Northedge, "AIG London Unit Not Regulated by FSA," *Independent*, Mar. 15, 2009.

39. Daniela Gabor, "The (Impossible) Repo Trinity: The Political Economy of Repo Markets," *Review of International Political Economy* 23, no. 6 (2016): 967–1000. See particularly pp. 10–1. The "run on repo" is widely reported. See, for instance, Bill Snyder, "The Role of 'Repo' in the Financial Crisis," Stanford Graduate School of Business, Mar. 12, 2012.

40. The legal opinion on repo hinged on a question: When one player takes cash in exchange for collateral (a bond, say) alongside a contract to "repurchase" that collateral soon afterward, is the original transfer of collateral a "true sale"? If so, then that bond "sold" in a repo operation would no longer be the property of the bank, so the bank shouldn't need to set aside capital against it, and the cash injection it gets in exchange for that bond is also an asset that can be used to flatter the balance sheet. Obviously, a repo isn't *really* a true sale; the "repurchase" contract creates an umbilical link between the bank and that piece of collateral. But Linklaters, for a large fee, provided Lehman with the legal opinion saying that it was.

41. The Valukas report, which examined the dissolution of Lehman Brothers, quoted Lehman's global financial controller Martin Kelly, who said he believed "the only purpose or motive for the transactions was reduction in balance sheet" and that "there was no substance to the transaction" (*Report of Anton R. Valukas, Examiner,* Mar. 11, 2010, jenner.com/lehman/VOLUME%201.pdf). Nathan Powell, an independent research analyst, said Lehman conducted toxic transactions in Britain "to take advantage of the lack of limits on re-hypothecation." See Emmanuel Olaoye and Christopher Elias, "MF Global Trustee Reviewing Firm's Practice of Repledging Collateral," Reuters, Dec. 21, 2011. On Ernst & Young earning $150 million, see Richard Brooks, *Bean Counters: The Triumph of the Accountants and How They Broke Capitalism* (London: Atlantic Books, 2018), 131–3.

42. As with money creation by the banking system, which is kept in check by reserve requirements, rehypothecation is theoretically kept in check by the "haircuts" involved in repo—so for Lehman's Repo 105, the bank would have to pledge $105 in collateral in exchange for $100 in cash.

43. See Manmohan Singh and James Aitken, *The (Sizable) Role of Rehypothecation in the Shadow Banking System,* IMF Working Paper No. 10/172, July 2010. A similar thing happened on a smaller scale when the derivatives broker MF Global went bankrupt in a financial crisis aftershock in 2011. Again, it was MF Global's loosely regulated London unit that was the epicenter of the disaster.

44. *Sustaining New York's and the US' Global Financial Services Leadership,* City of New York Office of the Mayor/US Senate, Jan. 22, 2007, nyc.gov/html/om/pdf/ny_report_final.pdf.

45. The quotes are also drawn from Charles E. Schumer and Michael R. Bloomberg, "To Save New York, Learn from London," *Wall Street Journal,* Nov. 1, 2006.

46. *The Global Financial Centres Index,* City of London, Mar. 2007, 3, 50.

47. Speech by the Chancellor of the Exchequer, the Rt Hon Gordon Brown MP, to Mansion House, June 20, 2007, available at webarchive.nationalarchives.gov.uk.

48. For information on inequalities, see Edward N. Wolff, *The Asset Price Meltdown and the Wealth of the Middle Class,* National Bureau of Economic Research Working Paper No. 18559, Nov. 2012, esp. tables 1, 12, 13. Also see Gillian B. White, "The Recession's Racial Slant," *Atlantic,* June 24, 2015.

49. The figures for US and global bank fines is from Kara Scannell, "US Haul from Credit Crisis Bank Fines Hits $150bn," *Financial Times,* Aug. 6, 2017, and "Banks Paid $321 Billion in Fines since Financial Crisis: BCG," Reuters, Mar. 2, 2017. The FCA data is based on a table I constructed from the FCA's and its predecessor the FSA's published data on fines levied from the UK National Archives website. This data also includes fines levied by the Prudential Regulation Authority (PRA). To save time I excluded all fines below £250,000, those levied on individuals, and those on nonfinancial institutions such as mining companies. My finding of zero fines related to crisis-related activities is a subjective assessment, based on activity type. I sent separate Freedom of Information requests on this specific point to the FCA, PRA, and Serious Fraud Office (SFO) on May 4, 2018; the Bank of England and the SFO replied on May 17 and June 12, respectively, both referring me back to the pages I had already used to collate this data. On the US data see *Quarterly Report to Congress,*

Office of the Special Inspector General for the Troubled Asset Relief Program, Apr. 26, 2018, sigtarp.gov/Quarterly%20Reports/April_26_2018_Report_to_Congress.pdf, and Georgina Lee, "How Many Bankers Were Jailed for Their Part in the Financial Crisis?" Channel 4, Nov. 20, 2017. As of January 23, 2019, four Barclays officials were on trial in London for misleading the market in a Qatari fundraising episode in 2008; this was, however, related to fallout from the crisis, not its causes. See Caroline Binham, "Former Barclays Chief Dishonestly Misled Market, Jury Hears," *Financial Times*, Jan. 23, 2019. Also see "Corporate Crime Gap How the UK Lags the US in Policing Corporate Financial Crime," Corruption Watch (UK,) March 2019.

50. That $880 million was just what they knew about; overall, HSBC excluded $60 *trillion* in wire transactions from money-laundering monitoring each year, according to *Too Big to Jail: Inside the Obama Justice Department's Decision Not to Hold Wall Street Accountable*, Republican Staff of the US House Committee on Financial Services, July 11, 2016, 180.

51. Qtd. in Matt Taibbi, "Gangster Bankers: Too Big to Jail," *Rolling Stone*, Feb. 14, 2013.

52. Qtd. in *Too Big to Jail*.

53. The Finger quotes are from my interview with him in Berlin, Jan. 19, 2017, and follow-up emails. The PwC report is *An Overview of Russian IPOs: 2005 to 2014: Listing Centres, Investment Banks, Legal Counsels, Auditors and Issuers' Jurisdictions*, PricewaterhouseCoopers, 2014, pwc.ru/en/capital-markets/publications/assets/a4_brochure_ipos_eng_print.pdf. For a more comprehensive look at these questions, see David Whyte (ed.), *How Corrupt Is Britain?* (London: Pluto Press, 2015).

54. See "Sir Ken Macdonald Attacks Regulation of City Bankers," *Telegraph*, Feb. 23, 2009. One anomaly in this pattern was the appointment in 2012 of David Green as head of the UK's Serious Fraud Office, who did appear genuinely to be seeking prosecutions of financial regulatory misconduct, despite a shortage of resources. On Green, see, for instance, Suzi Ring and Franz Wild, "Britain's White-Collar Cops Are Getting Too Good at Their Job," *Bloomberg Businessweek*, Feb. 28, 2018. See also "Serious Fraud Office Needs Funding Boost, Warns OECD," *Financial Times*, Mar. 23, 2017. Green was replaced in September 2018 by Lisa Osofsky, a former FBI lawyer.

CHAPTER EIGHT: WEALTH AND ITS ARMOR

1. See "FDIC State Profiles," Federal Deposit Insurance Corporation, fdic.gov/bank/analytical/stateprofile, which is regularly updated.

2. The "written by Citibank" quote comes from Nathan Hayward, from my book *Treasure Islands*, based on research in Delaware, which was South Dakota's main competitor. This research was carried out by me and by Ken Silverstein in 2009. Hunhoff spoke to me by phone on October 9, 2018.

3. See Zachary Mider, "South Dakota, Little Tax Haven on the Prairie," *Bloomberg Businessweek*, Jan. 9, 2014, and Kara Scannell and Vanessa Houlder, "US Tax Havens: The New Switzerland," *Financial Times*, May 8, 2016. The offices of Bret Afdahl, director of the South Dakota Division of Banking, sent me data via email on Nov. 16, 2018, showing total South Dakota trust company assets at $294 billion at the end of 2017,

25 percent up from a year earlier and roughly double the figure for 2012, and 95 trust companies employing 208 people (though it wasn't clear how many were part-time). The trust companies paid a total $961,635 in annual supervision fees in the 2017 financial year, plus $1.9 million in bank franchise tax.

4. In fact, the basic idea was probably imported from the Holy Lands: the prophet Muhammad is said to have endorsed a legal structure called a waqf, which is much like today's charitable trust.

5. Brooke Harrington, *Capital without Borders: Wealth Managers and the One Percent* (Cambridge, MA: Harvard University Press, 2016), 107.

6. This and subsequent quotes are from my interview with Meierhenry at his offices in Sioux Falls, Oct. 22, 2018.

7. Ronald A. Wirtz, "In South Dakota, We Trust," *Federal Gazette*, Federal Reserve Bank of Minneapolis, Feb. 26, 2013.

8. Adam S. Hofri-Winogradow, "The Stripping of the Trust: From Evolutionary Scripts to Distributive Results," *Ohio State Law Journal* 75, no. 3 (2014): 529–70.

9. On the IRS losing resources, see Paul Kiel, Jesse Eisinger, and ProPublica, "The Golden Age of Rich People Not Paying Their Taxes," *Atlantic*, Dec. 11, 2018, and David Cay Johnston, *Perfectly Legal: The Covert Campaign to Rig Our Tax System to Benefit the Super Rich—and Cheat Everybody Else* (New York: Portfolio, 2003), esp. ch. 10, "Handcuffing the Tax Police." In the slumber party case I cited, Johnston reported one girl, while the *Atlantic* reported several girls; it's not clear if they are referring to the same testimony. On life expectancy, see US Burden of Disease Collaborators, "The State of US Health, 1990–2016: Burden of Diseases, Injuries, and Risk Factors among US States," *JAMA* 319, no. 14 (Apr. 2018): 1444: "In 2016, Hawaii had the highest life expectancy at birth (81.3 years) and Mississippi had the lowest (74.7 years)." Comparisons with World Health Organization tables (methodologies may not be identical). For the data on billionaires, see for example Chuck Collins and Josh Hoxie, "Billionaire Bonanza 2018, Inherited Wealth Dynasties of the 21st-Century U.S.," Inequality.org, Oct. 30, 2018, inequality.org/great-divide/billionaire-bonanza-2018-inherited-wealth-dynasties-in-the-21st-century-u-s.

10. The South Dakota trusts data comes from an email from Afdahl to me on May 19, 2017 (the first of two sets of emails I exchanged with his offices). On Mitt Romney, see my article "Where the Money Lives," *Vanity Fair*, Aug. 2012. The limit on how much can be gifted over a lifetime is complemented by an annual gift exclusion, the maximum you can give to any individual in any year (you can give $16,000 to one individual, $32,000 to two, and so on).

11. See Zachary Mider, "GRAT Shelters: An Accidental Tax Break for America's Wealthiest," *Washington Post*, Dec. 28, 2013. Also see Collins and Hoxie, "Billionaire Bonanza 2018."

12. Jersey Finance, the official arm of the offshore center, said, "Over £1 trillion of assets are held in Jersey trusts and other asset-holding vehicles, of which £400 billion are held in private trusts and roughly £600 billion in corporate asset vehicles." From *Jersey's Value to Britain: Evaluating the Economic, Financial and Fiscal Linkages between Jersey and the United Kingdom*, Capital Economics for Jersey Finance, Oct. 2016. For a comparison

of jurisdictions by amount of trust activity, see *Annual Report*, Cayman Islands Monetary Authority, 2016, 21, "Table 4: Number of Licensed Trust Companies—Selected Jurisdictions, 2012–2015 Calendar Year-End." This showed Jersey, Guernsey, Isle of Man, the British Virgin Islands, and the Caymans as each having 150–190 trust companies (each trust company services many clients). For the UK total, see "Inheritance Tax Statistics," HM Revenue & Customs, gov.uk/government/collections/inheritance-tax-statistics, "Table 12.7—Assets Held in Taxpaying Discretionary Trusts at 10-Yearly Charge Date." The $9–$36 trillion estimates for the size of assets in tax havens are from Henry, *Price of Offshore Revisited*, updated in James Henry, "Taxing Tax Havens: How to Respond to the Panama Papers," *Foreign Affairs*, Apr. 12, 2016. Henry partly pioneered this method of estimation, triangulating using three separate statistical methods, combined with "investigative economics," which involves talking to players in the industry. The widely publicized estimates by Zucman, at the lower end, were published in his book *The Hidden Wealth of Nations*. Zucman uses a novel method to estimate assets in tax havens by using data on cross-border holdings of assets and liabilities and establishing mismatches between them. This number misses out on a large section of the data for several reasons: (a) many trillions are held in vehicles like trusts where the beneficial owner is not *un*recorded but *mis*recorded (e.g., in the name of the trustee), so no mismatch shows up in the cross-border data, even though the asset is offshore; and (b) banks will usually be quite happy handing over *aggregate* data on client assets to balance-of-payments data collection authorities like the BIS, which is the main international source used by Zucman, but they will be far less happy handing over client-level data to tax authorities, so his method misses a large amount of assets hidden from tax authorities. For further "missing" data, see Nicholas Shaxson, "How to Crack Down on Tax Havens: Start with the Banks," *Foreign Affairs*, Mar.–Apr. 2018, as well as John Christensen and James Henry, "The Offshore Trillions," letter to the editor, *New York Review of Books*, Mar. 10, 2016 (in response to Cass R. Sunstein's "Parking the Big Money," Jan. 14, 2016).

13. Emile van der Does de Willebois et al., *The Puppet Masters: How the Corrupt Use Legal Structures to Hide Stolen Assets and What to Do About It*, Stolen Asset Recovery Initiative, World Bank/UNDOC, 2011, 45–46. It said, "Investigators and prosecutors tend not to bring charges against trusts, because of the difficulty in proving their role in the crime. . . . Even if trusts holding illicit assets may well have been used in a given case, they may not actually be mentioned in formal charges and court documents, and consequently their misuse goes unreported."

14. See Dan Alexander, "The Mystery Of Wilbur Ross' Missing Billions," *Forbes*, Oct. 16, 2017.

15. There are no statistics outlining what proportion of trusts are discretionary, but pointers exist. Giles Corbin, a partner at Jersey-based Mourant, said, "Something like 90 percent of Jersey trusts we draft are fully discretionary ones"; a practitioner in the British Virgin Islands stated that "most British Virgin Islands trusts tend to be discretionary trusts." For both figures, see "Jersey: '90% of Our Business Is Discretionary Trusts,'" Tax Justice Network, June 12, 2013, taxjustice.blogspot.com/2013/06/jersey-90-of-our-business-is. html. McDowell told me that discretionary trusts were the "best" and "most flexible" kinds.

16. See Richard Murphy, "Northern Rock—The Questions Needing Answers," Tax Research UK, Sept. 17, 2007, taxresearch.org.uk/Blog/2007/09/17/northern-rock-the-questions-needing-answers. The distinction between ownership and control is outlined on p. 28 of *Granite Master Issuer PLC: Annual Report and Accounts for the Year Ended 31 December 2006*, where it states, "The Company's ultimate parent is The Law Debenture Intermediary Corporation plc, a company registered in England and Wales, the shares being held under a trust arrangement. . . . The Company's ultimate controlling party is Northern Rock plc . . . ." Also see Ian Cobain and Ian Griffiths, "A Twisty Trail: From Northern Rock to Jersey to a Tiny Charity," *Guardian*, Nov. 28, 2007; "Memorandum from the Financial Services Authority," Parliament.uk, Oct. 9, 2007, publications.parliament.uk/pa/cm200708/cmselect/cmtreasy/56/56we08.htm; and Paul Murphy, "The (Un)charitable Core of Northern Rock," *FT Alphaville*, Oct. 8, 2007. I contacted DSNE for comment (by email) on May 9, 2017, but received no response.

17. See *Report on Abuse of Charities for Money-Laundering and Tax Evasion*, Centre for Tax Policy and Administration, OECD, Feb. 24, 2009, 64.

18. On family offices, see "How the 0.001% Invest," *Economist*, Dec. 15, 2018. The HNWI data comes from Anthony Shorrocks et al., "Global Wealth Report 2018," Credit Suisse, Oct. 2018, principally fig. 1 on p. 20. The "six times" figure comes from Capgemini World Wealth Report (worldwealthreport.com/reports), showing the world HNWI population growing from 10 million in 2009 to 15.4 million in 2015, for a 7.5 percent annual growth, while World Bank annual population growth figures show an average 1.2 percent for that time period. On "ownerless wealth" not being properly reported, Credit Suisse does not mention trusts, foundations, and the like: it says it uses survey data (which it notes is unreliable) supplemented with "rich lists" such as the *Forbes* billionaires list, collated by journalists. *Forbes* says it measures holdings, wealth, and stakes but also does not explicitly mention trusts or foundations and the like (Kerry A. Dolan, "Methodology: How We Crunch the Numbers," Mar. 7, 2012). A trove of inequality data comes from Thomas Piketty, *Capital in the Twenty-First Century* (Cambridge, MA: Belknap Press, 2014).

19. Annette Alstadsæter, Niels Johannesen, and Gabriel Zucman, *Tax Evasion and Inequality*, National Bureau of Economic Research Working Paper No. 23772, Sept. 2017. In less egalitarian countries it may well be higher: a study of Credit Suisse by the US Senate found that 85–95 percent of accounts looked at were not declared to their tax authorities. See *Offshore Tax Evasion: The Effort to Collect Unpaid Taxes on Billions in Hidden Offshore Accounts*, US Senate Permanent Subcommittee on Investigations, Feb. 26, 2014, 64.

20. The plot, and my role in breaking the story, is covered in my book *Poisoned Wells* (in the Obiang Nguema chapter). In short, I revealed the fact that the government of Equatorial Guinea had captured some mercenaries following the arrest, a few hours earlier, of a planeload of them in Zimbabwe en route to Equatorial Guinea. The journalist friend who reported on Calil didn't want to be identified. He wasn't Ken Silverstein (who is also a friend of mine, and who did the best reporting on Calil's financial activities in his book *The Secret World of Oil*).

21. See Paul Krugman, "Understanding Republican Cruelty," *New York Times*, June 30, 2017. The "slash and burn" quotes come from Luyendijk, *Swimming with Sharks*, 104.

22. Alex Cuadros, *Brazillionaires: The Godfathers of Modern Brazil* (London: Profile, 2016).

23. See Benjamin I. Page, Larry M. Bartels, and Jason Seawright, "Democracy and the Policy Preferences of Wealthy Americans," *Perspectives on Politics* 11, no. 1 (Mar. 2013): 51–73. The authors studied wealthy people, based on interview material, and found "that they are extremely active politically and that they are much more conservative than the American public as a whole with respect to important policies concerning taxation, economic regulation, and especially social welfare programs. Variation within this wealthy group suggests that the top one-tenth of 1 percent of wealth-holders (people with $40 million or more in net worth) may tend to hold still more conservative views that are even more distinct from those of the general public."

24. Harrington, *Capital Without Borders*, 245.

25. From my interview with Gaydamak in Moscow in 2005. In addition, Global Witness reported in *All the Presidents Men* (Mar. 1, 2002) that Gaydamak "may have even visited the UK, possibly even as recently as late November 2001," despite the international arrest warrant being issued by France on Dec. 6, 2000. Gaydamak held an open press interview at the Dorchester Hotel in London two days afterward—with no action from British authorities.

26. Harrington, in an email to me, Aug. 26, 2016, following up my interview with her on June 29, 2016.

27. These quotes are from Eva Joly, *Notre affaire à tous*, Éditions des Arènes, 2000, iii, 20; and Eva Joly, *Est-ce dans ce monde-là que nous voulons vivre?*, Éditions des Arènes, 2003, 36.

28. See Daniel Kahneman and Angus Deaton, "High Income Improves Evaluation of Life but Not Emotional Well-Being," *Proceedings of the National Academy of Sciences* 107, no. 38 (Sept. 21, 2010): 16489–93, and Grant E. Donnelly et al., "The Amount and Source of Millionaires' Wealth (Moderately) Predict Their Happiness," *Personality and Social Psychology Bulletin* 44, no. 5 (May 2018): 684–99. Also see Andrew T. Jebb et al., "Happiness, Income Satiation and Turning Points Around the World," *Nature Human Behaviour*, Jan. 8, 2018, which said, "Globally, we find that satiation occurs at $95,000 for life evaluation and $60,000 to $75,000 for emotional well-being." The Carnegie quote is widely reported.

29. The Davidson quotes are from two telephone interviews with Davidson, on April 28, 2017, and April 23, 2018, and subsequent emails. The "self destruct" quote is from Brooke Harrington, "How to Hide It: Inside the Secret World of Wealth Managers," *Guardian*, Sept. 21, 2016.

30. On Manafort's daughters, see Natasha Bertrand, "Hacked Text Messages Allegedly Sent by Paul Manafort's Daughter Discuss 'Blood Money' and Killings, and a Ukrainian Lawyer Wants Him to Explain," *Business Insider*, Mar. 21, 2017.

31. Harrington, email to me, Aug. 2016.

32. The "confidant" quote is from Pierre Delalande, a French wealth and advisory manager, in Michel Pinçon and Monique Pinçon-Charlot, *Grandes fortunes: Dynasties familiales et formes de richesse en France* (Paris: Payot & Rivages, 2006), 14–16.

33. Brooke Harrington, "The Bad Behavior of the Richest: What I Learned from Wealth Managers," *Guardian*, Oct. 19, 2018.

CHAPTER NINE: PRIVATE OCTOPUS

1. The main sources for this are Anthony Gnoffo Jr., "Trenton's Old-Time Newspaper War: Complete and Sober vs. Sassy and Flashy," *Philadelphia Inquirer*, Aug. 20, 1989, and Iver Peterson, "Telling Shocking Tales in Trenton," *New York Times*, Nov. 23, 1992.

2. From various news reports, especially Bob Fernandez, "Philly's Digital First Papers Face Harsh Cuts, Potential 'Lights-Out Scenario,'" *Philadelphia Inquirer*, May 15, 2018, and Joshua Benton, "The *Boston Herald*'s Buyer Is a Vulture Capitalist," *Boston Globe*, Feb. 15, 2018. The Pew Research Center estimated in a June 2018 fact sheet that daily newspaper circulation in the United States had declined by about 27 percent during this period.

3. From my telephone interview with Reynolds on October 9, 2018.

4. See Ken Doctor, "Newsonomics: Alden Global Capital Is Making So Much Money Wrecking Local Journalism It Might Not Want to Stop Anytime Soon," Nieman Lab, May 1, 2018, niemanlab.org/2018/05/newsonomics-alden-global-capital-is-making-so-much-money-wrecking-local-journalism-it-might-not-want-to-stop-anytime-soon. The comparison with peers was uncertain, he said, because the company's secrecy meant it wasn't possible to get a breakdown of expenses and other components of its published data. Ray's estimate was not based on inside information, he said: he made a back-of-the-envelope guesstimate for me based on the $1.50 cover price multiplied by circulation numbers, minus staff numbers multiplied by $30,000-odd annual salaries, plus associated costs.

5. Julie Reynolds, "Leaked Financial Report Shows Jaw-Dropping Profits for 'Outlaw' Newspaper Owner," News Matters, dfmworkers.org/leaked-financial-report-shows-jaw-dropping-profits-for-outlaw-newspaper-owner, and Julie Reynolds, "Layoffs, Buyouts across DFM Newspaper Chain Follow Hedge Fund's Profit-Extraction Strategy," News Matters, dfmworkers.org/layoffs-across-dfm-newspaper-chain-are-part-of-hedge-funds-profit-extraction-strategy.

6. The history of KKR and LBOs is widely reported. On Smith's involvement, see Alison Leigh Cowan, "Bottom Fishing with R.D. Smith," *New York Times*, Mar. 29, 1991.

7. This was, as the Chicago-based private equity investor John Canning Jr. explained, "really a marketing concept" (Josh Kosman, *The Buyout of America*," Profile Books, 2010, ch. 1). Also in the early 1990s, as I was aware from my time working as a war correspondent in Angola, real military mercenaries were being rebranded as "Private Military Contractors." (The main mercenary outfit operating in Angola while I was there had the extremely corporate-sounding name Executive Outcomes.)

8. Jensen delivered the goods in two short pieces in the *Harvard Business Review*: "Eclipse of the Public Corporation" (Sept.–Oct. 1989) and "CEO Incentives: It's Not How Much You Pay, but How" (with Kevin J. Murphy, May–June 1990), a rousing defense of performance-based executive pay. Don't worry about workers, suppliers, taxpayers, or lenders, he said. As long as the company's financial performance delivered

returns to shareholders, all was good. He didn't mention Milken or Drexel. Morris is quoted from my interview with him on June 2, 2016, and subsequent emails. He added that Jensen's ideas resonated far beyond private equity: they allowed company CEOs to use what their peers were earning at private equity–owned companies as an argument for ratcheting up their own pay. In the early 2000s Jensen began admitting he was wrong about pay. Jensen did not respond to an emailed request for an interview for this book. Ludovic Phalippou, separately, used almost identical language to Morris, describing private equity as "the purest version of capitalism on steroids." See Javier Espinoza, "Spain Wrestles with a Private Equity Boom," *Financial Times*, Jan. 16, 2019.

9. Peter F. Drucker, *The Concept of the Corporation*, 2nd ed. (New York: John Day, 1972), 140.

10. There are endless takedowns of Friedman's and Jensen's ideas. See for instance Steve Denning, "The Origin of 'The World's Dumbest Idea': Milton Friedman," *Forbes*, June 26, 2013. For a deeper investigation, see Lynn Stout's *The Shareholder Value Myth: How Putting Shareholders First Harms Investors, Corporations, and the Public* (San Francisco, CA: Berrett-Koehler, 2012). Also see Ho, *Liquidated*, ch. 3 and esp. p. 124 onward. Jensen's "rainmakers" is quoted in Ho, 27.

11. On Jensen, see John A. Byrne, "The 'Barbarian' At Harvard Business School's Gate," Interview with Duff McDonald, Poets & Quants, Apr. 6, 2017, https://poetsandquants.com/2017/04/06/barbarian-harvard-business-schools-gate. Also see Clayton Christensen, "The New Church of Finance: Deeply Held Belief Systems and Complex Codes Must Be Changed," *Deseret News*, Dec. 9, 2012, and my phone interview with Christensen for *Vanity Fair*, May 24, 2012.

12. As Eileen Appelbaum and Rosemary Batt put it, "With the portfolio companies of most private equity firms located in many different industries, private equity's expertise is typically financial, not operational" (Eileen Appelbaum and Rosemary Batt, *Private Equity at Work: When Wall Street Manages Main Street* [New York: Russell Sage Foundation, 2014], 7–8).

13. Tobias Adrian, Fabio Natalucci, and Thomas Piontek, "Sounding the Alarm on Leveraged Lending," IMF Blog, Nov. 15, 2018, blogs.imf.org/2018/11/15/sounding-the-alarm-on-leveraged-lending, points to $1.3 trillion worth of high-risk "leveraged loans" in the market.

14. See Doctor, "Newsonomics." It said, "When Alden bought a majority of DFM, it bought a largely debt-free company. Since then, it has leveraged it up by borrowing."

15. For the Wilbur Ross episode, see Applebaum and Batt, 206–9, 233.

16. Various sources, including Helia Ebrahimi, "How Private Equity Plundered Profitable Greek Telecoms Company Hellas," *London Telegraph*, Jan. 7, 2012; "Another Greek Tragedy," *Economist*, June 20, 2015; "Private Equity's Trojan Horse of Debt," *New York Times*, Mar. 15, 2010; and court documents.

17. See Appelbaum and Batt, *Private Equity*, 83; "Private Equity Co. Uses Bankruptcy to Keep Friendly's Afloat," *New England In-House*, Feb. 24, 2012; and Jenn Abelson, "US Alleges Fraud in Friendly's Case," *Boston Globe*, Dec. 13, 2011.

18. The accounts show £148 million in revenues in 2017, equivalent to around $190 million. Trainline.com Limited is owned by Trainline Holdings Limited, which

is owned by Trainline Group Investments Limited, which is owned by Trainline Junior Mezz Limited, which is owned by Trainline Investments Holdings Limited, which is owned by Victoria Investments Newco Limited (Jersey), which is owned by Victoria Investments Bidco Limited, which is owned by Victoria Investments Midco Limited, which is owned by Victoria Investments Pikco Limited, which is owned by Victoria Investments Intermediate Holdco Limited, which is mostly owned by Victoria Investments Finco Limited (around 300 million out of 311 million shares; the remaining 11 million or so shares are owned by named French people linked to Trainline's operations in France). However, the Finco company is owned by Victoria Intermediate Topco Limited (Jersey), which is owned by Victoria Investments S.C.A. (Luxembourg). The general partner (GP) of this Luxembourg entity is Victoria Manager SARL (Luxembourg). All the companies so far are UK companies unless otherwise stated. The Trainline.com accounts for 2017 list Victoria Investments Finco Limited as the ultimate parent company and list KKR & Co. LP as "the ultimate controlling party, on behalf of the funds under its management." (It is possible that some details changed, since some of the annual returns outlining the shareholdings dated to as early as January 2016.) A prospectus for KKR Acceleration Aggregator LP (a company owned by KKR but otherwise unrelated to Trainline), published in Dec. 2016 by the German financial regulator BaFin, lists KKR Management LLC as the GP of KKR & Co. LP. It also lists several other companies that appear to be linked to Trainline: KKR Victoria GP Limited (Cayman), KKR Victoria Co-Invest LP (Cayman), Trainline International Limited, Trainline.com limited branch (Luxembourg), KKR Victoria Aggregator LP, and a Cayman exempted limited partnership, which is represented by its general partner KKR Victoria Aggregator GP Limited (Cayman). This adds up to twenty-two companies in the Trainline cluster. As of June 25, 2018, KKR listed 183 active (i.e., "real") portfolio companies on its website.

19. The limited liability game is often more complex than described here. Generally, contractual obligations can and often do feed liabilities up the ownership chain of limited liability companies. But this strategy can still be made to work by combining it with the Opco-Propco strategy. The Propco is where all the value is realized (and extracted), while the Opco, laboring under the burden of high rental costs, is worth very little. So, as Appelbaum and Batt explain, "the operating company has legal liability in the case of negligence or medical errors, but very little in the way of resources to satisfy patients' claims against it. Separating real estate assets from the operating companies is a strategy for minimizing exposure to patient litigation" (*Private Equity*, 71–2). On Anderson, see John Cassidy, "The Bain Bomb: A User's Guide," *New Yorker*, Jan. 13, 2012.

20. Normal companies typically use something like three times as much debt as "equity" (the owners' own money), while with private equity it's roughly the other way around. See Appelbaum and Batt, 77, which also has the 40 percent figure for enterprise value. Research shows that private equity firms are significantly more aggressive in using tax havens and other schemes to escape paying tax, and this is particularly true for the larger firms, which can afford the armies of lawyers and accountants to design the huge, complex schemes that really shake the taxman off their tail. See Brad Badertscher, Sharon P. Katz, and Sonja Olhoft Rego, *The Impact of Private Equity Ownership on Portfolio Firms' Corporate Tax Planning*, Harvard Business School Working Paper No. 10-004, Mar. 4, 2010.

21. The Randall and Barbara Smith Foundation, a philanthropic foundation founded by Smith and his wife, lists four main investments, including the Dubai firm. Almost no published information is available on the Dubai firm except that it was dissolved in 2013 and its company secretary was a local law firm called BSA Ahmad Bin Heezim & Associates LLP. The foundation's investments are from the IRS Form 990-PF return for the Randall and Barbara Smith Foundation, 2016, and SEC data.

22. Richard Marosi, "The Homex Story: A Boom and a Bust," *Los Angeles Times*, Nov. 26, 2017.

23. Julie Reynolds, "Another Form of Misery: Alden's Slumlord Investment in Mexico," News Matters, Feb. 20, 2018, dfmworkers.org/another-form-of-misery-aldens-slumlord-investment-in-mexico.

24. See Julie Reynolds, "Untangling the Web of Alden's Dubious Deals," News Matters, Jan. 8, 2018, dfmworkers.org/untangling-the-web-of-aldens-dubious-deals.

25. The basic data on Alden DFM SPV, Ltd., is available on secinfo.com, registered to Ogier Fiduciary Services (Cayman) Ltd. On the question of the United States encouraging dirty money, see my article "Where the Money Lives" on Mitt Romney (another private equity mogul), and James S. Henry, "The World's Largest Tax Haven? Guess Who," *American Interest*, June 18, 2018. On Alden DFM SPV, Ltd., there is also a second company with almost the same name, Alden DFM SPV LLC, based in the equally secretive Delaware. On the Solus story, see *Sola Ltd and Ultra Master Ltd v. MNG Enterprises, Inc.*, Delaware Court of Chancery, Mar. 5, 2018, and the summary in Julie Reynolds, "Hedge Fund Alden Siphoned 100s of Millions from Newspapers in Scheme to Gamble on Other Investments, Suit Says," News Matters, Mar. 8, 2018, dfmworkers. org/hedge-fund-alden-siphoned-100s-of-millions-from-newspapers-in-scheme-to-gamble-on-other-investments-suit-says.

26. The latest SEC filing (Form D), published in Nov. 2014, described Alden DFM SPV, Ltd., as an "exempted company with limited liability," which is now out of date, since the Ogier website has a section on Cayman Islands exempted companies (ogier.com/publications/cayman-islands-exempted-companies, Nov. 17, 2016), which notes that "Following the commencement of the Limited Liability Companies Law, 2016, an exempted company may not be registered using the abbreviation 'LLC' or the words 'limited liability company' in its name." On the vehicle's net asset value, Alden ticked the SEC box "decline to disclose." There appears to be no update on the SEC site.

27. Julie Reynolds, "Who Profits from Alden Global Capital? You'd Be Surprised," News Matters, June 11, 2018, dfmworkers.org/who-profits-from-alden-global-capital-youd-be-surprised.

28. Interview with Matt Stoller in Washington, DC, Oct. 23, 2018, and Eliza Ronalds-Hannon, Matthew Townsend, and Lauren Coleman-Lochner, "Behind the Breakneck Unraveling of Toys 'R' Us," *Bloomberg*, Mar. 16, 2018.

29. Appelbaum and Batt, *Private Equity*, 65; on employment growth, p. 233. Chapter seven, "Private Equity's Effects on Jobs and Labor," goes into these questions in more detail. The exception to this trend is in finance, insurance, and real estate, where earnings at least rose, yet the finance curse shows that those are precisely the sectors where high earnings are the most troublesome.

30. Daniel Rasmussen, "Private Equity: Overvalued and Overrated?," *American Affairs* 2, no. 1 (Spring 2018): 3–16.

31. See "Tamara Mellon Puts the Boot in to Buyouts," *Financial Times*, Apr. 6, 2012. On gender, see Theresa Whitmarsh, "My Locker Room Rally Cry for Women in Private Equity," World Economic Forum, Nov. 2, 2015, weforum.org/agenda/2015/11/my-locker-room-rally-cry-for-women-in-private-equity, and "Overview of the Health and Social Care Workforce," The King's Fund, kingsfund.org.uk/projects/time-think-differently/trends-workforce-overview. The comparable figure for investment bankers is 16 percent women. The statistic on women in hedge funds is from Rachael Levy, "Hedge Funds Have Few Women Investing for Them—and the Men Who Run Them Aren't Really Looking to Change That," *Business Insider*, Sept. 13, 2016. On the comparison with S&P 500 firms, see Cynthia Littleton, "Women on Wall Street Face Steep Climb to the Top," *Variety*, Apr. 6, 2016. These studies may have different measurement methodologies.

32. See Simon Lack, *The Hedge Fund Mirage: The Illusion of Big Money and Why It's Too Good to Be True* (Hoboken, NJ: John Wiley & Sons, 2012). Lack told me in an interview on June 23, 2017, that he expected returns to outside investors would have deteriorated since then, due to the larger amounts of money-chasing assets pushing up prices. (The comparison between "feeble" hedge funds and private equity returns is mine, not his.)

33. The 2 and 20 formula is especially lucrative for bigger funds, principally because the overheads are relatively smaller: it doesn't take twenty times as many people to run a $5 billion fund as it does a $100 million fund. The 20 percent profit share is usually taken only after an agreed "hurdle rate" of internal profit, typically 8 percent, is reached. Appelbaum and Batt estimate that two-thirds of the GPs' total revenue derives from the 2 rather than from the (performance-based) 20 (*Private Equity*, 52). The Paulson quotes are from Lindsay Fortado, "John Paulson Mulls Shutting His Hedge Fund," *Financial Times*, Jan. 22, 2019.

34. For an explanation of this, see Michael Fahy, "Dissecting the Truth About the Private Equity Market," Thomson Reuters, Apr. 8, 2018. As Professor William J. Magnuson of Texas A & M School of Law put it, the terms that LPs sign up to "effectively eliminate the ability of private equity investors to voice their opinions and participate in essential business decisions of the funds that they own. Near total control is vested in the private equity firm itself." See William J. Magnuson, "The Public Cost of Private Equity," *Minnesota Law Review*, 102, 2017. Forthcoming Texas A&M University School of Law Legal Studies Research Paper No. 17-28, May 2017.

35. Derek Thompson, "How Hollywood Accounting Can Make a $450 Million Movie 'Unprofitable,'" *Atlantic*, Sept. 14, 2011. On June 22, 2017, I asked Prowse for an update via his website, but he did not reply.

36. See Florencio Lopez-de-Silanes, Ludovic Phalippou, and Oliver Gottschalg, "Giants at the Gate: Investment Returns and Diseconomies of Scale in Private Equity," *Journal of Financial and Quantitative Analysis* 50, no. 3 (June 2015): 377–411, and Peter Morris, *Private Equity, Public Loss?* Centre for the Study of Financial Innovation, July 2010, 27. Phalippou said, in a summary of his 2017 book, *Private Equity Laid Bare*, "Headline fees are remotely related to the actual fee bill. Fees depend on how every single clause is

written and how each element is defined. Contracts are incredibly difficult to read and understand . . . recording (and discussing) headline numbers is pointless" ("Synopsis of *Private Equity Laid Bare*," LinkedIn, Dec. 5, 2017, linkedin.com/pulse/synopsis-private-equity-laid-bare-ludovic-phalippou). Also see Yves Smith, "Another Private Equity Scam: Clawback Language Does Not Work As Advertised," Naked Capitalism blog, Sept. 3, 2014.

37. The $3 trillion figure is from the Bain & Company's *Global Private Equity Report 2018* and the *2018 Preqin Global Private Equity and Venture Capital Report*, and the hedge fund figure is from James Williams, *The LP Blueprint 2018—Insights on Alternative Investments*, GFM Research/Intralinks, Sept. 2018. It is widely accepted that returns in both sectors are getting worse, largely because when investment funds were small, there was a rich menu of highly promising companies to choose from. The low-hanging fruit are now gone, and the more money there is, the harder it is to find good deals. The "outperform" data is from Rasmussen, "Private Equity."

38. Firms also like to use a metric called X, so they can say "I got 3x" or "5x," meaning they sold companies for three or five times what they paid for them. (Alden has said that it will consider selling properties if it can get 4x.) Two company officials with long experience with private equity told me how the new players chase high numbers especially hard: they start aiming for 3x or higher, to make a name in the market. Once they are known and trusted to deliver high returns, they can sit back and watch investors' money roll in, chasing their track record, and they rake in those easy 2 percent annual management fees. Appelbaum and Batt discuss the various studies of private equity performance in chapter six of their book.

39. There's also an inbuilt positive bias in the research, as the less successful funds are less likely to share their data with researchers. For example, a standard metric is the "value bridge," which systematically overstates performance. The value bridge seeks to split out successes into their component parts: general market increases, stock picking, market timing, financial engineering, and genuine operational skill. Even if the mathematics are usually correctly calculated, they capture only one dimension of debt. The details are beyond the scope here; see Peter Morris, *Evaluating Private Equity's Performance: Approach the "Value Bridge" with Caution*, KPMG International, 2016. Phalippou said the value bridge "is biased to exaggerate the contribution of earnings growth" ("Synopsis of *Private Equity Laid Bare*"). Most observers agree returns are likely to deteriorate because the huge amount of liquidity in global markets has made assets very expensive to buy: it will be very hard to sell them at even higher prices later down the line. Also, in the next downturn private equity's borrowing binge is likely to make the value of their assets fall further than more conventional funds and lead to more bankruptcies. See also Ludovic Phalippou, *Private Equity Funds' Performance, Risk and Selection*, Edward Elgar's Research Handbook on Hedge Funds, Private Equity and Alternative Investments, Phoebus Athanassiou, (ed.), July 8, 2010.

40. Appelbaum and Batt state, "GPs invest just $1 or $2 in the fund for every $100 invested by the fund's LPs, yet they claim 20 percent of the profit," (*Private Equity*, 51–2). See also Ben Protess and Michael Corkery, "Just How Much Do the Top Private Equity Earners Make?" *New York Times*, Dec. 10, 2016.

41. Simon Goodley, "Carlyle Group Offers a Slice of Its Own Brand of Controversy for $7bn," *Guardian*, Apr. 22, 2012.

42. The quotes from Phalippou, Lack, and the anonymous banker come from my interviews and conversations with them in 2013, mostly in March or April, and with subsequent correspondence with Lack on June 23, 2017. Back in 1989, the US Treasury secretary Nicholas Brady even alluded to this, slamming "a history of overcommitment driven by fees and fashion." See "Leveraged Buyout and Corporate Debt," hearing before the US Senate Committee on Finance, Jan. 24, 1989, 7.

43. One complicating factor here is that some of the biggest buyout funds, like KKR and Blackstone, are listed on the stock market. This gives investors ways to buy directly into the "titans," rather than being vulnerable "limited partners."

44. See Christine Perez, "Spire Realty's Caleb Smith: The Next Trammell Crow?" *D CEO* (Dallas), Mar. 2011.

CHAPTER TEN: BIG HOG

1. This history is mostly drawn from news stories, especially Mike Kilen, "Boondocks Closing: How a Legendary Family Truck Stop Met Iowa Travelers Halfway for 45 Years," *Des Moines Register*, Oct. 13, 2018. The story said it was due to close on October 20, 2018, though I visited on October 19 and the staff told me that was its last day. It was pure coincidence that I visited on that historic day. (I had fish sticks.)

2. See *From Great Recession to Great Reshuffling: Charting a Decade of Change Across American Communities*, Economic Innovation Group, Oct. 2018. On the impact of deregulation, see Clara Hendrickson, Mark Muro, and William A. Galston, *Countering the Geography of Discontent: Strategies for the Left-Behind Places*, Brookings Institution, Nov. 2018, esp. 12–3.

3. From my interview with Ikerd in Fairfield, Iowa, Oct. 16, 2018.

4. Global agricultural exports are now around seventy times larger by weight than they were in 1970. Exports data from Livestock, Dairy, and Poultry Outlook, USDA, Dec. 17, 2018. It recorded 5.6 billion pounds of exports in 2017, around 22 percent of US production, compared with 82 million pounds, or 0.6 percent of production, in 1970.

5. The Fetters' story came from the documentary *The Farm Crisis*, Iowa Public Television, 2013.

6. See Christopher Leonard, The Meat Rocket (New York: Simon & Shuster, 2014). The chapters "The Eden Crash" and "Expand or Expire" were most relevant for this section on chickenization. This superb book, focusing on Tyson and (mostly) the poultry business, originally inspired me to write this chapter (and thanks to Patty Lovera at Food and Water Watch for helping steer me towards hog farming and Iowa).

7. Ibid., 103–4.

8. Ibid., 114–5, 118.

9. Data from the US Department of Natural Resources and a printout given to me by Diane Rosenberg on October 16, 2018, "USDA Ag Census Figures 1920–Present." For US-wide figures, the number of farms that raised hogs fell from 512,292 at the 1978 agricultural census to 63,246 by the 2012 census. See Stephanie Mercier, "The

U.S. Hog Industry—Then and Now," AgWeb, Dec. 22, 2016, agweb.com/blog/straight-from-dc-agricultural-perspectives/the-us-hog-industry-then-and-now.

10. Quotes are from my interview with Miller at the Farm Bureau offices in Des Moines, Oct. 18, 2018, and from my interview with O'Brien at her farm in Atlantic, Iowa, Oct. 21, 2018. On the staggering rise in interstate banking, see Christian A. Johnson and Tara Rice, "Assessing a Decade of Interstate Bank Branching," *Washington and Lee Law Review* 65. no. 1 (Winter 2008), 76. The relevant piece of legislation was called the Riegle-Neal Interstate Banking and Branching Efficiency Act.

11. The Petersen quote is from my interview with him at his farm in Clear Lake, Iowa, Oct. 19, 2018.

12. On the chains of limited liability companies shifting risk and allowing secrecy, see Loka Ashwood, Danielle Diamond, and Kendall Thu, "Where's the Farmer? Limited Liability in Midwestern Industrial Hog Production," *Rural Sociology* 79, no. 1 (Mar. 2014): 2–27.

13. According to a Food and Drug Administration report from 2011, "80 percent of antibiotics in the United States are sold for agricultural purposes, and agriculture uses drugs from every major class of antibiotics used in human medicine." Typically supplied in low doses, the antibiotics fail to kill bacteria and are accelerating the rise of resistant strains. See *Factory Farm Nation* (Washington, DC: Food & Water Watch, 2015), 29. On MRSA, see Price, Lance et al., "Staphylococcus Aureus CC398: Host Adaptation and Emergence of Methicillin Resistance in Livestock." *mBio*. 3, no. 1. Jan./Feb. 2012): 1. It finds "strong and diverse antimicrobial selection associated with food animal production," and says this especially dangerous strain of MRSA appears to have acquired tetracycline and methicillin resistance in livestock. Ractopamine has been widely reported on, but see for example *Factory Farm Nation*, 31.

14. According to one estimate in *Factory Farm Nation*, CAFOs produced 369 million tons of manure in 2012, about thirteen times as much as the sewage produced by the entire US population. On comparisons with a municipal town, see an (undated) section on Ikerd's personal website johnikerd.com entitled "Responses to 20 Questions Frequently Asked by Defenders of CAFOs," http://johnikerd.com/responses-to-20-frequently-asked-questions-by-defenders-of-cafos. The hog house explosion is described in *Factory Farm Nation*, p. 24. On impaired waterways, see "2016 Map of Impaired Waters," available at "Section 303(d) Impaired Waters Listings," Iowa Department for Natural Resources, iowadnr.gov/Environmental-Protection/Water-Quality/Water-Monitoring/Impaired-Waters. See also Ted Genoways, "Hog Wild: Factory Farms Are Poisoning Iowa's Drinking Water," *Mother Jones*, Mar. 21, 2014, and "Gulf of Mexico 'Dead Zone' Is the Largest Ever Measured," National Oceanic and Atmospheric Administration, Aug. 2, 2017. Medical effects are widely reported. For example, see James Merchant and David Osterberg, *The Explosion of CAFOs in Iowa and Its Impact on Water Quality and Public Health*, Iowa Policy Project, Jan. 2018, summarized by its authors in "Impacts of the CAFO Explosion on Water Quality and Public Health," *Des Moines Register*, Jan. 24, 2018. The main report estimates that there are ten thousand registered CAFOs in Iowa, mostly for hogs, but the number is likely higher since satellite imagery shows numerous hog barns that haven't been registered.

15. The Animal Mortality Facilities are described in "Environmental Quality Incentives Program (EQIP): Key Practices for Iowa Confined Livestock Operations," USDA, nrcs.usda.gov/Internet/FSE_DOCUMENTS/stelprdb1256038.pdf. Rendering in the United States produces "approximately 11.2 billion pounds of animal derived proteins and 10.9 billion pounds of rendered fats. About 85 percent of this production is utilized as animal feed ingredients." See David L. Meeker and C. R. Hamilton, "An Overview of the Rendering Industry," in David L. Meeker (ed.), *Essential Rendering: All About the Animal By-Products Industry* (Alexandria, VA: National Renderers Association; Fats and Proteins Research Foundation; Animal Protein Producers Industry, 2006), 1–16. "Whole carcasses" are part of the mix.

16. From my interview with Petersen on October 19, 2018.

17. The Iowa Farm Bureau is (according to its Form 990 tax return) recorded as a 501(c)(5) tax-exempt body, a classification that provides a tax exemption for labor and agricultural organizations.

18. Information on FBL's corporate structure and shareholdings is from "Corporate Profile," FBL Financial Group, fblfinancial.com/CustomPage/Index?KeyGenPage=207924; FBL Financial Group, Inc., Notice of Annual Meeting of Shareholders, US Securities and Exchange Commission Schedule 14A, May 16, 2018, p. 14; and "Annual Statement for the Year Ended December 31, 2016, of the Condition and Affairs of the Farm Bureau Life Insurance Company," which provides a partial diagram of the corporate structure on p. 51. See also the *60 Minutes* piece on the Farm Bureau that aired on April 9, 2000, available at "60 Minutes: Farm Bureau (Part 1)," YouTube, July 1, 2009, youtu.be/c4iiV8e0Y6A.

19. The waterworks story was quite widely reported, which helped limit the damage. The bill's label subsequently changed from HF 316 to HF 484. See for instance MacKenzie Elmer, "Des Moines City Manager on Water Works Bill: 'We Need to Move Really Fast,'" *Des Moines Register*, Feb. 20, 2017.

20. "About IPCW," Iowa Partnership for Clean Water, iowapartnershipforclean-water.org/about-ipcw.

21. The quotes in this section are from my interview with Thicke at his dairy farm on October 16, 2018; from my interview with Mercier in Washington, DC, on October 24, 2018; and from my telephone interview with Fiegen on November 21, 2018 and subsequent emails. On "chickenshit" Democrats, it's telling that Jerry Crawford, who was the Iowa chairman for the presidential campaigns of Michael Dukakis, Bill Clinton, Al Gore, and John Kerry, and who ran Hillary Clinton's Midwest campaign in 2008, founded a law firm that has for years been Monsanto's top Washington lobbyist. OpenSecrets.org records an average $290,000 per year paid by Monsanto to his firm, Crawford, Quilty & Mauro, for lobbying purposes from 2009 to 2017. Data for 2017 was not given.

22. On the 2006 race, see Anne Fitzgerald, "New Iowa Ag Leader Expected to Champion Biofuels," *Des Moines Register*, Nov. 9, 2006. I wasn't able to find independent corroboration of her 15-point lead ahead of the election, though Thicke, who ran four years later, remembered O'Brien's lead at 14 points. The $319.45 check is documented in Dan Gearino, "Campaign Discounts Animal Neglect Charge," *Sioux City Journal*, Nov. 3, 2006.

23. Frerick, via email to me, Sept. 25, 2018.

24. On soil degradation, see Rick Cruse, "Cost of Soil Erosion in Iowa Is Not a Pretty Picture," *Mitchell County Press News*, Sept. 6, 2017. The data came from the Iowa Daily Erosion Project (DEP), a team of scientists from Iowa State University, the National Soil Erosion Research Lab, the USDA ARS National Laboratory for Agriculture and the Environment, the University of Iowa, and Colorado State University.

25. See Anne Weir Schechinger and Craig Cox, *Double Dipping: How Taxpayers Subsidize Farmers Twice for Crop Losses*, Environmental Working Group, Nov. 2017.

26. Telephone interview with Josh Flint, Oct. 8, 2018, ahead of my trip. According to *Successful Farming* magazine's ranking of "Pork Powerhouses 2018," the Maschhoffs was ranked number five behind Smithfield, Seaboard, Pipestone, and Iowa Select. The Maschhoffs, to its credit, seemed somewhat more open to talk than other large firms, which did not respond to requests for interview.

27. See for instance "Livestock Production Contract Checklist," Office of the Attorney General, Iowa Department of Justice, Jan. 1996 (recommended as a valuable current resource by Fiegen), or Susan M. Brehm, "From Red Barn to Facility: Changing Environmental Liability to Fit the Changing Structure of Livestock Production," *California Law Review* 93, no. 3 (May 2005): 797–846. Further information on the contracts came from my interviews conducted October 15–21, 2018, with Petersen, Van Winkle, Miller, Ikerd, Flint, Thicke, Schutt, Mercier, Aaron Lehman (president of the Iowa Farmers Union), Diane Rosenberg (executive director of Jefferson County Farmers and Neighbors), Larry Ginter (a retired farmer), and Mary Hendrickson, a rural sociologist at the University of Missouri and a recognized expert in agricultural markets and societies. For a similar issue in the chicken industry, see "Corporate Control in Agriculture," Farm Aid, farmaid.org/issues/corporate-power/corporate-power-in-ag, and the testimony by a chicken farmer named Kay Doby: "They give you the guidelines to raise the birds. You are on their schedule, you don't have a schedule of your own. What the grower's looking for is the day you get these [chicken] houses paid off, and then you can make some money. The bad thing about that is that time never comes, because when you get close to it, the company comes out and says, 'Oh . . . you need new heaters.' So they got you over a barrel."

28. See *Factory Farm Nation*, 11, for the 1995 figure, and a fact sheet published by the National Farmers Union entitled "Consolidation in Agriculture," Sept. 1, 2016, for the 2016 figure. The combined revenue figures are from annual reports from JBS ($51 billion), Hormel ($10 billion), Tyson ($40 billion), and Smithfield (estimated at $15 billion based on 2016 public data; the company has stopped publishing these reports).

29. A report called *The Economic Cost of Food Monopolies*, Food & Water Watch, Nov. 2012, estimated that concentration was higher in Iowa than the national average, at around 95 percent (fig. 3). (The "salvage market" quote is on p. 12.) That report cites numerous studies on the negative effects on the local economy, especially pp. 13–20. A meta-study of fifty-one such studies in 2007 summarized that "adverse impacts were found across an array of indicators measuring socioeconomic conditions, community social fabric, and environmental conditions. Few positive effects of industrialized farming were found across studies. The results demonstrate that public concern about

industrialized farms is warranted." See Linda Lobao and Curtis W. Stofferahn, "The Community Effects of Industrialized Farming: Social Science Research and Challenges to Corporate Farming Laws," *Agriculture and Human Values* 25, no. 2 (June 2008): 219–40.

30. On real estate values, a number of studies are summarized in John A. Kilpatrick, "Concentrated Animal Feeding Operations and Proximate Property Values," *Appraisal Journal*, July 2001. The 40 percent figure was from Dooho Park, Kyu-Hee Lee, and Andrew Seidl, *Rural Communities and Animal Feeding Operations: Economic and Environmental Considerations*, Department of Agricultural and Resource Economics, Colorado State University, 1998, cited in *False Promises! Costly Reality! What Hog Confinements Really Cost Iowa's Counties!*, Humane Society, m.humanesociety.org/sites/default/files/archive/assets/pdfs/care4iowa_false_promises.pdf. The study that found the 88 percent reduction was Mubarak Hamed, Thomas G. Johnson, and Kathleen K. Miller, *The Impacts of Animal Feeding Operations on Rural Land Values*, University of Missouri–Columbia Community Policy Analysis Center Report R-99-02, May 1999. (With thanks to Diane Rosenberg for the various documents.)

31. On alternative ways forward for de-financialized US agriculture, see for example Francis Thicke, *A New Vision for Iowa Food and Agriculture* (Fairfield, IA: Mulberry Knoll, 2010). (For per-hog prices of CAFOs versus alternative methods, see p. 25.) Also see D.G. Landblom, W.W. Poland, B. Nelson, and E. Janzen, *An Economic Analysis of Swine Rearing Systems For North Dakota* (Dickinson Research Extension Center, North Dakota State University, 2001) which estimated that "accounting for all business parameters," Open Pasture and "hoop structures" (a less intensive alternative to CAFOs) "returned 6.63% and 4.07% more income, respectively." Ikerd told me that a move to smaller high-tech farming operations, re-localised, with animals in pasture, and made efficient through an "Amazon model" of retailing, with government subsidies shifted from large agribusinesses towards supporting competitive local markets, if done right, would leave retail prices barely higher than today. (Ikerd's website, johnikerd.com, contains a range of resources on this.) On the impact on consumer prices, also see *Factory Farm Nation*, 27. (The American Farm Bureau Federation shows roughly the same statistic: farmers receive 15 cents per dollar spent on food, compared with 31 cents in 1980.)

32. See Paul Ramey, with Angela Huffman and Joe Maxwell, "Consolidation and the American Family Farm—Ohio," policy brief, Organization for Competitive Markets State Series, Sept. 2018.

33. On ADM, See Philip H. Howard, *Concentration and Power in the Food System: Who Controls What We Eat?* Bloomsbury, 2017, 72.

34. From my interview with O'Brien on October 21, 2018.

35. On market power enabling large integrators to indirectly reap the windfalls received directly by small CAFO farms, a US Small Business Administration (SBA) investigation of poultry growers found that the integrators had "such comprehensive control over the growers" that the subsidies were flowing not to the little guy but to the integrators (*Evaluation of SBA 7(a) Loans Made to Poultry Farmers*, SBA Report No. 18-13, Mar. 6, 2018).

36. Smithfield executives have denied being controlled by the Chinese Communist Party. But for evidence that this is so, see Nathan Halverson, "How China Purchased

a Prime Cut of America's Pork Industry," Reveal, Jan. 24, 2015, revealnews.org/article/
how-china-purchased-a-prime-cut-of-americas-pork-industry. Halverson obtained an
official company document, which laid out that "Shuanghui meets its obligations and
follows the path laid out by the Communist Party. . . . It receives directives from Beijing, and it follows them." See also Jeff Stein, "Trump Farm Bailout Money Will Go
to Brazilian-Owned Meatpacking Firm, USDA Says," *Washington Post*, Jan. 9, 2019.
On market power, the Smithfield website (as of December 7, 2018) boasted, "Vertical
integration is a key point of difference and a unique selling proposition for our products
and brands, allowing us to drive changes through the supply chain." On JBS, this is
widely reported. See for instance Pedro Fonseca and Ana Mano, "JBS' Batista Arrested
with Ex-Brazil Agriculture Ministers in Probe," Reuters, Nov. 9, 2018, or Jessica Brice
and Tatiana Freitas, "Brazil's Batista Clan: A Short Guide to an Empire Built on Beef,"
Bloomberg, May 18, 2017.

37. JBS Annual and Sustainability Report 2017 and WH Group 2017 Annual
Report. WH Group reported $923 million in US-sourced profits and $210 million in
non-Chinese worldwide income taxes, so a direct tax–profits comparison for the United
States was not possible. The 2018 report was available only in Chinese.

38. In one study of soy and beef production in the Amazon, 90–100 percent of
foreign capital in the operation had been routed in via tax havens. See Victor Galaz
et al., "Tax Havens and Global Environmental Degradation," *Nature Ecology & Evolution* 2 (2018): 1352–7.

39. On farmland speculation, See Jennifer Clapp and S. Ryan Isakson, "Risky
Returns: The Implications of Financialization in the Food System," *Development and
Change* 49, no. 2 (Mar. 2018): 437–60. For the Pittman quote, see David Kesmodel and
Jesse Newman, "Farmland Investments Take Root," *Wall Street Journal*, Aug. 4, 2015.

40. The Germany vs. USA data is from the 2016 national accounts data from
"Manufacturing, Value Added (% of GDP)," World Bank, data.worldbank.org/indica-
tor/NV.IND.MANF.ZS, with Germany at 20.6 percent of GDP and the United States
at 11.6 percent.

41. For a deeper exploration of the comparison between US and German manufacturing, see Suzanne Berger, "How Finance Gutted Manufacturing," *Boston Review*,
Apr. 1, 2014. One of Berger's arguments was that there was great value in big firms
keeping competences in-house rather than outsourcing them; in one sense, it was an
argument for "bigness." I put this dissonant note to the antitrust expert Gerald Berk,
who had recommended Berger's article, and he said my question was one that plagued
the antitrust lawyer Louis Brandeis a century ago, elaborated in a well-known set of
essays called *The Curse of Bigness*. As Berk argued it, "There are many more forms
of enterprise than the large, hierarchical corporation and the atomized, financialized
shareholder-value-driven model. Among them are cooperatives, mutuals, municipal
ownership, ESOPs, land trusts, industrial districts, and developmental (trade) associations. Brandeis was especially interested in cooperatives and trade associations. Each of
these forms necessitates very different sorts of regulatory institutions and, in my view,
none survives very well unless they can fend off predatory rivalry from the powerful—
hence the need for antitrust."

CONCLUSION

1. The 75 percent fall is from "Transformation of the Latvian Banking Sector (Customer Deposits and Payments)," Nov. 2, 2018, presented to me by Sandra Liepina, CEO of Finance Latvia Association, on November 29, 2018.

2. Almost immediately, on Geithner's appointment, the share prices of banks run by Geithner's friends and associates rose by over 10 percent. See Daron Acemoglu et al., "The Value of Connections in Turbulent Times: Evidence from the United States," *Journal of Financial Economics* 121, no. 2 (Aug. 2016): 368–91. They found an "abnormal return" for Geithner-connected banks of 6 percent after one day and 12 percent after ten trading days. "Foam the runway" was widely reported. On the bailout quotes, the "remotely backstopping" quote referred to the Primary Dealer Credit Facility, from Tooze, *Crashed*, 206, 208-209. Tooze said total lending under that facility came to $8.951 trillion (though on a different measure, daily collateral posting in repo markets, it peaked at $4.5 trillion in March 2008.) Among other bailout programs, he estimated that the share of foreign borrowers under the Term Auction Facility (TAF) was "well over 50 percent;" of the Single Tranche Open Market Operations bailout program the foreign share was over 70 percent, with Credit Suisse accounting for 30 percentage points; of the Term Securities Lending Facility, 51 percent of the collateral provided went to non-American banks; while some 40 percent of the Commercial Paper Funding Facility went to European banks (and 10 of that 40 went to UBS). What is more, 52 percent of mortgage-backed securities sold to the Fed under Quantitative Easing were sold by foreign banks, with Deutsche Bank and Credit Suisse the largest sellers by a healthy margin (Tooze, 207–210).

3. See Peter G. Peterson Foundation, "Per Capita Healthcare Costs—International Comparison," Aug. 10, 2018, https://www.pgpf.org/chart-archive/0006_health-care-oecd. It estimated per capita healthcare costs at $4,069 in OECD countries in 2017, compared to $10,209 for the United States.

4. From "Annual Corporate Tax Cuts," Americans for Tax Fairness, americansfortaxfairness.org/annual-corporate-tax-cuts, accessed Dec. 21, 2018. On the estimated $100 billion cost, see Jim Tankersley, "Budget Deficit Jumps Nearly 17% in 2018," *New York Times*, Oct. 15, 2018. See also "Analysis: The Trump-GOP Tax Cuts, One Year Later," Americans for Tax Fairness, Dec. 13, 2018, americansfortaxfairness.org/analysis-trump-gop-tax-cuts-one-year-later.

5. The Harvard numbers calculated from Harvard's website: tuition fees of $46,000, plus room and board and other expenses, for an estimated $72,000 total in the 2018–19 year. On further costs, first, growth rates after recessions are statistically faster than usual, and governments tend to cut taxes in recessions to restart faltering economies, leading to correlations between tax cuts and growth that falsely suggest it was the tax cuts that caused the growth. Second, US corporations are sitting on around $1.7 trillion in corporate cash piles, according to Moody's. Why would a corporate tax reduction—adding to these already vast, uninvested cash piles—spur corporations to invest? Cutting corporate tax is like pushing on a string. What is more, these piles have been growing at around 6 percent a year for many years, so older research from when piles

were much smaller won't reflect this factor adequately. This brings about the third point: much of the go-to data on corporate taxes is *old*. One of the most influential studies in terms of measuring impacts of corporate tax cuts is Ruud A. de Mooij and Sjef Ederveen, *Corporate Tax Elasticities: A Reader's Guide to Empirical Findings*, Oxford University Centre for Business Taxation Working Paper No. 0822, 2008—from ten years ago. The studies the authors cite have publication dates that range between 1985 and 2004 (and the data those studies use come from earlier years, including the 1970s). See also "Discussing Discussions around the Corporate Income Tax," Rasmus Corlin Christensen blog, Aug. 18, 2016, phdskat.org/2016/08/18/discussing-discussions-around-the-corporate-income-tax. Fourth, the data on how FDI responds to corporate tax cuts is systematically skewed in the pro-tax-cut direction because of "round-tripping." This happens when *local* investors who want to invest *at home* send their money offshore, hide their identity through financial secrecy or by diluting it in larger vehicles, then bring the money back home again—maybe piggybacking on a private equity investment, and thus fraudulently accessing tax breaks or other benefits that are only available to foreign investors. So a lot of what gets measured as FDI isn't FDI at all, but predatory behavior by locals. Fifth, foreigners own a significant portion of shares in US firms. So a significant share of the tax cuts will flow overseas. Sixth, another question muddies the corporate tax data further. It's about who bears the "burden," or "incidence," of corporate taxes. The owners or shareholders of corporations? Consumers? Workers? This "incidence" question is a hornet's nest of academic claims and counterclaims; suffice it to say that corporate-funded think tanks will tell you that corporate taxes make workers suffer, while independent ones will tell you that this is not so. See for instance Kimberly A. Clausing, "Who Pays the Corporate Tax in a Global Economy," *National Tax Journal* 66, no. 1 (Mar. 2013): 151–84. Seventh, much of the research uses GDP as a benchmark for the effects of corporate tax cuts on growth; this tends to flatter the numbers and elasticities by including profit shifting. Gross national income is generally a better measure, particularly for smaller economies which make up a large part of the dataset in many studies. An eighth issue involves the "lower bound" question: when interest rates are close to zero, a tax-funded spending increase ought to boost economic activity, in turn boosting taxes, while a tax cut is unlikely to do so. See for instance "But Do the Numbers Add Up?" Mainly Macro blog, May 17, 2017, mainlymacro.blogspot.com/2017/05/but-do-numbers-add-up.html. Ninth, when it comes to FDI flows in response to corporate tax cuts, a big chunk of recorded profit flows to the financial sector, which will deepen the finance curse and worsen future growth. For further points in this area, see Nick Shaxson, "Ten Reasons to Defend the Corporate Income Tax," Tax Justice Network, Mar. 18, 2015, taxjustice.net/2015/03/18/new-report-ten-reasons-to-defend-the-corporate-income-tax. On finance-related research, see also Chris Brooks and Lisa Schopohl, "Topics and Trends in Finance Research: What Is Published, Who Publishes It and What Gets Cited?" *British Accounting Review* 50, no. 6 (Nov. 2018): 615–37. They find that "almost all finance research is conducted using techniques from economics and mathematics, with virtually no use made of qualitative methods or interdisciplinary approaches."

6. From Daniel Yankelovich, *Corporate Priorities: A Continuing Study of the New Demands on Business* (Stamford, CT: s.p., 1972).

Index